Happy

Cor Wagenaar (ed.)

Happy
Cities and Public
Happiness
in Post-War
Europe

NAi Publishers, Rotterdam

Contents

Happy

Beach Cities

Re-inventing the European City?

Preface

Sometimes, architecture and town planning are used to promote public happiness. There is no shortage of bright, attractive, and also tricky and subversive imagery presenting yesterday's vision of tomorrow's cities as places where everybody will be happy. This book is the result of a simple, but as it turned out highly controversial idea: that the transformation of the European city after 1945 has been guided by this type of imagery. The urban landscape reflects specific ideals about happiness. Not, however, of the private happiness one may experience in the intimacy of one's home, but of *public* happiness. Many of the examples collected here – the authors speak of *icons* – can be seen as instruments especially devised to win the people's minds while trying to make the imagined prospects come true. If happiness becomes a public affair, the public domain is the setting where town planners stage their icons, and all these icons carry promises of happiness. Who defines these promises? Obviously, the clients: politicians, developers, marketing experts. Does that corrupt these icons? If so, does it diminish their appeal?

If these promises are inspired by the specific conditions from which they emerged and mirror the views of the clients who commissioned them, the usual solid scientific work in libraries and archives would not provide adequate tools to come to grips with this fascinating phenomenon. Something else is needed, studying the existing body of knowledge is not enough. What began as just an idea soon developed in to a major enterprise, involving architects, historians, town planners, and sociologists from all over Europe in a different way. Looking for icons of public happiness, they had to travel the entire continent. The result of this undertaking is unique in many ways, but probably most of all because the authors decided to present the results of their work in the form of a travel guide. As they toured Europe, they discovered the unknown treasures of the countries in Central and Eastern Europe that until 1989 had been subject to the 'socialist experiment'. This explains why a disproportionate number of projects collected in the book comes from that part of Europe. It's paradoxical that many of the ideas that apparently inspired them seems to have originated in the United States. This book is an invitation to the reader to take some time off, hire a car, buy a train ticket or take a plane, and start. There is an entire world to be discovered – so, why wait?

Kristin Feireiss

Happy

Moscow •

Kaunas
•

Kiev •

• Lviv

íjváros

Artek   Gori •
Bucharest •   Tbilisi

Happy

Rotterdam, September 19, 2002.

People are lining up in front the auditorium, hoping to find a seat. Hardly anybody speaks. At the far end of the room, opposite the entrance, two men sit behind a table. Donald Mitchell, the famous Mahler expert, is supposed to interview Valery Gergiev, who has just finished conducting the Rotterdam Philharmonic in Mahler's Sixth Symphony. Fumbling with the things on the table, Mitchell and Gergiev appear to underline the silent interlude between the concert and the discussion that is about to begin. Probably few people know more about Mahler than Mitchell does, but as soon as Gergiev starts speaking, Mahler is no longer the topic. Gergiev sketches the outlines of his personal universe, painting a panorama of a living body of music, created by composers who, long before audio recordings, fast trains, the internet and air transportation brought them all together in what resembles a giant virtual chat box, already formed a close-knit community. They were well aware of each other's compositions, and they visited each other, listened to each other's work, and read the musical scores that were easily available in all the major cities. This body of music, Gergiev continues, reflects man's living conditions, whoever he is, wherever he lives, whatever his work is. It follows history, registers opportunities, dilemmas, tensions, frictions – no matter what their nature and origin may be – and anticipates the tragic events of the future – Mahler's Sixth Symphony foreseeing the drama of the First World War, Shostakovich's Fourth, the reign of terror in the Soviet Union in the mid-1930s. Gergiev stresses that the composers reacted to real issues; their music is not about petty family affairs. The street, the city, the masses, that's what it's about. Keeping this body of knowledge alive is the joint responsibility of contemporary composers and conductors. They should reinterpret it, discover hidden possibilities. This body of music is not a luxury, it is a part of life, communicating basic things about the world we live in. Outside Europe and the United States, Gergiev goes on, huge masses live in poverty. These masses will make themselves known. They cannot be stopped. There is no reason why they should accept that six multinationals own most of the planet's energy resources; there is no justification for deny-

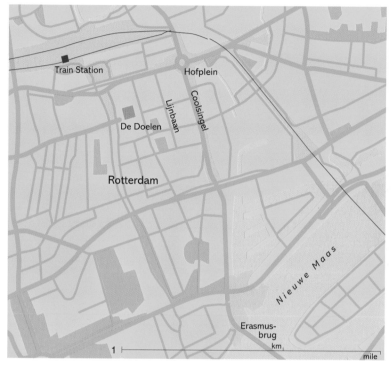

Train Station

Hofplein

De Doelen

Lijnbaan

Coolsingel

Rotterdam

Nieuwe Maas

Erasmus-
brug

1

km

mile

Happy

ing them their rights. They are not aliens, but our fellow men. According to Gergiev, we, living in Western Europe and the United States, are not more progressive than they are, we only have progressed a little further than they have until now. Before losing himself in political rhetoric, Gergiev goes back to the living body of music, expressing his view that it is imperative for the masses outside Europe and North America to share it, add to it, enrich it. Then the interview is over. Baffled by Gergiev's rhetorical avalanche, the audience again lines up before the auditorium doors, now trying to get out, to leave the concert hall that opened in 1966, expressing the city's ambition to become one of Holland's main cultural centers, and not merely the world's largest port. As the audience flocks to the square in front of the white marble maze that is so characteristic of this building, the last regular trains leave Rotterdam's main station, streetcars screechingly head for the terminus, and the famous conductor undoubtedly starts thinking about his performance of the next day. **C.W.**

Artist impression of J. Hoogstad's reconstruction project of De Doelen

Happy

Cities and the Pursuit of Public Happiness An Introduction

Cor Wagenaar

However diverse the personal views of the authors of this book may be, they all share the belief that there is indeed such a thing as a 'body of architecture,' a vast and expanding container of knowledge and experience. That defines the basic attitude all the articles have in common: they attempt to analyze what appear to be the fundamental characteristics of the actual activities of architects and town planners, of their efforts to create the urban imagery that surrounds us every day of our lives, and of the intentions that lie behind this imagery. Naturally, this is only one layer of this immense body of knowledge, but an essential one. At this level it does indeed function in much the same way as the musical universe Gergiev referred to, i.e., as a joint responsibility for all architects, town planners, historians, urban sociologists, critics and the general public, as something that escapes national boundaries as well as petty personal concerns, and as something that registers historical experience. This book explores the communicative potential of architecture and town planning and focuses on the public domain as the stage where this quality manifests itself most clearly. The way architects and town planners design streets, squares, housing estates and occasionally a commune of rebellious beatniks, represents some of the most essential characteristics of their work. The public domain is for architecture and town planning what the concert hall is for music. It is a manifestation of the views and ambitions of those who order plans for it, the skill and experience of the designer, their ability to reinterpret inspiring examples from the past, society's financial and economic potential to realize these plans, and the public's perception of the city of tomorrow. A more telling story than the one told in the public domain is hard to imagine.

It is true that the meaning of the public domain has changed in the last decades. Compared to fifty years ago, it seems to have become less effective as a public stage where society expresses itself, its culture, its image of itself, its social and political ambitions. Already

Happy

in 1960, the famous American novelist Saul Bellow noted that 'the greatest human qualities' no longer manifested themselves in the streets and squares of the city. 'A modern mass society has no open place for such qualities, no vocabulary for them, and no ceremony (except in the churches) that makes them public. So they remain private and are mingled with other private things that vex us or of which we feel ashamed.'[1]

Recently, Jonathan Franzen went even further, stating that the private domain has all but conquered and expelled the public domain. Roaming through streets

[1] Saul Bellow, 'The sealed treasure' (1960), in: *It All Adds Up. From the Dim Past to the Uncertain Future*, New York 1994, 59, 60.

and squares, people no longer relate to each other; instead, they chat with their friends and colleagues, shouting to their cell phones as if they were alone. Whatever message may be conveyed by the public domain or the architecture that defines it, will never get across to this lonely crowd. Communication seems to have ended, and what once was a powerful medium now seems to be fading away. Making things even worse, there is no alternative for the communicative properties of the public domain. Franzen denies that its role has been taken over by television and the internet. For him, they represent the private realm in a shameless, exhibitionist way. Before the camera, people behave in ways they would never dare in public. They would be ashamed of themselves, for in the public domain they would be acutely aware of all the people watching them. Complete visibility of all who are there and everything that happens is the distinctive quality of the public domain. 'A genuine public space is a place where every citizen is welcome to be present and where the purely private is excluded or restricted.'[2] Naturally, this implies certain rules of conduct.

[2] J. Franzen, *How to be Alone*, London 2002, 50.

In a way, the public domain imposes these rules and therefore may be seen as a civilizing force. On the other hand, this may be the reason for people to want to escape from it and seek refuge in the private domain. Even so, the public sphere never completely lost its public functions, and relative to other 'media' it even seems to have become more important. It may very well be the only realm that resists the overwhelming tendency, inherent in the electronic multimedia, towards the virtual privatization of practically everything. That is why we decided to focus on the use of the public domain as a medium that conveys fundamental characteristics of society. This book deals, in other words, with the concert hall qualities of public space.

As a medium, the public domain contains many messages, but we were interested in only one specific type: those that embody promises for a better future, that point towards ideal, or idealized, ways for people to live in a community, whether it is society at large, the city, the neighborhood or the commune. Cities symbolize the pursuit of public happiness. That tends to give our subject matter a utopian ring. Even so, none of the projects presented here was invented out of the blue. All of them were designed as concrete answers to concrete needs, and all commissioned by clients who knew very well what they were aiming at. Often they took existing examples as sources of inspiration. Some of the utopian projects were actually built, though sometimes only fragments were realized, and often they were simply discarded because political changes or the emergence of new commercial strategies made them obsolete.

Happy

When they were built, they sometimes inspired powerful counter-utopia's, fragments of which were sometimes also built – one of the most striking sequences in this respect is undoubtedly provided by the reconstruction of Rotterdam. One of the distinguishing features shared by the multitude of urban utopias presented in *Happy. Cities and Public Happiness in Post-War Europe* is that they are indeed part of the universal 'body of architecture', that they are closely linked to each other, following the same life cycles, the same fashions. That is why instead of calling them utopias we much preferred to label them 'icons'. Icons are vehicles that connect our innermost emotions, needs, wishes and dreams to their outward manifestation in the city. Some of them are historical and others are very recent. Although they are real, their fundamental power is tied up with the messages they convey, and these messages are, to a large degree, utopian. In other words, they are real as a medium and utopian as a message. We're interested mainly in their function as media. Whether they are modern, traditional or historical, old or new, built and subject to the intricacies of history, or frozen in beautiful drawings waiting to be enshrined in a museum or canonized in a book on architectural history, what makes them especially appealing is their capacity to visualize a brighter future for everyone. They cover all aspects of everyday life. From this, they derive their seductive power, and, reduced to the scale of the concrete situations that constitute our daily behavior, they make it easy to identify with the imagery they present. A wedding on scaffoldings at the building site of a new housing estate is, naturally, more appealing than a map of tomorrow's city, even though such map may indicate all that is needed for a happy, secure and untroubled life.

Icons expressing hope for a better future: Europe after 1945 This book is, among other things, an anthology of images showing the way to a completely new world, seen as a prerequisite for people's individual and collective happiness. Nevertheless it focuses on Europe and starts in the ruins left behind by the Second World War. Why Europe? Why the last five decades? Isn't there a happier era, a less burdened place? Did European architecture and town planning in these years contribute something special to our 'body of architecture?' And isn't the need to limit the scope of this book strangely at odds with the universality of our 'body of architecture?' Not at all. The framework we chose only underlines it. The impact of what happened on the European stage was felt all over the world, and the most influential innovations in, for instance, the United States and the Soviet Union left their mark in Europe; and though the willful elimination of the past was a striking quality of post-war architecture and town planning everywhere, the vast body of knowledge and experience accumulated before 1945 remained a powerful source of inspiration. Europe, however, provides the richest treasure of icons that communicate images of a better society – the focus of this book. And that is no coincidence.

In 1945, Europe lay in ruins. Millions had died, the holocaust had wiped out most of the Jewish population, political boundaries had moved across Europe as if they were nothing more than lines drawn at a conference, hundreds of thousands of people were on the move, and refugee camps were either hastily constructed or set up in what not long before had been

Happy

concentration camps. In 1944, J.L. Sert believed that European cities were doomed. His *Can Our Cities Survive? An ABC of Urban Problems, Their Analysis, Their Solutions. Based on the Proposals Formulated by the C.I.A.M.* contained mostly American examples – he wrote his manifesto in the States – but what he was saying clearly referred to European cities as well.[3] Sert did not refer to the air raids, the bombings, the calamitous destruction brought about by the war, however.

3 J.L. Sert, *Can Our Cities Survive? An ABC of Urban Problems, Their Analysis, their Solutions. Based on the Proposals formulated by the C.I.A.M.*, Cambridge (Mass.) 1944.

He was convinced that the collapse of the cities was determined by their haphazard growth in the recent past and the way they were planned – or rather the way planning had failed. The bombs simply finished what the processes of congestion, pollution and economic depression would have done anyway. This was Sert's doom and gloom scenario in 1945. And in 2000? Had his premonitions become reality? They had not. In 2000, only a few decades later, things had changed dramatically. Europe had become the world's richest economic region, most people were either unbelievably wealthy or confident that they were on their way to shake off the poverty of times immemorial. Even the Balkans showed some signs of quieting down. European cities flourished. By and large, their story has been one of surprising success, bringing them progress and prosperity. The cities may not be perfect, but they improved beyond what anyone could have imagined. If Sert wrote his treatise as an urgent plea for planning, his lessons surely took effect, for Europe became something like a town planning paradise. The unremitting efforts to rebuild and improve the European city were part of a far more ambitious program: a campaign to construct – literally – a completely new world. Planning was the magic word. Planning extended to all realms of human activity: the economy, social relations, communities, architecture, the city. The ultimate goal was a society of a type that had never existed before. Something so new, in fact, that guidebooks were written to make sure people would know how to survive. *The intelligent man's guide to the post-war world*, for instance, taught people how to make the most of the revolutionary opportunities offered by this new world – it took no less than 1143 pages to explain everything in detail.[4]

4 G.D.H. Cole, *The intelligent man's guide to the post-war world*, London 1947.

By definition, cities are social phenomena. They are the result of the collective efforts of the societies that produce them. If these efforts are to be successful, people will have to support them. They have to be convinced that they should cooperate – or at least not obstruct the way to a better world. What, then, is the best way to engage people? Here our icons present themselves as powerful tools. They lay claim to the future, and they embody a vital promise: that it is possible, literally, to build this future. They epitomize what the German philosopher Ernst Bloch called 'the principle of hope.' Attacked by die-hard Marxists for his 'utopian' attitude, Bloch insisted that history was often propelled by the seemingly unrealistic prospects of a brighter future. Instead of escapist dreams, these visions mediated between people's hope and realistic possibilities to make these hopes come true; they are examples of what Bloch called 'anticipating consciousness.'[5]

Happy

5 H. van den Enden, 'Inleiding: Blochs marxisme van de hoop', in: H. van den Enden (red.), *Marxisme van de hoop – hoop van het marxisme? Essays over de filosofie van Ernst Bloch*, Bussum 1980, 13. Not unlike Robert Musil years before him, Bloch sees history as a field of countless possibilities, but unlike Musil's 'Möglichkeitssinn', Bloch's hopeful perspectives served the specific purpose of realizing what he, faithful to the Marxist dogma, saw as the inevitable outcome of history: a classless society where nature and society would be in perfect balance. R. Musil, *Der Mann ohne Eigenschaften*, Reinbek bei Hamburg 1987 (first published 1930).

The icons presented here gave these cities the vigor to rise from the grave. Enormous amounts of thought, energy and money have been invested in their survival, and that would never have happened if they had not served some clear and distinct purposes, that, at the most abstract level, might well be characterized as the pursuit of happiness – obviously a universal human quality.

An American Dream and a Socialist Paradise
Between 1948 and 1989, the 'iron curtain' split Europe in two. This semi-impenetrable barrier separated two socio-political systems that for many years were engaged in the Cold War. Each system had its own specific vision of a new world. So, instead of one model, there were at least two (not counting the national variations within each of the two blocs). Both systems were powered by forces outside the traditional heartland of European culture (though Russia had become an influential exponent of European culture since the late nineteenth century at the latest, and American culture was long considered an offshoot of European culture even by the Americans themselves). Even so, the heyday of Europe as a cultural superpower belonged to the past. Our survey starts in the middle of what has rightly been termed the American Century.[6] It can hardly be a coincidence that most of the icons show a strong American influence – that is true even for those from the socialist countries. That is less surprising than it may seem. Social improvement and material prosperity were pretty much the essence of the bright new future ushered in by postwar reconstruction, and the American Dream offered the most appealing images of these hopes becoming reality. They were also at the heart of the socialist utopias. A carefree, leisurely lifestyle, comfortable houses and nice cars, and readily available consumer goods came to epitomize the Welfare State since the late 1950s. For the vast majority of the European working classes, this was what paradise looked like. Whether socialist, social democrat or capitalist, the European political establishment could hardly come up with a more attractive vision. All that had to be done to adapt the American Dream to the cultural realities of the Old World was to stress the collective effort necessary to realize its inherent promises – which gave them a strong political ring even in Western Europe – and to replace their suburban qualities by a more urban setting (especially in the socialist sphere). In this way, the American Dream was integrated into the public domain. Striking examples are, for instance, the presentation drawings of the Stalin Allee in Berlin, some of which show the new boulevard through the windshield of an American car driven by a gorgeous blonde.

6 The American Century was the topic of two exhibitions in 1999 at the Whitney Museum of Modern Art in New York. They were accompanied by two interesting catalogues: B. Haskell, *The American Century. Art & Culture 1900 – 1950*, New York, London 1999; L. Phillips, *The American Century. Art & Culture 1950 – 2000*, New York, London 1999.

Happy

What has made the American Dream so appealing is its promise of individual prosperity, of progress. Progress is hard work – or is it? Socialism also promised progress, but presented it as the inevitable outcome of a historical process that could not be stopped. In the years immediately after 1945, socialism was immensely popular all over Europe. It promised a one-way street to a better future and was powered by a very seductive political philosophy that by then had developed an effective iconography of symbols, colors, songs, and architecture. Socialism promised progress as a side-effect of an ideology on the march, and the heroic stories of economic development and the construction of new towns all over the Soviet Union gained credibility thanks to the Red Army's having become the single most powerful factor in beating Nazi Germany. Especially after 1948, when it virtually annexed part of the heartland of Europe, the Soviet Union became an even greater power on the European theatre, underlining its claim to superiority by beating the United States in conquering space; Yuri Gagarin's solo flight in the Sputnik caused a shock. The immense prestige of communism partly counteracted the sometimes brutal consequences of the use of international political power during the Cold War. However fundamental some of the differences with the rest of Europe may have been, socialism in the East Bloc also showed some striking similarities with the latter: the unquestioned belief in planning, and the promise to set free the lower classes (called the 'working classes' in socialist countries, whereas their counterparts elsewhere were usually referred to as the masses of the 'common men'). This helps to explain the striking similarities between the icons all over Europe. America's imagery of wealthy citizens merged seamlessly with communism's vision of tomorrow's world. The emergence of the socialist version of the Welfare State in the 1970s – however poor compared to its Western European counterpart – triggered an avalanche of commercial advertising clearly inspired by American examples. Superimposed on this basic layer of a vista of a better world, shared by all utopias, were some characteristically socialist ideals: the public domain should also testify to the historical struggle of the working classes and to its driving force, namely, the communist party and its leaders. Apart from that, the public domain should demonstrate the evolution of historical materialism: historical monuments should mark society's evolution in the past, and the new architecture and town planning should mark how history's goal was being approached.

Careful maneuvers in a mine field Working on this book has been a fascinating experience, though it has also entailed many difficulties. Easiest to solve were the practical problems. In some regions, traveling required strenuous efforts, and obviously we faced the inevitable, virtually insurmountable language barriers. By adding local experts to our team we could overcome these difficulties. There were, however, more fundamental issues at stake. Focusing on the communicative qualities of architecture and town planning implies a distinction between medium and message – one that is not always easy to make. The icons collected in the book are not only attractive and captivating design strategies; they are also highly controversial. Their controversial qualities stem from the way they address people's innermost feelings and sentiments. Happiness is a purely individual emotion, a state of mind as the Hungarian

Happy

author and urban sociologist György Konrád put it. Our icons connect these sentiments to specific political, (sub-)cultural or commercial forces, seemingly corrupting them in the process. Promising to fulfill whatever needs people may feel, politics makes use of the iconography of the joyous city to buy people's consent, inducing them to cooperate. Commercial advertisements use the same imagery for similar purposes, their aim being a bigger share of the market or an increase in profits. Ironically, the widespread abuse of these icons does not diminish their beauty, appeal or evocative potential in the least. Even if some of our icons may have been devices to lure people into a 'happy' state of mind, instruments to buy their consent or at least diminish their readiness to revolt, they can still be very convincing and sometimes even beautiful pieces of design, in much the same way as Prokofiev's *Zdravitska cantata* in the honor of Stalin's sixtieth birthday, for instance, is brilliant even though the purpose it served was not. The intentions of those who commission, create and use the icons and their actual effects appear to exist on two separate levels. There is little doubt that the imagery thus created affects people's individual ideals, setting in motion complex interactive processes.

This book is about the 'body of architecture' as an expression of life, of people's aspirations and the ways to fulfill their ideals, in short, an expression of history. History is a fundamental and natural component of architecture and town planning, expressing itself on two levels, at least. The work of the planners always reflects the aspirations of those for whom they work. At the same time, it is rooted in the knowledge and experience these disciplines have accumulated. Even so, this is definitely not a history book. Its subject matter transcends history.

Compiling a book that canvasses the contributions of architecture and town planning to the way we experience the European city, we composed a different story from the one based on the usual textbook cliches. We discovered many phenomena that until now seem to have been ignored. Why are they not better known? Evidently because the history of architecture is itself part of the machinery that propagates some icons and ignores others, taking the side of those who designed them and, therefore, tacitly supporting the views of the authorities who ordered their construction. In doing so, history has to some degree been corrupted in a way very similar to the sometimes corrupted nature of the icons. Thorough scientific research wasn't necessary to reach this conclusion (which in part explains the critical tone of this book). Visiting cities all over Europe as our reporters did make clear how urgently our body of architectural knowledge needs to be revised.

Is it possible to write a book on 'happy' architectural and town planning icons that is not at the same time a sanctimonious celebration of modernism? The very thought infuriated some of our colleagues. For them, modernism is synonymous with esthetic perfection, social justice, economic feasibility, democracy and moral righteousness. They are convinced that only modernism can contribute to a better world. For them, this book is pure heresy. Nobody can deny that the epochal works of Le Corbusier, Mies van der Rohe, Taut, Oud, and many others have left their imprint on postwar architecture, but this alone does not explain the appealing quality of the icons presented in our book. It would be quite absurd to trace the joyous, care-

Happy

free imagery of a world free of the collective misery of the recent past back to the utopian views of modernism. The story is not that easy. For one thing, the seductive powers immanent in political and commercial perspectives have to be taken into account (even if we wish to refrain from commenting on politics or the mechanisms of business, big or small). In ways we may never grasp, they address fundamental qualities; the knowledge, skill and creativity needed to produce Konrád's happy state of mind is definitely not a monopoly of modernism.

Writing this book has been like entering a minefield. Our reporters were well aware of that. Deeply rooted emotions are involved in many of the phenomena we encountered. Plunging head over heels into the complex biographies of cities and their inhabitants, we could not avoid questioning our own beliefs and attitudes. They proved to be as diverse as the personalities involved and the topics studied, and we had to accept the impossibility of imposing uniformity on them. They color the articles in this book. The authors alone are accountable for their contents. The editor takes full responsibility for the composition of this book as well as for the short essays that comment on some of the phenomena we encountered. None of these analyses, and hardly any of the articles, claims to be scientific. *Happy* is a travel book, and that is all it is.

A travel guide

A travel guide This book is the result of a journalistic expedition, carried out by more than twenty reporters who traveled the entire European continent, from Finland to Portugal, form Italy to Ireland, from the Urals to the Atlantic. Most of them are architects, town planners, historians and sociologists, recruited mainly in the countries that they were asked to study. All they were allowed to take with them was a so-called 'matrix' identifying a number of themes.[7] Exploring the continuous dynamic processes, unraveling the codes and conventions of the European city, coming to terms with the ambitions and views of the authorities who guided its transformation, our team revealed unknown treasures all over the continent. They collected dozens of icons – each and every one a part of its own microcosm. Instead of illustrating general movements and trends that unfolded all over Europe, spreading, so to speak, horizontally from one region to another, we leap from icon to icon, relating stories that are always unique, trying to see through the various layers of their evolution in what could be defined as an experiment in vertical analysis. All the icons tell stories that evolve at the crossroads of universal human needs, political geography, economic opportunity, technology and the techniques of representation. Often they are milestones in the continuous process of change that is characteristic of cities, marking a specific phase within the process. Nevertheless, each of our icons

7 The themes listed in the matrix were: 1. L'Europe Blessée: Between Ruins and Tabula Tasa (ruins, tabula rasa, rebuilding, celebrations and festivities) 2. The Transformation of the Historical City (the old city, monuments and symbols, tradition as model) 3. The Consumer Society: Progress for All (shopping places, life style) 4. Other Cultures: From Migrant Worker to Squatter (migrant workers, groups from former colonies, student revolt and squatting, existing in niches) 5. The City as Stage: From the Political Rally to the Permanent Festival 6. The Traffic Society: Movement for All (with the car, with the train) 7. Living in the City (mass housing, one-family house) 8. Work in the City. From Steelworks to Computer Screen (work as production, work as consumption) 9. Leisure Time in the City (recreation, sport).

could be substituted by a different one. They were not selected because of their outstanding qualities as works of art, but rather because they expressed their message in a particularly eloquent way – a message they shared with numerous other examples that might have been chosen instead of them. Our icons are, in other words, typical rather than exceptional, even though all of them are unique. *Happy* reads as a travelogue about a mysterious country, a guide to cities unheard of, and an introduction to a curious world where people lead their lives in unfamiliar ways. Many of these cities have been forgotten. They disappeared behind the iron curtain, or were alienated from us by the joint forces of politics, geography and the history of modernism. Excavating them, rediscovering broken links, our reporters found themselves engaged in a wonderful adventure that has only just begun: the re-discovery of architecture and town planning as highly communicative, interactive disciplines much in the same way as Gergiev's international body of music.

The foundation *Happy* is a very simple historical construct leading from the collective utopias of the reconstruction years to the individual and allegedly more personal and lifestyle-oriented utopia's of the present. These two extremes are separated as well as connected by the subcultural utopia's of the 1960s and 1970s. The articles in this book have been arranged against the background of this simple, almost Hegelian structure (collective, countercultural collective on a small scale, individual). Chronology has not been strictly observed, though the first entries focus on reconstruction icons and the public domain as a manifestation of ideals that, at the time, were considered to be more or less universal, whereas the articles that conclude this report concentrate on the life-style oriented, very diverse urban models, where the public domain has come to resemble a collage of semi-individualized ideals and the stage for festivals that are likewise oriented at specific groups. If the public domain can be seen as a concert hall, the first works that this book offers have the qualities of a symphony of hope flourishing above dark undertones of the memories of war and holocaust; the book concludes with a suite of various movements spiced with reminisces of countercultural rebellion, and sometimes performed simultaneously.

How should one structure a book like this? Most of it is made up of articles written by our reporters: long ones, short ones, bird's-eye views, in-depth analyses, some sociological in nature, others historical or conceived from a designer's point of view. A more or less uniform whole was nevertheless the editor's goal. Submerging the articles in a sea of even more text was not an option. Instead, two types of text have been inserted, both of them clearly differentiated from the main body of articles. Short introductory captions introduce the cities, the main characters in this book. They give an impression of what our reporters encountered when they were doing their research. They give a hint of what one might encounter today. Then there are more analytical passages. They have no scientific pretensions whatsoever and are intended only to give some background information. Never more than quick scans of easily available information, they only illustrate how much more research still has to be done. Like the short introductions, this investigative journalism underscores the book's character as a preliminary report. Like all travel books, it unveils some of the mysteries of the unknown territories it covers and leaves the wonderful experience of discovering the many other hidden treasures to the reader.

Happy

Eliminating the Traces of the War!

Rotterdam-Berlin, October 5, 1999.

On board a train to Berlin — the walkman is playing Steve Reich's *Different Trains*, and the landscape unfolds as a sequence of idyllic rural scenes. Different trains, trains on their own tracks, metaphor of life: in the end their destination always seems to have been

inevitable, no matter at how many points they could have taken off in other directions. Reich, who often traveled on trains across the USA as a child, imagined trains simultaneous crossing Germany.[1] Different trains, different destinies: soldiers on their way to the battlefield, cargo being directed to the armament industry, people headed for the extermination camps. And in the skies at night huge fleets of bombers cruising towards the cities. Osnabrück, Hannover, Berlin. Destruction at an unprecedented scale, and, as it turned out, practically without effect on the German war effort, strengthening the morale of the victims rather than break-

ing it. However devastating the air raids, the trains could not be stopped. Senseless, counterproductive, irrational but unavoidable, the mechanisms of war followed their seemingly predetermined course. Ruins were their universal manifestation. Now the ruins are gone. Osnabrück has been repaired, Hannover was replaced by a spacious urban landscape, and Berlin became the scene of two competing reconstruction campaigns. Like all reconstructed cities, they resulted from the daring visions emanating from the ruins. On board a train heading to Berlin in 1999, you marvel at the urban landscapes dreamed up in the visions of yesterday's politicians, town planners and architects. Sometimes alive and in perfect shape, sometimes worn down and obsolete, these dreams define the character of all these cities as they float past the window one after the other, until finally you reach Berlin. **C.W.**

---

1 'When I was one year old, my parents separated. My mother moved to Los Angeles and my father stayed in New York. Since they arranged divided custody, I traveled back and forth by train frequently between New York and Los Angeles from 1939 to 1942 accompanied by my governess. While these trips were exciting and romantic at the time, I now look back and think that, if I had been in Europe during this period, as a Jew I would have had to ride very different trains.' Steve Reich, *Different Trains (for string quartet and tape)*, Kronos Quartet, WEA 7559-79176-2 (CD-booklet).

Happy

26

RUINS

Centuries of political and military competition between the European nations culminated in the Second World War. Europe, once the generator of cultural movements that swept all over the Western world – from Greek antiquity to international modernism – lay in ruins, a third world war seemed inevitable, and the atomic bomb threatened to complete the work of destruction began by the air raids. Cities had become primary targets in modern warfare: for decades the remains of burnt-out buildings dominated once-prosperous towns from the heart of Russia to southern Italy. The ruins were believed to mark the end of an era. They were deplorable, but they were not deplored. They were celebrated as the end of a terrible nightmare. From all over Europe, there are pictures of children playing in the ruins. The ruins mark the end of the war, of the Holocaust, and what was generally believed to be their fundamental cause: an obsolete society where many felt like second-rate citizens excluded from the advantages that the middle classes and the upper strata of society enjoyed. The children represented the future, a society very different from the one that now lay in ruins. The ruins were a relief. Buildings that survived the war were seen as obsolete, the sad remains of a dead past waiting to be demolished as soon as they could be missed. Fueled by the same sentiments, architects and town planners initiated wholesale demolition campaigns that cleared even larger areas than the bombs had done. If the old society had to make way for a new one, much of the old cities had to go, too.

Bathers on the ruined Danube bank, 1945

Happy

Budapest, 1945

Happy

Germany, 1948

Germany, 1940s

Happy

Germany, 1940s

Happy

Kiev, May 1, 2002.

Lots of people have gathered in the center of Kiev. Labor Day is being celebrated. People enjoy their day off and they walk along Kreshtchatik Street. Kiev's main boulevard has been transformed into a pedestrian thoroughfare for their spontaneous parade. Bands are playing, and somewhere a choir is singing. On the square at the end of the boulevard, a different scene is unfolding. Red flags, portraits of Lenin and Stalin and the occasional, lavishly decorated military uniform enliven a demonstration clearly organized by what remains of the Communist Party. Most of the demonstrators are elderly people, many of whom have come by bus or train. They are outsiders now. Gone are the days when they paraded on Kreshtchatik Street. Somebody is scolding the demonstrators: go to Russia where you belong! Haven't you brought enough misery to the Ukraine! Their eyes filled with tears, some of the demonstrators return to their buses, embracing photographs of Lenin. C.W.

'We want to eliminate all traces of the war!'

Post-war Reconstuction in Soviet Posters

Bogdan Tscherkes

The greater the tragedy, the brighter the visions of paradise. In the Soviet Union, tragedies were in ample supply in the 1930s and 1940s. The consequences of the war only highlighted a disastrous series of events that had begun long before. The future outlined in the reconstruction posters was, in every respect, the counterpart of all this misery. At the same time, they neatly mirror the changes in the political situation in the Soviet empire.

More than 30 million people lost their lives during the Second World War. Of all the countries involved in it, the Soviet Union suffered the most: nearly 20 million of its people died. The number of cities that were destroyed reached 1,710, 70,000 villages were lost, and 25 million people lost their homes.[1] After a catastrophe of this magnitude, it was only natural that the construction of new houses, cities and villages became one of the most urgent tasks. To achieve this, it was essential to involve everybody who was capable of doing the work. Every means available was used to stimulate building activity, including the use of extensive propaganda campaigns. Posters are among the most intriguing tools in these campaigns. Feelings of despair and depression were to be suppressed and the widespread sentiment of apathy and sadness had to be tackled. One method was to create evocative images of building a happy future for everyone. The Soviet posters succeeded very well in fulfilling these tasks. Analyzing those from the first postwar decade, one is struck by the vast differences in the way they were made, the feelings they convey and their contents. What accounts for this fascinating phenomenon is the historical moment in which they evolved.

The first posters devoted to reconstruction were made during the war years and printed in 1944. One of the best was made by I.A. Serebrjanskij: 'Come on, let's do the job!' It shows

1 N.P. Bylinkin, A.V. Rjabuschin (ed.), *Geschichte der so
wjetischen Architektur I,* (1917-1954), Moscow 1985, 172.

Happy

33

I.A. Serebrjanskij, 'Come on, let's do the job'

T.F. Belozvetova, 'We want to rebuild our home town'

a young woman who looks us straight in the eye while carrying with both hands a basket filled with building materials. Her face reflecting hope and confidence, she asks us to help her and take up her basket, which contains the symbols of the building trade: bricks and trowel. The woman is depicted as an idealized figure, looking forward to the future peace, and, in spite of her work clothes, she looks like a pin-up girl. The poster radiates humanity and optimism, at the same time showing the dramatic situation caused by the war, which still lingers on. The women are left alone. There are not nearly enough workers available. All the men have gone; they are either fighting on the battlefield or have already died there. But the vitality of this woman, her beauty and her resolute call 'Come on, let's do the job!' bear witness to her faith in the prospects of rebuilding the ruined country.

Happy

Two other posters, also from 1944, are dedicated to the same theme. They differ not only in their artistic arrangement and mood, but also demonstrate the different strategies in coping with reconstruction in the city and in the countryside. The expressive poster by T.F. Belozvetova, 'We want to rebuild our home town!' still shows the impact of wartime heroism. His main heroine passionately calls the viewers to work, to help rebuild the cities and overcome the poverty and the ruins that are also shown. The poster proposes to tackle reconstruction in much the same way as the war was fought, anticipating a massive military campaign that is now not directed against the enemy, but to the titanic operation of clearing the rubble and rebuilding the cities. A completely different approach is reflected in a poster by V. Ivanov and O. Burova, 'We want to rebuild our villages, which were destroyed by the fascist invaders.' It shows an idyllic scene of life in a reconstructed Russian village: a pastoral wooden building, a clear blue sky, the famous Russian birch trees, and smoke coming from a chimney symbolizing the domestic warmth that could not be enjoyed for such a long time. All the posters from 1944 feature women, for they played a vital role in the reconstruction of Russian cities and villages in this period.

V. Ivanov, O. Burova, 'We want to rebuild our villages, which were destroyed by the fascist invaders'

The posters from 1945 display an attitude different from the one seen in those made during the war. A different mood had emerged. Human emotions disappeared, and triumphant heroism was now the main theme. The image of the Soviets as superior human beings developed. Not affected by doubts of any kind, they believe in themselves, and are always in a good mood.

Happy

ВИКТОР ИВАНОВ-45.

ОТСТРОИМ НА СЛАВУ!

V. Ivanov, 'Let us rebuild for our own glory'

However, they are also face-less. Women are still a major feature, but their feminine qualities are gone. They symbolize victory and have become working class idols. Illustrative for this tendency is a poster by V. Ivanov, 'Let us rebuild for our own glory!' After demobilization, more men appear on the posters. As was the case everywhere else after the war, the Soviet Union faced the challenge of re-integrating them into a society that was trying to get back to normal. The heroes of yesterday had to become the workers, architects and engineers of tomorrow. This very difficult process of reconstruction is the theme of another poster by V. Ivanov, 'For peaceful and constructive work!' It shows two soldiers returning from the battlefield. This topic is repeated in a poster by B. Muchin, 'We want to eliminate all traces of the war!' Again we see a former soldier who wears workman's clothes over his uniform and is laying bricks for a new building. By showing the fragment of a complete city full of cranes and brigades of workers, this poster goes beyond the purely symbolic visualization of bricks and ruins. There are still some ruins, but parts of streets have already been rebuilt. They paint a picture of peaceful life, and the former soldier, who is now a construction worker, proudly points to this panorama. It is the result of his own work, and it anticipates future happiness in the rebuilt Russian cities.

The victory of the Soviet Union and the subsequent success of the reconstruction program between 1946 and 1950 were always associated with Stalin, thus strengthening the personal cult that had already grown up around him in the preceding years. His image replaced both the women who, in the wartime posters, were represented as construction workers, and the returning soldiers on the posters from the early phases of the reconstruction. Stalin was shown

Happy

V. Ivanov, 'For peaceful and constructive work!'

B. Muchin, 'We want to eliminate all traces of the war!'

Happy

B. Beresofskij, M. Solovjov, I. Schagin, 'Under the leadership of Stalin the Great - forward towards communism!'

N. Petrov, K. Ivanov, 'Praise the great Stalin, the architect of communism!'

Happy

as leader and master planner. Examples are posters by B. Beresofskij, M. Solovjov and I. Schagin, 'Under the leadership of Stalin the Great – forward towards communism!' (1951), and by N. Petrov and K. Ivanov, 'Praise the great Stalin, the architect of communism!' (1952). The high-rise buildings of Moscow became the architectural symbols for this period and Stalin loved being depicted in front of them. The first poster shows them as they were being constructed, and on the second, Stalin towers above the skyscraper that D. Tscheschulin, A. Rostovskij and I. Gochman completed on the Kotelnitscheskij in 1952. The visual hierarchy put Stalin in the foreground, in front of the result of his creative genius, the high-rise buildings of Moscow. He even dwarfs the Spasskij Tower of the Kremlin, although the tower is much

I. Golovanov, 'My friend, the best qualities of our souls we dedicate to the fatherland!'

closer to the spectators. The veneration of the skyscrapers as the work of Stalin is also manifested in the heroic poster by L. Golovanov, 'My friend, the best qualities of our souls we dedicate to the fatherland!' (1952). In front of the new skyscraper of the University of Moscow, built in 1953 by L. Rudnev and P. Abrosimov, two young people are shown in a dramatic, romantic pose. In their hands is a book of proverbs by Lenin and Stalin *On youth*. The silhouette of historic Moscow is seen in the background, surrounded by the towers of the new, Stalinist capital.

The glorification of Stalin's spendthrift postwar building campaign ended with his death in 1953. In 1954, Nikita Khrushtchev declared war against this 'sugar pie style' in architec-

Happy

O. Savostjuk, 'We live up to the norm - what about you?'

Happy

В наших планах – радость созидания,
Вдохновенье мирного труда.
Для народа строим эти здания,
Новые возводим города.

O. Savostjuk, 'Build fast, well and inexpensively! Next pages: N. Boschko, 'With the help of everyone we develop Soviet trade!'

ture, and a year later the Communist Party published the famous declaration 'On abolishing waste in planning and construction'. Again, the mood expressed by the reconstruction posters and the heroes depicted on them changed. The symbols of Stalinist architecture remained, but women reappeared, as can be seen on O. Savostjuk's 'We live up to the norm – what about you?' Finally, a poster by N. Boschko, 'With the help of everyone we develop Soviet trade!' even showed family life and the small pleasures of being happy at home. In 1955, a completely new topic appeared in O. Savostjuk's poster 'Build fast, well and inexpensively!' Here we find poems that seem to reject the heroic rhetoric of the Stalinist poster:

'Our plans are inspired by the joy of creation
Our dedication to peaceful work
For our people we build these houses
And create new cities.'

The Soviet Union entered a new phase that was inaugurated by Nikita Khrushtchev and the battle against Stalin's heritage. Instead of painting illusory pictures of future happiness, symbolized by sumptuous palaces and luxurious architecture, daily labor is now shown as a source of genuine happiness. This happiness is associated with attempts to reduce building costs by introducing industrial techniques, and with the start of the vast building programs that, in the years to come, were to transform the cities of the Soviet empire once more.

Happy

BUILD!

The act of building is the topic of thousands of photos, paintings, films, and even ballads. It is an act of creation, of literally materializing the city of tomorrow. It also boosts productivity: factories, roads, bridges, and healthy homes all contribute to the generation of future wealth. No human activity, moreover, has a more direct impact on the economy. In most economic plans — and in the 1940s and 1950s, these were made by the dozen — the construction industry is used to steer the entire economy, correcting short-term cycles and channeling money, building materials and the labor force into the sectors destined to become the engines of tomorrow's economy. A more direct contribution to future prosperity would be hard to imagine.

The Netherlands, 1950s

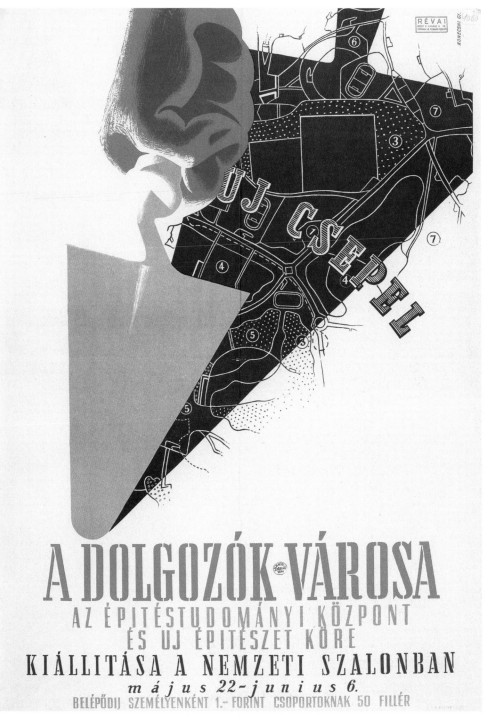

New Csepel, the town of the workers. The exhibition of the Center of Building Science and the Circle of New Architecture, Artist: Konecsni György

Happy

Woman Carpenter near Stalingrad, 1959

Happy

Soviet Union, 1963

Minsk, 1973

Happy

Socialis

Palace

Comm

t-Realist
s for the
on Man

SOCIALIST-REALIST PALACES FOR THE COMMON MAN

In the late 1940s, as the Soviet empire in Middle Europe consolidated, the authorities in Moscow wanted to celebrate the introduction of socialism as a victory for the common man. What better stage on which to present this historical fact than the heart of the city? What better means than creating spacious boulevards lined with luxurious houses that looked like palaces? The appropriate style for this festive architecture had already evolved in Russia in the 1930s. Where architects in Western Europe celebrated the virtues of abstract modernism as the key to a new (international) style that fitted the needs of modern planning, socialist realism addressed popular taste. The term 'socialist realism' was coined during a writer's conference in Moscow in 1934 and marked a shift in the paradigm that governed Russian art and architecture: technology was replaced by humanism.[1] In the terminology of socialism, art expressed social consciousness during the epochal historical transformation from capitalism to socialism, focusing on the driving force behind this transformation, the working classes.[2] Socialist realism had forced M. Stam, J.B. van Loghem, E. May and many others to leave the Soviet Union in the 1930s. However eager they had been to 'build socialism,' their work did not strike a chord with ordinary working people. Something else was needed, something appealing, a style that gave the people the happy impression that they were the new kings, that they represented the power that determined history. The message the new architecture should convey should supersede the hard material facts from which it originated. Architecture was to become a popular mass medium that should encourage the people to enjoy the role assigned to them by the principles of Marxism-Leninism. Socialist-realism was to be the style of socialism everywhere. The need to manifest its inherent message was all the more urgent in the conquered lands east of the Iron Curtain. There, the cities destroyed by war were to be reconstructed in a socialist-realist fashion. The first of the famous 16 principles of town planning, issued by the East German Ministry of Building

Happy

in 1950, is revealing. It celebrated the city as the ultimate expression of political life and of the national spirit, transforming the architect into a 'representative of the political needs of his people, a statesman in the truest sense of the word.'[3] His task was to endow each city with its own specific identity. That called for something else than the application of abstract schemes. Out of the ruins left by the war, the palaces of the common man should arise, and they did. The Marszalkowska in Warsaw, the Stalinallee in Berlin, the numerous 'Magistrales' in East-German cities: all of them were historical symbols. They were inaugurated with people's festivals, and they were the setting for an endless series of parades, with the May Day festivities marking a climax in the socialist calendar of celebrations.

Naturally, architects and town planners in Western Europe were shocked. Not, however, because they deemed the results of socialist-realism ridiculous. Only in the middle of the 1950s did the defamation of socialist-realism as humbug sugar-pie architecture become fashionable. Nor did they see this style as an unacceptable deviation from orthodox modernism – modernism not yet having established itself as the dominant style in the countries west of the Iron Curtain. They feared socialist-realism because of what it was: a very rich popular style that symbolized the successful emancipation of the common man. It symbolized the realization of a goal Western European countries shared with socialism. Luckily for worried Western politicians, the lavish palaces soon turned out much too expensive, and in the middle of the 1950s socialist-realism gave way to a rather basic form of modernism.

1 J. Düwel, *Baukunst voran! Architektur und Städtebau in der SBZ/DDR*, Berlin 1995, 24.

2 G. Conermann, *Bildende Kunst in die soawjetischen Besatzungszone. Die ersten Schritte bis hin zum sozialistischen Realismus im Spiegel der Zeitschrift "bildende kunst" von 1947-1949*, Frankfurt am Main 1995, 41.

3 'Vertreter der politischen Forderungen seines Volkes, zu einem Staatsmann in höchsten Sinne des Worts', 'Grundsätze des Städtebaues', in: *Bau/Holz*, August 1950. Quoted in *J. Düwel, Baukunst voran! Architektur und Städtebau in der SBZ/DDR*, Berlin 1995, 85.

Happy

The Kreshtchatik

Bogdan Tscherkes

Even though the Kreshtchatik is much more than just a simple street, it bears the name 'street'. In the eyes of the town planner, the Kreshtchatik presents itself as a combination of a main traffic thoroughfare with wide sidewalks, a boulevard lined with chestnut trees, three squares and high-rise buildings stemming from different periods and reflecting various stylistic trends. Eighteen streets branch off from the Kreshtchatik, which is 1,200 meters long, its width varying widely, from 52 to 420 meters, but averaging 75 meters.

These facts do not tell us a lot. Everywhere, even in Kiev, there are streets and boulevards that are longer and wider. What is it that makes the Kreshtchatik something special, that attracts people and makes this street a symbol of Kiev and the Ukraine, indeed the main street of the entire country? Something here unites the homeless and the intellectuals, politicians and prostitutes, communists and nationalists, immigrants and patriots. Visiting Kiev without strolling along the Kreshchatik means not visiting Kiev at all.

Ruins of Kreshtchatik street, 1944

Happy

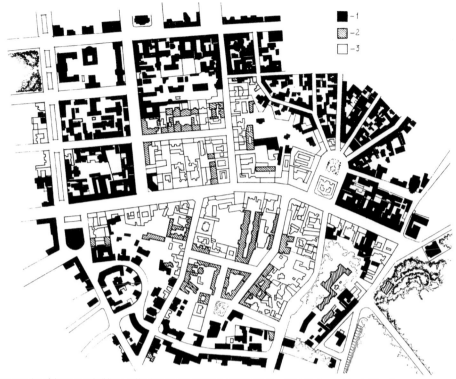

Documentation of damages to buildings on Kreshtchatik street after the 2nd World War, 1944 (dark: remaining buildings)

The Kreshtchatik originated in the eighteenth century and developed into something of a main street in some of the reconstruction plans made after the catastrophic fire of 1811. When Kiev developed into a boomtown in the first half of the nineteenth century, however, the Kreshchatik did not benefit from the beautification plans: the university, the opera and the new cathedral lined the new boulevards that were created elsewhere in Kiev. The construction of the Kreshtchatik was entirely the work of the private entrepreneurs who owned the land in this part of the city. The only contribution the state made was a master plan drawn up in 1837, in which the width of the street was fixed at 34 to 44 meters. The economic boom did the rest.

The Kreshtchatik filled a void between the three distinctive areas that make up Kiev, and when they slowly started to merge, the Kreshtchatik became the new central artery. Not even its less than perfect topography – it was liable to flooding – could keep the street from becoming the heart of Kiev's new urban core. The city's growth was phenomenal: 65,000 people lived there in 1861, and 632,000 in 1914. Kiev joined

Clearance work on Kreshtchatik street, 1944

Happy

Moscow and Petersburg, becoming Russia's third capital city.

The nineteenth-century Kreshtchatik was a mixture of every conceivable style then fashionable in Europe. Most of the buildings were designed by architects who had studied in Petersburg, and their work reflects the impact of the capital. The First World War and the Russian Revolution of 1917 stopped the rapid development of the Kreshtchatik. Since the people of Kiev

Nikita Khrushtchev during the 1st of May Parade, 1946

opposed the new regime, the capital was moved to Charkiv, 500 kilometers to the east and closer to Moscow. Investments poured into Charkiv, and only after a combination of military and economic strategies paved the way for Kiev to resume its traditional role as the capital city did it come back to life. Only a few buildings were erected on the Kreshtchatik, the most notable one being a late constructivist department store designed by Alexey Scusev's office

(D. Fridman and L. Metsojan) in 1936. This building is also the only link between the historical Kreshchatik as it developed until the late 1930s, and the completely new 'Magistrale' that was designed as part of the plans to reconstruct Kiev after its partial destruction in the Second World War. The Kreshtchatik was secretly mined by the Soviet army and when these

Project under device 'Golden Star' for the competition to Kreshtchatik street, 1944

Happy

mines exploded on September 24, 1941, killing all the inhabitants and about 300 German soldiers, the old street was no more. What buildings remained were destroyed during the Battle of Kiev in November 1943.

On June 22, 1944, Nikita Khrushtchev, then leader of the Ukrainian Communist Party, organized a competition for the reconstruction of the Kreshtchatik. The plans were designed to mesh with the political aspirations of Stalin, who wanted Russia, White Russia and the Ukraine to join the United Nations as independent states, a development which would give him three votes. Making the Kreshtchatik look like the main boulevard of a real capital city meant that the new buildings had to be principally representative in character. The most prominent architects of the Soviet Union submitted plans, and in January 1945, an exhibition of 22 projects and 252 exhibits was organized in Kiev's museum of Russian art. Three groups were allowed to continue to the second round. Especially promising was the work of some relatively young architects: Aleksandr Vlasov, Vladimir Zabolotnyi and Aleksej Tacij, all of them winners of the Stalin Prize. The impact of this competition for the reconstruction of cities in the Ukraine can hardly be overestimated. Its results included a treasury of design solutions that were emulated all over the country. Although it was initiated in June 1944, more than a

Dimitriy Tshechulyn, Project for the Main Square on Kreshtchatik street, 1944

Aleksander Vlassov and partners, final project, perspective of Kreshtchatik street, 1949

Bird eye's view of Kreshtchatik, 1956

The laughing people on Kreshtchatik street during the 1st of May Parade, 1953

Happy

Aleksei Taziy and partners: Bird eye's view of Kreshtchatik, competition project, 1944

Viktor Orechov and partners, bird eye's view of Kreshtchatik, competition project, 1944

year before the war ended, all the plans it produced display triumphal arches, monuments and towers – no one seemed to doubt the impending victory of the Soviet Union. After the competition dragged on for two more rounds, A. Vlasov received the assignment to make the final plans for the Kreshtchatik, but when Stalin called Khrushtchev to Moscow, Vlasov soon followed suit, becoming the city's chief architect. The task of finishing the plans for the Kreshtchatik was now entrusted to Anatolij Dobrovolskij. When Stalin failed in his ambition to procure three votes in the United Nations, he no longer needed the Ukraine to look like an autonomous state, and the idea of endowing the Kreshchatik with public buildings was abandoned. In 1946, a giant statue of Lenin had been erected at one end of the street, and it seemed like a good idea to put Stalin's statue up at the opposite end; some of the planners believed that it was quite appropriate to begin the Kreshtchatik with Lenin and end it with Stalin, or the other way around. The everyday life of 'homo sovieticus' would unfold between the two statues. The Stalin monument was never built; instead, in the 1980s a giant steel arch was erected, which was meant to symbolize the reunification of Russia and the Ukraine. (To the inhabitants of Kiev, however, it is known as the 'Yoke of Moscow.')

The Square of the October Revolution (now the Square of

Petro Slota, view of Kreshtchatik, etching, 1956

Serhiy Shyshko, Kreshtchatik, painting, 1973

Alla Sidenko, Kreshtchatik, etching, 1972

Happy

Dancing on the Kreshtchatik, May 2, 1955

Demonstration, May 1, 1955

Youth carrying a model of the Sputnik and a picture of Gagarin, May 1, 1961

Europe) is the monumental climax of the Kreshtchatik. The dense urban tissue that used to exist here was destroyed during the war. The Square's huge dimensions and the way it connects the historical city with the new boulevard always attract people. It is a focus of urban life, and most of the plans made for the Kreshtchatik concentrate on this climax in the city's urban landscape. Drawings made by Vlasov in 1949 already show all the features of the future square.

The Kreshtchatik soon became the role model for all the Magistrales in the Soviet empire, culminating in the Marszalkowska in Warsaw and the Stalinallee in Berlin. As the countries of Eastern Europe were added to the empire in the late 1940s, their architects had to be taught the essentials of socialist-realist architecture and town planning, and the main 'street' of Kiev was seen as one of the most compelling examples. Even today, the people of Kiev like the Kreshtchatik, which is seen as an essentially Ukrainian work of art and architecture. In the early 1990s, hatred of the socialist regime was directed not at the street – even though its Stalinist architecture leaves no room for doubt about its origin – but mainly at the Lenin statues. Apart from some very big ones, there were also a number of more modest monuments. They are all gone now. After the Ukraine became in independent state in the

Fireworks, May 1, 1960

Youth dressed up in cosmonauts' suits, May 1, 1963

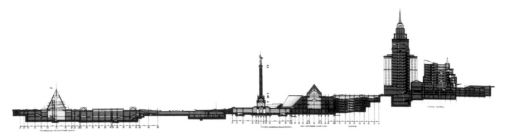

Alexander Komarowskij, design for the reconstruction of Independance Square, section, 2000

Happy

Square of the October Revolution (now Independance Square), october 1978

early 1990s, the Kreshtchatik rapidly became the symbol of political and economic revolution: expensive shops, luxurious shopping malls underneath the square and the street, and a column celebrating Ukrainian independence now dominate the scene, and of course there has been an invasion of commercial billboards. There are plans to build super-modern office towers on the empty plots near the Kreshtchatik, but the hotel on the southern perimeter of the main square that had been planned as a skyscraper but was never finished is now expected to be completed according to the original plans.

Happy

Inauguration of the Lenin statue on the Square of the October Revolution, (now Independance Square), October 1977

Happy

Aleksander Komarovskiy and partners; Independence Column on Independence Square, Kiev, 2001

Leonid Kutchma, president of the Ukraine, and children during the inauguration of the Independence

Column, Kiev 2001

Happy

Warsaw, March 28, 2000.

Tuesday. Back to Warsaw at last! The place where two of my great-grandmothers lived in 1922 and where I arrived for the first time in 1957, witnessing the early freedom movement that found a moderate voice in Gomulka. How strange that family links are felt through generations. Having grown

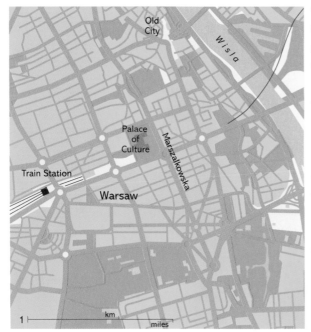

up in the fifties in undefined urban spaces, with ruins making place for green corridors, and having been educated as an architect in the sixties, I felt extremely comfortable on Constitution Square: this was socialist happiness in built form. But almost nobody seemed inclined to agree with me. Political correctness demanded sacrifices: the Stalinist legacy and the terror associated with it acted like a veil over people's memories, and over the built environment. Janusz Durko, the director of the Historical Museum of Warsaw, was the only one who admitted that that day was a beautiful day, the 22nd July 1952 – 'everybody was happy and me too.' So was I after the interview, as my nostalgic longing for defined urban spaces had found a measure of support. Happiness in Warsaw in the year 2000 was, in fact, tied to other places and events. A veritable flood had swept the city with memorials and the Pope had graced the city repeatedly: places for and moments of happiness had been created for every taste. No need to tie events, heroes and people together. What a relief! N.G.

Happy

THE
MARSZALKOWSKA
IN
WARSAW

Niels Gutschow

The movie that celebrated the opening of Marszalkovska Boulevard on July 21, 1952 radiates joy. The socialist world congratulated itself, for the communist paradise appeared to be at hand. A lavishly illustrated book, with large photographs on almost every page, shows the faces of happy people: construction workers on the building site, architects and civil servants giving orders, politicians, children in the bath, families in richly furnished living rooms, people roaming around in shops filled to the top with everything one could wish for. Moving from barren barracks to palatial apartment buildings, from poverty to abundance, everyone had experienced a great leap forward and now belonged to a happy community where everything would be taken care of.[1]

1 *MDM- Marszalkowska 1730-1954*, Warsaw 1954.

Propaganda? Authoritarian regimes are based on suggestion. The chosen ones, who could move to their new homes, were also the protagonists of a 'new mankind', and in return they displayed unquestioning loyalty. There is no doubt that they were happy, at the same time that they were acting the role of being happy. Only much later, when the political context had changed, did they appear to have been collaborators, and become ashamed of their happiness of earlier years.

Socialism: life is a festival
The plans for a new Moscow in 1935 made clear what Stalin expected from a socialist city: it should be compact and endowed with many impressive public squares. A 'beautiful' city would be full of 'captivating motifs,' such as power, greatness,

elegant simplicity and cheerful optimism. Optimism was justified, of course, given the wide-spread conviction that the future socialist society was going to excel in wealth and abundance. In the meantime, Stalin made sure that more and more people participated in the 'modern cult of town planning'. The plans should be partial realizations of the society of the future,

offering the people concrete samples of what such a society could be like. They were built promises of future happiness, characterized by beauty and prosperity. The workers would live in palaces, and life would be transformed into a never-ending festival. Stalin concluded benevolently: 'Life has improved, my friends, life has become more cheerful. And when life is cheerful, it is easier to work hard.'

Warsaw 1952 Already in February 1945, Khrushtchev, who was then secretary of the Ukrainian Communist Party, came to Warsaw with a generous promise: the reconstruction of the city would be Stalin's gift to Warsaw. It took, however, more than five years before the 'bourgeois' architects, who were inspired mainly by British town planning models of the decentralized, open city, gave up their resistance to Stalin's socialist-realism. In June 1949, the special Russian emissary Edmund Goldzamt proclaimed that Polish architecture, too,

Happy

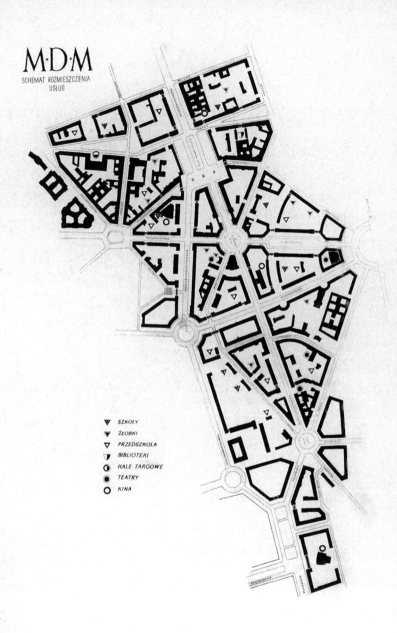

MDM
SCHEMAT ROZMIESZCZENIA
USŁUG

▼ SZKOŁY
▼ ŻŁOBKI
▽ PRZEDSZKOLA
◿ BIBLIOTEKI
◐ HALE TARGOWE
◉ TEATRY
○ KINA

projekt zostaje zatwierdzony.

MDM to budowa: 12 żłobków i 4 Ośrodków Zdrowia!
22 przedszkoli i 11 szkół!
200 sklepów, barów, restauracji i cukierni.

Happy

should be 'national in its design and socialist in its contents'. Only then did the end of 'Anglo-Saxon anti-urbanism' become inevitable. Twenty-one Polish architects were invited on a tour of Moscow, Leningrad, Kiev, Stalingrad and Tiflis to see some prime examples of socialist-realism with their own eyes. Shortly before, in March, the architects Zygmunt Stepinski and Jan Knothe, and the town planners Stanislaw Jankowski and Jozef Sigalin, had been assigned to draw up plans for the principal grand boulevard, Marszalkowska Dzielnica Mieszkaniova, the MDM. Already on July 22, the sixth anniversary of the Declaration of Lublin, President Bierut approved their plans, and work started on the first of August. In his very first speech to the people of Warsaw, shortly after its liberation in 1945, Bierut had promised them a great future: 'Warsawa! We promise you today, while standing amidst the rubble of your beautiful buildings, streets and squares, that we will do everything, we, who love you, to erect a monument worthy of your fame in history.'

In the 23 months that remained until the opening of the MDM, the construction site was filmed and photographed, articles appeared, and poems were written about it. Goldzamt had promised the people 'palaces for the working classes' that would be cheerful in their architectural design. Jankowski, one of the town planners, spoke of an 'unprecedented giant' that would act as an 'island' in the destroyed city.

Construction site and planning
The most important element in the urban plan was a metropolitan square that should serve as a forum for festivals and parades of the people until, one day, the 'Stalin Square' in front of the 'Palace of Culture' – a gift of the Soviet Union – would take over this role. The design of the palace dates from the same time as the plan for the Marszalkowska and was made in an architectural office in Moscow. Contrary to earlier promises, not all of the reconstruction was paid for by the Soviets, but this palace definitely was. East of the new 'Constitution Square,' the boulevard became somewhat less wide to enable the planners to integrate some remaining fragments of buildings and the historical 'Plac Zbawiciela.' In the immediate vicinity, 45,000 houses were scheduled to be built in the course of the Six Year Plan. These, the homes of the official heroes of the working class, were provided with all the

Happy

luxury one could wish for. What was expected from them was that they would do everything they could to increase productivity and break record after record, emulating the example of their famous Russian colleague Stachanov who had given his name to the phenomenon of the 'Stachanov-worker.' This continuous competition between the working population, however, soon became a farce, as Andrzej Wajda demonstrated much later in his movie *Man of Marble*.

In the spring of 1952 no less than 70,000 'volunteers' crowded the construction site of

Happy

the MDM. When a journalist asked a passerby what the purpose of all this activity could be, he was told that the Marszalkowska was going to be the 'central artery in the urban organism' and the climax of 'metropolitan socialist life', the 'center of socialist Warsaw.'

Problems arose when the square was being furnished with cheerful, bigger than life-size statues that were to give it a socialist ring. It proved very difficult to find an appropriate theme. A trio of the usual type, for instance Marx, Engels and Lenin, seemed an obvious choice, but apparently the authorities did not dare to transform the Polish capital into a memorial for Lenin. Less controversial themes, such as 'Silesia, Sea and Capital City' were then put to the test, since they represented the nation in a more general way. This theme was also abandoned. Three enormous candelabra, which were finished just in time, took their place. In the end, the world of socialism could be seen only in a few sculptures showing happy workers.

Happy

The festival on July 22, 1952 The main square was inaugurated on July 22, 1952, the eighth anniversary of the Lublin manifesto. A seemingly endless parade, a 'Defilada', formed by 'young builders of the People's Republic', and guests from all the other People's Democracies, marched through the square. The next day, a new constitution was proclaimed, giving the square its new name: Constitution Square.

Only a few months before, the city had witnessed the usual May Day parade. As always, it followed a route across the Ulica Jerozolimskie, along the city's east-west axis. A model of the new subway was carried along in the parade; it showed a subway car full of jubilant children, framed in a cut-away subway tunnel – a scene that pointed forward to the future, when all

subway stations would look like festival halls. On this occasion, the new route was inaugurated, running southward towards Constitution Square, which stood out like an island in a sea of ruins. A young boy in short trousers crosses the square to hand flowers to the President. The spacious square with its brilliant architecture, the party leaders seated on a tribune, the pioneers who kept on cheering, and the best athletes from the communist empire – everything and everyone radiated optimism, cheerfulness and joy. The young Heroes of Labor carried with them a model of the Palace of Culture, making people aware of this gift of the Soviet Union. Andrzej Wroblewski described the scene as a 'sea of light' and an 'orgy of stone', urging the people to let themselves be seduced by this light, this square and this bright open space.

Happiness and Unhappiness If the Soviets had hoped to seduce the inhabitants of Warsaw into becoming faithful communists, their strategy sadly failed. The motto 'more beautiful than ever' made the bright future look imminent, but history took a different turn. The palaces were much too expensive for the common workman, and so they were allotted to a new class of privileged party members. The white island of the blessed remained an isolated fragment and soon became a symbol of Stalinist oppression. After Stalin's death on March 5, 1953, and

Happy

his subsequent, vehement denunciation by Khrushtchev, the Stalinist urge for wasteful extravagance came to an end. Suddenly, the Marszalkowska and Constitution Square were seen as scandalous mistakes. Denouncing this 'nightmare' became a way showing resistance against the regime.

In March 2000, when we first started to look for the origins of the Six Year Plan and the documents that could tell us more, we met a lot of skepticism in Warsaw. These public places, which were the setting for Stalin's visions of happiness, had undoubtedly become places of unhappiness and shame. This explains why Constitution Square was badly in need of maintenance. After 1989, it had been taken over by dozens of small shops and kiosks. Cheap merchandise

Happy

71

took the place of ideology, and the happiness of consumerism without limits captured Warsaw. Shop windows and billboards praised Lego and Barbie, and a giant photograph of Claudia Schiffer, suspended over the entire square, spoke of a new world of happiness: her phrase 'because I'm worth it' (in Polish: 'jestem tego warta') announces a new perfume that, in the very same words, is advertised in Paramibo, Fukuoka and Groningen.

The way the square has been repainted reminds the visitor that its name refers not only to the constitution of 1952, but also to those of 1797 and 1997. It took quite an effort to prevent the square from being renamed after Ronald Reagan, since in Poland it is the general conviction that the country owes its freedom solely to that American president. One of the very few people we met who readily admitted that he had experienced the square's official opening in 1952 as a joyful event was Janusz Durko, the director of the Museum of the City of Warsaw. 'The sun was shining, the people were cheering.' The historian Jolanta Niklewska remembered the peaceful, happy days she spent there as a child. Her parents, on the other hand, were ashamed of it. A cab driver told us he liked the square, but did not think the architecture was Polish. Wojciech Bruszewski, an architect, thinks that the square is 'at odds with the rest of the city,' an 'implantation'. What is considered most unforgivable is that the axis of the MDM does not lead in the direction of the church on the old Zbawiciela Square. What these critics forget is that the eastern part of the project respects the old building lines. The anger of Warsaw's residents, however, knows no planning history and is concentrated only on failure and guilt. It has only one goal: to get rid of the trauma of Stalinism. The only person we encountered who had a broader outlook was Zygmunt Stepinski, a prolific writer and the son of an architect who had worked on planning the square. He sees the square as an important document of

Happy

European history. He even saw himself obliged, in order to protect his father's heritage, to threaten the city council with a lawsuit in case the original layout of the square was not restored after the removal of the small shops and kiosks.

The inhabitants of Warsaw have more than enough opportunities to identify with good and happy places, and, on the other hand, to rally against what they see as bad and unhappy ones. The city's extremely precarious history seems to elicit this attitude. Almost no one accepts the city, its history, its public places and its heroes as a single entity. Everybody is on the lookout for small fragments of a mosaic that make up an image of a happy past. Hidden in this way of dealing with the city and its past is, perhaps, a continuous dialectical process in which the elements of happiness and unhappiness are forever newly assembled and disassembled. Often, historical distance transforms happiness into unhappiness, and this transformation can be experienced as a relief. A relief from hollow phrases, from masks that hide one's true face, and from grand, theatrical gestures. When the people of Warsaw have felt ashamed long enough, maybe they will rediscover the Marszalkowska and Constitution Square as places to be proud of.

Sources

Bohdan Garlinski, *Architektura Polska 1950-1951*, Warsaw 1953; Andrzej Wroblewski, 'Nowe Domy, Nowi Ludzie', in: *Nowa Kultura*, 24, August 1952; Stanislaw Jankowski, *MDM – Marszalkowska Dzielnica Mieszkaniowa*, Warsaw 1954; Edmunt Goldzamt, *Architektura Zespolow Srodmiejskich i Problemy Dziedzictwa*, Warsaw 1956.

Happy

Science, Technology, and the International Style

SCIENCE, TECHNOLOGY, AND THE INTERNATIONAL STYLE

There are probably few historical epochs that have been as deeply affected by the belief in science and technology as the first decades following the Second World War. (There are precedents, of course. One needs only to think of the last quarter of the eighteenth century, when science also determined the mentality of the epoch.) All aspects of society became subject to the scientific method of solving problems. If problems were surveyed, goals defined, the means calculated, and the plans drafted and checked, then, it was felt, nothing could stop society from moving forward. The evolution of science and technology is a linear process, with the latest inventions and discoveries always improving upon the existing body of knowledge and technical skills. Relying on science, technology and planning, society, too, could evolve in a linear way; the past was condemned as the domain of prejudice, scientific misconceptions, and still unmastered dark impulses. People were fascinated by the promise of science and technology. Television series showed the wonderful world of tomorrow, in which technical gadgets have eliminated tedious housekeeping jobs, medical science has successfully fought hitherto incurable diseases, nuclear physicists have revealed the unlimited sources of atomic power, and the Russians have led the way to the exploration of space. Space represented the new frontier. Planet earth had disclosed all its secrets, and television was bringing the whole world into everyone's living room. An endless series of exhibitions showed how science, technology, planning and modern design were revolutionizing society, and how they would make everyone's life easier. They helped to foster a new brotherhood of mankind that paid no regard to political or economic borders.

No architectural 'style' seemed to be better suited to express the belief in endless progress than the International Style, the Americanized variant of modernism. Apart from a short-lived socialist-realist intermezzo, the postwar era in Europe was completely dominated by modernism. The fact is so overwhelming that it seems perfectly natural, whereas it is actually one of the most striking phenomena

Happy

in the history of architecture and town plan-ning. Before 1945, modernism did not account for more than about 5% of what was built, and probably a lot less; and in the 1930s its share sank dramatically as it was practically banned from Germany, its heartland, and from the Soviet Union. Only the Italian variant survived, as well as the modernist movements inspired by it (in Poland, for instance, and most notably in Hungary). Prewar modernism had been very criti-cal of the political establishment, and its critical attitude partly coincided with the leftist political views of many of its protagonists. By the 1950s, the modernist-inspired 'International Style' had become the household style of the capitalist establishment as well as of the socialist countries in Eastern Europe. How can one explain this sudden breakthrough? The forces behind it are complex, but clearly one of the keys to understanding what happened can be found in the United States. In the 1930s, when the Second World War was already brewing, many leading modernist architects left Europe to settle in the United States. Sigfried Giedion, Walter Gropius, Werner Hegemann, and Erich Mendelsohn were among those who tried their luck overseas. The immigrant architects were warmly welcomed, and acceptance of European modernism gained momentum after 1937, when J. Hudnut, a dean at Harvard University, founded the famous Graduate School of Design and invited Gropius to become its leader.[1] Even so, the victory of modernism was still a long way off. The famous exhibition 'The International Style. Architecture since 1922,' organized by New York's Museum of Modern Art (MoMA) in 1932, had been severely criticized for introducing what was seen by many as an anti-American cultural import. During the early years of their American adventure, many of the former pioneers of European modernism still believed that the United States was culturally backward and in need of their help. Franklin D. Roosevelt's New Deal helped to create more favorable circumstances for modernism. Catering to the needs of the 'common citizen' naturally implied building for the masses, which in turn necessitated experimentation with mass production, industrialized

Happy

77

building techniques and planning – innovations that were characteristic of modernism. In the 1940s, the war economy made the introduction of modern production techniques even more urgent; and hundreds of thousands of Americans had to move to the centers of the war economy, where new housing estates had to be erected for them. Modernism's apparent compatibility with the requirements of mass production and its adoption by MoMA and at Harvard University, two of the most highbrow, elite institutions in the United States, paved the way for modernism there, but it gained popular appeal only after the publication in 1943 of Ayn Rand's *The Fountainhead*, an immediate bestseller. The movie based on her novel, starring Gary Cooper and Patricia Neal, did the rest. Released in 1949, it was an instant success. By then, the rise of modernism to the position of dominant house style of American capitalism was almost complete. It culminated in the late 1940s when its new status was explicitly confirmed in a broad propaganda campaign aimed primarily at Europe. Remarkably, this campaign continued where the wartime propaganda had left off. Official institutions such as the 'United States Information Agency' and the 'Congress for Cultural Freedom' adopted the design language of the former avant-garde as the style best suited to express democratic capitalism, advocating it as the alternative both to 'traditional' architecture, which was now seen as symbolic of the obsolete prewar societies, and to socialist-realism that was promoted at the time as the quintessential socialist style. The International Style promised to be the ideal alternative to both, all the more so since its origins lay in Europe. Part of the strategy to promote the International Style was, therefore, a strong emphasis on its European roots. The intermediate years, when modernism had been expelled from Europe, were usually presented as a regrettable interlude that coincided with the rise of totalitarianism, both rightwing and leftwing. This, naturally, implied a strong and inherent relationship between the International Style and anti-totalitarianism or, in other words, democratic capitalism in its new, socially revolutionized form. However questionable this

Happy

interpretation may be, its impact has been tremendous, and nowhere more so than in Germany, where Gropius was sent in the early 1950s as a special emissary, working mainly in the American occupation zone. He was soon accused of securing all the important posts for former members of the Bauhaus.[2] Despite a short-lived controversy during which the International Style was accused of being anything but democratic, modernism's emergence as the only style that was compatible with the new social and political circumstances was not hampered by the opposition it encountered.

The tremendous prestige of the USA and the efforts to promote the International Style as the cultural expression of the rejuvenated democracies may help to explain the return of modernism to a continent from which it had been virtually expelled in the 1930s. Yet, modernism might still have failed to take hold if its ideology had not coincided with the ideals of constructing a totally new society, an ideal reinforced by the urge to undo the damage of the past. The desire to break away from the past has always been one of modernism's inherent qualities. Its strong and willfully destructive undertones found an outlet in the demolition of entire urban districts in the 1950s and 1960s. The overwhelming success of modernism in the years of reconstruction was, moreover, greatly enhanced by the close alliance its proponents forged with the new professional layer of managers and planners. The planner's ideal of purifying society by eliminating everything that appeared to be irrational was reminiscent of the way modernism had stripped architecture and town planning of everything that could be seen as contingent. The mental attitude underlying modernism was very compatible with the planner's mind. The need to reconstruct almost the entire European continent called for industrialized, modern building techniques on an unprecedented scale, and that obviously called for a modernist approach. What, then, could be more logical than that the International Style become the leading design fashion of the first three decades after 1945? Most of the pioneers of prewar modernism were happy to claim the heritage ofmodern design as their own.

Happy

Some were embarrassed, however, because the claim clearly doesn't hold. Others, J.J.P. Oud, for instance, were quite pleased about the way architecture and town planning had been revolutionized but refused to call the resulting buildings 'architecture' – at best, it was a way of creating interesting and comfortable contraptions that were, however, bereft of intellectual and cultural qualities.

One of the more enduring benefits modernism derived from its ascendancy, however, was the moral prestige it acquired from being declared the cultural expression of the quest for a revolutionary new organization of society. Claiming to be an essential factor in defusing the kind of explosive social tensions that had already caused so much harm, modernism now undertook what could very well be seen as a moral mission that coincided with that of the planners. This also may help to explain the shock wave of moral indignation that arose when postmodernism first made its appearance. Postmodernism represented not just bad taste: it was a social outrage, light years away from the high ideals of postwar modernism. In the meantime, the International Style had been adopted in the socialist countries as well, where, of course, it was seen as a style based on the production processes of mass housing and, firmly rooted as it was in the economy, as a contribution to the new, socialist society. The palaces inspired by socialist-realism fell out of fashion. They were replaced by housing estates built with industrially-produced, prefabricated panels. Perhaps the knowledge that this type of modern production technique was also being adopted in the West helped to make it acceptable – if it was standard practice on the other side of the Iron Curtain, then, at least, it could hardly be considered a totally irrational practice.

1 J. Pearlman, 'Joseph Hudnut's Other Modernism at the "Harvard Bauhaus"', in: *Journal of the Society of Architectural Historians*, December 1997, 458.

2 W. Nerdinger, 'Das Bauhaus zwischen Mythisierung und Kritik', in: *Die Bauhausdebatte 1953. Dokumente einer verdrängten Kontroverse*, Braunschweig/Wiesbaden 1994, 14.

Happy

Budapest, October 28, 2000.

Andrassy Street, once known as the 'Street of the People's Republic,' leads from the center of the city to the Hösök Tér, the Square of the Heroes. Part of the master plan of the 1870s, it is lined with the most luxurious and extravagant apartment buildings, the famous opera house and the ballet theater.

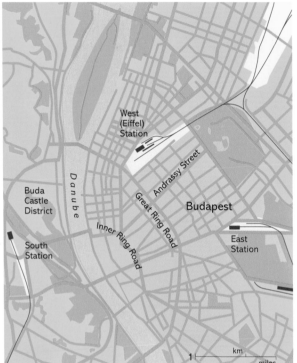

Underneath Andrassy Street runs the first subway of the European continent, and the first electric one anywhere. Built in 1896, it must have carried tens of thousands of civil servants, for they formed the heart of the Austrian-Hungarian Dual Monarchy that evolved after the Compromise of 1867. They were k.k., kaiserlich (imperial) and königlich (royal), and the two 'k''s explain why this huge empire is also known as Kakania. Kakania collapsed in 1914, but its spirit still lingers on. It has become a mental and physical rather than a political entity, and even today it is not hard to imagine that modern bureaucracy is a Kakanian invention. Budapest is still one of the two capital cities of Kakania – Vienna is the other one – and around 1900 it was both the richer and the bigger of the two. Its phenomenal urban structure made it a source of inspiration for the American City Beautiful movement; its unparalleled growth in the last quarter of the nineteenth century, on the other hand, made Budapest the most American of the European metropolises. In a way, Andrassy Street is Budapest in a nutshell. The first two stories of one of the old apartment buildings on the street have been turned into the Ring Cafe. A fat elderly man sits at a table near the entrance, dressed as a farmer would be if he had go to a funeral or a wedding. His voice sounds hoarse, no doubt the result of heavy drinking. He doesn't speak; he barks commands. Two young men, probably in their thirties, sit next to him. The old man is their boss. They remove the ashes from his sleeves if he drops some on them. They bring him his drinks when he orders them – cheap brandy guaranteed to scorch one's throat. A beautiful young woman enters the bar. Her hair is cut the way Sinead O'Conner used to wear hers in the days when *Nothing compares 2U* was on all the hit parades. The old man's two servants jump to their feet, making sure the young woman does not approach their boss. He is in a very bad mood today. On the far side of the bar, she takes off her fur coat. Underneath it she wears the kind of outfit one would expect to see in a nightclub. When she opens her mouth to order a drink, two teeth appear to be missing. A young man enters the cafe and, starting at the back, hands all the guests a small paper card. 'Please help, I'm deaf and I cannot speak' it says in several languages. When he comes near the old man,

Happy

ignoring the warnings of the assistants, he is immediately in trouble. The old man, furious, gets up surprisingly quickly and appears to be about to knock him down. His assistants barely succeed in pushing the young man out of the way. He leaves the bar, his cards lost. Before the door closes behind him, he utters some sounds. He may not be the king of rhetoric, but it is clear what he wants to say: 'Mafia! Mafia!' Shocked and angry, he is on his way. The old man orders a taxi. When he leaves, taking with him his servants and the girl, the bartender is visibly relieved. C.W.

Happy

For the country! For the victory of the Popular Front, 1953

Happy

With the Five-Years Plan for the Happy, Stong, Independent Hungary! On the way of the people's democracy for the socialism!

Happy

Vote for the Five-Years Plan. Vote for the Popular Front!, 1949

Happy

We build the socialism!, 1948

Never forget your past when build your future! Building workers, be among the first ones! Subscribe for peace loan!

Happy

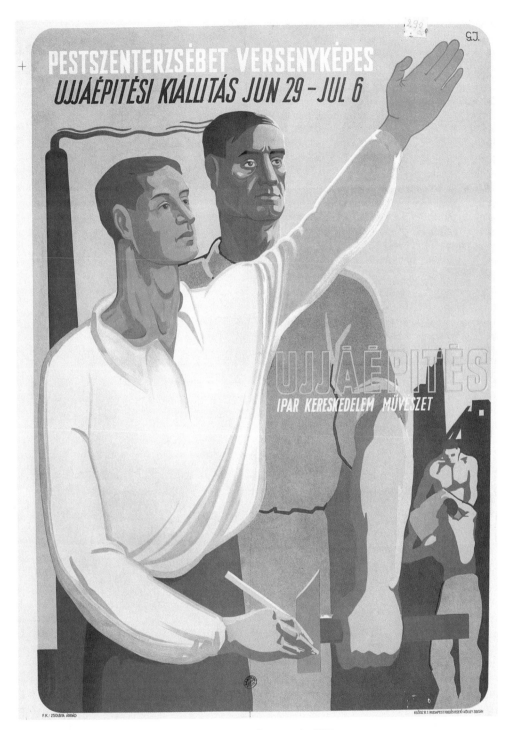

Rebuilding exhibition from 29th June to 6th July. Rebuilding – Industry – Commerce – Art, 1947

Happy

Come to work for the building sites of roads, railways, bridges and canals. You can volunteer at the council and at the recruiter of the company, 19

Happy

Kaunas, September 10, 2000.

Sunday: Before I realized it, I had arrived in a former military zone, where I met the city architect, Nerijus Vlatkevicius, in his office, which is located just behind the reinstalled statue of the legendary figure of Lithuanian history, Witold the Great, who once rulded Europe between the Baltic Sea

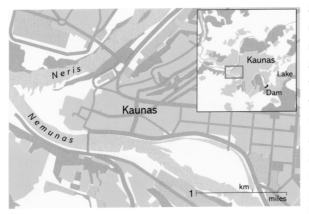

and the Black Sea. I had to learn that memory makes one happy, that one needs heroes to identify with. This was a surprise for me, coming as I do from that other world, where all heroes have vanished in reaction to their over-promotion. The discussion was short, the answer clear: Yes, happiness, 'Laime,' arrived at Kaunas with electricity. From darkness to light — Lenin's promise was fulfilled. The search for happiness became an overwhelming vision: electricity not only lights inner and outer spaces. Light is more than that. It brings forth a new promise of liberation. Was not Stalin seen as a beacon of liberation? With these thoughts in mind, I strolled along the Avenue of Freedom, past shops advertising Gucci, Chanel and Sony: an avenue once named after Stalin and, still earlier, after Kaiser Wilhelm. Now freedom. To do what? N.G.

HAPPINESS IN THE LIGHT. THE CONSTRUCTION OF A NEW POWER PLANT IN KAUNAS, LITHUANIA, 1959

Niels Gutschow

In Rotterdam or Berlin, people hardly ever think of electricity as something special. It is simply there, and apparently always has been. Even during the Second World War, when the bombs destroyed so many cities night after night, the lights never went out for more than a couple of hours. Today, if because of some accident a cable is damaged and the computer doesn't work for a few minutes, people are at a loss.

Less than half a century ago, things were quite different in Europe. Seen from Western Europe, there were still many dark spots behind the Iron Curtain, where, cut off from 'progress' and 'development', the only sources of light were candles and oil lamps. Upon these black spots, the proletarian October Revolution of 1917 built its myth of 'electrification' as a symbol of progress and even revolution. Was it not Lenin himself who stated that communism was equivalent to 'the power of the Soviet Union plus electrification', or, put differently, 'Revolution with electrification'? The pioneers of the Revolution also spoke about 'electrification and the abolishment of illiteracy.' Of course,

And page 92-93. Inauguration festival of the new power plant, 1959

Happy

Construction of the dam

the development of the Soviet Union required electricity, but the ambiguity of the word 'light' epitomized a social program: electricity would, literally, carry the light of the revolution and demonstrate the wealth of the communist era to come. To read by the light of an electric lamp and, thus educated, to belong to the socialist community of mankind – that also was part of the program. The power plant in Kaunas was meant to be a precursor of this bright vision. The light was to lead the way to an epoch of abundance, the happy state of the future. The electrification of Lithuania would stimulate traffic and industry, transforming cities and villages into radiant symbols of light. From now on, wealth and progress would determine the course of the Lithuanian nation. Kaunas (Kovno, in Russian and Polish, Kauen in German), ideally situated at the confluence of the Nemusas and Neris Rivers, has a fateful history that can be traced back to the twelfth century. Between 1920 and 1940, the city was the provisional capital of the equally provisional independent Lithuanian state. With more than 400,000 inhabitants, it is today the country's most developed industrial city. Already in 1926, a new power plant had been planned on the Nemusas, and only a few years later a disastrous flood demonstrated once again the necessity of taming the power of the river, at the same time making use of it for the production of electricity.

In September 2000, when I explained the plans for this book to members of the city government and the technical university, the town planner Nerijus Valatkevicius spontaneously exclaimed that the real carriers of happiness in Kaunas were the dam that had been built in the second half of the twentieth century, protecting the city, and the power plant that, literally, had brought light to the city.

Happy

Since its incorporation into the Soviet Union in 1944, Lithuania has depended on the centrally organized production of energy, including electricity. In 1955, the central offices of the 'Hydroenergy Project' in Moscow decided to build both the dam and the power plant, and on the 23rd of October, 1957, a series of festivities marked the opening of the construction site. Two years later, the dam was finished and the level of the water behind it began to rise as far as 82 kilometers inland, forcing farmers to move to newly built villages elsewhere. The 2,000 construction workers and the work force of the power plant were housed near the dam in a new village, which, of course, was designed to demonstrate the ideal ways of living appropriate for a socialist state. Attaining an output of more than 500,000 kilowatts, the power plant reached its full capacity in April 1960. Each phase of its construction was celebrated with elaborate opening rituals, and these festivities were celebrated in a fascinating movie that highlights the glory of the entire enterprise in its title: *Light of the Nemusas*. It tells the gospel of a light that not only shines in the city and the villages, but also illuminates the country's bright future. A series of postcards, produced in the year of the opening, shows the power plant as it towers above the river, transforming the latter's former destructive potential into useful energy that is distributed via transmission towers to the remotest villages of the land.

In 1959, students of the technical university who worked on the construction site during the summer period, organized in 'Brigades,' wrote an opera, which, however, remained unfinished and was never performed. Set to music by V. Telksnys, the lyrics of Jurgis Bucas glorify the students' life in the *Tents of the Students* (as the opera is called), and the happiness of the light that will soon be shining:

Happy

Thousands of years in Kaunas
the rapid water of Nemunas
surrounds the Motherland of Lithuanians
like a silver belt

Passing the gardens of native land
and new settlements
sparkling with flashes
he waves into the lagoon

New constructions in Kaunas
dammed up swift Nemunas
Nemunas flooded like a lagoon
celebrates new life

He washed away many dreams
of Lithuanians into the lagoon,
he accumulated deep flow
to turn the turbines

New constructions in Kaunas
dammed up swift Nemunas.
Nemunas brings light
and happiness to cities and villages.

Construction of the dam

Happy

Though the opera was never finished, the songs were played on the radio and even today they remind people of the happy times when the power plant was built. Algirdan Brazauskas, once head of the Lithuanian Communist Party, then president of the independent state of Lithuania, and since July 2001 Prime Minister, remembers how the construction site helped to strengthen the political structure of the socialist establishment: it was at the building site that the political leadership saw its own visions of happiness realized.

As so often happens, heaven and hell, happiness and unhappiness seem close to one another. Forty years after the opening of the power plant, there are people who see in its construction a diabolical plan of the former Soviet Union: the secondary dam that would have protected the city in case the main dam collapsed was never built. The building that brought the light represented at the same time the threat of a devastating flood. Would not the Russians be happy to destroy it, if the Lithuanian people revolted? For more than thirty years, these fears remained silent rumors. After the fall of the Soviet empire, these suspicions came out into the open. In the 1990s, they helped to destroy the myth of the power plant as the carrier of the light. New, immaterial values came to the fore: 'freedom' now captured the minds of the people.

Happy

New village for the construction workers of the dam and the power plant

Happy

Searching for Star Happiness: A Fairytale

Bogdan Tscherkes

Stars do not always live only in Hollywood. Once upon a time, when the Soviet Union still existed, some of them lived in Russia and they were searching for star happiness. On April 12, 1961 the first man ever flew into space, the Soviet pilot Yuri Gagarin. To make this happen, other events had to take place previously: starting in October 1957 manmade satellites were sent into orbit around the earth, and then, in 1960, the first living beings followed. They were dogs. Hence the fame and glory of having discovered the cosmos can be claimed neither by the Americans nor by the Russians, although, to be sure, the dogs carried typical Russian names: 'Bielka' and 'Strielka.' Their picture was broadcast from space to TV screens and printed by all the important newspapers in the world, and artists portrayed them, as well. What they did not get, were parades and poems. This came later and was done for human beings, because, no matter how cruel man can be to his fellow beings, he still loves his own kind best.

Gagarin spent 89.1 minutes in space. This is, of course, a very short time compared to the many months astronauts spend in space nowadays. But never again did a space flight cause such happiness, such admiration and delight on this earth:

Happy

With his hand touching sun and stars,
He races above the Earth,
And all the Earth fell silent
Ready to listen forever to the voice from universe...

We love the one
Who was the first to fly into the starry distance
To whom we eagerly listened and for whom we waited,
We love the one
Whose flight is our hope and glory,
Who told the stars about the dreams on Earth

This poem was written by the Hungarian poet Antal Gidash in admiration of Gagarin's flight.[1] In the cities there were spontaneous gatherings of enthusiastic people. It looked as if tomorrow, or if not tomorrow then the day after tomorrow, everybody was going to fly into space, and with that all worldly problems would be solved or simply disappear. People in general like to forget or leave behind their worldly problems if they cannot solve them, and all of a sudden such an opportunity came up! 'Earth is the cradle of reason, but you cannot live for all eternity in a cradle. The time has come and man has left his cradle and opened the road to the planets!' exclaimed Alexander Nesmejanov.[2] Everybody wanted to become an astronaut: to fly, to fly off, and to fly away!

1 Antal Gidash, 'Rukoj kasajas zviozd. Stihi o pervom kosmonavte' (The Hand that Touches Stars. Poems about the first astronaut), in: *Pravda*, 15 April 1961.

2 Alexander Nesmejanov, The Road to the Planets is Open, in: *Pravda*, 13 April 1961.

The first living beings in space:
Bielka and Strielka

Oh yes! Only yesterday Yuri Gagarin was an unknown major in the Soviet army, and today he is the hero, the star, the idol of many! People talk about him, write about him, and everywhere they show his photos and his portrait. The leader of the Soviet Union himself, Nikita Khrushtchev, cuts short his vacation in Sotchi to fly to Moscow and gather with the other members of his government and the leadership of the Communist Party and the Supreme Soviet of the USSR at the airport in Vnukovo to meet the hero. Everywhere a sea of people, flowers, flags and portraits of Lenin, Khrushtchev and Gagarin. And then, on April 14, 1961, at 12:37, an expectant murmur rises on the airfield: 'the airplane, Gagarin's airplane!'. Accompanied by an escort of jets, the Iljushin 'IL-18' approaches the airstrip. The airplane makes a loop over Moscow, and a military orchestra intones 'Welcome in Moscow,' written in Gagarin's honor. The air-

Happy

ДОРОГУ К ЗВЕЗДАМ
ПРОКЛАДЫВАЮТ
КОММУНИСТЫ!

Khrushtchev presents Gagarin at the Red Square

plane lands close to the red carpet, and Major Gagarin swiftly walks down the runway. He takes a hundred steps to the red carpet and stops in front of Khrushtchev, who takes off his hat and kisses the hero. Khrushtchev and Gagarin parade among the many rows of spectators on the Moscow airfield. After a few minutes, Khrushtchev and Gagarin and his wife climb onto a light blue car with the top down, decorated with festoons of red roses. The car heads off towards Moscow. Everywhere along the way from Vnukovo to Red Square, hundreds of thousands of happy and enthusiastic Muscovites welcome the motorcade 'Hurray to the hero of space!' They arrive at an unusually beautiful Red Square. A huge billboard with a portrait of Lenin and another one with a picture of the spaceship and its pilot Gagarin towers over it. On blood-red flags one can read 'Honor and Glory to Comrade Yuri Alexeievitsh Gagarin – the conqueror of space!'. Tumultuous ovations thunder across Red Square.[3]

For the first time, such an event is broadcast live from Moscow to Europe: 'For the first time yesterday millions of people from 14 European countries – England, France, Italy, Czechoslovakia, Poland, Belgium, Sweden, Denmark, German Democratic Republic, Switzerland, the Federal Republic of Germany, Finland, and the Netherlands – saw Moscow on their TV screens, watched how the Soviet capital honored the first astronaut in world history, Yuri Alexeievitsh Gagarin. 'Today we report a moment of history', a BBC reporter announced when he began the broadcast. Moving moments of the festive welcome of the world's first astronaut at Vnukovo airport take place before the eyes of Londoners. Also broadcast is the rally on Red Square, the moving

3 'Yuri Gagarin reports. A festive welcome in Moscow; The heroic deed will live forever! Demonstrations and rallies on the Red Square,' in: *Pravda*, 15 April 1961.

Happy

appearance of Gagarin, the splendid speech of the leader of the government of the USSR, Khrushtchev, the festive parades of the Muscovites in front of the grandstands at the Mausoleum. According to our data, three to four million people in London watched the program in London.... 'Attention, this is Moscow' – sounded the voice of the newscaster, and the citizens of Paris, Bordeaux, Marseilles, Lille, and of hundreds of other cities and villages in France could watch with their own eyes the reception given by the Muscovites to the hero of space....[4]

Gagarin's appearance and the interview with him were nothing special. He said what the Soviet ideologists had prepared for him and what they wanted to hear: 'I experienced an enormous happiness when I was trusted with this flight. Like many Soviet people, I had asked to be the one to fly into space. And indeed, the Party, the Soviet people entrusted me with such a task which had never been undertaken.... Long before that memorable spring morning, I decided in my heart to dedicate the impending flight to our Communist Party, our people....'[5]

In August 1961 the second Soviet astronaut, German Titov, flew into space. Starting with the year 1962, space flights gradually became routine. However, until his early and tragic death in an airplane crash in 1968, Gagarin was a most appreciated and sought after guest 'from space' in all the lecture halls of the world. Unfortunately, the topicality of the event faded and it became clear that man had to look for his happiness on Earth. But the first astronaut will always remain a symbol for people looking for star happiness.

4 'The world listens, the world applauds,' in: *Pravda*, 15 April 1961.

5 'Yuri Gagarin reports,' in: *Pravda*, 14 April 1961.

Postcard of Gagarin

Poster 'Unparalleled Flight to the Stars', with showing Gagarin and the festivities in Moscow. Artist: Ch.K. Mistakidi

Happy

Brussels, August 31, 2004.

In Brussels, a peculiar feeling came over me. It was caused by an avalanche of impressions, not unlike the experience you sometimes have in a crowded department store. I think about the nineteenth century, accumulations, contradictions, differences. Brussels is always different, yet always the same.

Ceaseless demolition, new things on top of the old, different styles side by side, a mixture of concrete and brick. The popular element is being lost, the common people are leaving; the petit bourgeois, foreigners, the overwhelmingly rich and the appallingly poor, people bent on showing off, as well as paupers, diplomats, interpreters, civil servants are trying to start a new life here. The Atomium, Koekelberg, the Palace of Justice: a skyline of symbols, and less and less of modern skyscrapers. And, not far from the sea: rain. Cars are everywhere. In Brussels you get lost in the city, in eating and drinking in filthy streets, and in the stalls selling second-hand books and reproductions of old and new masters. P.U.

Happy

Expo '58

Pieter Uyttenhove

Not only did the World Expo of 1958 celebrate progress in an unequivocal way; above all, it expressed an indestructible belief in universal welfare and the eagerness of all people to cooperate in order to enhance their shared ideals. All nations, it was said, should be able to

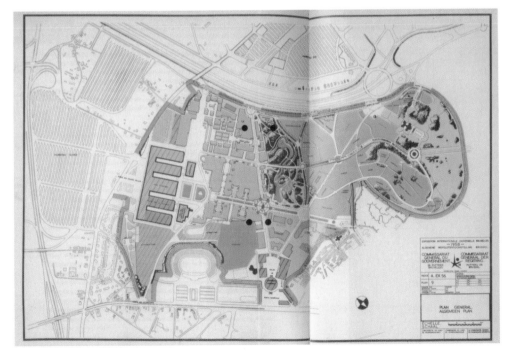

Plan of Expo '58

present their own ideas about happiness and the ways to achieve it. If politics is tantamount to promoting happiness, so the organizing committee declared, then all nations should be given an opportunity to show how they conceived happiness and how they thought about the material and moral conditions necessary to realize its promises. The means of communications were improving, diminishing the physical and mental distances that once separated people; the speed of transportation was increasing, and the sources of energy becoming ever more abundant; technology was advancing ceaselessly; and standards of living were rising. In short, modernity was paving the way for a future where the dramatic consequences of the war could be overcome. The aim of Expo '58 was to usher in a new historical epoch enlightened by universal human ideals. Never before or since have the hopes and expectations fostered by development plans for Europe's oversea colonies, encompassing the social, cultural and economic realms, flourished more abundantly than they did at this period – Belgium, the exhibition's host country, was proud of its achievements in central Africa. All countries should embark on a common voyage on board the same ship, and improving conditions in the underdeveloped world would, it was assumed, help enable its peoples to get on board as well. The epoch that witnessed Sputnik, rock and roll, and television, was symbolized by the Atomium: a building 150 billion times the size of a molecule – a surreal and materialistically inspired practical joke in steel and aluminum.

Match, cover

French pavilion

Happy

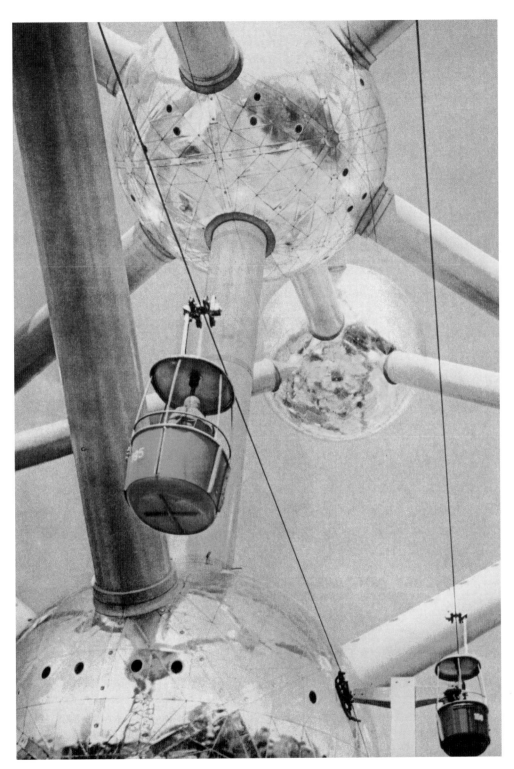

Atomium, Brussels

Happy

Moscow, June 23, 2001.

Even today, the subway station is called VDNKh, Exhibition of the Successes of the People's Economies in the Soviet Union. Once built as a permanent showcase of the superiority of socialism, the site has now become a favorite gathering place for successful Russian entrepreneurs. Now, Western luxury is on display in pavilions richly decorated with socialist symbols – and nobody cares. All the signs of the old socialist iconography are still there: the red star, working men looking like bodybuilders, the proud farmer's wife carrying a plucked chicken, the hammer and sickle, the Fountain of Friendship between the peoples of the earth. They are now the setting for Mercedes, Sony and Gucci. Nothing has changed in the way the buildings look; even the speakers that are hidden in the golden spikes are still there. The propaganda that once reminded the labor force of its great historical mission, however, has died down, replaced by the kind of shopping mall music that accompanies the lust for material consumption. J.D.

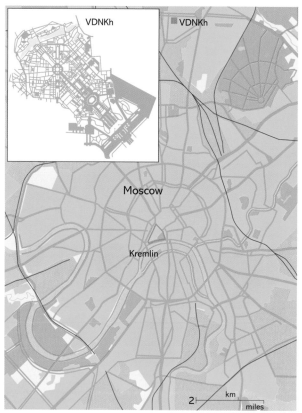

VDNKh

VDNKh

Moscow

Kremlin

km
2
miles

Happy

Exhibiting the Achievements of the People's Economy in the Soviet Union

Jörn Düwel

The first exhibition to celebrate the achievements of the people's economy of the Soviet Union – as it was called to emphasize it's socialist nature – was organized in Moscow in the 1920s. The new Soviet empire was eager to show that a socialist society could boast a strong and healthy economy, and obviously there was no better place to demonstrate the virtues of Soviet industry than in Moscow, capital of the first socialist state. The show was meant to be a permanent one. The area where it took place was continually expanded, and once in every ten years or so the pavilions were demolished and replaced by bigger and more beautiful ones. The exhibition reached its climax in the early 1950s. Now that the 'great patriotic war' had been won, it became imperative to commemorate victory and stress the new self-consciousness

The VDNKh in the 1950s

Happy

of the Soviet Union. Almost all the pavilions were replaced, and new ones were added. All the Soviet republics were asked to create displays about themselves in their own national buildings. To these, a series of thematic pavilions was added, including, for instance, the Hall of Mechanization, the Pavilion of the Economy, a building for the communist youth organization, and pavilions for the huntsmen and agriculture. The exhibition drew many visitors, attracted not only by the expectation of seeing fascinating new products, but also by the opportunity to escape their everyday routines. Spacious parks with many cafes surrounded the pavilions, and an existing subway line was extended, with terminals named after the exhibition.

In the late 1950s and early 1960s, the exhibition in Moscow was emulated in most of the capital cities of the Soviet republics, although the size and luxury of the Moscow example was never equaled. The aim was always the same: to present an idealized picture of the economic capacity of the Soviet Union, showing respect, of course, for the current political framework. The evolution of socialist man, a new type of human being, was always the central topic of these shows, which were obliged to demonstrate new ways of life, based entirely on socialist values. Extensive programs were designed, ranging from the way the exhibits were presented to a specific iconography, and numerous surviving paintings, mosaics, relief tableaux and sculptures still testify to the collective character of these exhibitions.

The VDNKh in the 1950s. Fountain of Friendship between the People of the Earth

Happy

'Rotterdam Ahoy'

Evelien van Es

To commemorate the reconstruction of the port of Rotterdam, the municipal administration, marking its ambition that the city become the world's largest port, decided to organize a major exhibition in 1950, named, appropriately, after a shipboard term: 'ahoy'. No limits were placed on the amount of resources made available for showing how the port had grown in the past, and how it was expected to continue to grow in the near future. The use of cheap materials was out of the question; only real objects were to be shown. The internationally renowned architects Van den Broek and Bakema were engaged to supervise the plan for the show, which was held in a park near the river. The centerpiece was a series of pavilions that demonstrated the whole range of activities that go on in a port the size of Rotterdam. The most spectacular was a huge basin that contained models of all the seagoing ships registered in Rotterdam. A bridge led to the park, where visitors could gaze at a diorama representing the hibernation of Willem Barentsz and his crew, who survived the harsh winter on Nova Zembla after his ship had been wrecked by drifting ice, (one of the most heroic events in the seventeenth century, Holland's Golden Age). Another pavilion evoked the sight one might encounter when traveling underwater in a submarine. A 'joyous corner' brought back memories of prewar Rotterdam. At a quay near the river, full-size parts of modern ships could be admired, and one could also board a ship for a trip through the port. One and a half million visitors saw the show, and they were deeply impressed by it. 'Rotterdam Ahoy' demonstrated that Rotterdam may have lost its center during the air raid, but not its spirit. The show radiated confidence in the future, when the port would continue to flourish and grow.

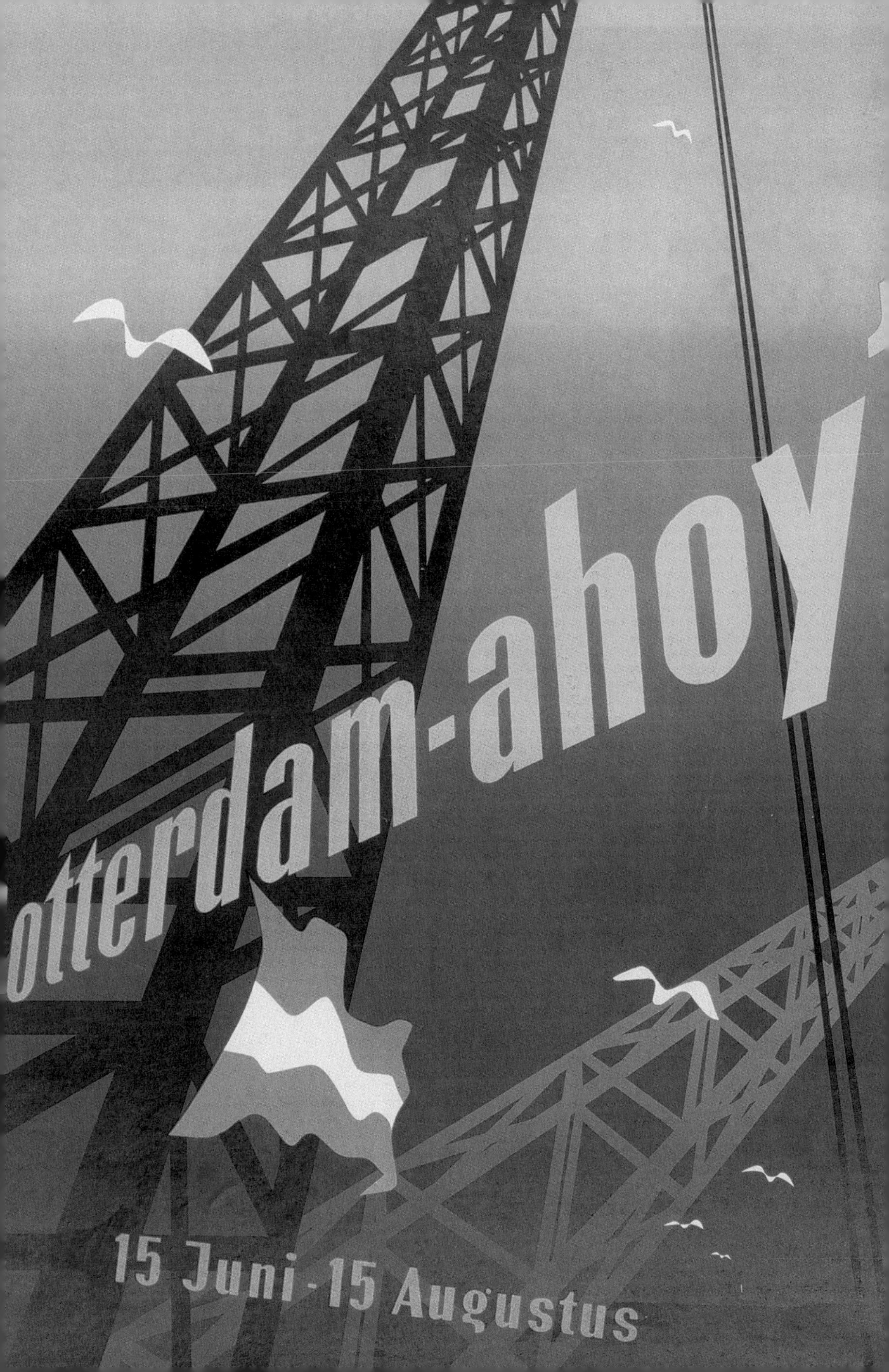
otterdam-ahoy
15 Juni - 15 Augustus

Happy

Happy

The
New
Community

COLLECTIVE HAPPINESS

If the tragedies of the fateful years after 1939 had been man-made, it was not enough to focus on the political make-up of society, to correct chaotic and irrational nature by introducing modern planning, or to think about a wholesale cultural renaissance. Man himself had to be addressed. No wonder, then, that the interaction between the individual and his social and physical surroundings – with the latter often being treated as a foundation for the former – became the overriding theme of the 1950s and 1960s, in literature, photography, the visual arts and, especially, in architecture and town planning. Naturally, modern architecture and town planning appeared to be exceptionally well equipped to contribute to these new relations. The functional layout of the public domain was seen as a powerful tool to promote a new community spirit. It demonstrated how a planned community fosters social relations by bringing together different social groups and providing opportunities for people to meet each other. This repositioning of mankind, this 'situated modernism,' to quote a phrase coined by Sarah Goldhagen, derived its urgency from the belief that it would contribute to removing the mechanisms that had led to the war and, left unattended, might result in further catastrophes of a potentially even more threatening nature. Architecture and town planning became instruments in situating man in his social environment, in the city, in nature, and even in the cosmos (which in these years became a popular fascination and posed a new frontier for scientists to explore).

A consequence of this attempt to reposition the individual in his social environment was the almost complete collectivization of society. In the socialist countries that made up the Soviet empire, the collectivization of life was almost complete. Youngsters were induced to join the pioneers, a socialist phenomenon that excelled in luxurious holiday resorts, some of them offering, for instance, miniature railway lines operated by retired railway workers, or, as in former East Germany, special trains that carried the pioneers all over the country. The party and the labor unions provided a comprehensive network of social clubs, political organizations and cultural institutions that left very little opportunity for private initiatives in any aspect of life. Paradoxically, these all-encompassing, collective undertakings were not unique to socialism. For decades, they were also something like a cultural ideal in the capitalist democracies of Western Europe and the United States. The collective nature of Western society was fostered by the totalitarian nature of modern planning, the belief that a cultural renaissance required a homogeneous society, and the fear that the existence of social groups that did not share the fundamental values of the community at large could easily lead to social upheaval – for decades, the rise of fascism was referred to as the nightmarish outcome of social disintegration. However collectivist Western society may have been in the years of reconstruction, it never resorted to repression, political trials or censorship, McCarthy's short-lived red scare in the United States being the only exception. In the words of one of Philip Roth's characters in his novel *I Married a Communist*, McCarthyism inaugurated '…the postwar triumph of gossip as the unifying credo of the world's oldest democratic republic. In Gossip We Trust. Gossip as gospel, the national faith. McCarthyism as the beginning not just of serious politics but of serious *everything* as entertainment to amuse the mass audience. McCarthyism as the first postwar flowering of the American unthinking that is now everywhere."¹ In terms of repressive machinery, however, McCarthyism was incomparable to what was going on in Central and Eastern Europe.

The welfare state that was to be the Western equivalent of socialism also necessitated the construction of large-scale collective arrangements that were increasingly difficult for the individual to evade. The number of civil servants engaged, for instance, in the administration of the social security systems increased as these systems expanded, subjecting the majority of the people to a growing number of compulsory measures. Work life changed, too, as scientific management techniques grew more important, assigning each employee a specialized part of the work and reorganizing modern enterprises through the development of sophisticated processes the efficiency of which depended on planning and coordination. The result was a change in the quality of life and the emergence of *The Organization Man*, to quote the title of William H. Whyte's well known book. The organization man displayed three specific qualities: 'a belief in the group as the source of creativity; a belief in belongingness as the ultimate need of the individual; a belief in the application of science to achieve the belongingness'.[2]

One of the characteristics of modern mass society was, not surprisingly, its uniform quality, a consequence of the standardization of people's needs and wishes that is also manifest in the uniform qualities of some of the most widespread icons of urban happiness. In *The Lonely Crowd*, David Riesman, Nathan Glazer and Reuel Denney explained this unifying tendency by the 'other directed' psychological make-up of the organization man. 'What is common to all the other-directed people is that their contemporaries are the source of direction for the individual – either those known to him or those with whom he is indirectly acquainted, through friends and through the mass media.'[3] The media greatly contributed to the collective character of postwar society and they did so not because they enforced uniformity, but because organization man longed for it. Evidently there was no need for the sometimes elaborate systems of control and suppression established in some of the socialist countries.

Contrary to what one might expect, most politicians, planners and scientists regarded this shift as beneficial and necessary. Some even saw it as the next phase in evolution. B.F. Skinner, whose ideas were quite influential in the 1950s and 1960s, claimed that the essential feature of the next phase in evolution should be the scientific exploration of the last domain that still escaped man's complete understanding: human behavior itself. This was all the more important since the tragedies of the Second World War had not been the consequence of some kind of natural disaster. This greatest of all catastrophes had been entirely man-made; in other words, it was the result of man's behavior. Since planning promised to reshape society, what was most urgently needed was a 'behavioral technology comparable in power and precision to physical and biological technology.'[4] Obviously, what distinguished this latest phase in evolution was that it was determined by man himself, and not by the blind forces of natural selection.

Astonishingly, the strong belief in planning and in the need to make scientifically-based decisions was mirrored in the contemporary visions of Richard Neutra, the Austrian born architect who settled in California in the 1930s. 'Design,' Neutra claimed, 'is the specific responsibility to which our species has matured, and constitutes the only chance of the thinking, foreseeing, and constructing animal, that we are, to preserve life on this shrunken planet and survive with grace.'[5] The captions in the book are revealing: 'Mankind precariously floats to its possible survival on a raft, rather make-shift as it is, and often leaking: Planning and Design,' or 'From a baby carriage to a metropolis, our man-made surroundings, top-heavy with technological trickery, have become our mold of destiny – and a source of never-ending nervous strain.'[6] There was no need for despair, however, since 'Individual and social psychology will ultimately merge with BRAIN PSYCHOLOGY, TO GUIDE THE DESIGNER IN THIS OBSERVATION AND CREATION RESPONSE PATTERNS,' and, to conclude: 'THE ART OF DESIGN can associate itself with scientific skill, and do so WITHOUT AN INFERIORITY COMPLEX.'[7]

1 Philip Roth, *I married a communist*, London 1998, 284.

2 W.H. Whyte Jr., *The Organization Man*, New York 1956, 7.

3 D. Riesman, N. Glazer, R. Denney, *The Lonely Crowd. A Study of the Changing American Character*, New York 1956, 37.

4 B.F. Skinner, *Beyond Freedom and Dignity*, New York 1971, 5.

5 R. Neutra, *Survival Through Design*, New York 1954, 6.

6 R. Neutra, *Survival Through Design*, New York 1954, 17, 23.

7 R. Neutra, *Survival Through Design*, New York 1954, 202, 381.

Happy

Turin, January 25, 2003.

The *Pinacoteca* on the roof of the Lingotto, where the Agnelli family has chosen to display the body of Giovanni Agnelli after his death, is just three months old. Renzo Piano's building is the latest step in a series of architectural interventions that have reshaped Fiat's factory during the last twenty years. It was

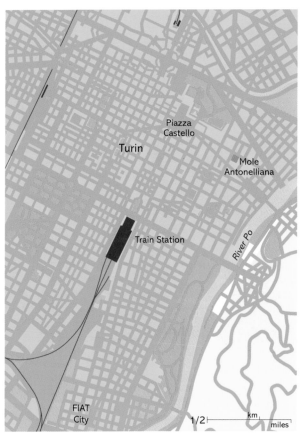

built to host Giovanni and Marella Agnelli's collection of paintings. We do not know how many people have visited the collection in the past few weeks, but certainly there are many more coming now. Journalists have been surprised. They report that no less than 100,000 people have gathered to say goodbye to the *Avvocato*, a number which amounts, roughly, to one ninth of Turin's population. People pass in front of the body, cross themselves, shake hands with the members of the family. Giovanni Agnelli's body was meant to stay here for a few hours; the family, over-whelmed by the popular participation, has decided to keep the gallery open all night. The men and women waiting in this long, silent line have lived most of their lives in a city where Fiat was almost everything. Giovanni Agnelli has been a familiar figure (sometimes beloved, sometimes hated) for all of them. His is, in many ways, the funeral

of a king. His death marks the end of an era, and everybody around us seems conscious of that. The Agnellis' and Fiat's future is uncertain. Turin is doing its best to become less and less Fiat-dependent. The spectacular, 1 km-long Lingotto building has been turned, since production ceased in 1982, into many things at once: an exhibition center; a congress center; an engineering faculty; a five-star hotel; a shopping mall; a multiplex cinema; a concert hall... Projects have changed over time, and new ones are underway: Turin's first subway line will come here within a few years, and the surrounding area will be a key location during Turin's 2006

Winter Olympic Games. The Lingotto is becoming important in Turin's new, 'post-industrial' geography, and the Pinacoteca may very well be the only part of the building where its link with the Agnellis can still be perceived. But this long, silent line indicates that it will probably take quite a long time to cancel the traces of the industrial city from people's lives and memories. P.S., F.d.P.

Happy

Fiat Torino

Filippo de Pieri, Paolo Scrivano

'Per Avandero [...] la città era un mondo perso, una macina per produrre i mezzi d'uscirne quelle poche ore e poi tornarci. [...] La storia della sua vita [...] era la storia dei suoi mezzi di trasporto: prima una bici a motore, dopo un motoscooter, poi una moto, adesso l'utilitaria, e gli anni a venire erano già segnati dalle previsioni di automobili sempre più comode e veloci.'
ITALO CALVINO, *LA NUVOLA DI SMOG*, 1958

Turin's association with automobile production is often taken for granted by its inhabitants, an attitude that has remained almost unchallenged even after the crisis suffered by the automotive industry in the last decade. Obviously, given the complexity of the social fabric of a city of nearly 900,000 inhabitants (around 1,500,000 including the metropolitan area), Turin could not be described as dominated by a single economic system, but its social rhythms and dynamics have undoubtedly been significantly influenced by the overwhelming presence of that industry. The decisive emphasis on manufacturing, however, is a relatively recent phenomenon in Turin's history. In fact, the origins of the automobile industry, between the end of 19th century and the beginning of the 20th, are tied to Turin's conversion from a bureaucratic to a manufacturing center. First the capital of a strongly centralized country, namely, the Kingdom of Sardinia, and then of a new national state, Italy, Turin suffered a reverse when the Italian capital was transferred to Florence in 1864. The loss of activities related to the state administration and the consequent population decline condemned the city to almost two decades of decline.

Turin recovered from the crisis thanks to the presence of certain previously state-owned activities such as the arsenal and the railway workshops, industries that required skilled workers and that consequently were later able to generate employment for the local labor force. By the turn of the twentieth century, more than a hundred small companies manufacturing bicycles and other sorts of vehicles had been established. Fiat (Fabbrica Italiana Automobili Torino – Turin's Italian Car Factory), for example, was founded in 1898. Even though only a few of these companies survived the first decade of the 20th century, at that point the social and economic profile of contemporary Turin had been defined. Moreover, during World War One demand from the armed forces strengthened the importance of the manufacturing sector. It was only after World War Two, however, that Turin began to take on the appearance of the *città dell'automobile*, the Italian variant of *Motown*, in a process that was accompanied by dramatic transformations. In fact, few Italian cities experienced as great an urban mutation as did Turin after 1945. The change was, in part, a consequence of wartime events; for allied air raids had

Happy

destroyed or heavily damaged more than 10,000 buildings. But war damage alone was not responsible for the changes that affected the city: in the postwar years, Turin's transformation was related mainly to an impressive immigration that nearly doubled the population of the city, increasing the number of its inhabitants from less than 700,000 in 1946 to 1,025,000 in 1961.

page 124: Felice Casorati, Fiat 600/Notturno torinese, 1956

page 125: Advertising for the Fiat 500 and 600 series

Population growth obviously went hand in hand with intense building activity. Construction between the end of the war and the mid-1950s was in general dominated by a number of professional figures, mostly engineers or *geometri* (professionals with a college-level degree and certain limitations as regards design competency); the presence of architects, measured by the number of building permits granted by the municipality, never exceeded 11% of the total. In this context, architects seemed to have concentrated on a limited number of isolated interventions. In fact, the majority of buildings designed by architects were confined to a precise segment of the real estate market: a 'niche' demanding high quality detailing, good technical performance and an aesthetic that identified the architecture in question as 'designed', thus differentiating it from the mass produced market and developers' speculative building. Architects such as Passanti and Perona, Carlo Mollino, Gabetti and Isola, Gino Becker, Jaretti and Luzi are good

Happy

representatives of this tendency. For all these reasons, Turin's architectural culture seemed to exist in a condition of marginality, outside the operations of the mass market.

Advertising for the Fiat 500 and 600 series

In the postwar years, two possible faces of the city seemed to emerge. On one hand, in fact, immigration strengthened the image of Turin as a manufacturing and working-class town, while, on the other, the city struggled to maintain its 'bourgeois' identity. The equilibrium between these two seemingly opposed tendencies was found through the creation of a new model of citizen, a worker and a bourgeois at the same time: maybe still a worker as purchasing power but already a bourgeois as aspirations. If the immigrants coming from the East or, in a larger number, the southern areas of the country became the new proletariat, a social shift turned the local, former blue-collar workers into members of the lower middle class (thus nourishing further expectations on both sides). This transformation took place at the end of the 1950s and the beginning of the 1960s: as a result, the city's identity evolved from production to both production and mass consumption.

In the novel *La nuvola di smog* (The Smog Cloud), Italo Calvino well described Turin's cultural and social environment in the late 1950s (the book was published in 1958). The protagonist

Happy

lives in an unnamed industrial city where the effects of pollution (dirt and dust) dominate every moment of daily life. Despite the anonymity of the place, it is hard not to recognize Turin: from the description of the streetscape to the sociological and psychological representation of the characters, everything seems to accurately portray the subalpine town. It is probably one of the protagonist's colleagues, Dr. Avandero, who best reflects the new social attitudes of the city's inhabitants. A passive and aloof employee but a devoted Alpine skier, he waits for the first snow to have a reason to leave the city. And after the end of the winter season – as the protagonist of *La nuvola di smog* ironically puts it – he substitutes the mountain sports by other outdoor activities, such as excursions, trout fishing or photography, anything that brings him far from the place where he lives and works. Although the product of the writer's imagination, Avandero renders the behavior and aspirations of the emerging consumer society better than any scholar could.

At the time of Calvino's depiction, the automobile had already entered the imagery of the city at all levels. For example, a 1956 painting by Felice Casorati ('Fiat 600/Notturno torinese', 'Fiat 600/Turin's nocturne') associates two classic images of Turin – the grid-shaped urban fabric as seen from the hill that encircles the city on the east, and the Alpine crests – with a novel and powerful icon: a grey Fiat 600, in fact, one of the first to be built, as evidenced by the characteristic 'against-the-tide' door opening. In the painting, human figures seem to be familiar with the car, and the image of the 600 appears as an integral element of Turin's traditional landscape. But this implicit message is not limited to Casorati's work. The images used in the 1955-58 advertising campaigns of the Fiat 500 and 600, for instance, seek to communicate a sense of innocent familiarity: the car in fact seems to complete the images in a natural manner. The campaigns indulge in a representation of a society where happiness is associated with the car and the latter, in turn, is presented as a symbol of social status and of the opportunities that mobility seems to offer. In one of the most powerful series of photographs, a happy worker leaves the factory and heads towards his family, who are waiting for him with a brand new Fiat 500: he precedes by some meters a crowd of fellow workers, some of them with a bicycle at their side. This image recalls a famous painting of the Italian Ottocento, Giuseppe Pellizza da Volpedo's *Quarto Stato* ('Fourth Estate', that is to say, the proletariat). The similarity is striking, but while the workers in the painting are symbolically marching towards socialism, the happy employee has a different objective: consumerism.

Sweeping Alpine panoramas or romantic views of the country, anodyne filling stations or joyful scenes of hunting, skiing and picnicking: these are the images the campaigns endlessly repeat. In these images, values of modernization alternate with (or are attenuated by) continuity with the past. But if modernity is represented by mechanical mobility as well as by women's hair color (blonde) or mononuclear family structures (father, mother, son or daughter), tradition is embodied by landscape, at least the suburban and rural one. From this point of view, the cityscape is depicted ambiguously as the scene of both old and new symbols. Perhaps this was a deliberate choice on the part of the campaigns' inventors; for in such a context the car becomes a quintessential element of the city, validating Turin's nickname of *città dell'automobile*.

Happy

Berlin, Zoologischer Garten, January 6, 2004.

I'm getting out of the train from Amsterdam while an empty freight train passes through the station with a thundering noise. The loudspeakers refrain from Hulot-like jokes, barking commands at passengers heading

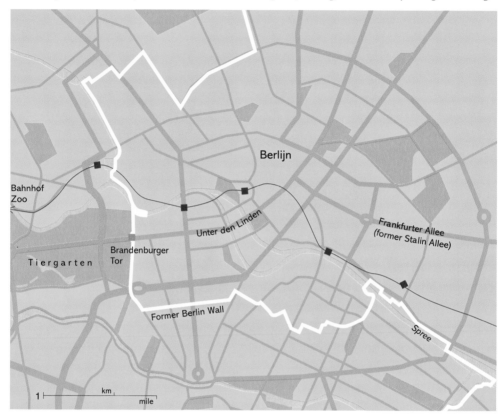

for Stettin, Cottbus, Vienna, Prague, and Breslau. The station's main hall greets its guests with the national specialties: *Bratwurst*, beer and sweat. Leaving the station, I'm harassed by blacks dressed as missionaries, trying to sell me jewelry, postcards and outdated maps of Berlin. As night falls, the gates of the *Zoo* are slowly growing dark. This reminds me of a passage in a book by W.G. Sebald, where he describes the terrible scenes that took place here during the air raid of November 1943. Rumors spread that the lions had escaped and that they were roaming around the Kaiser-Wilhelm-Gedächtniskirche. Later they were found suffocated and charred in their cages. For some reason, I cannot choose between the underground and the regional trains, and take a cab to Pension Funk in Fasanenstrasse. Lying in bed, I start to read *Die Stadt als Gabentisch. Zwischen Manhattan und Berlin-Marzahn.* E.T.

Happy

Henselmann, a Socialist Superstar

Ed Taverne

What kind of happiness can exist outside the official framework of 'really existing socialist society?' Clearly none. As history propels itself forward to its final fulfillment in a communist paradise, it traverses a number of historical stages expressed by specific architectural and town planning concepts. This implies that architecture and town planning reflect the inevitable course of history, and if the Party's task is to help realize the ideologically prescribed course of history, it should also define how to represent this process in architecture and town planning. If the Party succeeds in creating the proper style, happier architecture and town planning cannot be imagined – if only because this style would be in tune with history. Determining what is the politically correct style, however, is not all that easy.

In the German Democratic Republic (GDR), the 'socialist state on German territory' as it was often referred to, state and party-controlled institutions operated simultaneously as scientific research groups and planning offices. They analyzed the technological and economic as well as the architectural aspects of building in the GDR, adapting their findings to the specific needs of socialist politics. This resulted in an impressive series of studies, their topics ranging from the industrialization of the building process and the layout of housing estates and housing typologies, to the conservation of historical monuments, from reconstruction of town centers and villages to future trends in traffic. Most of this research was carried out by the so-called 'Architekturkollektive'; private initiatives were rare.[1] This clearly reflected the practice of building and planning, which was also monopolized by 'design collectives' and by the real estate development departments of the big public housing administrations. The research that was generated by the official institutes displayed some peculiar characteristics. Urban sociology, for instance, was notoriously lacking, whereas the collective's interest in the 'esthetics of information' developed surprisingly early.[2]

1 H. Barth, '"Portraits in miniature"'. Architekten und Stadtplaner in der DDR', in: H. Barth (hg.), *Grammatik Sozialistischer Architekturen. Lesarten historischer Städtebauforschung zur DDR*, Berlin/Erkner 2001, 21-50; H. Barth, Th. Topfstedt u.a., *Vom Baukünstler zum Komplexprojektanten. Architekten in der DDR. Dokumentation eines IRS-Sammlungsbestandes biographischer Daten.* (Dokumentenreihe des IRS, nr.3), Berlin/Erkner 2000.

2 G. Braun, M. Heider, H. Schwenger, 'Deutsche Demokratische Republik', in: Chr. Engeli, H. Mazerath (Hrsg.), *Moderne Stadtgeschichtsforschung in Europa, USA und Japan. Ein Handbuch*, Stuttgart, Berlin, Köln, Mainz 1989 (Institutionen, Hilfsmittel und Literatur zur Stadtgeschichtsforschung), 279-302; *Stadt und NS-Zeit in der DDR und in den neuen Ländern*, (Themenheft der Informationen zur modernen Stadtgeschichte IMS), 1, 1999.

However rigid and monolithic the socialist system may have been, it did allow at least some people to develop and even publish their personal ideas outside of the official channels, sometimes covertly criticizing the official line. Best known among them is Hermann Henselmann (1905-1995). He was the only more or less accepted star architect in the GDR, a chameleon-like personality who combined an ideologically motivated devotion to the Party with an independent posture comparable to that of Le Corbusier. A veritable 'Baukünstler' (literally 'building artist'), Henselmann also possessed remarkable litarary skills, as his numerous essays and his active correspondence with, among others, Brigitte Reimann illustrate. In 1960, he published a short essay on the everyday practice of the planning, designing and building of a housing estate in the northeastern periphery of Berlin: *Wir bauen an der neuen Stadt* ('We're Working on a New City'). Written in the then fashionable, unimbellished 'Altagssprache' – the language people use in everyday life – the booklet illustrates the debate on the program and the form appropriate for the 'socialist city', topics that politicians and architects alike felt deeply insecure about since their peers in the Soviet Union seemed to have lost their sense of direction.[3]

3 H. Henselmann, *Wir bauen an der neuen Stadt*, Berlin 1960, in cooperation with Ernst Blumerich, Hans Tuchtenberger and Iris Klemm. Blumerich and Tuchtenberger appear on al list of Henselmann's assistants. Henselmann himself illustrated this publication with cartoon-like drawings and photo's of the model.

The story of *Wir bauen an der neuen Stadt* is not very complicated and reads like a socialist version of advocacy planning. A planning collective of four ideologically highflying if not downright fanatical architects reports on the planning and design processes of an imaginary satellite town near Berlin. Their discussions, interviews and calculations result in a detailed model meant to encourage future inhabitants to participate in the planning process. They are induced to come up with their own ideas to make the new estate even more beautiful and, even more importantly, to enrich its program – an ambition that, one should note, contradicted contemporary practice in the GDR's public housing and town planning at the time. *Wir bauen an der neuen Stadt* is written in the form of a fable. In it, Henselmann paints an optimistic picture of the way a planning collective like the one that was responsible for the 'real socialist city' of Hoyerswerda – the town of Brigitte Reimann's novel *Franziska Linkerhand* a decade later, should function.[4] Reimann's 1973 novel is less idealistic and more dramatic than Henselmann's epic. In its own unique way, his book is best compared to the so-called 'Produktionsstück' (production piece) rather than to a utopian novel.

4 B. Reimann, *Franziska Linkerhand*, Berlin 1974. An unabridged edition was published by Angela Drescher in 1998 for the Aufbau-Verlag in Berlin. In this novel, Henselmann figures as the beloved genius, Professor Reger. B. Reimann, H. Henselmann, *Mit Respekt und Vergnügen. Briefwechsel*, Berlin 2001.

As is typical for this literary genre, the lack of drama is compensated by the abundant use of dialogue.

What drives the four architects is their ambition to use the most up-to-date planning techniques

Happy

wir

bauen

Hermann Henselma

an

der

neuen

stadt

BRIGITTE REIMANN

Franziska
Linkerhand

ROMAN

Happy

and building technology as tools for the creation of a completely new neighborhood of about 100,000 inhabitants. Their sources of inspiration range from the best socialist examples – Magnitogorsk and Moscow in the Soviet Union, Eisenhüttenstadt and Hoyerswerda in the GDR – to state-of-the-art town planning in Western countries (Levittown in the USA, Harlow New Town in Great Britain, Vällingby near Stockholm in Sweden). These are the examples that needed to be tested and improved upon in order to create a new entity in the cultural politics of the GDR: the socialist city. But what was meant by this? What concept of urbanity underlies their concepts? Henselmann's fable is an investigation into the basic characteristics of the socialist city. It is a fascinating project that, while it accepts the findings of the research conducted by the official institutions, takes a certain critical distance from them; it also shows that Henselmann was trying to find a theoretical basis for his own work as Berlin's Chief Architect in the second half of the 1950s. To broaden the scope of this heroic quest, Henselmann leads his four 'positive heroes' through all the aspects of contemporary town planning.

Architecture for the common man. *Wir bauen an der neuen Stadt* begins with an inventory of the social and cultural requirements the new housing estate has to meet. Ignoring the research methods then current in Western sociology, this survey addressed the common man directly. While strolling along the street or sitting in a milk bar, the interviewee is asked what his housing conditions are, and how he would like to see them improved. The underlying assumption is that the traditional role of the family should be changed. In the capitalist world, the family was needed as a safeguard against the dangers inherent in that type of society, whereas under socialism the family could be replaced by the new category of the 'Hausgemeinschaft': a small-scale community composed of a number of apartments or individual homes. Thus, the introverted character of the family could be replaced by the higher level of existence attainable in socialist society, where solidarity and openness reign supreme. Information on what should constitute such an open society was provided by official institutions, namely, the 'national front' (political education) and the 'free German youth' (the youth movement). They were not only expected to provide all types of statistical data; they were also to assist in thinking about suitable formal solutions, about the 'Gestalt' of the new estate. Its layout should accommodate the structural changes that were expected in almost all spheres of public life, whether cultural, legal, or in the realm of outdoor sports. The first chapter of the book outlines the way a plan should be developed. Interviewing the man in the street should be part of the procedure, and Henselmann specifically praised the democratic virtues of this approach. The second chapter focuses on the theory and practice of socialist town planning. Naturally, the first examples to be studied were the most recent experiences and the latest concepts in the Soviet Union, especially those pertaining to Moscow. Most, if not all of the procedures and operations of physical planning that were guided by socialist planning notions originated there. Unlike the Western economies, where ownership of the land is among the most powerful forces in architecture and town planning, the Soviet Union could boast of a long tradition in which – to quote Stalinist rhetoric – the needs of the working people are

Happy

Hermann Henselmann, perspective of Strausberg Platz, 1951

Happy

Happy

decisive. In the 1920s and 1930s, numerous daring projects were considered, urban models that often contained the most radical proposals for the complete collectivization of urban life. N.A. Miljutin's design for Sotsgorod and, more generally, his ideas on the construction of a socialist city exemplify this radical phase. Henselmann starts his study with these plans, but he goes on to analyze the examples of collective living that were motivated by shortage and need rather than by high ideals. Henselmann's protagonists are sympathetic to Khrushtchev's 1954 plea to part with the old ideas and concepts and concentrate instead on the construction of spacious new towns modeled after the English garden cities.[5] Why continue to build monumental boulevards based on the esthetic canons of the eighteenth and nineteenth centuries? Obviously Berlin's planning collectives could not avoid comparing the satellite towns near Moscow with their counterparts near London or Stockholm. Even though they admired the Western examples for their technical perfection, they did not recommend them. What was lacking in them was the possibility of '…shap[ing] and express[ing] as perfectly as possible man's relation to his family, the state and the entire community.'[6] These new towns provided the basic material necessities, nothing more. What signaled the specifically socialist character of the satellite towns surrounding

5 The impact of Soviet models for town and country planning on the GDR has been analyzed by W. Durth, J. Düwel, N. Gutschow, *Ostkreuz. Personen, Pläne, Perspektiven. Architektur und Städtebau der DDR*. Band 1, Frankfurt/New York 1999, and *Aufbau. Städte, Themen, Dokumente. Architektur und Städtebau der DDR*. Band 2, Frankfurt/New York 1999. A concise history of Soviet planning is attempted in R.A. French, Plans, *Pragmatism & People. The Legacy of Sovjet Planning for Today's Cities*, London 1995.

6 'Die Bindungen, die der Mensch zur Familie, zur Staat und zur ganzen Gesellschaft eingeht, so vollkommen wie möglich zu gestalten.' *Wir bauen an der neuen Stadt*, 33.

Moscow was, apart from their spacious layout and extremely low density, the way they expressed their inhabitants' political engagement with society at large. Socialist planning, like all forms of planning, aims to fulfill the needs of the individual as completely as possible, but it doesn't stop there: it accepts a moral obligation to accommodate all of society, not just the privileged few. What that amounts to is demonstrated by the first satellite town of 150,000 inhabitants in the northwestern fringe of Moscow. It is made up of so-called kwartaly, clusters of highrise slabs that were conceived as 'micro-regions' of (ideally) 2,500 inhabitants. These micro-regions are grouped together in so-called 'regional housing units' ('zhiloy rayon') that contain all the necessary amenities for a population of at least 30,000 people. When the scale of a city makes it necessary, these units can be combined to either 'regional' regions or 'urban' regions, the 'gorodskoy rayon'. The regional plan for Moscow of 1971, for instance, projected no less than eight 'regional regions.'[7] Though this type of planning, in which the required functional equilibrium is defined at various levels, is very similar to contemporary capitalist planning models such as the neighborhood unit, Henselmann and his four architects conclude 'that the fundamental differences are precisely those that define the connection between the smallest unit and the entire organism

7 B. Kreis, *Moskau 1917-1935. Vom Wohnungsbau zum Städtebau*, Berlin 1985; J-L. Cohen., 'La Forme Urbaine du "Réalisme Socialiste,"' in: J-L. Cohen, M. de Michelis, M. Tafuri, *URSS 1917-1978: La Ville, l'Architecture*, Paris 1978, 140-170.

Happy

of the city. Most Soviet plans are based on groups of five hundred to one thousand inhabitants, usually in a small central green area that is often connected to a larger green area in which schools, a kindergarten, smaller sports fields and playgrounds are located. The center is always linked to a park containing a house of culture, to which a sports stadium is often joined.'[8] For the Berlin planners, the new satellite towns in the Soviet Union – the ones that were published, that is – were inspiring examples because they did not suffer from the repetitive and mechanistic qualities so often found in Western housing estates. The careful design of visual perspectives, the footpaths through greenery, and the distribution of architectural highlights testified to an almost Sittesque sensitivity in creating the 'close relations' between the smallest and the largest housing units.

8 '...dass die wesentlichsten Unterschiede eben in jener Verbindung der kleinsten Wohneinheit mit dem Gesamtorganismus der Stadt bestehen. Fast alle sowjetischen Pläne schaffen Gruppen von fünfhundert bis tausend Einwohnern, meistens einer kleinen zentralen Grünanlage, die oft auf einen grösseren Grünzug mündet, auf dem die Schulen, Kindergärten, die kleineren Sportanlagen und die Spielplätze untergebracht sind. Das Zentrum ist immer in Verbindung mit einem Park gestaltet, in welchem sich ein Kulturhaus befindet, dem sich in manchen Fällen ein Stadion hinzustellt.' H. Henselmann, *Wir bauen an der neuen Stadt*, Berlin 1960, 28.

Cartoon from *Wir bauen an der neuen Stadt*

Working patterns The third chapter of *Wir bauen an der neuen Stadt* concentrates on the actual planning of a new neighborhood in the specific context of the GDR. The ambitions of the people of East Berlin as well as of the political organizations are carefully considered and translated into a functional program that defines densities and formal solutions for housing, traffic and, especially, public amenities. Naturally, the experiences in the socialist heartland were taken into account, but they were not simply imitated. Guidelines and methods for determining the desired densities were openly discussed. Whereas it is general practice in Western countries to relate densities to the various levels of wealth of the future inhabitants,

Happy

the Berlin planners, Henselmann foremost among them, wished to use zoning as a tool to accommodate the living patterns of different groups in a dynamic socialist society. With respect to this point, the collective openly criticized the rigid planning schemes that were then standard practice in the GDR and that resulted in new towns like Stalinstadt/Eisenhüttenstadt and Hoyerswerda proving to be too inflexible to accommodate the social and economic changes prescribed in the Seven Year Plan of 1959.[9] Starting in 1955, the so-called 'Schemaentwürfe' (schematic designs) served as the basis for new living quarters ('Wohnkomplexe'), which, with their 5,000 inhabitants, were considered to be the least expensive town planning units, partly because that size was optimal for industrialized building techniques. The planning collective designed a new category, the 'Wohngruppe' (living group) and did not refrain from using this alternative as a polemical device in criticizing current practice. The 'Wohngruppe' was conceived as the physical equivalent of the Soviet 'Hausgemeinschaft'. Intended as a unit of no more than 1,250 inhabitants, it reads as a combination of the 'Wohnzelle' (living cell) that had been developed as part of the famous 'Kollektiv- plan' (collective plan) of 1946, and the concept of the 'micro-region' that was the smallest unit in the Russian housing estates. Above all, however, the 'Wohngruppe' served as a corrective for the obsolete planning practices introduced in *Die sechszehn Grundsätze des Städtebaues* (1950) ('The Sixteen Basic Rules of Town Planning'), that had been detailed in numerous studies by the Deutsche Bauakademie, most notably in the schemes designed by Kurt Junghans (1954) and Hans Schmidt (1958/59).[10] The Grundsätze and all planning documents based on them distinguished only two levels in the layout of living quarters: the neighborhoods ('Wohnkomplexe') and the districts ('Wohnbezirke').

9 W. Durth, J. Düwel, N. Gutschow. Ostkreuz. Personen, *Pläne, Perspektiven. Architektur und Städtebau der DDR.* Band 1, and *Aufbau. Städte, Themen, Dokumente. Architektur und Städtebau der DDR.* Band 2, 357-431 (Stalinstadt); 488-507 (Hoyerswerda); J. Palutzki, *Architektur in der DDR*, Berlin 2000, 93-112 (Stalinstadt); 148-160 (Hoyerswerda).

10 J.F. Geist, K. Kürvers, *Das Berliner Mietshaus 1945-1989*, München 1989, 384.; W. Durth, J. Düwel, N. Gutschow, *Ostkreuz. Personen, Pläne, Perspektiven. Architektur und Städtebau der DDR.* Band 1, and *Aufbau. Städte, Themen, Dokumente. Architektur und Städtebau der DDR.* Band 2, 462.

In this model, the neighborhoods figured as the smallest planning unit (5,000 inhabitants) and the basic component of the program as well as of the design of the new estates. Henselmann believed this dual system to be far too inflexible. His planning collective subdivided the neighborhood into smaller units, defined by an optimum scale that allows the inhabitants to experience human relations more fully in the new estates. This scale was determined by 'movement diagrams' of specified groups – such as elderly people, children. 'The number of children should be sufficient to create groups of children playing together. As is well known, this stimulates social contacts in the neighborhood. The number of elderly people should enable them to socialize. And what applies to children and the elderly is equally valid for all other groups: working people, housewives, and adolescents.'[11] These arguments motivate the size of the living groups, which should not exceed 1,250 inhabitants. Consequently, this became the level where all the necessary amenities should be provided.

Happy

Cartoon from *Wir bauen an der neuen Stadt*

11 'Die Anzahl der Kinder müsste so gross sein, dass sich echte Spielgemeinschaften bilden. Das trägt bekanntlich zur Vertiefung der Nachtbarschaftsbeziehungen wesentlich bei. Die Anzahl der älteren Menschen müsste so gross sein, dass sie untereinander Kontakt finden. Und das, was für die Kinder und die alten Menschen gilt, das gilt natürlich für alle anderen ebenso, für die Berufstätigen, die Hausfrauen und die Jugendlichen.' H. Henselmann, *Wir bauen an der neuen Stadt*, 38.

Henselmann developed his ideas against the background of the official rules and current practice in the GDR. In practice, the models that had been developed by the statistical experts of the Deutsche Bauakademie determined the character of the housing estates in the GDR. The many discussions they provoked went beyond the level of academic and technological hairsplitting, since they focused on the essence of the new socialist society: 'the ambition to link people together through town planning, doing full justice to the need to do so in the most economical way.'[12] Naturally, the members of the Berlin collective could not ignore this principle nor did it wish to do so. Taking 1,250 as the ideal number of inhabitants, they arrived at a total of 375 families in each living group, assuming an average of 3.2 people per family. For the extensive level of public amenities they envisaged, this was hardly enough, but they refused to let themselves be frustrated by a rigid numerical requirement, preferring to reserve sufficient space in the new neighborhoods for the buildings that might be needed later (for the kindergarten, schools, political education, etc.). Such an approach would endow these neighborhoods with sufficient flexibility to adjust to the goals laid down in the Seven Year Plan. Four living groups make up a 'socialist housing complex' of about 4,800 inhabitants, less than the maximum decreed by the Institut für Städtebau und Siedlungswesen.'. The planners were satisfied with their calculations of the number of schools and other public buildings that would be needed, although

12 'Die Sorge um den Menschen mit der Forderung nach grösstmöglicher Wirtschaftlichkeit im Städtebau zu verbinden'. W. Durth, J. Düwel, N. Gutschow, *Ostkreuz. Personen, Pläne, Perspektiven. Architektur und Städtebau der DDR*. Band 1, and *Aufbau. Städte, Themen, Dokumente. Architektur und Städtebau der DDR*. Band 2, 500-504.

Happy

Henselmann, who had a lot of experience in building schools, recommended fewer restrictions in choosing the size and shape of the plots for schools. The number of students was bound to vary, and the education models were destined to change following the inevitable evolution of socialist society. Having concluded the discussions on zoning and land use in the living group, the authors analyze same topics at the district level the. A district comprises five living group housing complexes for a total of about 24,000 people, which meant in practice that they numbered 7,500 dwellings in 20 living groups. These numbers are sufficient for a community center containing a wide array of high quality public amenities, which, in turn, call for architectural and town planning highlights. The program for these centers hardly differs from the official guidelines, though the planners emphasized the need for cultural facilities. Apart from their functional meaning, they provided the architects with opportunities to enrich the new neighborhood with architectural centerpieces with strong symbolic value. This induced them to strengthen the visual relation to the community, where the House of Culture served as the 'best building in the area'.[13]

13 S. Hain, St. Stroux, *Die Salons der Sozialisten. Kulturhäuser in der DDR*, Berlin 1996.

Completing the socialist town How critical Henselmann was of the GDR's town planning standards becomes quite clear in the passages analyzing the location of the new estates, in his description of the design of the new estates, and in his unfriendly remarks on their architecture. The young design team of

14 A. Kaminsky, *Wohlstand, Schönheit, Glück. Kleine Konsumgeschichte der DDR*, München 2001, 36-70.

Wir bauen an der neuen Stadt makes it clear from the start that they are launching their proposals as part of the 'Seven Year Plan for Peace, Welfare and Happiness'.[14] Part of this program was an ambitious 'Plan for the socialist reconstruction of the Building Trades' that was focused primarily on the reconstruction of existing urban areas (historic centers as well as housing estates in the urban periphery). Obviously, as the capital of the GDR, Berlin was to benefit most. Its transformation from a capitalist inferno into a socialist paradise should coincide, they asserted, with a new distribution of urban densities. The center should

Cartoon from *Wir bauen an der neuen Stadt*

Happy

become less crowded (the number of inhabitants per hectare should decrease from 1,400 to 500), whereas the density in the periphery should increase from 50 to about 350. This redistribution of densities was the key element of the cultural program proposed by the four planners: a completely new, socialist city, the perfect counterpart of the architectural reconstruction of the central areas between the Brandenburg Gate and Alexanderplatz. There was only one major obstacle: where could they possibly find a suitable location for the huge new housing estates that were necessary to realize these ideals? What kind of geographic characteristics should this location possess? The plan defined a set of criteria: apart from correcting the imbalances caused by the years of capitalist development, the location should guarantee easy connections to the urban center and to the areas that provided employment, as well as offer the possibility 'of completing the overall image of the city.' Henselmann identified a suitable location in Hohenschönhausen (in the Weissensee district) in the northeastern outskirts of Berlin. The nature of the terrain and the amenities already there made it possible to construct a housing estate there of about 120,000 inhabitants, with a density averaging 300 people per hectare. The area was perfect for the application of the rapidly developing industrial building processes now available for constructing public housing. That would save costs, and this incentive became even stronger when the idea emerged of establishing a large 'Baustoffen-kombinat' (a factory for the industrial production of large-scale building components) in the immediate vicinity. If all the housing units allotted to Berlin in the Seven Year Plan were built there, all the conditions needed to realize the ideal of the socialist city would be met. 'When we visit other cities, Moscow or Stockholm to name but a few, we are always led to certain neighborhoods. We get to see the southwestern district of Moscow, which is presented as the most perfect expression of what our comrades in the Soviet Union see as socialist town planning. In Stockholm they show us around in Vällingby to illustrate how they envisage modern living conditions in Sweden. Not a single metropolis on earth is perfectly designed from one end to the other. Why shouldn't we create in Berlin, for this very reason, a complete urban area that in its overall plan, its architecture and the way it is built, in its apartments and its public buildings makes perfectly clear what we mean by a new city?'[15] A rhetorical question, obviously, but one that leads the four planners directly to the design of their city of tomorrow.

Dialectics In one of his letters to Brigitte Reimann (June 21, 1963), Henselmann claims that most of what goes wrong in architecture and town planning in the GDR should be attributed to the inability to think dialectically. He adds: 'Yet we, wholive in a

15 'Wenn wir andere Städte besuchen, Moskau oder Stockholm, um nur irgendwelche zu nennen, dann führt man uns doch auch zu bestimmten Stadtteilen. Man führt uns in den Südwestbezirk von Moskau, der am vollkommensten das ausdrücken soll, was sich die sowjetischen Genossen unter sozialistischer Stadtplanung vorstellen. In Stockholm führt man uns nach Vällingby, um uns dort zu zeigen, wie man sich in Schweden das Leben der Menschen unter neuzeitlichen Bedingungen denkt. Es gibt keine Grossstadt der Welt, die von einem Ende bis zum anderen auf einmal vollkommen gestaltet ist. Warum sollen wir nicht in Berlin ebenso einen in sich geschlossenen Stadtteil schaffen, der schon in der Art und Weise des Städtebaues, der Architektur und der Baumethoden, dem Zuschnitt der Wohnungen und der öffentlichen Bauten Auskunft gibt über das, was wir unter einer neuen Stadt verstehen'. H. Henselmann, *Wir bauen and der neuen Stadt*, 51-52.

socialist society, have at least as many favorable conditions as people elsewhere.'[16] The plan published in *Wir bauen an der neuen Stadt* can be seen as a perfect example of what Henselmann refers to as dialectics. It is determined by the mutual relations between stable, clear life patterns, neatly contained within the framework of the living group, on the one hand, and, on the other, the collective centers of the neighborhood, the district and the city, each of them characterized by their instability and the specific nature of their architecture. The spatial container for the plan was not hard to define: five units of 25,000 inhabitants, separated by infrastructure but connected by continuous bands of greenery. In the socialist city, social reality is not based upon the traffic infrastructure; it is determined by carefully organized collective programs, including childcare, education, culture, sports and shopping. This is the lesson Henselmann learned from the first generation of socialist cities in the young republic: Stalinstadt/ Eisenhüttenstadt and Hoyerswerda. His plan is an answer to their failure. The same is true of the way he lets his team of planners work on the details of the smallest unit, the living group. Living groups are composed mainly of buildings of four stories, to which, in each living group, two buildings of two stories are added for the elderly. Their layout varies, but this variation does not follow from different combinations in housing typologies, as one would expect, nor from preconceived esthetic guidelines (seriality, for instance), but rather from the desire to break away from the rigid monotony inherent in the procedures prescribed in the Seven Year Plan. Since the introduction of the latter, housing typology had been reduced to a set of standard plans that were determined by the use of large construction panels ('Block- and Plattenbau').[17] The optimum use of the crane at the building site became the leading design principle, and the ensuing wish to minimize the distance between the buildings resulted in a grid of 200 meters – a pragmatic decision that immediately received an ideological justification, since it resulted in spatial relations that could be understood in one glance, thereby displaying one of the key characteristics of socialism: clarity 'Überschaubarheit'. In the words of Henselmann: 'We, socialist town planners believe that these visual relations are very important, because in smaller spaces, people more readily feel at home.'[18]

The differences in the layout of the living groups are motivated mainly by the ambition to open up their introverted character, to connect them to the public domain, and to solve the design issues in ways that are specific to each living group. The public domain, with its schools, shops, workshops and clubs, is usually designed as a green zone of a more or less haphazard shape, in which the buildings appear to have been placed at random. The wish to

16 'Doch gerade wir im Sozialismus haben doch so viele günstige Voraussetzungen als irgendwo anders.' B. Reimann, H. Henselmann, *Mit Respekt und Vergnügen, Briefwechsel*, Berlin 2001, 7-10.

17 Th. Hoscislawski, *Bauen zwischen Macht und Ohnmacht. Architektur und Städtebau in der DDR*, Berlin 1991; Ulrike Passe, 'Stadtentwicklung und Wohnungsbau in Ost-Berlin seit 1945', in: K. Dörhöfer (Hg.), *Wohnkultur und Plattenbau. Beispiele aus Berlin und Budapest*, Berlin 1994, 33-53.

18 'Wir sozialistischen Städtebauer sind der Meinung, dass diese Blickbeziehung sehr wichtig ist. Denn im kleineren Raum wird der Mensch leichter heimisch.' H. Henselmann, *Wir bauen an der neuen Stadt*, 55.

Happy

concentrate these buildings outside the living groups, however, was motivated primarily by the needs of the building industry: without them, the groups could be constructed more easily. Even so, an ideological motivation was, once again, not difficult to find: this way of designing housing estates illustrated the 'provisional' character of the lifestyles under 'really existing socialism.' The new living conditions created by socialism were transient and dynamic by definition, and contrasted sharply with the stability and bourgeois complacency so typical of capitalism.

Whereas, from a planning point of view, use patterns in public housing and the associated standardized design solutions are relatively stable, the various educational programs were expected to be very dynamic in nature. The Seven Year Plan optimistically anticipated vast changes in production and consumption, too, as can be seen in its almost Archigram-like visions of the future.[19] The evolution of a new society might very well result in new building types and totally new amenities, and the town planners must be prepared for this. The planning collective was very excited about these perspectives, because instead of merely accommodating whatever was thought of as necessary, its members wanted to express the provisional character of society as a symbol of the undreamed of promises for the future. They discovered the motif of the village green: an extended open space waiting for these future promises to materialize. The village green was appealing inasmuch as it evoked a widely-shared image of the homeland ('Heimatbild'), but instead of addressing the historical associations connected with it, the planners wanted the people to accustom themselves to the vision of unknown future opportunities.[20] This type of thinking helps to explain why the green zones became the structural backbone of the town planning concept. They should entice the inhabitants of the living groups into leaving the shelter of their homes and going to their neighborhood centers, and from there to the center of the urban district with its new collective spaces and public buildings. This way of opening up the living groups and connecting them to the urban core epitomizes what Henselmann meant when he spoke about dialectics. The catalyst of this dialectics is the tension between the intimacy of the home and the 'spaciousness of public life' ('Weiträumigkeit des gesellschaftlichen Lebens'). In the urban center, this dialectical tension receives architectural expression in the diversity and richness of the public buildings. The home is mass-produced, while the public building is atypical, unique.

One of the problems that had to be solved was the precise nature of the architecture of the socialist city. After the somewhat artificial debates between realists and formalists in the early 1950s and the denunciation of socialist realism in 1955, it was quite

19 This echoes the attitude in books like K.Böhm, R. Dörge, *Unsere Welt von Morgen*, Berlin 1959. Here one finds, among other things, phantasies of 'Warenparadiese.' A. Kaminsky, *Wohlstand, Schönheit, Glück. Kleine Konsumgeschichte der DDR*, 54-55.

20 The Heimat ideology in the GDR in discussed in G. Lange, *Heimat und Aufgabe*, Berlin 1973; the way the cinema used it has been described in H. Blink, 'The Concept of "Heimat-GDR" in DEFA Feature Films', in: S. Allan, J. Sandford (ed.), *DEFA. East German Cinema*, 1946-1992, New York, Oxford 1999, 204-221.

21 W. Durth, J. Düwel, N. Gutschow, *Ostkreuz. Personen, Pläne, Perspektiven. Architektur und Städtebau der DDR*. Band 1, and *Aufbau. Städte, Themen, Dokumente. Architektur und Städtebau der DDR*. Band 2, 470.

Happy

clear that historical references were out of the question. The time of 'picture painting' ('Bildchenmalen') was definitely over.[21] Henselmann, himself frequently the victim of the ideological controversies in the decade before, succeeds in evading this issue in *Wir bauen an der neuen Stadt*. He refrains from theoretical statements, only mentioning movement as a theme in the architectural composition, and construction as a tectonic principle. What accounts for the urban feel of the center is the way the park systems culminate there, in the construction of terraces, platforms and passages that heighten the esthetics of movement. The buildings in the center should radiate joy, the spontaneous optimism that is referred to as 'Heiterkeit'. At the time, hardly any example of this joyous architecture could be found in the GDR, with the possible exception of some entries in design competitions, among them Henselmann's own proposals for the new center of Berlin (1959).[22]

22 W. Durth, J. Düwel, N. Gutschow, *Ostkreuz. Personen, Pläne, Perspektiven. Architektur und Städtebau der DDR.* Band 1, and *Aufbau. Städte, Themen, Dokumente. Architektur und Städtebau der DDR.* Band 2, 261.

Since the development of architecture in the GDR had become completely determined by the industrialization of the building process, building technology and construction had been ideologically examined with an eye to gleaning from them the criteria for a socialist style. This occurred first in large-scale public housing, where standardization and mass production introduced a new scale, a new tectonic, and an astounding uniformity, in short all the characteristics that would forever symbolize socialism's victory over the 'Mietskaserne' (tenements). This encompassed one of the goals of the Seven Year Plan: to liberate the last inhabitants of the Berlin slums by 1965. It called for a complete overhaul of the building industry and necessitated a dramatic increase in the productivity not only of construction workers, but of architects as well. The first result was to be the development of a rather primitive construction system based on the use of large prefabricated panels ('Großblockbauweise') and the transition to technically more refined systems of a higher quality for use in the public buildings in the centers. No wonder, then, that the planners in *Wir bauen an der neuen Stadt* wished to set the architecture of their public buildings apart from that of public housing. By leaving the construction of market halls, swimming pools, clubs, stadiums and cultural centers out of the planning schemes of the Seven Year Plan, they could buy some time that could be used to enrich the science of architecture with innovations from other fields: mechanics, chemistry and nuclear physics. Ongoing research in non-Euclidian geometry, for instance, might prove to be of value for the development of the differentiated spatial structures generated by the emerging socialist society.

The fibers and synthetic building materials that were developed by chemists might enable the architects to construct efficient and at the same time very sculptural structures. In a socialist society, this type of synergy of technology and science does not lead to science fiction, but instead fosters public architecture of a highly ideological nature. Anneliese, the only woman in the planning team, stated in this regard: 'I believe that these new possibilities might open ways for us to imagine what communist architecture could be like. I imagine buildings that express the joy and dignity of the communist people in a very special way. Just imagine this:

Happy

3 'Ich finde,' so Anneliese, the only woman on the team, 'dass
iese neuen Möglichkeiten uns die Wege öffnen könnten für
as, was ich mir unter der Architektur des Kommunismus
orstelle. Mir schweben Gebäuden vor, die auf eine ganz
esondere Art die Heiterkeit und Würde derjenigen Menschen
usdrücken, die im Kommunismus leben. Stellt euch das einam
or: frei von der Furcht vor Kriegen und Not. Aller Schemerz
nd alle Trauer können wieder ein meschliches Mass erhalten.
as muss sich doch auf irgendeine neue schöne Weise in der
aukunst ausdrücken.' H. Henselmann, *Wir bauen an der neuen*
tadt, 72.

being free of the fear of war and need. Pain and mourning can regain a human scale. All this should express itself in architecture in some beautiful new way.'[23] Perhaps at this date Henselmann had already begun to conceive what was to be one of his best architectural projects: the 'Kongresshalle' in Berlin of 1961. When he wrote his book, however, he knew of no better building to illustrate his ambitions than Pier Luigi Nervi's sports palace in Rome!

Trying to escape the ideological stranglehold

This sketchily presented utopia of a new communist architecture is the heart of the book. At a time when architecture had all but succumbed to the dominance of the building industry, Henselmann, the architect-artist, tried to rescue it by associating it with the imagery of technology, science and culture instead of that of planning, power and the party. In doing so, he transformed architecture into a democratic tool for community planning ('Gesellschaftsbau') that is meant to express the construction of a new society. It does so by designing a new housing estate on a symbolic location in the socialist city. This view was anything but common in the GDR, and that explains why a story that at first glance is rather harmless was in fact a very antagonistic architectural manifesto.

What triggered the publication of Henselmann's vision of the architecture of the socialist city was the 'Big change in Building' in the GDR in 1954 and 1955.[24] Henselmann, who had been appointed chief architect of East Berlin in the wake of the uprising of June 1953, went though a critical phase in his career when architecture designed to celebrate the state made way for mass-produced public housing aimed solely at satisfying the most basic material needs. In 1955, he felt compelled to warn against the tendency to overrate architecture's symbolic and ideological meaning. The monumental architecture he designed for the Stalinallee had not even been completed, and he still headed a research group at the Institut für Theorie und Geschichte der Architektur of the Deutsche Bauakademie that was seeking to define the theoretical foundations of socialist realism. What was at stake was not only a style, but the more fundamental issue of the socialist qualities of the urban environment at a time when industrialization and standardization had taken command.[25] On the occasion of the third congress of the SED on March 25, 1956, Henselmann presented a project for the 'Wohnkomplex Friedrichshain', a district between the Stalinallee and the Ostbahnhof, planned for 1,600 apartments and 5,000 inhabitants. The plan was completely determined by the technical requirements of industrialized public housing.

24 W. Durth, J. Düwel, N. Gutschow, *Ostkreuz. Personen, Pläne, Perspektiven. Architektur und Städtebau der DDR.* Band 1, and *Aufbau. Städte, Themen, Dokumente. Architektur und Städtebau der DDR.* Band 2, 177-182.

25 Geist, Kürvers (1989), S. 387ff.; W. Durth, J. Düwel, N. Gutschow, *Ostkreuz. Personen, Pläne, Perspektiven. Architektur und Städtebau der DDR.* Band 1, and *Aufbau. Städte, Themen, Dokumente. Architektur und Städtebau der DDR.* Band 2, 510-511.

Happy

Henselmann projected simple buildings stripped of complicated additions and without shops on the ground floor. By connecting the buildings to galleries – just as in his earlier designs for an apartment building on the Weberwiese – he created spacious views of the schools, Kindergarten and libraries in the open terrain between the buildings. He eased the widespread fear of monotony by a sculptural composition of high-rise slabs and towers, culminating in four 'point houses' in the Swedish fashion: vertical accents in a sea of four-story buildings.[26]

26 S. Hain, 'Berlin Ost: "Im Westen wird man sich wundern", in: K. Beyme et al. (ed.), *Neue Städte aus Ruïnen. Deutsche Städtebau der Nachkriegszeit*, München 1992, 32-75.

This experimental design ignored the official rules laid out by the Bauakademie, but newspaper articles that published Henselmann's plan proved to be an ideal channel for addressing the people. 'How do we want to live in the future?' Henselmann asked himself frankly, and the reactions of the people made him aware of their many desires and ambitions, and ultimately providing him with source material for *Wir bauen an der neuen Stadt*. Unlike what politicians and architects tend to believe, the general public showed a lively interest in public housing and town planning. While Henselmann's colleagues were preparing their ritual battles over high-rise apartment buildings or stylistic details, the people in the living quarters, the working men in the nearby factories, and the National Front discussed everyday practical problems: how to make the daily rituals of childcare, shopping and going to the movies easier? Henselmann challenged them by asking simple but fundamental questions: 'How does man live in modern society, that is to say, a society like ours'?[27] What do people like to do in their spare time? What makes a bar look nice and cozy without becoming cramped and confining? One of the conclusions of the discussions about the Friedrichshain project was that it

27 'Wie lebt eigentlich der Mensch in der modernen, d.h. einer unserem Ordnungsbilde entsprechende Gesellschaft?' W. Durth, J. Düwel, N. Gutschow, *Ostkreuz. Personen, Pläne, Perspektiven. Architektur und Städtebau der DDR*. Band 1, and *Aufbau. Städte, Themen, Dokumente. Architektur und Städtebau der DDR*. Band 2, 472.

would be best to separate housing and the public buildings, and this notion became one of the principal design guidelines in *Wir bauen an der neuen Stadt*. The public debate on Friedrichshain taught Henselmann that the general public is not as narrow-minded as architects, whose visions are often blurred by theoretical dogmas, seem to think. People want a much more open and spacious way of town planning than the rules and regulation allow; traffic should be banned from the living quarters and public buildings should be concentrated in central areas. Henselmann believed these to be valuable suggestions, and he called upon his colleagues to design new concepts that took seriously the wishes of the inhabitants. For the time being, however, his fellow architects only criticized the all too open, suburban character of Henselmann's plan. They feared that the metropolitan qualities of the Stalinallee would be lost forever. Henselmann's references to examples from non-socialist countries, for instance his flirtation with the 'Stadtlandschaft' (urban landscape) and the highrise apartment building provoked only sarcastic remarks.

Happy

Photo from *Wir bauen an der neuen Stadt*

Henselmann's successful visit to Hamburg, which led to the last joint initiative for a competition for a housing estate in the northeast- ern periphery of Berlin (Lichtenberg, not far from the location he chose for the imaginary new town he presented in *Wir bauen an der neuen Stadt*), fueled the opposition against him.[28] How could he refer so openly to planning con- cepts that had nothing whatsoever to do with socialism? The competition for Lichtenberg went ahead nevertheless. 'Architects from all over Germany are going to give Lichtenberg a new face' was the watchword of this town planning contest for an urban area of about 73.5 hectare and 4,400 houses'. The entrants were asked to investigate the best ways to solve the practical problems ensuing from the Five Year Plan, which envisaged a building program for Berlin of 14,000 apartments. The cultural challenges were at least as interesting; for the competition would result in the confrontation of widely different solutions to a problem that had been defined entirely in terms laid down by the socialist planning bureaucracy. Henselmann chaired the jury, and Ernst May of Hamburg was awarded first prize — a highly provocative decision, since shortly before this May had been denounced in the GDR as a despicable representative of Bauhaus formalism! Historians have pointed to the jury's sensitivity to the urban values conveyed by the green zones that May used as the structural element in his plan, and to the way he concentrated all the public build- ings in urban centers, two themes that also characterize Henselmann's 1960 publication. Sadly, Henselmann failed in his attempt to depoliticize town planning in general, and the plans for Berlin, in particular. The competition might have been the best way to arrive at a more pragmatic approach, but the ideological obstacles proved too strong. Henselmann's next attempts were a plan for the second part of the Stalinallee and his book *Wir bauen an der neuen Stadt*.

28 W. Durth, J. Düwel, N. Gutschow, *Ostkreuz. Personen, Pläne, Perspektiven. Architektur und Städtebau der DDR*. Band 1, and *Aufbau. Städte, Themen, Dokumente. Architektur und Städtebau der DDR*. Band 2, 476-480; Geist, Kürvers (1989), 392-396. *Prämiert und Ausgeschieden. Dokumentation eines IRS- Sammlungsbestandes zu Städtebaulichen Wettbewerben in der DDR (Dokumentenreihe des IRS, nr.2)*, Berlin/Erkner 1998, 62.

Happy

A tale of two cities The debate on socialist architecture and town planning was greatly energized in the following years, when the Bauakademie decided to re-evaluate the famous 16 principles of town planning, especially those concerning the design of socialist housing estates. Hans Schmidt played a leading role in this remarkable process, which was further stimulated by the desire to make plans for improving the center of Berlin that would counter West Berlin's provocative move of hosting an international competition for 'Haupstadt Berlin' from which architects from the GDR had been excluded. The net result was that, once again, all debates on architecture and town planning came under the spell of politics and ideology, a tendency that Henselmann tried to resist in two urban projects: one was for the second part of the Stalinallee (1957), and the other was the proposal he offered in *Wir bauen an der neuen Stadt*.

At first glance, Henselmann's project for the missing link between the Stalinallee and Alexanderplatz looks like an uneasy combination of a monumental boulevard and a residential quarter set in a green space.[29] The boulevard that splits the new housing estate in two is no longer lined with classicist palaces for the workers but by sober, industrially-built apartment buildings. Two zones of seventy meters separate them from the actual street, and here Henselmann projected eight 'point houses' as intermediate elements connecting the towers of Strausbergerplatz with the future monumental high-rise buildings on Alexanderplatz. The housing estate is designed as a composition of free-standing high-rise apartment buildings randomly distributed in an open park-like landscape. His plan looks remarkably free, especially compared to the plans, diagrams and abstract schemes then being produced by the Institut für Gebiets-, Stadt- und Dorfplanung (DBA), which employed among others Hans Schmidt, Edmund Collein, Gerhard Kosel and Kurt Liebknecht. Henselmann presented his plan as an experiment, the result of his attempts to find suitable concepts for the socialist city, and in no way intended it as the final result of this quest. This same attitude characterizes his explanation of the plan, written in a literary, informal style. Instead of proposing a rigid planning process, he recommended a provisional approach, governed by the limited availability of building lots (the foundations and underground infrastructure had not yet been removed), and the impossibility of foreseeing in what direction the building industry would develop. The plan is informal: it simply accepts the inherent discrepancies between the metropolitan feeling that results from the large scale of the industrial building processes on the one hand, and the social and urban imagery architects and the general public usually associate with big cities, on the other. This discrepancy is an example of Henselmann's dialectical way of thinking, which grappled with the many contradictions inherent in a socialist society. For example, there were the slowly increasing demands of the population and the gradual development of different lifestyles in confrontation with the static solutions provided by the socialist planning bureaucracy. This dichotomy was especially notable in public housing. 'In the minds of many citizens, who desperately wait for a house, ideas exist that are strangely at odds with their

29 W. Durth, J. Düwel, N. Gutschow, *Ostkreuz. Personen, Pläne, Perspektiven. Architektur und Städtebau der DDR*. Band 1, and *Aufbau. Städte, Themen, Dokumente. Architektur und Städtebau der DDR*. Band 2, 508-514; J.F. Geist, K. Kürvers, *Das Berliner Mietshaus 1945-1989*, 396-403

Happy

wish to get a house as soon as possible.[30] Naturally, even in socialist societies a need was foreseen for single family houses, but as building technology improved, this type of home was expected to become less popular, because a not insignificant part of what made it attractive was the way it contrasted with the Mietskaserne, and thus once the latter were gone, the single family home would inevitably lose some of its appeal. This was one of the many dialectical paradoxes Henselmann encountered during the many interviews he did while preparing *Wir bauen an der neuen Stadt*. His project, however, was unacceptable. Its democratic character, evident in the way he presents his findings, implicitly questioned the GDR's power structure. To quote him on this point: 'The victory over front and back so typical of the housing conditions under capitalism includes the victory over above and underneath, over government and being governed.'[31] The discrepancies he allowed in his plan as signs of changing social relations were seen as irreconcilable with current planning practices.

Indeed, the contrast with the most recent official theories, which urged that socialist housing estates be built 'with a uniform building technology and [in a uniform] style' could hardly be more striking. Henselmann's plan was rejected, and a collective composed of Collein, Dutschke, Englberger, Funk, Hopp and Paulick took over. On October 6, 1959, the first stone was laid for the second part of the Stalinallee, at virtually the same moment that Henselmann sent the manuscript of *Wir bauen an der neuen Stadt* to the publisher!

30 'In den Köpfen vieler Bürger, die dringend auf eine Wohnung warten, bestehen tief eingewurzelte Vorstellungen, die in Widerspruch geraten zu dem Anspruch, recht schnell zu einer Wohnungen zu kommen.' J.F. Geist, K. Kürvers, *Das Berliner Mietshaus 1945-1989*, 398.

31 'Die Überwindung des Vorn und Hinten im Wohnen der kapitalistischen Periode schliesst auch die Überwindung des Oben und Unten, des Regierens und Regiertwerdens mit ein.' J.F. Geist, K. Kürvers, *Das Berliner Mietshaus 1945-1989*, 399.

Sources

W. Durth, J. Düwel, & N. Gutschow, *Architektur und Städtebau der DDR*, 2 vols, Frankfurt a.M., New York 1999

H. Henselmann, *Gedanken, Ideen, Bauten, Projekte*, Berlin 1978

T. Hoscislawski, *Bauen zwischen Macht und Unmacht. Architektur und Städtebau in der DDR*, Berlin 1991

J.F. Geis, K. Kürvers, *Das Berliner Mietshaus 1945-1989*, Berlin 1990

F. Rogier, 'The Monumentality of Rheroric: The Will to Rebuild in Postwar Berlin', in: S. Williams Goldhagen, R. Legault, *Anxious Modernisms. Experimentation in Postwar Architectural Culture*, Montréal, Cambridge (Mass.) 2000, 165-190

Happy

THE RATIONAL CITY

In the 1950s, town planning was seen as a tool for correcting urban problems (a task it always had), an instrument for accommodating urban growth, channeling the lower-class laborers who streamed into the cities into housing estates that, at least from a town planning point of view, guaranteed the best possible conditions for decent large-scale housing projects (a role it acquired in the second half of the nineteenth century), and an artistically inspired discipline that aimed at creating the groundwork for representative, monumental architecture reflecting the city's political, economic and cultural make-up (an ambition that was especially strong around 1900). These were the long-established features of a discipline that now, once again, had to re-invent itself. Saturated, by definition, with ideas about the city's future, it now was joined by a powerful group of likeminded people: the planners and managers who represented the managerial revolution in the mid-twentieth century. It was only natural, then, that town planning started to emulate the mentality and adopt the working premises of the new bureaucratic elite. If a social revolution – whether the creation of the welfare state or of the evolution of socialism – was at the heart of the new society, it can hardly be surprising that social concerns came to dominate town planning. If this revolution was supposed to result in a new, democratic community it was only to be expected that the city as a work of art should represent this community, and not merely provide occasions for the privileged few or the institutionalized authorities to represent themselves. The modern city was built by all the people who work and live in the city. 'The architects of the new urban landscapes are lawyers and people who represent the legislature, economists and merchants, hygienists and doctors, teachers, captains of industry, and last but not least craftsmen, small business men, retirees and all the other small business people who commission buildings.' The city was the 'collective work of the citizens'.[1] If modern planning wanted to doaway with everything irrational and contingent, it was no wonder

Happy

that the days of what had come to be considered artistic excesses were numbered. Surveys and research became all-important (either complementing the personal genius of the individual designer, or replacing it). Since the authorities responsible for the plans for the reconstruction and extension of cities invariably presented themselves as democratic, whether in the Western, parliamentary democracies or in the socialist single-party systems, town planning, a powerful tool in their hands, had to be considered democratic as well.

The modern city, then, is ideally a smoothly functioning organism made up of zones dominated by one function only, be it housing, work or recreation, with the 'municipal functions' concentrated in the city center. Traffic is what gives life to the modern city, a clear reflection, in the ideal case, of the citizens' daily timetables. In the morning, the traffic flows are directed toward the working places – the offices in the center or the industrial areas in the outskirts. In the evening, everyone streams back home. Complementing this basic rhythm are the weekly outings to the beach or the woods, or the new recreational facilities near the cities, along with the annual vacations. For the great masses of people, the opportunity to go on a holiday was one of the blessings of the social revolution of the 1950s, triggering the construction of modern holiday resorts like la Grande Motte in France and Artek in the Ukraine. The perfect modern city functions like clockwork, once all the technical problems have been solved by modern town planning.

Zoning implied the end of the hectic, chaotic metropolis of the nineteenth century. Planning would bring it under control, greatly reducing the density of its most built-up areas. Complementing the rigid zoning strategies was the ideal of decentralizing the overcrowded city. Both strategies reflect the strong sentiment that existed against anything the nineteenth century had produced and the urge to break away from a past that was dominated by it. The urban community, it was thought, should be re-assembled at a scale that allowed social contacts to flourish: that of the 'Hausgemeinschaft' in the socialist countries, or of the neighborhood unit in Western Europe. The rational city was, ideally, a collage of modular suburbs that were conceived as basic components of the city as a whole.

1 'Die Baumeister dieser neuen Stadtlandschaften sind Juristen und Gesetzgeber, Wirtschaftler und Kaufleute, Hygieniker, Ärtzte, Lehrer, Industriekapitäne und nicht zuletzt kleine Handwerker, Gewerbetreibende, Rentner und all die kleinen Bauherren…' F. Jaspert, Städtebau', in: *Handbuch moderner Architektur*, Berlin 1957, 37.

Amsterdam, August 24, 2003.

People from all over the world – Africa, Suriname, the Dutch Antilles – and also some locals from Amsterdam, flock to the Kwakoefestival in Bijlmer Park. Around the soccer field, lots of stands have been set up, where exotic food can be eaten and where one can relax and enjoy African beer, lying in the hammocks suspended between little huts that people have built for themselves. Young preachers try to lead you straight to God, while a steel band from the Antilles invites you to dance. The finale of the soccer championship is the climax of a tournament that has lasted for five weekends. Hilltop wins the final match, and now the party really starts. When the festival is over, everybody slowly returns to the concrete realities of the apartments in the Bijlmer. M.v.R.

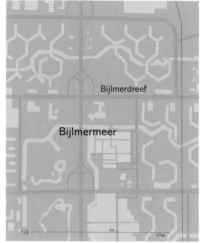

The Bijlmer

or Exercises in Giving Life to a Rigid Urban Plan

Marieke van Rooy

'Nowhere in the world has a more beautiful and modern city of a comparable size been built. The opportunity is there: a project for the most pleasant living quarter one can imagine.'

G. van Hall, Mayor of Amsterdam, 1964

The Bijlmermeer is an idealistic housing estate dating from the 1960s, located in the urban periphery of Amsterdam. It has developed in a completely different direction than the one the planners originally envisaged; for since its inauguration, social problems have overshadowed the ideals of the makers. The multicultural nature of the community and the spontaneous changes introduced by the inhabitants are likewise usually ignored. Yet, these have been the very things that have made the Bijlmer a unique place.

From polder to housing estate In the first decades following the Second World War, living conditions in Amsterdam were far from idyllic. An ambitious plan was made for the renewal of the densely populated nineteenth century neighborhoods, where hygienic conditions left a great deal to be desired. At the same time, plans were made to build new housing estates. In the 1950s, construction of the western garden cities began, based on Van Eesteren's famous General Extension Plan of 1935. The new neighborhoods, mostly made up of four-story apartment buildings, could not solve the housing shortage, and consequently Amsterdam faced the challenge of accelerating its expansion program. Since it was felt that the city could not accommodate future growth, the only way to secure sufficient space was to look for suitable locations in neighboring municipalities. The Bijlmermeer, a polder located between Diemen and Weesp and part of the municipalities of Weesperkarsel, was considered the best option.

Happy

Unfortunately, this polder did not border on Amsterdam, a minor detail that, nevertheless, did lead to the national government becoming involved in the matter. The national authorities refused to add the Bijlmermeer to Amsterdam, fearing that a satellite town separated from the nuclear city would create problems. For Amsterdam, however, the issue was of vital importance. So vital, in fact, that the municipality tried to gain the support of the inhabitants by sending them an open letter: 'You can probably guess that there must be a good reason for the College of Mayor and Aldermen to address all the inhabitants directly. There is. Have you ever thought of the problems those 25,000 families are facing, which, according to a very careful survey, live in un-acceptable conditions because their houses are, in fact, slums? The same survey showed that there are horribly poor living conditions in our city, and that in various parts of the historic core and the neighborhoods dating from the nineteenth century 25,759 houses can be found that do not deserve to be called houses. Have you ever thought about the agony of bringing up children in slums? Did you know that in Amsterdam's older living quarters there are 9,000 houses that have only one room, in which your fellow citizens live, often with their family? Did you know that 38,000 inhabitants of Amsterdam live in houses with only two rooms? You can imagine that we are now deeply concerned that slum clearance and the elimination of these inhuman conditions may not be possible, as long as the Government refuses to grant us permission to build new houses in the Bijlmermeer. Your good city of Amsterdam – and who isn't proud of our city – should build new houses for at least 100,000 of our citizens as quickly as possible.'

When the Government finally did grant permission, an agreement was made in which the city rented the polder for twelve years. By that time, the municipal department of town planning had already completed its plans. The first steps were supervised by Van Eesteren, who was the chairman of CIAM until 1947, and the project was completed by Siegfried Nassuth, his succes-sor. The principles of CIAM's 1933 Charter of Athens guided its planning. Living quarters, recreational facilities, working places and traffic zones were separated, and they alternated with green zones. CIAM's pleas for high-rise construction in a time of housing shortage was also taken to heart.

Festival in the Bijlmer Park

Happy

Aerial view of the Bijlmer

A promising design 'The Bijlmermeer is going to be a special city. A city free of the smell of gas. A city in the greenery, but close to the center of Amsterdam. A city with attractive shops and lots of spaces for playing and walking around. A city where today's man can already experience tomorrow's living conditions.'

Queen Juliana inspects a model of the Bijlmer

This quote is taken from a promotional pamphlet of the 1960s. The design of the Bijlmer aimed at creating a pleasant living environment with lots of amenities for its inhabitants. It was based on an integrated concept in accord with which the apartment buildings, the public spaces and the traffic arteries were planned as a unified system. The plan is marked by clearly arranged architectural elements in a contrasting sea of greenery, featuring high-rise buildings and an efficient traffic system of elevated streets and subway lines. The ten-story buildings are angled, giving the estate its typical honeycomb structure, a layout chosen because it guarantees the

Happy

inhabitants maximum exposure to the sun, and allows them easy access to the adjacent parking garages. From the elevated streets, drivers are led directly to the garages, a system that was seen as a crucial element of the neighborhood's design. The stops of the public transportation system are situated near the garages, and shopping centers are located on the ground floor. The garages provide access to internal streets that lead to the elevators.

The apartments are remarkably spacious and have large windows, big balconies and neatly designed living rooms. They also contain two novelties: a corridor for children to play in, and a combination kitchen-dining room. Since the Bijlmer was meant to accommodate the typical Dutch family of the time, most of the apartments have four or five rooms – the project dates from the years of the baby boom. The buildings contain internal storage rooms for all the apartments, and a 'box' on the ground floor for parking bicycles. Collective amenities are a major feature of the original plan. They were thought necessary to replace the meeting places so common in the nineteenth-century neighborhoods, from which, it was assumed, most of the future inhabitants would come. Portions of these public areas were located near the internal street, and others were situated in pavilion-like buildings in the greenery. These were the places for the kindergarten, hobby clubs, theater companies and bars. All this, it was hoped, would stimulate a rich social life.

Whereas the architecture was quite hard-edged, the greenery between the flats was conceived of as pleasant and soft. The idea was to create an agreeable atmosphere where the inhabitants relax, undisturbed by automobile traffic. Only bicycle lanes were allowed to cross the green zones.

Problems The first inhabitants who moved to the Bijlmer were pioneers who were interested in the experiment. However, this modern-minded, progressive group remained relatively small. Most of the people for whom the Bijlmer was built moved elsewhere, to the new towns and commuter villages outside Amsterdam, preferring the small-scale, low-rise houses built there. It became clear that the idealistic concepts of the high-rise-residences appealed only to a small number of people, and definitely not to the middle classes in general. They appeared to be unsuitable for families with children, and, apart from that, the rent was considered too high. Moreover, the contractors underestimated the actual construction costs, and it also cost quite a lot of money to manage these complexes. As a result, some vital components were never realized. Fewer elevators were installed, fewer garbage disposal facilities were provided, and a floor was added to the buildings. Collective facilities in each block were now considered to be less important. In 1974, a report was still urging that they be built, but four years later it was decided to eliminate them from the plans for the residences that still had to be built. Public transportation was also a cause for concern: only in 1980 did the direct subway line to the center go into service.

To keep the apartments from remaining vacant, the housing corporation accepted whoever wanted to live in them. Instead of the middle classes, the urban poor flocked to the Bijlmer, many of them illegal immigrants. For them, the Bijlmer was an ideal place to live in

Happy

and remain virtually unnoticed, and extensive networks of their countrymen took care of them when they got into trouble. For many immigrants, the Bijlmer has been the first stop in the Netherlands, and also the last.

Informal networks The concentration of a large variety of different groups living side-by-side in the Bijlmer accounts for the neighborhood's unique character. They represent about 107 different nationalities, although people from Surinam, Ghana and the Dutch Antilles dominate. When the weather is warm and people come to buy some ice cream at the ice cream parlor, the Bijlmer gives the impression of a tropical country far away from Holland. The anonymous, concrete apartment buildings provide the setting for exotic events. The Kraaiennest, a shopping center, offers a wide spectrum of wigs in an Afro shop, the butcher has complete goats for five euros a kilogram, mail-order firms send money and all kinds of goods to countries overseas, and the video shop stocks only African titles. The inhabitants of the Bijlmer have taken possession of their neighborhood by investing it with their own spirit. They have even built their own rooms in the parking garages, where they sell second-hand things, run a sports school and repair cars. Less visible networks offer services and activities in the apartments themselves; including, for example, a 24-hour kindergarten and take-out restaurants. There are also bars, brothels and all kinds of shops. Nationality and culture define these informal networks. This is the Bijlmer today: built for the white middle classes and now inhabited by people from a variety of far-distant countries trying to find happiness in Holland.

Radical innovations With its concentration of so many relatively poor groups, the Bijlmer was known from the outset as a problem neighborhood in constant need of attention. For years, the authorities tried to curb crime rates, vandalism and drug-related problems by a policy of tailor-made improvements. At the time, poor management was blamed for most of the trouble. In the middle of the 1980s, it had become clear that this approach wasn't working, and Rem Koolhaas, an admirer of the Bijlmer, was asked to develop a plan for its reconstruction. Instead of directing his attention to the residences, he tried to integrate the greenery, the traffic structure and the facilities offered in the Bijlmer. In his view, the architecture was wrongly blamed for the problems. Recreational facilities, for instance, were inadequate: all the Bijlmer offered was a park-like environment serving as the setting for a totally outmoded way of spending one's leisure time. Instead of the demolition of a portion of the buildings, as some had proposed, he suggested that the 'program' of the Bijlmer should be enriched, and a new concept for the project was developed, partly inspired by this vision. However valid Koolhaas' solution may have been, it could not prevent some of the buildings from being torn down. Their demolition was accelerated by the tragic crash of an El Al plane on October 4, 1992, in which one of the buildings was destroyed and 43 people were killed.

Whereas the original plan was created in the city's central planning office according to one overall concept, the renovation plans are diverse. Designed to tackle certain specific problems, they have been produced by a number of different teams of architects and town planners.

Happy

Remarkably, most of them appear to agree with Koolhaas: they do not consider the residences to be the source of all evils. Rather, they found that the facilities that should contribute to the neighborhood's vitality has fallen victim to faulty management, specifically the parking garages and the shopping centers underneath the elevated streets, most of which will be closed.

Where the apartment buildings are torn down, low-rise rows of houses are replacing them, most of which are sold to immigrants who have succeeded in making money. The planners stress that they do not want to replace the apartment buildings with urban villas for upper-class whites, a group which is conspicuously lacking now in the Bijlmer's social make-up. Their aim is to preserve its unique, multicultural character.

Plans to demolish the flats are strongly opposed by a group of 'Bijlmerbelievers'; many of whom were among the earliest residents, and thanks to their activity some of the apartment buildings will remain. Attempts to upgrade these focus on the ground floor and the first floor with its internal street. These two levels are being transformed into luxury apartments, some with their own private gardens. The complexes that will be restored have been labeled the 'Bijlmer Museum, a permanent memorial to the ideals that inspired the original town planning experiment.

Low-rise housing replacing the blocks of flats

Happy

To conclude   The difficult history of the Bijlmer is not unique. Many similar neighborhoods throughout Europe have failed in the same way. Why? Because the planners failed to predict the social changes that occurred in modern society. They built their dreams on a belief in the socializing effects of the architectural environment and the readiness of the future inhabitants to participate in the social processes that were an essential condition for these projects to succeed. It turned out, however, that people appear to attach much more value to their own individuality and have no need to spend a lot of time outside their homes. How do they use the facilities near home? What do they do to support the public domain? Apparently, they couldn't care less. In a neighborhood that seems to ignore the human scale, this attitude becomes quite evident. It is ironic that most of the Bijlmer's inhabitants come from countries where it is quite normal to use both individual apartments and the public areas for meetings and all kinds of activities. They are used to sharing their lives with their fellow citizen and are less individualistic than the Dutch. When they found that the Bijlmer did not accommodate their need for meeting places, they spontaneously transformed their apartments and reshaped the public domain, thereby adding a personal touch to the anonymous neighborhood. It was only because these informal networks seemed to induce a certain level of criminal behavior that their efforts failed. The corporations that own the Bijlmer saw no other remedy than to start an ambitious renovation scheme, hoping to eradicate the illegal practices. In the future, typically Dutch norms will dominate the Bijlmer, leaving little room for personal intervention. Some of the Bijlmer's inhabitants will feel better, while others will undoubtedly deplore the loss of the semi-illegal parallel world. However that may be, the mixture of dozens of different groups of people will always set the tone. Some of the more exciting aspects may be lost; but the exotic character of the Bijlmer is here to stay.

Cumbernauld, April, 2002.

The crumbling walls of Cumbernauld Station, empty of advertisements, announce by their void state that the resources of the once 'revolutionary' town have long since declined. That in itself is no marker of anything in the UK, where even affluent areas are served by run-down, unmanned railway stations. I temporarily suspend judgment. A short walk in the crisp spring air along a path lined with bracken leads to

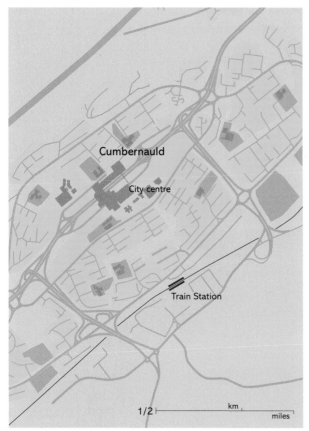

the archive. There is no museum – there never has been one - but you get friendliness and a nice cup of tea and a biscuit inside this shed packed with rarely visited memorabilia. But there are no nicely framed shots of the town at its peak. Memories of the town from the RCAHMS archive in Edinburgh, stored in twenty boxes with tantalizing photographs and press clippings about Copcutt's wonderfully futuristic social experiment, swirl around my head, but somehow the stuff here doesn't add much. The real questions can only be answered by the politicians in power over the course of the last five decades who didn't pass the baton. Public transportation links between the town and Glasgow and Edinburgh were never good, a sign that this is an urban place that lost its status a long time ago. Being 'popular among architects': is that what brought on the curse of national embarrassment, or was it being recently voted Scotland's 'Ugliest Town'? I did get fresh air. I needed it. I remembered the breathtaking natural beauty of the 'satellite village' of Abronhill, a high point to the northeast, where in the film Gregory's Girl the teenagers Gregory and Dorothy go and lie side by side on the grassy slope, pretending that by cycling their legs in the air they can feel, or even help to keep, the earth spinning. That film was made in 1981, six years before the town's development corporation began pushing its attractiveness as a 'powerful business community', and a good place to invest. Cumbernauld -- a new way of living, the brochure on display at the door, which dates from 1987, when over 50,000 people lived there, promised that even though it wasn't a new town, 'the ideals are still there'. 'Everything's on our doorstep'. But they weren't there for very long, and they aren't there now. I found two alternative Cumbernaulds that made a better connection with the town I had studied. Artists Gair Dunlop and Dan Norton constructed an online environment, www.cumbernauld.nu. Here, in this space inspired by the town's architect, you can play in 'the entropic utopia' and visit his drawings. These two artists also worked with landscape architects Gross.Max (long time

Happy

Edinburgh-based Dutchman Eelco Hooftman and Scotswoman Bridget Baines) on 'Grow your own Town'. This proposal for Cumbernauld, made in 2003 (included in The Lighthouse Centre's Re:motion, new movements in Scottish architecture exhibition), examined its perceived negative factors, and turned them into positive ones. In this space, rooftops become sheep farms, motorways evolve into drive-in gardens, and the wind energy of the hilltop town finally gets used. It becomes a hybrid of nature estates and housing reserves. Glasgow could not play this card, that's for sure, even if its cultural ambience is intact. The earth spun too fast for Cumbernauld, but at least there have been imaginations that didn't.   L.B.

CUMBERNAULD:
TOMORROW'S TOWN TODAY

Lucy Bullivant

Cumbernauld can be viewed as a transitional urban model, a highly integrated compact urban design that aimed to achieve a balance between individual and collective happiness. The New Town of Cumbernauld, which is located 14 miles northeast of Glasgow, was built in the early 1960s on a windy hogback-shaped hilltop two miles long and one mile wide. Designed by urban planner Sir Hugh Wilson, it featured maverick architect Geoffrey Copcutt's multi-level 'megastructure' town center, the first of its kind built anywhere in the world. Citadel-like in shape, 'a vast layer cake of structure', the center was the focal point of the town, a 'giant supermarket on stilts,' and a social hub which was built with a £70m budget, and provided with a bold, complex road system to keep the car at bay.

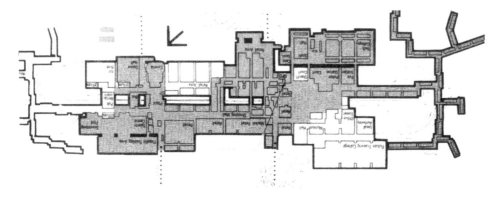

Town center, plan

Cumbernauld was designated a New Town in 1956, and the first phase of the town center — representing one fifth of the projected total — was completed ten years later, just two years before the effects of the events of 1968 began to be felt. Very soon after it opened, it was held

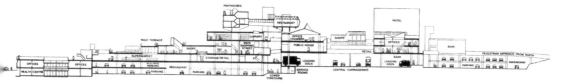

Town center, cross section

Happy

up as an exemplary model of community architecture by its planners, critics, and even the American AIA (which in 1967 gave it an award for Community Architecture, in competition with the cities of Tapiola and Stockholm). A blueprint, therefore, for city planning at the time, it was built to house a population of 70,000 (with space allotted for 5,000 vehicles). The intention was to alleviate the housing problem in Glasgow (from which it was envisaged that four fifths of the residents would come), creating a town with the tenth largest population in Scotland. At the time of Cumbernauld's designation as a New Town, the indigenous population was 3,500. The planners' aim was that by the 1980s, 50,000 people would be living in the main area, with another other 20,000 living in satellite villages, ultimately reaching a limit of 100,000.

The town pioneered not only freedom to leave the growing urban periphery, but new ideas in social and economic development, anticipating the beginning of Scotland's transition from a heartland of traditional industry to the site of a new age of flexible, light industries, in which urban centers would be the seedbed of new high technologies. A compactly planned development, its housing was combined with private gardens, in most cases located in named neighborhoods (with a corner shop for every 400 homes), and totally separated not only from busy roads but from factories. These neighborhoods 'radiated' from the town center in contiguous but self-contained areas that prefigured contemporary structured suburban developments. A clearly defined perimeter marked the town off from the surrounding landscape, while its split-level form gave it an excellent vantage point from which one could view and tour the surrounding countryside. Surprisingly, it was the only British New Town to break ground during the 1950s. It was the product of an interdisciplinary meeting of minds: professors of physics, economics and sociology contributed significantly to the design of the first phase, which was opened in 1966.

Happy

Instead of a neighborhood system of planning or anything resembling a housing estate, Cumbernauld was designed as an integrated town in which dwellings were grouped closely around the central area within a continuous, unobstructed landscape. The idea was that the population, served by a road system in which pedestrian and vehicular routes are separated, would have easy access to the major shopping, commercial, administrative and cultural buildings while also being in close contact with the countryside. This divorce of footpath and main road system allowed Cumbernauld's Development Corporation officers to describe the town as aspiring to be the safest town in Great Britain.

The principles on which the design of the town is based attained their fullest expression in the town center, which contained the principal shopping, business, entertainment and public buildings and services. This extraordinary structure, sited along the ridge of the hill, was demolished by bulldozers in the spring of 2001 (a local resident exclaimed: 'it's like Beirut up there'), testimony to the reality that it had reached the end of its useful life and that the retail spaces were not attracting enough incoming tenants. The structure had long since been viewed by inhabitants as an anachronistic place created at a time they weren't necessarily very sentimental about; and yet, back in the optimistic climate of the early 1960s, it seemed an ideal formal solution that was also a 'social condenser.' Early sketches of the basic concept for the town center, widely described as 'futuristic,' show the initial formulation of the idea of 'penthousing,' cradled on an umbrella structure inclined towards the south. Beneath this cradle, multi-level shopping facilities were situated on walkways, among them an attractive blue and brown-tiled health center, a hotel, an ice rink, a technical college, and police, fire and ambulance services, all spread out over a total of eight levels. Modern sculptures and murals deco-

Happy

Aerial view

rated the wall surfaces throughout. Beneath this, at ground level, was a multi-lane, 2-way service road with car parks underneath running parallel to an expressway. This road passes through the center without interfering with pedestrian movement or car parking.

The megastructure, as Miles Glendinning has explained, was 'an artificial landscape governed by the ideals of communication and flexibility: a massive rigid frame with shifting, changeable contents.' It was the center stage of a new urban development that took into account society's demand for a more dense and sophisticated response from the planners than those espoused by either the pre-modern Garden City or the 'early modern', CIAM schema of the interwar period. Seeking to get away from the densely interconnected forms of the old 19th century city, the planners clustered the town's elements, leaving behind the old denser, segregated 'neighborhoods,' while still encouraging a culture of mobility. The earliest areas built attained a density of 95 people per acre, increased to 120ppa in the more urban areas built a bit later. These are roughly similar to the tenement schemes built in Glasgow in the 1950s, and to the level of density in the contemporary re-planned down-at-heel Gorbals area of the city.

The impulse behind Cumbernauld's design was to make it an attractive dwelling place, as well as an area of intense activity, guided by an imported modernist vision, but still embracing

Happy

Aerial view

heterogeneity. The town center's attenuated, linear structure included many features that are now standard in shopping centers; in fact, it packed even more functions into one structure than the latter do. Although not monumental, it nonetheless had an ambitious layout: its row of crowning penthouses did not keep it from appearing rather like 'a vast terminal facility', as Copcutt described it. He proposed that its interpenetrating decks should contain a variety of furnishings and 'a kaleidoscope of advertising,'speculating that if pedestrian-based shopping centers became obsolete in the future, then his center 'could become a gigantic vending machine through which the motorized user drives to return revictuallised' – an astute anticipation of today's highway service station, in fact. The on-site Cottage Theatre offered a bit of live drama, and the Kerkagogos, church-organized discos – opened at a time when the church's pastoral outreach activities were increasingly popular – provided a hip and relatively open-minded social environment for the younger inhabitants. The mix of urbane center and traditional housing areas at Cumbernauld made it a compelling hybrid in this period. Nonetheless, there remained a shortage of commercial entertainment in comparison with Glasgow (half an hour away by road or rail), and the lure of the big city's edgy heterogeneity could never be supplanted by something that was more suited to young families interested in residing in a more pastoral, less frenetic environment. Both Robin Crichton, who made the film *Cumbernauld Town for Tomorrow* in 1970, and Murray Grigor were fascinated by the promise of Cumbernauld's architecture. Grigor made a somewhat ridiculous, almost surreal crime thriller set in the town; although it appears downright cheesy to our 21st century eyes, it is nonetheless a telling drama. A vivid 'period piece,' inasmuch as it is an example of television's employment of contemporary urban context to assist a dramatic plot, it starred the diva-like Fenella Fielding in the implausible story of the town's takeover. The decks and ramps of the town center lend themselves very readily as a cinematic backdrop, especially for the dramatic car chases, being both an innovative, cosmopolitan and secure locale and an architect's personal homage to road culture.

Happy

Set entirely away from the center, housing at Cumbernauld consisted mostly of low-rise groupings of rather traditional appearance (including many 'small sturdy cottages set to the wind,' as Robin Crichton describes it in *Town for Tomorrow*, which conveys its ideals in some detail, adding that every 400 houses had a corner shop, every area its own community room), but there were some higher towers. From the beginning, the population of Cumbernauld was very mixed, and people were allowed to buy plots and build for themselves. The landscaping around the housing areas is spacious, and there are no hermetic, back-to-back gardens, although

the many patio houses included in the town have sizeable courtyards. The success of centers of this kind in the New Towns of Coventry and Stevenage and, further afield, in Rotterdam had already proved to the Development Corporation that people like to do their shopping away from the noise and danger of automobile traffic. Replacing the hectic struggle in crowded streets by pleasant conditions where shoppers can stroll and chat made the design an even more clearly community-oriented, providing them easy access by car and bus (via ramps), and the opportunity to park their cars within a short distance of the shops.

From the time of the town's inception, the Development Corporation issued a continual flow of promotional literature about 'Britain's new industrial showplace,' outlining the financial benefits to businesses moving to the New Town, endowed as it was with highly attractive social amenities, government grants and the easy availability of loans, while a concurrent stream of journalists, architects and planners from all over the world visited the town from the early 1960s onwards. Demographically, the most pronounced feature of the early residents, predominantly from Glasgow, was that one third of them were under 15; and only 5% were elderly. Space, sunlight, privacy, and sturdy, split-level housing oriented to with-stand the wind: all these qualities were exploited to the full. In his film, Crichton talks about the 'engineering for pedestrians,' referring to the complete segregation of footpaths and roads, and calls it 'brilliantly legible,' doing away with the need for traffic lights, not to mention traf-fic police.

Writer Mary Gilliatt visited the town in the autumn of 1966, reporting for Country Life,

Happy

just after the first phase of the town center had been completed. 'There still seems to be too much monotone, too much grey everywhere, too little change in the light and shade that are essential if character and individuality are to be given a town built over a period of years not centuries.' However, she acknowledged that fade-free paint in such a blustery climate had limited the color choices, and she was convinced by the overall appearance, giving due praise to the 'white pebble stone facing the point blocks with the rolling, brooding background of Kilsyth and Ochil hills, and the gleaming massed cube structure of the center.' She also lauded

Gros.Max, Grow your own town

Cumbernauld's 'astonishing variety in house types and shapes with thoughtful gradations of roofs so that everyone gets a fair share of sunlight and a view down the hill to the woods.'

Alastair Borthwick, another well-known writer of this period, found it disappointing at first. 'I saw houses with blank walls at street level and windows in unlikely places upstairs.' But soon he became converted: 'the oddly positioned windows let in sunlight while the main windows looked north to the view. And the children I saw (they went about in shoals) were having a whale of a time with never a car to bother them.' For him, Cumbernauld's chief advantage was that it was actually planned as a whole. They designed the town first, he pointed out, and then they thought about the houses, in each case for convenience and comfort, so

Happy

that the needs of a dwelling place were made to harmonize with a variety of patterns of movement. Conventional street patterns were avoided in favor of roads in and around each neighborhood. These were each given a new name. For instance, Seafar is an old farmland, while others took the names of writers and poets. This method of development struck him as quite 'a different matter from starting at one end in the accepted fashion and churning out houses until they came out the other end.' The other aspect which greatly impressed him was that the houses were arranged in such a way that they did not overlook each other. Privacy in a council house garden was unheard of in Scotland until the Cumbernauld planners went to work, so this was truly radical, and again, a key quality of more recent suburban developments. The road system, he noted, had the virtue of not being 'patched together after the houses were built, as it has been in nearly every housing scheme in the land. It was worked out at the beginning, before one brick was laid on another. The traffic is just one more part of total planning, of a town thought as a whole. The ingenuity of the thing attracts me.' The landscape architect, too, was encouraged to exercise his imagination, something which had not previously been seen in Glasgow. Grass, expensive to keep tidy, was not ubiquitous, but interspersed with cobbles, rectangular granite stones and paving. Shortcuts were discouraged by planting heather instead of grass, and big boulders were left for children to play on instead of being taken away.

Borthwick suspected Cumbernauld might well be windy (as indeed today's Greenwich Millennium Village in London is, too, and likewise built to withstand the wind), with slow buses, and he observed that the 'place is still a one-class town where the boss lives somewhere else. It couldn't have been much fun being in at the early stages and waiting years for the big shops and the public entertainments to arrive,' he speculated. However, he still viewed it as unique among New Towns. 'In the others they have built mostly neighborhoods, self-contained districts with their own schools and small shopping centers catering for many thousands of people, with a big shopping center in the middle of the town to serve the lot.' By contrast, Cumbernauld's town center was on everyone's doorstep. 'Privacy and bright lights within ten minutes of each other is something no other town has.' It was the creation of a new urban model, a hybrid, that impressed him the most: 'Cumbernauld is neither country nor town, but something completely new, a kind of town-country that has never happened before, a place that has the neighborliness of Glasgow without its grubby streets' and 'the privacy and freshness of the countryside without its loneliness.'

In Scotland, the provision of mass housing needed to take account of a tradition of migration, to mainland Europe and Ireland. Low-rise housing was not challenging to investors. The concept of placing industrial plants not in the middle of a city like the old urban centers, but tucked away beyond residential areas remains a valid approach. Demographically, Cumbernauld, while still an important area for business, has changed dramatically, and the pioneering quality of its 'self-made culture' has gone. It seems ironic that Cumbernauld, dubbed a town designed to facilitate people and cars, should end up becoming a social anachronism due to its very facilitation of mobility. As Crichton poignantly observed,

Happy

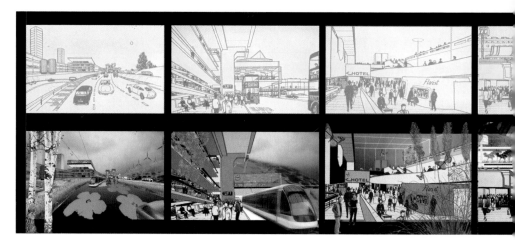

'There is a limit to what planners can do. They provide the framework – and people make it live'. Self-made culture moved on from Cumbernauld back to the metropolises of Glasgow and Edinburgh, rather than growing in this design's nurturing environment, which outlasted its usefulness, a social experiment that inevitably ended after its test phase. The idea that one small town can demonstrate a pattern for the future has also become anachronistic, hard to take seriously and even worrying, particularly in an era when heavily planned commercial developments – like the Bluewater shopping center built at the edge of a chalk pit in Kent in the late 1990s – can give the appearance of asteroids.

The desire to make a clean break between town and country and preserve the country's 'green and pleasant land' is a sentiment deeply etched in the British psyche. Ironically, this urge to avoid urban sprawl is currently being subjected to challenge from the UK's Deputy Prime Minister in southeastern England, as he gives the green light for new building for London and the Southeast to provide at least 90,000 new homes by 2006. He has earmarked four areas for expansion, all outside London, including the other New Town, Milton Keynes. Residents fear the expansion will lead to a significant loss of open green spaces, and, with their own sense of a happy environmental balance being daily eroded by commercial forces, oppose what one of them has called 'this blurring of town and countryside.'

This romantic concept of a firm town/country division is combined at Cumbernauld with an application of zoning that was central to Le Corbusier's Ville Radieuse plan. Residential buildings are placed in the outskirts, with a commercial center set high on a central hilltop. It seems extraordinary that in such a location a late-Modernist attempt should be made to radically reshape the concept of an urban center on multi-level 'megastructural' principles, and to have it serve as the central nodal point of a highly integrated social vision. The other strand of Cumbernauld's identity was the idea of creating a town that would be easy to add to or dismantle, and flexible enough to cope with changing economic or social patterns. The dismantling of the town center in 2001 in order to pull apart the megastructure and transform it into something more like an open shopping street, along with the filling in of the central expressway, shows that the plan, which revolved around a heavily interiorized concept of

Happy

social space that initially transcended a purely commercial function, could no longer be sustained by the local council, North Lanarkshire, which took over once the Development Corporation was dissolved. The destruction seems not to have been the result of any coordinated plan, just as new housing has been haphazardly creeping into the residential areas in the form of little brick boxes designed by speculative builders.

The original projections in 1956 for Cumbernauld's population growth were never fully reached. By the end of the 1980s, 50,000 people were living there, and private developers, who began moving in even before North Lanarkshire took the reins, built 1800 new houses in two years, anticipating a rather more modest increase, and this has led to unexceptional additions to the early schemes.

Any consensus that might exist today concerning the idea of the 'social' leads us away from the centralizing visions of the 20th century. Global capitalism, market-driven property forces, compliant councils, and, above all, changing perceptions of time and place and the emergence of widely differentiated cultural landscapes, with more centralized, commercial visions, have led to cities sprawling beyond their historic boundaries. In the United Kingdom, the idea of the high-density, big city district, thriving thanks to its reinvigorated industrial roots and reinvented building stock, has supplanted the neat concept of a rural mono-cultural town with everything in one physical location.

The vision for Cumbernauld that was once so effective as a provisional urban model seems parochial in the light of our 21st century nomadic inclinations. However, the social ideas behind its planning can be seen reflected in more recent suburban developments. The suburb, as much as people like to criticize its parochial qualities, has proved, thanks to many of its best examples, to be a more durable model. In Scotland's changing society, the brilliantly legible solution to the conflict of cars and people that Cumbernauld forged became more of a hindrance than a gateway to social satisfaction. Tomorrow's Town Today became something else in a world that was simply less and less interested in thinking legibly about cultural planning as a community-oriented enterprise.

Happy

Rome, July 20, 2001.

Both the inhabitants and the authorities of Rome have often tried to equal the impressive remains of antiquity. Not so long ago, they were still driven by this desire. If you want to see what this has led to, the best thing to do is to rent a scooter (preferably a Vespa, to give the trip a really authentic touch), and to start with the Roman Forum. Then you pass the Monument to Victor Emmanuel II, nicknamed the typewriter, or the wedding cake. It was erected here at the end of the nineteenth century. On your way to the EUR district initiated by Mussolini and saturated with museums, ministries and, of course, the 'square colosseum' (the Palazzo della Civilita Romana), you notice the Circus Maximus and the Baths of Caracalla. If you park your Vespa at the Palazzo della Civilità and mount the steps, you will see the Nuove Corviale apartment complex lying precisely in its axis. From here it takes only ten minutes to get there. This impressive building was designed in the 1980s and marks Rome's southern city limits. Only green countryside extends beyond it. This voyage through time, from the old Roman center to the new 'city wall' takes only forty minutes of your precious time. M.v.R.

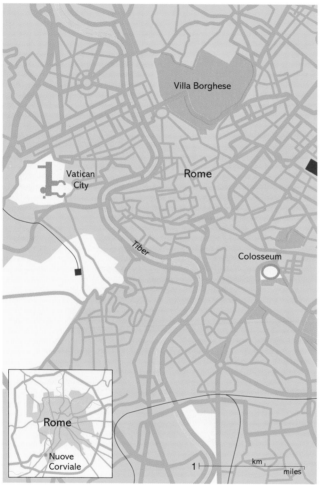

Happy

Il Nuovo Corviale, a Utopian Project in the Roman Periphery

Marieke van Rooy

'If future inhabitants expect to find a paternalistic structure of the type where everything is taken care of and they do not have to invest anything themselves, Corviale is destined to fail, because it is quite clear that it cannot be managed in a paternalistic way.'[1]

MARIO FIORENTINO, 1982

Il Nuovo Corviale, a huge housing estate for about 8,500 inhabitants in the outskirts of Rome, refers to the old Roman aqueducts that appear in the landscape

1 Mario Fiorentino, in: *Roma: Nuovo Corviale*, Nicoletta Campanella 1995, 79.

as symbols of man's victory over nature. The ideals incorporated in this project recall those of the Romans in the heyday of their empire. Il Nuovo Corviale has been designed as a self-sufficient unit that does not depend upon the neighboring communities. Shops, schools and recreational facilities are part of the design, and are meant to attract people from outside.

A housing shortage fueled the construction of a parallel city in the 1950s, parts of which still exist today. Thousands of illegal barracks, usually lacking even the most rudimentary public amenities, were built wherever the municipal authorities decided to tolerate them. In 1962 the municipality decided to build five large-scale housing projects in the city's outskirts. Corviale was the last to be built and is distinguished from its predecessors by its unique design: a monolithic block surrounded by a green oasis. This approach can be seen as a reaction against the proliferation of illegal shanty towns.

The roman architect Mario Fiorentino was supervisor of the project. In his work, he tries to strike a balance between historical urban structures and technological innovations. That explains why Corviale has been organized as a traditional city. It is surrounded by greenery, and includes a concrete amphitheater, a church, a sports center, a theater, a market and a movie theater. Some of the apartments are located in two three-story blocks, but most of them are located in the project's most visually striking element, a ten-story apartment building with a total length of one kilometer. The fourth floor, designed for shops and offices, divides the building into two parts. The building is a concrete structure of prefabricated elements. A diagonal structure of receding parallel lines displays the prefabricated panels of the outer walls. Concrete also dominates the interior spaces, where it alternates with glass tiles. Color is provided by signs on the walls, which indicate to visitors where they can find what they are looking for. Blocks of elevators divide the building into five volumes. In front of them small

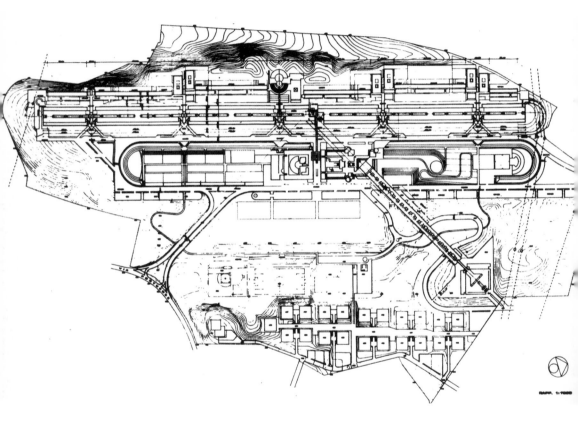

squares were planned, intended as meeting places for the inhabitants. Each of the five volumes is organized around an open patio, where the galleries that provide access to the apartments are located.

The network of corridors is a vital part of the project. Bridges connect the various parts of the estate, and the result gives the impression of a genuine micro-city. The corridors are not merely traffic routes; they are also intended as places where the inhabitants can spend leisure moments. Near the elevators, concrete benches are installed that are reminiscent of Herman Hertzberger's work. The design offers numerous occasions for social contacts and is testimony to Fiorentino's belief that society is something that can be planned and designed.

Happy

The aim, obviously, is to create a pleasant environment where the architecture fosters the inhabitants' social well-being. A similar attitude marks the work of contemporary projects in, for instance, Amsterdam (De Bijlmer) and London (Robin Hood Gardens), to name but two that now are usually seen as proof of the failure of modern architecture. Even so, I would hesitate to accuse the architects of these projects of naivete. Mario Fiorentino, for instance, knew full well that the success of this type of project depends on many factors. 'If one wants to design real neighborhoods instead of dormitory cities, it is necessary to invest considerable

sums of money in public services, and to acknowledge that running a project like this requires good management and the availability of a trained staff (for service, cleaning, the garden, and maintenance in general), and makes it necessary to conceive and program these aspects as being as important as the architectural design.'

In 1982, when the first houses were completed and Mario Fiorentino died (providing the occasion for the myth that he committed suicide when he had to confront the failure of his work), most of Corviale was still surrounded by scaffoldings. The elevators didn't work, electricity and gas failed regularly and the nearest bus stop was three kilometers away. Many apartments remained empty and were subsequently occupied by 700 families of squatters.

Happy

After they were chased away, some of them decided to set up homes at the doorsteps of the building. They stayed there for more than a year and only the bitter cold of a hard winter made them leave. Occasionally the public areas were occupied by distinct groups, for instance people from Peru or Croatia. The most dramatic in this series of events started in 1989 and still lingers on today: in that year, 64 families occupied the fourth floor. They not only moved there; they also redecorated the entire floor to fit their specific needs. Some even invested a considerable amount of money to transform their part of the floor into an actual palazzo. Parts of the public galleries were privatized and added to the private domain of the apartments. From the outside, the fourth floor is immediately recognizable by the small makeshift residences that were created there. They vary in color and material and add a fascinating note to the complex. Some of these units are quite spacious, and far bigger than the 'official' apartments on the other floors. While generally the apartments are easily accessible to everyone – the intercom system does not function so everybody can enter – the fourth floor is closed off by fences that block the way to the galleries. This keeps strangers outside, and also acts as a defensive line against the police – after all, the entire floor is occupied illegally. The squatters

Happy

created their own realm on the floor that was originally intended to be the central social meeting place for all the inhabitants of Corviale. For the last few years, their example has been followed in the remaining public areas of the complex. The kindergarten and the school are now being used as a boxing gym, the workshop for a theater, the council of the residents of Corviale, and a meeting place for the elderly.

Fiorentino warned the inhabitants not to count on help from the traditional paternalistic structures and institutions. They were expected to invest time and energy in making the project a success. And so they did. They literally repossessed the building. On the one hand, this illustrates the failure of the management and the responsible authorities, but, on the other hand, one may condemn their expectations as being too utopian. Did one expect too much of the individual inhabitant in this 'housing machine?' Throughout the years, the people living in Corviale have established a special relation with the 'monster' and they oppose the negative evaluation of this experimental complex. Nevertheless, they would like nothing better than the implementation of the original concept, which would guarantee more security and better opportunities for organizing all kinds of activities.

Happy

Dunaújváros (Sztalinváros), March 14, 2004.

Spring is in the air, and the last patches of snow are melting away. As we approach the center of Dunaújváros, one of the half dozen 'Stalintowns' built in the former Soviet Union and its satellite states, we have to find our way

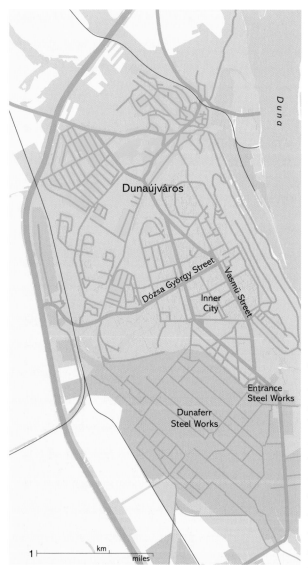

Dunaújváros

Dózsa György Street

Vasmü Street

Duna

Inner City

Entrance Steel Works

Dunaferr Steel Works

1 | km | miles

through a thick layer of industrially produced apartment buildings. Churches have been built in the wide open spaces characteristic of town planning in an era when all land had been nationalized. To describe them as ugly would be the understatement of the new millennium, but they are there, fulfilling people's religious needs after decades of supression. Then, finally, we arrive at our goal: in the small but elegant core of Dunaújváros, built according to the principles of socialist realism and probably one of the most successful town planning projects in postwar Hungary. Dunaújváros is now seeking to exploit its unique architectural features. In addition to trying to attract tourists to its local museum, the city invites them to take a walk through the luxurious green parks surrounding the kindergartens and schools, to take a look at the movie theater and the town hall, and to stroll along the city's central axis, which is somehow too friendly to be called a 'Magistrale' and which leads towards the huge steel works that was the reason why the city was built in the first place. In a way, this old Stalin City was part of a huge conveyor belt that linked specialized regions in the vast Soviet empire in a centrally planned economic machine on a continental scale. Today, the latter is gone, but the factory is still operating and the city is still alive. **C.W.**

Happy

Stalintown

Henriett Szabo

Since the Second World War, the number of Hungarian towns has doubled, an odd phenomenon closely related to the socialist regime that was established in the late 1940s. The first Five Year Plan that was issued in 1948 already projected a number of new socialist towns, laying the foundations of Hungary's new economic and industrial system. No less than eleven new towns were built: Ajka, Kazincbarcika, Komló, Oroszlány, Ózd, Salgótarján, Százhalombatta, Tatabánya, Leninváros (now Tiszaújvaros), Várpalota, and Sztalinváros (now Dunaújváros). All of them were created to serve specific goals within the new socialist economy; they attracted most of the finances invested in public housing in these years; and since they were free of the physical constraints often hampering the development of existing cities, they were experimental playgrounds where the principles of socialist town planning were put to the test. They reflected the demands of the new socialist bureaucracy and marked Hungary's road to industrialization.

Ten years of Stalintown

The steel works

Everything was determined by the National Planning Office, which was virtually a part of the Communist Party, then under the leadership of Mátyás Rákosi. The Planning Office's authority was absolute; counterproposals made by experts, for example, those at the Budapest University of Technology, were usually simply discarded. Part of the Planning Office's strategy was aimed at distributing industry more equally over the entire national territory, in an attempt to solve the traditional imbalance between the capital city and the rural countryside. One of the advantages believed to be inherent in this strategy was that it would create pockets of industrial labor in areas that, so far, were dominated by agriculture; this would increase support for the regime in regions where communism was not yet very popular. Metallurgy, the machine tool industry, chemical engineering and the railway system were assigned a pivotal role in this effort to politicize the countryside.

The project for Stalintown was one of the biggest and most ambitious of this period. Originally, the city was to be located further south, near the border with Yugoslavia. Political

The main boulevard

Happy

and military reasons forced the Planning Office to reconsider these plans; and when a ban on the construction of important industrial complexes in the regions bordering on Yugoslavia and Austria was issued, Stalintown moved to its present site, some 60 kilometers south of Budapest.

Stalintown was designed by Tibor Weiner, who before the war was one of the Hungarian students at the Bauhaus in Dessau. In the 1930s he worked in the Soviet Union, where he specialized in designing elementary schools. During the war he worked in Chile, where he was appointed professor at the University of Santiago in 1946. In 1948 he returned to Budapest. The Institute of Town Planning chose him to design Stalintown in 1950, and he worked on it for two years. The first sketches show a city of about 25,000 inhabitants, while the final proposals envisaged a city of about 40,000 people.

The ironworks is the all-important element in Stalintown. As work is the essence of socialist life, and the huge factory almost a temple of labor, everything in the New Town is

Working for the community

Building site

focused on the factory. The main street runs directly from the city to the factory, which is separated from it by a green strip. The street looks disproportionately wide, because it is not only the main thoroughfare of Stalintown but also the Magistrale where political demonstration were enacted. A second main street crosses the Magistrale at right angles and leads from the railway station to the Town Hall Square. These two boulevards are the city's main structural elements. The major buildings of Stalintown make it clear that it was not all that easy for Hungarian architects to adopt the new style of socialist-realism dictated by Moscow. Like Weiner, many had their roots in prewar modernism, which was now heavily criticized as capitalist and formalist, whereas the new style was promoted as socialist and close to the people. The new ideology claimed to combine socialist contents and national forms, the international proletariat and patriotism, modernity and tradition. The apartment buildings have high-pitched roofs, an ornamental frieze, main entrances set in wide frames, and windows also set in large frames (and usually divided into two sections). Columns and semi-columns are used to accentuate the entrance; and the balconies derive their particular character from large corner columns, and the thin iron bars in between.

Today, Stalintown (now Dunaújváros) is embedded in a ring of industrially-produced housing estates, built according to the principles propagated by Khrushtchev in December

Happy

Putting up the flag

Happy

1954. In recent years, several churches have been inserted in the green areas between the apartment buildings. The original social-realist town with its pleasant scale, its modest architecture and abundant greenery stands out as by far the most pleasant part of the city. People prefer it to the housing estates that were added later, and the municipality has discovered that the architecture of its oldest areas can be used to promote Dunaújvaros as something special – and special this New Town surely is.

Socialist-realist buildings in the heart of the city

Happy

Hoogvliet, February 9, 2004.

In the subway, opposite me, a girl from the Dutch Antilles is sitting. About 20 years old, she wears her hair in braids and she is immaculately dressed. Her clothes look brand new and are lavishly decorated with all kinds of things. Next to her is parked a baby carriage with a small child. He is too big for

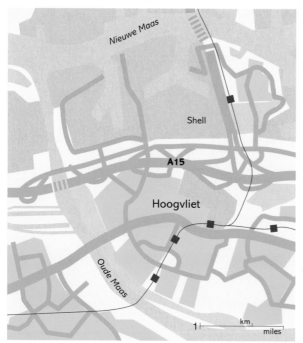

this contraption, a trendy tricycle; as he keeps on whining, his Nike cap falls to the floor. His mother gives him a bag of potato crisps and he quiets down. At the next stop on this early Monday morning, a scraggy-looking couple enters the train, quarreling about ten euros. It is difficult to understand what they are saying, as both of them are missing several teeth. Elaborately, they pile the contents of a plastic bag on their lap: a newspaper, a sheet of silver paper, a small tube, a lighter. Finally they stop nagging about their ten euros, lighting their 'sket'. The other passengers look slightly embarrassed as the smell of heroin, homeopathically small though the doses may be, drifts their way. Then the train enters Hoogvliet. Naturally, the escalator is out of order. The entrance to the stairway is blocked by three cantankerous middle-aged Dutch ladies, dressed uniformly in beige and yellow. Although none of them is older than fifty, they nevertheless have a walker. Leaning against it, they smoke their cigarettes, refusing to step aside — after all, they are handicapped, aren't they? Outside the station, the steel-grey sky works like the natural setting for the row of dull single-family houses and the sad, disconsolate shops near the bus station. Luckily the crow that is always there isn't absent today, but is begging for something nice to eat, not afraid at all. I give him a piece of bread, but he prefers a tray of French fries with mayonnaise that has fallen out of the garbage can. He looks at me as if he wants to peck out my eyes, yelling: 'I want nothing of you, go away!' Typically Hoogvliet. M.P.

Happy

HAPPY
HOOGVLIET

Michelle Provoost

Only six kilometers long, Rotterdam's subway line was the shortest in the world when it opened in 1968, but, not surprisingly, the city still took great pride in having built the Netherlands' first subway. It was yet another sign of the city's agility in re-inventing itself after the devastating air raid that had destroyed its historic core in 1940. It showcased the two pillars of Rotterdam's carefully cultivated image: modernity and progress. A new urban core, dominated by buildings designed for business and spacious new housing estates, fostered the city's self-esteem. The subway was welcomed as a technical improvement that strengthened this new image. Starting in the rebuilt center, the line crosses the river, revealing the old working-class estates on the southern bank. It continues to the postwar housing estates, which are composed of an endlessly repeated series of identical or very similar units (which were appropriately labeled 'stamps'). For the time being, the line ended at Slinge station, located in one of the world's most famous housing estates: Pendrecht, which is a major highlight of Dutch urban planning. The initial designs for Pendrecht had been prepared by a team in the vanguard of modern architects associated with CIAM: Van den Broek & Bakema and Lotte Stam-Beese. The purity of the design and its widely praised spatial concept had turned it into a model for similar experiments all over Europe. The subway line was soon extended beyond the city's municipal borders, starting with the stations in Rhoon and Poortugaal. Even though at this point we have barely left Rotterdam behind us, the city looks light-years away. Small villages line the dikes, and there are small shops, churches, and quite a number of farms: a typical Dutch pastoral scene. Green pastures show up on both sides of the subway line, willows mark the course of narrow country roads, and sheep graze the banks. Then, all of a sudden, one of the new housing estates appears and we are back in Rotterdam. Station Hoogvliet is lined with towers and large apartment buildings. It is the city's farthest outpost, 12 kilometers away from the center. Hoogvliet is a veritable New Town, an autonomous urban unit designed in the late 1940s according to the principles of the English New Towns near London.

The motivation for building Hoogvliet this far from the existing city was the passionate desire to do more than simply repair the destruction caused by the war: the port of Rotterdam was to become the largest in the world. To achieve this ambitious goal, huge new harbor

Happy

189

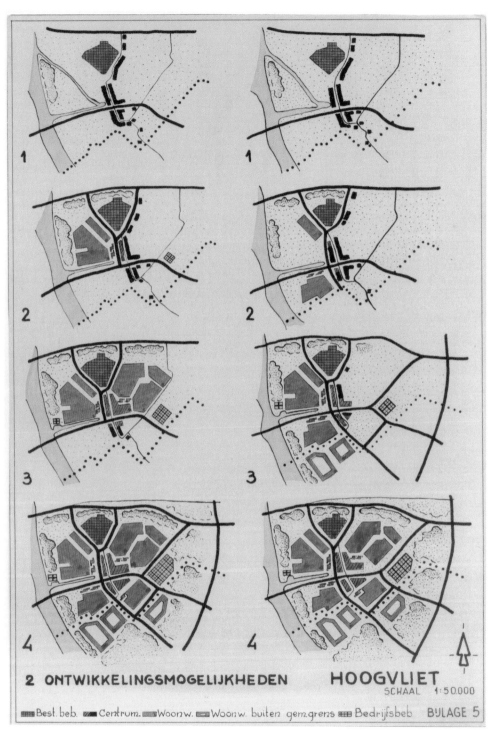

Development strategies for Hoogvliet

Happy

The old village giving way to the New Town

basins were created in the Botlek and Europoort areas and complemented by new industrial complexes. The small medieval village of Hoogvliet, situated in the immediate vicinity of the Shell refinery, was singled out as a 'nucleus of growth', suitable for housing the labor force required by the expanding port. Gradually, the old village was to be replaced by a completely new Hoogvliet. The historic port was filled in, historic farms and the characteristic small houses along the dikes were demolished. As a prelude to these grand ideas, the old core near the seventeenth-century church (which itself escaped demolition) was destroyed to make place for the New Town's shopping center. The scale of this shopping mall was quite large: the plan envisaged shops, high-rise apartment buildings, cultural buildings including a musical center, and a sports stadium. Hoogvliet was to become a regional center, a sparkling magnet attracting people from the neighboring villages. Lotte Stam-Beese's drawings of Hoogvliet radiate a worldly, urbane atmosphere comparable to Harlow or Stevenage, quite different from that of the famous Pendrecht housing estate. Hoogvliet was to be a proud and independent urban core next to Rotterdam.

Successes and failures In its urban layout, Hoogvliet clearly reflected the ideals of the neighborhood unit. The social hierarchy of family, neighbors, the neighborhood community and the urban society was mirrored by the physical hierarchy of the individual house, the street, a group of streets with a small shopping center, the neighborhood and, finally, the city at large. All the housing units were designed as parts of a balanced community comprising

Happy

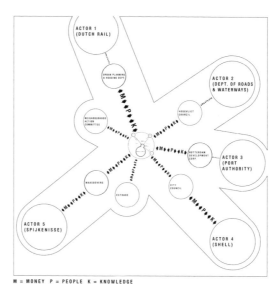

ACTOR 1
(DUTCH RAIL)

ACTOR 2
(DEPT. OF ROADS
& WATERWAYS)

ACTOR 3
(PORT
AUTHORITY)

ACTOR 4
(SHELL)

ACTOR 5
(SPIJKENISSE)

URBAN PLANNING
& HOUSING DEPT

NEIGHBOURHOOD
ACTION
COMMITTEE

HOOGVLIET
COUNCIL

ROTTERDAM
DEVELOPMENT
CORP

MAASOEVERS

ESTRADE

CITY
COUNCIL

M = MONEY P = PEOPLE K = KNOWLEDGE

Organization Scheme

various types of houses. The architecture of the houses, schools, and shops was uniform and sober. This functionalist feeling was greatly enhanced by the industrial building methods that were applied in Hoogvliet. Apart from that, the town expressed one of the great ideals of the time: social equality. An abundance of open spaces and communal gardens compensated for the small houses; and the transparency and openness of the public greenery represented a new, open urban society. Naturally, traffic was organized according to the latest ideas on efficiency. Cars, bicycles and pedestrians were provided with their own dedicated lanes. These were combined to create wide traffic arteries provided with ample greenery, a modern version of the American parkways. All the components of the urban structure were endowed with the qualities of modernism and efficiency; but, at the same time, they can be said to embody an idealistic social model.

Like most postwar utopias, the ideal New Town of Hoogvliet soon experienced serious difficulties. Instead of fostering social cohesion, the neighborhood units promoted a feeling of alienation. In nearby Vlaardingen, sociologists discovered that inhabitants identified with their street and its immediate surroundings, but not with the social module of the neighborhood. To make things worse, the size of the houses was seen as too small. Lacking an extra room that could be used as a study, the houses offered in Hoogvliet were, they contended, bound to have a devastating effect on the development of the individual personality, at the same time hampering opportunities to enjoy a harmonious family life. This was all the more serious because the population of Hoogvliet was made up of a curious mix of dockworkers from Rotterdam and immigrants from the agrarian provinces of Drenthe and Zeeland. The latter had their own dialect, clung to their own lifestyles and were a source of continuous friction. Finally, the notion of transforming Hoogvliet into an autonomous New Town was questionable right from the start. Rotterdam was nearby, and after the construction of the subway line and

Happy

192

Logica

Happy

Campus ('toornend')

new highways in the 1960s, the inhabitants of Hoogvliet were no longer dependent on the amenities offered in Hoogvliet. In addition, what had been conceived of as one of the advantages of Hoogvliet, its situation at a stone's throw from the Shell refinery, turned out to be a major drawback, as a series of accidents and the continuously polluted air demonstrated. On January 20, 1968, an explosion shattered most of the windows in Hoogvliet, dramatically altering its image: a city once seen as friendly, efficient and modern suddenly bore the stigma of being the kind of place that one would do well to avoid.

Even before Hoogvliet lost its utopian image, the town planners had understood that its location was far from ideal. At the beginning of the 1960s, when new housing estates were still being added and the population of the New Town was growing rapidly, the planners decided that the original vision of a city inhabited by some 60,000 people had become problematic. They decided to extend the subway line, adding one more stop to create Spijkenisse, at a safe distance from the industrial complexes. Spijkenisse was to develop into a New Town of approximately 80,000 people. The housing estates originally intended to be part of Hoogvliet were transferred to Spijkenisse, and, as a result, Hoogvliet definitively lost its image as an optimistic, desirable housing estate. Hoogvliet never had more than 37,000 inhabitants, and just a limited number of shops were built, the only vestiges of the ambitious plans for a shopping mall with numerous cultural and recreational facilities. Decades later, rows of terraced

Happy

houses were built on the area that was left open. Even today, the area near the church gives the impression of a suburban wasteland and is only used for parking. Instead of the urban, even semi-metropolitan character originally meant to distinguish Hoogvliet's housing estates, the last ones that were built display a typically suburban character, defined by small, meandering streets lined with single-family houses. Lost within one of these estates and stuck between the remnants of old dikes, the subway station is a far cry from offering direct access to a truly urban center, as was originally planned. The entrance to the city is marked by a vast, desolate square that is used as a bus station, where, in a surreal scene, 10 bus stops all serve the same line: no. 78. Whoever enters Hoogvliet at this point cannot help but remember the feelings of the town planners in the late 1960s. Hoogvliet is a town planning accident. It has become a mutant: half New Town, half suburb.

Ghetto It may be true that Hoogvliet failed to live up to its promises as a New Town, and it is hard to deny that the dream of the modernist city became discredited here even before half of the project had been realized. Even so, Hoogvliet does exist and is here to stay. In the mid-1990s, over 30,000 people lived there, some of them the middle-aged 'pioneers' of the 1950s and 1960s. They liked Hoogvliet because to them it was a quiet place at a comfortable distance from the increasingly problem-ridden metropolis of Rotterdam. Many of the former inhabitants of Hoogvliet – those who could afford to move – left the tiny, noisy homes and settled in the bigger houses of the surrounding cities. The inexpensive houses of Hoogvliet attracted new

The Estate Hoogvliet, brick house

Happy

inhabitants, as Hoogvliet became a refuge for immigrants, many of them from the Dutch Antilles. They took up residence in the northern parts of Hoogvliet, where their different lifestyles soon caused trouble. It did not take long for a real schism to develop between the suburban, white, well-to-do southern parts, which were mainly inhabited by native Dutch people, and the northern parts that were increasingly dominated by socially weaker groups. 'Nieuw Engeland', the 'oil' estate, epitomized this new trend. In 1951, so-called fan-shaped apartment buildings had been erected here, lining streets named after regions rich in oil: Caracas Street, Texas Street, etc. The homes in this area were especially small, built in somber brick and located in the least desirable part of Hoogvliet, close to the oil refinery alongside the highway. In the 1990s, these streets changed into what soon became known as a ghetto. Junkies, drug dealers, and vandalism made Nieuw Engeland an ideal topic for a documentary on Dutch television that further strengthened the image of Hoogvliet as a sad, lost neighborhood.

Revitalizing Hoogvliet To stop the downward trend, Hoogvliet proclaimed itself a disaster area in the mid-1990s. First of all, the fan-shaped apartment buildings were raided by the combined forces of the police, the public health service, tax collectors and bailiffs, who combed through every apartment in an attempt to stop all illegal activities. Drug dealers were imprisoned, defaulters indicted, and illegal tenants chased away. Subsequently, the remaining inhabitants were offered better houses elsewhere in Hoogvliet, and apartment buildings were I manner that was meant to set an example for the other projects. The local authorities and the two housing corporations that had recently been privatized and owned most of the housing stock in Hoogvliet cooperated in an attempt to improve housing conditions. No less than 5,000 houses, 30% of the housing stock, were to be demolished, mainly apartments of 56 square meters or smaller that could no longer satisfy the expectations of the inhabitants of the 1990s. Likewise, the 'maisonette' apartments and the homes for the elderly that in the 1960s had been built around small courtyards – all of them miniature houses with only one small living room and an even smaller bedroom – were marked for demolition. Marketable homes were to take their place. The authorities hope that by creating a more diverse palette of housing types and reducing the proportion of subsidized tenement housing (which used to be 70%), they could coax a more diverse, well-to-do population to move to Hoogvliet.

The revitalization campaign for Hoogvliet was clearly an answer to specific needs, but it also reflected fundamental changes in the Dutch Welfare State. The state withdrew from public life, a move that led public housing to become almost completely privatized. The housing corporations shed their traditional role as social organizations and started to be run as semi-commercial companies. This happened not only in Hoogvliet; in almost all the postwar housing estates that have undergone revitalization, strategies have been adopted that are determined more by administrative and commercial concerns than by social ideas. As Jacqueline Tellinga puts it in a recent publication on 'The Big Make-Over': 'Since their privatization in 1995, the corporations have turned into real estate companies in which decisions on investments are taken at the highest level. They evaluate their possessions as part of their complete holdings,

Happy

regardless of their specific setting.[1] This is why they choose a generic approach for all reconstruction projects, no matter how different the original situations might be. Everywhere, high-rise buildings and apartment buildings are substituted by low-rise, mostly single family homes; private gardens replace collective greenery, and small neighborhood shopping centers disappear, replaced by large, central shopping malls. Last but not least, low-cost tenement houses are eliminated, and expensive owner-occupied houses are strongly promoted.

Jacqueline Tellinga, 'Corporaties zijn sinds hun verzelfstandiging in 1995 vastgoedmaatschappijen geworden waarbij e investeringsbeslissingen op hoog niveau in de organisatie orden genomeen. Ze beoordelen hun bezit vanuit hun complete vastgoedportefeuille, niet op buurtniveau', in: J. Tellinga, e Grote Verbouwing. Verandering van naoorlogse woonwijken, otterdam 2004, 20.

The revitalization of Hoogvliet followed along similar lines. To overcome the negative image, it was decided to replace most of the urban structure, the public spaces and the housing stock by something with a more 'contemporary' look. The characteristic composition of basic building forms floating in space, so typical of the modern city, was considered out of date. They were replaced by enclosed spaces and traditional urban elements: the city street, the return of the building line as the main organizational principle, the square, the boulevard. The original concept of an introverted pedestrian shopping mall was to be turned inside out by moving the shops to the boulevard. The free-flowing public space that washed through Hoogvliet's urban tissue was to be framed by new blocks of houses, streets and cozy courtyards. Communal spaces, a fundamental principle in postwar town planning, had to make way for private gardens. Everything reminiscent of the original 'collective' ideals was banished. From now on, the individual and his personal lifestyle were to set the tone in Hoogvliet.
In short, the most characteristic feature of the revitalization scheme was the urge to eradicate the modern model on which the original plan for Hoogvliet had been based. Everything associated with it was seen as negative. The town planners' main aspiration now was to reinvent Hoogvliet. Even though they returned to tested traditional models, their ambition to bulldoze most of the existing New Town out of the way is reminiscent of the tabula rasa mentality of their colleagues who built Hoogvliet in the 1950s. The new plan did not relate to the existing situation any better than the original concept had related to the historic village it was designed to replace.

WiMBY! In 1999, the alderman for city planning, at the time a representative of the Dutch green party, offered a motion urging that the municipal government mount an International Building Exhibition modeled on the German examples of the Internationale Bauausstellung (IBA) in Berlin and the Emscher Park exhibition. It was a brave attempt to counter the prevailing notions in urban politics and the town planning profession, which were entirely focused on spectacular and highly prestigious projects in Rotterdam's inner city. His goal was to direct attention to the slum-like conditions in many of the postwar housing estates, and his motion proved to be the starting point for the WiMBY! project: Welcome in My Backyard. Since 2000 the management team has been led by Felix Rottenberg, former chairman of the

Happy

SchoolParasites: Onix

Happy

Dutch Social-Democratic Party, and the contents of the enterprise have been defined by two architectural historians of Crimson, Michelle Provoost, author of this article, and Wouter Vanstiphout.

Even though the famous German undertakings inspired WiMBY!, it soon became clear that neither Berlin nor Emscher Park could provide a model for Hoogvliet. Not only was WiMBY! never more than a miniature version of these projects; the context was also very different. Whereas the Emscher Park project worked in a virtual vacuum – both industry and population tended to move away from the Ruhr region – Hoogvliet was bombarded with reconstruction proposals. There was more than enough money available, and revitalization had already begun. The local political board, the housing corporations and the commercial realtors were engaged in what they called the 'Hoogvliet conspiracy', a conspiracy that promised to be very successful.

Then came WiMBY! What could WiMBY! possibly add to a planning apparatus that was already in full swing? Its special assignment was to improve the quality of the revitalization scheme, to introduce innovative concepts on various levels – social, economic, architectural, urban – and, most importantly, to make their proposals really happen. Visits to Emscher Park helped to give the participants some clues as to what was expected: industrial ruins turned into cultural attractions, the promotion of high tech industries that built striking modern offices, beautifully designed public spaces and magnificent lighting installations that attracted carloads of tourists from all over Europe. However, was this really what Hoogvliet needed? What kinds of projects were possible, feasible, and necessary here?

It soon became clear that it would be of no use to establish yet another, separate organization, a real WiMBY! institute, to join the already existing organizations. That would only have led to time-consuming, competitive strife. Deciding, instead, to concentrate on the existing planning mechanism's weak points, we initiated a series of coordinated events that would, we hoped, have a marked effect on Hoogvliet. First and foremost, the projects that we embarked upon were to have a direct bearing on Hoogvliet and set an example for similar projects elsewhere.

Apart from engaging in specific projects, we also wanted to change people's mentality. Our focal point was the existing substance of Hoogvliet, both physically (the buildings) and socially (the people). As in so many reconstructed housing estates, there had hardly been any time to reflect upon the object of so much planning fervor: the original New Town of Hoogvliet. Nor had the results of research by sociologists, traffic experts, and town planning historians been properly assessed. WiMBY! identified the need to correct this as a prerequisite for reinterpreting the worn out New Town. It wanted to rediscover its now hidden qualities as an unknown, captivating new urban entity with its own peculiarities, and thus the reinterpretation and reuse of what was already there were to be the guiding principles in the reconstruction process. As a result, some projects – the Domain Hoogvliet, Hoogvliet inside out, the WiMBY! Week – bordered on engaging in communal social work. Sometimes initiatives that bore no direct relation to architecture were most effective in presenting alternative approaches

Happy

for sometimes overly ambitious, large-scale reconstruction projects. Temporary interventions, cultural reprogramming or a onetime event could help people to rediscover the New Town's hidden but positive qualities. Above all, such activities bring to light unexpected urban potentialities that can inspire future strategies. This potential is located both in the inhabitants and in the existing urban fabric. It remains an open question as to whether or not a program based on costly suburban houses can ever generate such vitality.

Anti-tabula rasa We were absolutely sure that if Hoogvliet was to become a new, vital and attractive city in ten years, nothing could be more counterproductive than to start from scratch. The tabula rasa mentality that wants to do away with everything it encounters, from buildings to the underground infrastructure, may have been useful in the era of postwar reconstruction, but in this case it was totally useless. Using existing qualities would help to prevent the New Town from becoming generic, something that could have developed anywhere, in a suburb near Leeuwarden as well as in Enschede or Amersfoort. While the planning machinery set in motion by the corporations went on preparing the demolition of thousands of homes, championing the values of the new, quiet, suburban middle-class Hoogvliet that was to be created in their place, WiMBY! worked on a totally different concept. Hoogvliet was to resemble itself and should not try to emulate other cities. It had to find ways to deal with its green, village-like character and the ethnic make-up of its inhabitants, and it should cherish whatever positive opportunities presented themselves. This approach called for a thorough analysis of Hoogvliet, focusing not only on problems and difficulties, but also on its positive aspects. By stressing the negative qualities, the large-scale reconstruction process that had been going on for some time ignored the positive characteristics. Nobody mentioned the profuse greenery — public gardens were only seen as wasteland waiting to be developed. Nobody drew attention to the potential of the large community of people from the Antilles; for the problems of recent years only left room for negative feelings. Thus, many qualities that could have inspired the revitalization process were simply discarded, an example of the approach that seems inherent in Rotterdam's 'progressive' tradition.

2 *WiMBY! Welcome Into My Backyard. Internationale Bouwtentoonstelling Rotterdam-Hoogvliet*, Rotterdam 2000.

Our dissenting views on Hoogvliet were first published in 2000 in a book entitled *WiMBY! Welcome into My Backyard!* Its cover illustrated our intentions: Hoogvliet's historical church is shown adjacent to a vast expanse of Stelcon slabs, symbol of the failure of the New Town but at the same time conveying its own peculiar beauty.[2] This beauty is enhanced by Hoogvliet's unfinished character and can be seen in many places: the dike that had to make place for the subway line, but simply continues on the other side of it; farms that look out of place between the apartment buildings; geese and sheep grazing in a setting of 1950s architecture. The WiMBY! strategy demonstrates precisely these qualities by exaggerating even the tiniest specimens of it and by highlighting those aspects that the official planning machinery sees as problematic. This analysis had distinct therapeutic features because it showed the

Happy

inhabitants just how special their New Town really is, thereby attempting to heal their ingrained inferiority complex. We sought to promote a change of mentality that might help to reverse the purely negative way of dealing with the existing situation. One of the earliest urban projects carried out by WiMBY! seems to confirm that this strategy may be successful.

Logica Believing that Hoogvliet has many positive qualities, we sought a different type of town planning document than the all-encompassing master plan. What was required was a set of instruments that could help to guide the processes already at work, directing and channeling them into a coherent policy. The most pressing task was to create some logic in the often conflicting projects initiated by the many institutions working on Hoogvliet. This is the origin of Logica, a town planning manual for Hoogvliet, which was produced by the Rotterdam-based architectural firm of Maxwan Architects and Planners. Time and again, Logica emphasized the need for a joint approach to the 'Hoogvliet project'. Logica asserted that as long as a coherent vision was lacking, the revitalization campaigns could only result in a chaotic, unremarkable generic city in which the most important characteristics of the New Town would be lost. Accordingly, Logica identified the qualities that should be seen as Hoogvliet's main characteristics, singling out four urban elements that, it was believed, could yield a consistent structure: the green buffer surrounding the New Town, guaranteeing a rural setting on all sides; the isolated location of the neighborhoods, endowing each of them with its own particular values; the green areas between the neighborhoods containing the New Town's infrastructure; and, finally, the overall green quality of Hoogvliet, a result of the fully mature trees in the open spaces and communal gardens.

Logica presented clear choices: each of the four structuring elements were put to the test. Were they to be respected, or could one do without them? These issues were addressed in the so-called Logica committee, which was made up of representatives of all the parties involved: the municipal planning board, the local political board, two corporations and the development agency of Rotterdam. The same issues were put before the inhabitants on the WiMBY! website. Thus, Logica changed from a plan into a negotiating process, which concluded with a binding selection of one of the 24 models that could be composed by combining the variables offered in the process. Remarkably, the strategy selected was that of conserving and enhancing all the existing qualities. Hoogvliet's green neighborhoods were to retain their self-contained qualities, flanked by wide parkways and surrounded by a recreational zone alongside the Oude Maas River.

New collectives While Logica addressed Hoogvliet's urban and physical qualities, other aspects of WiMBY! focused on its social qualities. Like the physical qualities, these were being grossly neglected, no matter how many publicity campaigns and inquiries the official planning machinery organized. WiMBY! wanted more. We wanted to show what the inhabitants themselves had to offer. We wanted to exploit their creativity and make them responsible for projects we developed in consultation with them. In doing so, we discovered that the concept of

Happy

the collective was much more important than the official reconstruction campaign took it to be. Working with single mothers from the Antilles community, we found that they needed forms of houses that combined the individual home with collective amenities and collective public spaces. The reconstruction campaign's implicit mantra: 'collective spaces have become impossible to maintain because the contemporary New Town lacks a collective mentality' may be true for the average Dutch family commuting from one place to the other in an ever expanding network city, but it does not apply to other groups. Judging from the growing number of communes, even among native Dutch citizens, there appears to be a growing need for collective arrangements. These considerations fostered three projects that we organized with the support of the corporations. They are intended to accommodate new collective housing arrangements. In one of the 'maisonettes' – the most endangered type of house from the 1960s – a group of single mothers from the Antilles is provided with their own individual homes and a collective room that can be used as a crèche, a study or a café. Parts of the surrounding public spaces will also be brought under collective control and designated as safe places for children to play and mothers to eat or party together. In another maisonette flat in the same part of Hoogvliet, homes for young people are planned that follow the so-called 'Foyer' model which provides spaces for living, education and work. The third initiative attempts to attract categories of people that so far have avoided Hoogvliet. Even though Hoogvliet is easily accessible and has a lot to offer, its negative image puts off the more affluent and creative layers of Rotterdam's population. How can one make Hoogvliet more attractive to these categories, thereby increasing its social diversity? The usual type of single-family house with a garden can be found anywhere. In itself, it cannot induce anyone to move to Hoogvliet. We believed that a form of co-housing might do the trick. This is a form of housing that combines twenty individual homes and a collective amenity that is assigned to them and managed by the twenty households living there. The nature of this amenity is decided collectively. It can be either a day-care center, an ecological garden, a car repair hall, or a sports facility. Thus, a new meaning is given to the term 'collective housing.' The oppressive connotations associated with the collective arrangements of the 1950s are replaced by self-defined contemporary forms that combine individual homes with a wide variety of opportunities to use public space.

Collective substance Judging from the way Hoogvliet appears in its overall planning and in its architecture, one would be inclined to think that its population must be homogenous. It is not. Behind the anonymous facades from the 1950s and 1960s, lives a rich palette of people. They differ in income, ethnicity, and lifestyle and express these differences in the way they dress and the way they decorate their homes. The photo project 'Hoogvliet inside out' asked dozens of people to have their pictures taken in a circulating photo tent. The elderly with their rollators, mothers with a perm, hip hop boys acting tough – all kinds of people showed up. These portraits were complemented by interior photographs taken by designers Gerard Hadders and Edith Gruson. Subsequently, the portraits and the interior photos were

Nearby oil refinery

blown up to larger-than-life billboards that were placed near the highway and as traffic signs at street crossings. Apart from that, they were used as propaganda for the WiMBY! week that was organized in December 2002 in a now demolished row of homes for the elderly, where all the WiMBY! projects were presented, while half of the U-shaped row of houses were still occupied. The facades of the empty houses were used as huge billboards for the interior photos. Each of the empty houses was dedicated to one of the WiMBY! projects, while in others movies were shown. In one of the houses, people could have their portraits made while the elderly people living nearby provided them with coffee. In this way, WiMBY! week not only

Happy

displayed a variety of WiMBY! projects, but also revealed the broad diversity of people living in Hoogvliet.

Education What are the elements that make a city worth living in? The quality of the housing stock and the shops, the facilities one finds there, the surroundings, the population – all these things matter. In a depressed area, educational facilities are particularly important. A great deal needed to be done to bring Hoogvliet's schools up to date. Most of them had been built in the 1960s, many according to the standard types then designed by the municipal authorities. They are inconspicuous buildings in which the classrooms are connected by

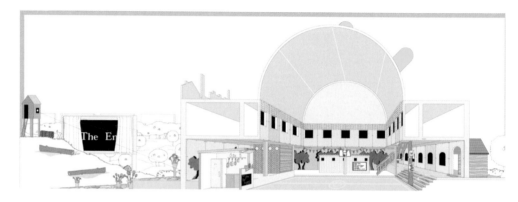

The Estate Hoogvliet

long corridors. The special rooms needed in present-day educational programs are usually lacking. It is difficult to find a suitable place for teaching pupils on an individual basis, or for libraries, music performances, etc. The shabby concrete classrooms designed as temporary solutions when the schools became too small are hardly suitable for these purposes. The need for special classrooms is further increased by the changing make-up of Hoogvliet's population. More often than not, children from various groups arrive at school without having eaten breakfast. Provisions need to be made to help the parents, and after school or during holidays, pupils have to be taken care of. Improving the facilities for primary schools, WiMBY! developed the so-called 'SchoolParasites', which were designed in cooperation with the Parasite Foundation. For three schools, beautiful facilities were created where the pupils can cook, eat, work by themselves or rehearse plays. These facilities, built to plans developed by Barend Koolhaas, Onix and Christoph Seyferth, can be industrially produced, and, apart from educational purposes, they can serve to accommodate neighborhood celebrations, meetings and gatherings of parents.

For secondary schools a special initiative was already underway: the concentration of three schools on a single campus. This enabled them to share, among other things, sports facilities and an auditorium. WiMBY! urged the participating parties to build this campus near the subway station. This was seen as a remedy for the disadvantageous location of the subway station, adding thousands of potential passengers, contributing to make the station safer, and giving the campus a function for the entire region. The campus, we believe, will make Hoogvliet a more attractive place: nice houses can be found almost anywhere, a nice campus is something special. Urging the schools in Hoogvliet to cooperate far more intensely than they were accustomed to, the Campus project tried to improve Hoogvliet's educational system by encouraging pupils to move from one school to the other. This should reduce the terribly high dropout rate. The subway station is presently framed by apartment buildings that are scheduled for demolition, and the campus will be integrated into the housing program that is going to replace them. This will result in an ensemble of attractive, small-scale school buildings and communal facilities such as a library that can be used by both the schoolchildren and the neighborhood inhabitants.

To conclude: the Estate Hoogvliet   What will happen to Hoogvliet once all our projects have been realized? Will the results differ fundamentally from the outcomes of revitalization schemes in other New Towns? Or will our efforts prove to be but incidents that are bound to disappear in the vast reconstruction work carried out by the official planning bureaucracies? Are they but romantic visions seeking to illustrate the merits of an old New Town? Is it at all possible for a small organization like ours to alter the course of these bureaucracies, as WiMBY! claimed it would? The Domain Hoogvliet will probably be the ultimate test case. Everything that WiMBY! has stood for the last four years culminates in this project. In conclusion, let us turn to the Hoogvliet Estate, a summer park intended to provide recreation and entertainment, situated in the green buffer between Hoogvliet and the highway in the periphery of the 'oil' neighborhood. Developed in close cooperation with various groups of people in Hoogvliet, it comprises several components, including a tree collection, a graveyard for pets, a natural playground, sports fields and a villa. The local inhabitants not only initiated all these amenities; they will also be engaged in building, managing and maintaining them. In the park itself there are spaces for all kinds of activities, as well as picnic tables, barbecues, and a pond for paddling. In the center of the Estate the villa acts as a visual focus. It was designed by the London-based firm of FAT architects, which also planned the park. Purely narrative in character, the ornamental facades have elements that refer, for example, to the original village-like, green Hoogvliet, the chimney of the Shell refinery that triggered the idea of building Hoogvliet, and the geometrical facades of 1950s architecture. It is a Venturian decorated shed containing the symbols and signs of a popular and recognizable visual language that can be understood by everyone.

Even for fleeting passerby, the need for a facility like the Estate is easily grasped, for in Hoogvliet nothing ever happens. The shopping mall boasts of a brasserie where one can drink a cup of coffee, but for younger people there is absolutely nothing to do, least of all during evenings and nights. The villa is going to change this. There will be musical and theatrical performances, and family celebrations can take place there as well. Like the park, the Villa has something for everyone.

We believe that by keeping ourselves submerged in the wonderful world of Hoogvliet and engaging in a never-ending pursuit of the creative forces inherent in it, our WiMBY! Initiative can contribute to a renaissance of the old New Town. Hoogvliet's negative image of a city inhabited by a dull NiMBY! population will be transformed into the positive image of a city with an unusual and intriguing mix of young and older people, including many people from the Dutch Antilles, and of nature and industry—a place that makes its inhabitants proud and visitors eager to see more.

Happy

Ljubljana, October 24, 2000.

The bar is not particularly crowded. Six people are there, four at a table that is almost crushed by the weight of all the bottles of beer, wine and stronger stuff, and everybody looks completely drunk. A girl by the name of Tatjana frees herself from her table and starts a general discussion

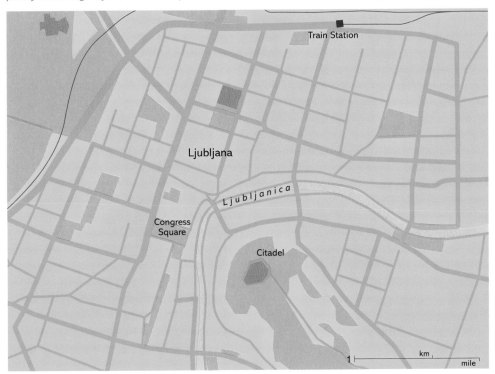

about everything, which soon becomes a specific discussion about Dutch drug policies, which she favors, the benefits of natural living as opposed to commercialism and Americanism, and the need to have a central point in one's life. Hers is Ljubljana, where she returned after all her travels. And she had done a lot of that, looking for unspoiled ways of life. She has even been to Nepal, visited Amsterdam (where she enjoyed Dutch policy on soft drugs – 'how can people be so stupid to think they are the same as hard drugs'), liked Sweden, but not Swedish drug policies, and was very happy to live in Ljubljana ('a village, not a city, but everybody needs a home'). What am I up to? No use explaining the 'happy' project in a not very sober situation like this. Better to say something general, in a broad sense, about enjoying architecture. Did I know that there is an architect in the bar. I did not. But there he is, standing right next to me. An interior architect, he explains, who once had a lot of contact with the university. Now, however, this is no longer so. Now he imports Italian design furniture for those who can afford it. It's the best, the world standard of interior design, he explains, and then he wants to know what to do about modernism in Slovenia. For it is simply not there, he complains. Once there was Plečnik , who was something like the big boss in his days. Now the only one who can be the new Plečnik is Boris – do I know Boris? – Boris Podrecka. Another great Slovenian guy, but hardly ever in the country. And do I know why? Because they do not want him. Who are they? They are the university people (because in becoming the new Plečnik, Boris would have to be a university teacher

Happy

as well). And why do they not want Boris? Because if Boris would become the new Plečnik , all the others would look second-rate and be out of business. All the best jobs would go to Boris. So now we know Podrecka will never be the new Plečnik . C.W.

Citizen Urban the Search for Happiness

Lucka Azman

In ancient philosophy, happiness is defined as having a body free from pain and a spirit free from disturbance. Epicurean hedonism results in a calm and tranquil life. According to Epicurus, happiness is a personal concern. Questions of collective delight (versus individual pleasure) as well as mass happiness (versus the satisfaction of an average citizen) and consequently issues stemming from disregard for the wishes and dreams of individuals besides oneself, are not his concern. The world and community of Epicurus are introverted, unconcerned with the polis, its rules and order. The only thing that is valuable in this egoistic ethic is an individual's pleasure. In Epicurean philosophy, happiness is the highest good connected to desire and satisfaction. There are two strategies for pursuing any given desire: either one can strive to fulfil the desire, or one can try to eliminate it. Although Epicurus prefers the second strategy, the inevitable desire for food and shelter leads to the adoption of the first.

Citizen Urban is the central (and only) character of the film of that name, produced in Slovenia by the architect Jože Bevc in 1963. The film is devoted to showing changes taking place in the city of Ljubljana, Slovenia in the 1950s and 60s. Epicurus personified, citizen Urban is a man searching for shelter in a quickly urbanizing environment, specifically, in the centre of the capital of the Republic of Slovenia.

    The character and role of the main actor are indicated in the etymology of citizen Urban's name. In Latin 'urbs' means city; therefore citizen Urban is a member of the city/community and at the same time a holder of the basic rights and duties in the city/community. His calm and tranquil life is represented by the idyllic surroundings of a municipal park, Zvezda, and by the act of feeding pigeons, which are unexpectedly interrupted by the bustle and dust of the city's building sites.

After the Second World War came the period of urban renewal, but also of urban sprawl in the suburbs. Attitudes towards everything old could be described as follows: the old is unworthy, worn out and consequently should be demolished. The old has lost all validity.

Happy

Baroque buildings are old-fashioned too. Thus, the Kozler mansion is pulled down to make way for modern public transport and traffic running through the city center.

The new construction in the city astonishes citizen Urban. His sweet dreams are cut short by the crash of a demolished wall. In the background rises the dreadful and monotonous façade of a new building. Moving at a very fast pace, workers on the building site hurry to clear away citizen Urban's personal property, while bulldozers clear away the ruins. The construction is going so quickly that citizen Urban hardly has the time to get dressed and to look at himself in his Biedermeier mirror. Away with tradition!

Here begins the first Epicurean strategy and citizen Urban's journey. His voyage consists of seven attempts to fulfil his wish for a calm life, and, above all, one he can call his own. The action takes place at seven locations:

(1) In the newly built environment.
(2) In a cellar in the old city.
(3) In the planning authority's office.
(4) In an attic in the old city.
(5) In a tent at the edge of the city.
(6) Close to the railways tracks.
(7) Finally, in nature, in a tree.

In accord with the new social and urban development after 1945 – when his apartment in the old city centre is demolished for the sake of new business and commercial areas, where new employment would be provided and consequently collective prosperity of the community would follow – citizen Urban is granted an apartment in a newly built housing estate. In a spanking new, crisp apartment block of the new age, on the fourteenth floor of a skyscraper,.

This new apartment and its whole setting, their characteristics and overall quality are as distinct from the old city as can be. First of all, this is a sterile environment. Everywhere there is concrete – just buildings, no greenery. When citizen Urban explores these new things, he finds that they are inert and worse than anything previously used. The elevator is out of order, and the tenants moving in have to walk up to the fourteenth floor, carrying all their belongings with them.

Nevertheless, citizen Urban adopts a sympathetic attitude; for despite all the troubles caused by his new environment, he has some positive experiences as well. From his apartment he can look out through the window or from his balcony and enjoy a fantastic view over his changing city: a city in a new perspective or a new perspective on the city.

Besides new city regulations, there is also a novel relationship between society and the individual. Judging from the payment provisions and amount of rent for the new apartment, our hero is confounded by the reality of paperwork and bureaucracy. The rent is too high, much higher than the skyscraper. Reality pulls the rug out from under citizen Urban's feet.

Paralyzed with astonishment, he is brought down to the mover's truck along with his property. The newly built is too expensive, too high, too alienating, and it doesn't work.

Happy

His journey takes him back to the old town, which is full of life. Citizen Urban even accepts that he has to keep his Biedermeir possessions in a cellar, in order that he may experience the vivacity of the city. But the collective spirit of the new society is pitiless. The city, with its Baroque characteristics, is in ruins. The hostility of the buildings also ruins culture's fundation. Our character has to find his way out of the ruins again.

Citizen Urban tries to find the next solution at the planning authority's office. The master plan of the city of Ljubljana as well as execution of its urban policy were elaborated and supported by the Office for the Regulation of Ljubljana, established after 1945. Another District urban planning institution was established in 1960 to elaborate a strategy for the city's further development, which, given its rapid growth, was sure to be extensive and hasty. The intention was to provide an urban vision combined with some degree of control. Debate on the overall urban plan began in 1962.

Many experts criticized the urban planning document, which, for citizen Urban, took the form of trying to negotiate the planning authority's building. This building is round and it has no entrance. Both its form and non-existent entry symbolize the activities taking place inside it: people going around in circles, with no outside participation wanted.

When our hero finally finds his way through the planning authority's hallways, the passage for clients is turned around. Skilled planners draw patterns, which appear felicitous if considered as artistic designs, but which fail to function in real life. Following such a path a person walks in circles. Epicurus looked down upon all purely scientific pursuits, and he declared mathematics useless, since it has no bearing on the conduct of life. For Epicurus, but obviously for citizen Urban, too, mathematics is not substantiated by sense knowledge, since in the real world the geometer's points, lines and surfaces are nowhere to be found. For him, sense knowledge is the fundamental basis for all knowledge, and the fundamental criterion for truth is perception.

Epicurean man is supposed to be the creator of his own happiness, something he achieves through calmness of mind and emotions or ataraxia. He prefers an individual search, thereby freeing himself from public life and emotional bonds. However, his personal involvement in the events of the city's growth as they are occurring forces him to resign himself to such a fate. In his last place of residence, in an attic in the old city, he helps the surveyors and holds their measuring instruments with his head. He is prepared for any contingency, with his foldup bed, chair, chamber pot, and portrait, all ready for immediate removal. Finally, our tragic figure gives away his Biedermeier household furniture.

Clutching his baggage, citizen Urban stumbles out of the city, crossing the crumbling structures in his path. He finds a vacant meadow, where he puts up a tent, but the spreading of the city's suburbs is as rapid as the renewal of the city center. Here housing estates are scheduled to be built, including apartment houses and small apartment towers, row houses and detached homes. When he crawls into his tent, excavators storm in and a crane lifts him up in the air.

Happy

Worn out by events, our hero looks for another way out. Finally, he finds a dark, quiet, cosy nook, next to the railway tracks, where not much traffic is expected. In the morning, however, he wakes up to discover himself in the middle of a new road, in an underpass – everything was built overnight! The city itself is unrecognizable; the designs of its new structures resemble boxes. The period between 1945 and 1965 was marked, in fact, by the extension of traffic infrastructure and service utilities.

Citizen Urban next finds himself looking up at the open sky, between heaven and earth. Is he searching for special powers, which the gods have over the lives and affairs of people? Will he get any help? Epicurus did not have faith in any deity, but he had an Epicurean garden. Epicurus offers citizen Urban one last opportunity.

Despairing, our tragic figure stands by a tree. Ropes are hanging from the branches. The events have been enough to drive anyone to despair. Surprisingly, citizen Urban has found his new home in the tree. First he waters the plants, than he loosens the rope with a chair tied to it and sits down. The treetop holds his Biedermeier furniture again.

In spite of the long search and almost tragic end, citizen Urban finds a solution and in his own, individual way solves the dilemma. Citizen Urban has found his happiness again.

Citizen Urban's calm and tranquil life: soon disturbed by massive urbanization in the city

No time to sleep or pack: workers and excavators clear the ruins.

Citizen Urban is granted a flat in a newly built housing estate.

Planning Authority's office: where is the entrance?

URBANISTIČNI URAD

Skilled urban planners drew patterns, which appear felicitous as patters pertaining to fine arts. Do they function in real life?

Citizen Urban is carrying his luggage, stumbling out of the city.

Citizen Urban is ready for any contingency: folding bed, chair, chamber pot, portrait, all ready for immediate removal.

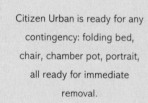

When he crawls into the tent on a vacant meadow, excavators storm in and a crane lifts him up in the air.

In the middle of a new road
in an underpass...

The events were enough to
drive anyone to despair, but
Citizen Urban has found his
new home and happiness
in a treetop.

A car for everyone

A CAR FOR EVERYONE

Traffic is the heartbeat of the city. Ideally, it reflects the layout of the rationally planned urban community, directing traffic between the functional zones. Since the 1950s, traffic has become almost synonymous with the automobile. At some point in these years, people exchanged their bicycles and scooters for cars. The first car in a family was not just a car; it was little short of a revolution. More expensive and technologically advanced consumer goods than cars were hard to imagine. As car ownership spread to the lower social levels of society, it marked the success of the new society that was so desperately desired after 1945. Everyone now had the privilege of buying a car, and the car was a symbol of progress, of emancipation and of freedom. What distinguishes the car from the train, the revolutionary nineteenth century invention, is not its speed, nor the comfort it offers. Whereas the train rapidly developed into a means of mass transportation, the car is privately owned and can be used by one person alone – and usually is. Whereas the train runs according to strict timetables, one can use the car whenever one feels like it. The train depends on a network of stations, but the car, which doesn't require stations, can stop anywhere. The use of the train is limited by the railway network, while the use of the car is limited only by the much more extensive networks of roads and highways. From a town planning point of view, the effects of train and car are completely different. The train favors concentrated growth near the nodes in the railway networks, but the car does not. If people prefer living in the countryside or in suburbs far away from the urban centers, the car is perfectly suited to fulfill these wishes. Since car ownership has become ubiquitous, suburbia has become impossible to contain, and urban sprawl has tended to escape the planner's control. The combination of railway systems and railway timetables gave planners a tool to direct urban growth and to regulate traffic. It is a much more complicated matter to regulate the use of the privately owned car. Regulating traffic has become a specialty within the town planning discipline, revolving around a variety of complex issues: does zoning dictate traffic, or is it the other way around? Is it possible to direct urban growth by building roads, or should the networks of roads and highways be seen as a consequence of existing urban structures?

Happy

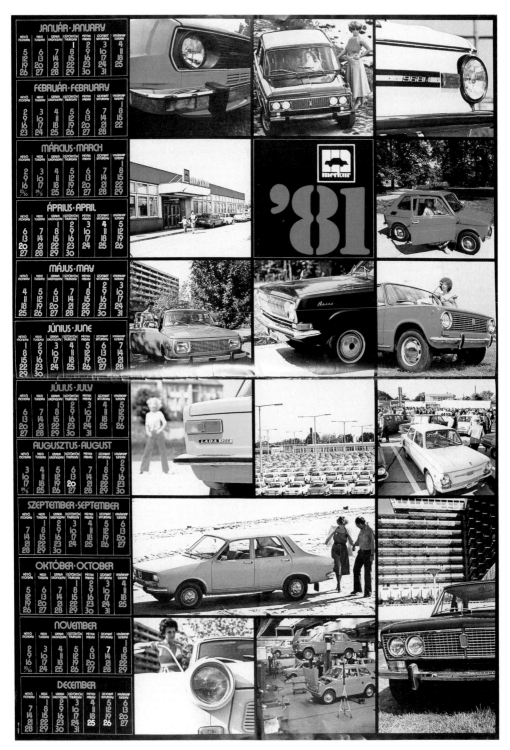

Calendar, 1981

Happy

Happy

Advertising campaigns for the Fiat 500 and 600, late 1950s

Happy

Novara, August 1, 2004.

Autogrill sandwich recipes for beginners. **Ischia:** *ciabatta* bread, grilled eggplant, grilled zucchini, tomatoes, lettuce, asparagus cream. **Capri:** *focaccia* bread, cooked ham, mozzarella cheese, tomatoes, oregano, lettuce, mayonnaise. **Camogli:** *focaccia* bread, cooked ham, Emmenthal cheese. **Belvedere:** anchovies, red hot peppers, garlic, olive oil. **Rimini:** *piadina* bread, Parma ham. **Positano:** pizza-style bread, mozzarella cheese, Parma ham, oregano, basil. These sandwiches are available for 2.90 euros in every Italian Autogrill. One of them does not exist. Guess which one? P.S., F.d.P.

The Italian Autogrill

Filippo de Pieri, Paolo Scrivano

'Ma chi gliel'avrà data la laurea a quell'ingegnere che ha fatto 'sta roba qua... Ti fanno girare tutto il palazzo avanti e indietro per dopo entrare da quella porta li...'
Robe da matti....

Ugo Tognazzi in *Il pollo ruspante,*

episode of *Rogopag,* 1963

The characteristic silhouette of the Autogrills is familiar to at least two generations of Italian motorists and probably to many foreign tourists, as well. At the speed limit of 130 km/h and from the deformed perspective of our windshield, just a handful of seconds separates their first appearance from their sudden disappearance (unless we continue our observation from the car's mirrors, defying the ultimate limit of the highway experience —a crash). This familiarity has deep, if recent, roots: the construction of the Autogrill chain – filling stations with a restaurant and bar annexed – along Italian motorways is part of the history of the construction of the country's physical as well as social landscape after then Second World War.

The first Italian motorways, located mainly in the northern half of the country, were opened in the 1920s, but at the end of the war Italy's highway system was still nothing compared to the American interstate system or the German Reichsautobahnen network. It was between the mid-1950s and the early 1970s that the largest part of the modern network of the autostrade was actually built. Its date of birth can be located around 1954. That year an engineering society (the Sisi, Sviluppo Iniziative Stradali Italiane SpA) was constituted to study a scheme for a road linking Milan to Naples via Bologna, Florence, and Rome. Behind the initiative were four protagonists of Italian industry, Eni (oil), Fiat (cars), Pirelli (tires), and Italcementi (concrete). Despite the resistance of the leftwing opposition, a bill concerning a plan for the construction of a national highway network was approved by the Italian Parliament in 1955.

The first stone of the new highway – emphatically called Autostrada del Sole, the 'Highway of the Sun' – was laid during a ceremony held on May 19, 1956. On that occasion, one hundred meters of the infrastructure were inaugurated in the presence of the President of the Republic, Giovanni Gronchi, and of the Archbishop of Milan, Giovanni Battista Montini (the future Pope Paul VI). Not surprisingly, the ceremony took place at the Milanese edge of the artery, at San Donato Milanese, the site of the headquarters of Eni. Behind the ceremonial display, with all the paraphernalia of military bands and film crews, there was, however, quite little of substance. Not only did the first segment of the highway end in the open country; work on the project for the following kilometers and on the tentative plan for the route towards Rome was still unfinished. Before its completion in 1964 the 'Autostrada del Sole' had to face the resistance of local interests and national bureaucracies, and the interference of political lobbies – not to mention the technical problems posed by the crossing of the Apennines.

The story of the Autogrills began around those same years: its protagonist was Mario Pavesi, a self-made man who created a small business empire starting from his Novara-based cookie company (the Pavesini biscuits were a familiar product to many Italians of the time). In 1947 Pavesi opened a small shop at the city limits of Novara, along the Turin-Milan highway. It was intended as a retail store for the company's products. Three years later, the store was transformed into a bar-restaurant. Prophetically blending English with Italian flavor, Pavesi named it Autogrill.

In the following years the Pavesi company commissioned the study and design of several 'punti di ristoro' (travelers' restaurants), the first two of which were built in 1958 in Lainate, near Milan, and in Giovi, on the Milan-Genoa highway. They were built on only one side of the road, and shared many architectural traits: a glass-walled cylinder with the restaurant and the bar, and a streamlined metallic structure containing the shop. The functional organization was determined by the attempt to give the buildings some sort of 'totemic' quality. These facilities were the work of a Milanese architect, Angelo Bianchetti. Graduated from the Politecnico di Milano in 1934, Bianchetti already had a solid experience in the design of fair pavilions and exhibition installations and, more generally, in advertising. In the previous years he had become very familiar with the Milanese world of graphic designers, well represented by two very influential figures, Xanti Schawinsky and Marcello Nizzoli.

When the Pavesi company began to consider the expansion of its Autogrill chain, an analysis of the best known experiences in this domain was carried out on North American models, which seemed to be the most relevant ones. Around 1958 Bianchetti embarked on a journey to the United States, and during a tour of the East Coast he examined in detail

Autogrill at Giovi

Happy

several models of American 'turnpike diners', most notably the restaurants of the Howard Johnson chain. Part of his photographic survey still survives, documenting that the Italian visitors were specifically focused on the signage system as well as on the organization of the kitchens and the distribution spaces. In Bianchetti's subsequent work for Pavesi the American influence was clear, and the architect himself never tried to hide his preference for American examples. In a short report of his trans-Atlantic experience published in an issue of the magazine *Quattroruote* (a publication closely affiliated with the Italian car industry), he tried to explain why the German model would be hard to adapt to Italian conditions.

US influence on Italy in the postwar years had changed around the mid-1950s: from the institutional involvement of US agencies in the reconstruction, it had turned into a more subtle form of cultural manipulation. Bluntly stated, Americanization took the form of a 'commodification' of Italian society. The diffusion of consumerism in Italy was marked by the success of supermarkets in the second half of the 1950s: the first 'American-style' supermarket in Europe opened in the summer of 1956 in Rome in a pavilion of an exhibition at the International Congress of Food Distribution (supplies, merchandise and equipment were provided by American companies). In the following months, the Roman prototype was successfully reproduced five times in Rome and then adopted in Milan.

At the beginning of the 1960s Italy was ripe for mass consumption, and architects and planners soon became aware of this new field of opportunities. After the publication in 1960 of Shopping Towns USA, Victor Gruen's ideas on the localization of shopping malls in relation to demographic tendencies and transport systems provided useful guidelines, as an article published in *Casabella* as early as 1961 well demonstrates. Although the first Autogrills were built before the publication of Gruen's work, the impact of his theories represented a significant step forward for Italian architects, who in this manner learned how to understand the interactive processes between modernization and traffic.

Back in Italy from his journey to the USA, Bianchetti designed the first Autogrill with the characteristic bridge structure, probably drawing inspiration from a model prototype prepared by the Standard Oil Company (an image of which was reproduced in the *Quattroruote's* article). Built in Fiorenzuola d'Arda, in the Po plain near Piacenza, along the Milan-Bologna part of the Autostrada del Sole, the Autogrill was inaugurated on a snowy and foggy day in 1959: newsreels of the time show the head of the company, the designer, and members of the government (the Novara deputy Oscar Luigi Scalfaro, destined to become Italy's ninth President of the Republic in the 1990s) surrounded by prelates, Carabinieri in dress uniform, and white-jacketed waiters holding trays full of Pavesini.

At Fiorenzuola – unlike the American examples – the restaurant, filling station and parking area were elevated above the highway (the Standard Oil prototype had all the facilities positioned on an embankment). The bridge solution had at least two advantages: it allowed a single building to serve both sides of the highway, thereby reducing the size of the plot as well as the number of employees needed. The originality of Bianchetti's proposal sets it apart from earlier examples. Norman Bell Geddes, for instance, in his Magic Motorways of 1940,

Happy

had advocated the use of a traffic control system to regulate the speed and movements of cars on highways, with control stations located about five miles apart on bridge structures.

Even more decisive for the success of the bridge form adopted by the Autogrills were the symbolic implications of eating in a restaurant floating over the highway – an experience which combined the rhetoric of 'modern' mobility with an ideal of resting-while-contemplating-the-street, which was itself modeled on the urban experience. In a more general sense, Autogrills seemed to combine the two main elements on which the process of the modernization of Italy was based: mobility and consumption. The motorist/consumer could stop at the Autogrill to buy gas, have a meal, and purchase all sorts of merchandise. This last activity was clearly the main goal of both the designer and his client: the Autogrills obliged their visitors to walk through the retail store (now a small supermarket) before they could come to the bar and restaurant area.

The Autogrills became a quintessential symbol of the rise of consumerism in Italy. Surprisingly, Italian critics rarely attacked the Autogrills as such. Among the rare examples was *Rogopag*, a movie of 1963 that featured four episodes written and directed by Roberto Rossellini, Jean-Luc Godard, Pier Paolo Pasolini, and Ugo Gregoretti. (The title is composed of the initials of the four authors.) In the episode directed by Gregoretti, *Il pollo ruspante* (The Free-range Chicken), starring Italian actors Ugo Tognazzi and Lisa Gastoni, the protagonist (Tognazzi) struggles with Autogrill personnel (and its rigid organization) to have a non-stan-

Kitchen of the Autogrill at Novara; page 230/231: Postcard of the Autogrill at Novara

Happy

PAY

Bar Ris

Postcard of the Autogrill at Novara

Autogrill at Fiorenzuola

dard meal: a chicken, free-range, if possible. The whole episode portrays the Autogrills as vehicles for the growing Americanization of Italian habits. The most penetrating part of it deals with the organization of the internal spaces of the Fiorenzuola building: the protagonist of *Il pollo ruspante* is obliged to buy several objects in order to make his kids stop crying.

In the first years of operation, the Autogrills were very successful. Between 1959 and 1962 the Pavesi company built at least a dozen other Autogrills, all designed by Bianchetti. Some of them were based on the bridge system (these include a substitute for the old Novara retail store). A sign of the success of the Autogrill was that it was soon imitated, for instance, by the Mottagrills, run by the Motta confectionery company.

The decline of the Autogrills started in the 1970s, independently of the oil crisis and in response to the increasing speed of cars (and shorter length of car trips). The Autogrills had been designed to serve a specific kind of client: the traveler/consumer who could travel around freely and was prepared to spend quite a bit of time for lunch or coffee breaks. Until the 1960s a stop at an Autogrill was tantamount to the experience of traveling: an activity that had an autonomous social meaning, independently of the practical and functional reasons for traveling. The advertising campaigns of the Autogrills depicted happy families (the husband-wife-one child structure was de rigueur) sitting at tables with decorated tableware (decorations might reproduce the image of the building). That a stop at the Autogrill could be considered a social event is shown by post cards representing the entire chain: while buying gas and having a light meal, the automobilisti could send them to friends or relatives, proving that they had been on the road.

Happy

INAUGURATO SUL TRATTO ROMA - FIRENZE AL Km 39
DA MILANO E AL Km 158 DA ROMA IL NUOV
• AUTOGRIL PAVESI • DI
MONTEPULCIANO

Autogrill at Montepulciano

Nowadays, the average time spent at an Autogrill is probably the same as that spent in other kinds of filling stations with a restaurant and bar, determined by the need of both the engine and the driver to refuel. The flamboyant interiors of some of the stations built at the end of the 1950s have been substituted by standardized and rather anonymous fixtures and equipment.

The Autogrills stand today as forgotten monuments of another era. In their 'golden age' they represented a 'romantic' phase of the Italy's transition to modern capitalism and mass consumption. At that time, perhaps, 'happiness' was a less artificial experience than in our days.

BISCUTER,
MOBILE HAPPINESS FOR THE MASSES

Helma Hellinga

Have you ever heard of the Biscuter? Only in Spain did anyone ever think of producing a car as odd as the Biscuter. The name sounds like 'two scooters', and that is precisely what this contraption looks like: two scooters welded together to form a car. The design dates from 1949 and originates with the French aircraft pioneer, car producer and designer Gabriel Voisin. It proved impossible to produce the Biscuter in France, but a group of industrialists from Barcelona considered the car a tool for extending the benefits of mobile happiness to the poor people of Spain. In 1953, with the support of the Franco regime, they founded the 'Auto Nacional S.A.' with the intention of producing the Biscuter. The front of the car resembles the Deux Chevaux of Pierre Boulanger. The Biscuter, however, is even more basic. It has no doors, no electrical starter, no bumpers, no rear window, no mileage indicator, no direction signals, no rearview mirrors, no fuel gauge, and no upholstered seats. Nor could it boast of having a roof, though it did offer the possibility of stretching a piece of canvas over the driver's head. Parking was very simple: one simply lifted the car and parked it on a suitable spot. The lack of a rear window made this the safest solution in any case. Its maximum speed was 60 kilometers an hour, which made the car unfit for trips abroad, but appropriate for domestic vacations. However simple the Biscuter may have been, it was supposed to become the pride of Spain and a monument to Spanish straightforwardness and functionality. The Biscuter never equaled the success of the Deux Chevaux, nor that of the Citroën Mehari that may have been inspired by it. It probably was simply too ugly and too reminiscent of a model car. It was produced for only a few years, from 1953 to 1958. Various models were designed, ranging from a van to a fiberglass vehicle. In the 1960s the 'Auto Nacional' changed its policy and started to produce one of the world's most expensive cars, the Pegaso. The firm now preferred mobile happiness for the happy few.

Happy

Happy

Essen, June 2000.

Friends warned me: if you want to drive from Dortmund to Essen, take the B 1, but avoid the rush hour. I followed their advice and drove on a Sunday. Green, leafy stretches alternated with suburbs and industrial areas along the motorway. Stopping at a filling station, I noticed a McDonald's full of young families with little children: local traffic.

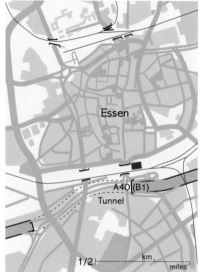

Essen

A40 (B1)

Tunnel

1/2 | km | miles

The tarmac radiated warmth in the sunshine. As I drove on, the residential districts became more densely built-up. Soon I reached the urban center of Essen, where I took the next exit. I wasn't in a hurry, so I followed the minor roads back the way I had come, ending up in a cul-de-sac. In front of one of the houses an old man was sitting in the sunshine, taking his mid-day nap. The smell of Sunday lunches wafted out through open windows. Behind a hedge was a playground; in the sandpit were two little girls. It all seemed idyllic, but in the background – even on a Sunday – there was the continuous roar of traffic. The B 1 ran directly behind the houses. However, the people there didn't seem to be bothered; they didn't even seem to notice the noise. For them it was probably a quiet day, compared with what they experience from Monday to Friday. When I asked the little girls in the sandpit what they were building, they told me it was a castle – but they already knew the word for baffle boards. D.M.

Heart Beat of the Ruhr: the B1

Doris Müller-Toovey

A motorway at the heart of the Ruhr region – can this possibly be a happy place? Stuck in a traffic jam near Essen-Kray, crawling along while listening to the traffic bulletins on the radio, you would not think so, however jolly the voice on the radio announcing that the situation is unlikely to improve. A thoroughfare of about 70 kilometres, connecting Duisburg-Kaiserberg to Dortmund-Hauptfriedhof via Bochum, Essen and Mülheim an der Ruhr, the A 40 (even today better known under its old name, B1) runs through one of Europe's most densely built-up areas. The B1, officially opened in the 1920s as a main road and now seen as a continuous traffic jam, dominates the conversation of the local people, at least of those who drive.

Opening ceremony of the tunnel, 1970

In 1997, it was the subject of a documentary film entitled *This Terrible Street*. Even so, in the minds of those who use this stretch of it, something sets the B1 apart from all other motorways. Where else is a street endowed with a name of its own that has survived all its subsequent names and rankings in the hierarchy of main roads and motorways? Few use its present official name, the A 40, apart from those from outside the region. For the inhabitants of Dortmund, Bochum, Herne, Gelsenkirchen, Essen, Mülheim an der Ruhr, Oberhausen and Duisburg, the B1 will always be the B1. They detest it, they curse it occasionally, but they still use it and some would have no idea of how to get from Essen to Bochum without the B1.

In recent years, the Ruhr conurbation has become much more diverse than the wholly industrial area which it is generally thought to be. The service-based economy has grown throughout the region, which can be seen as a pattern of transport, communication and economic networks. Combined with the urban and suburban areas, the industrial buildings, the green areas and the recreational facilities, these networks are unique. In the eyes of the people who live there, the combination of smaller towns and larger cities gives the whole region an urban character. Since the 1920s, attempts have been made to give it the name 'Ruhr City.'

The B1 runs through it along an old route between Duisburg and Dortmund. In 1876, responsibility for this road passed from the national to the regional authorities. Initiated by the regional planning authority of the 'Ruhrkohlenbezirk,' work started in 1927 to transform the road into the central axis of the area. It was named the 'Ruhrschnellweg' (literally: Ruhr fast road) and was six to nine metres wide, with three lanes overall. In 1934, it was endowed with the sobriquet national road number 1 and in 1953 it was renamed the B1 (Bundesstrasse 1). After World War II, Professor Korte of the Technical University of Aachen, who was responsible for the technical aspects of the new and rebuilt sections, called for the street to be extended, in anticipation of an increase of traffic. It was planned to widen the lanes of the motorway again and separate them with a central reservation. This was done between 1954 and 1962. The most ambitious project, however, was the construction of the city tunnel in Essen. 1020 meters long, this was opened in 1970 and celebrated as Europe's longest urban tunnel. In 1977, the B1 was upgraded into a new category as the A 430; at about the same time it was widened to six lanes overall for stretches and the installation of baffle boards (noise reduction barriers) was begun. Even so, the street – again renamed in 1992 and since then officially known as the A 40 – can hardly accommodate the ever-growing number of cars.

In the minds of the Ruhr region's inhabitants, the B1 is the 'irreplaceable traffic artery' of the area. Until recently they admired the elegant curves of the flyovers, the design of the pedestrian bridges crossing the street and the way the tram runs parallel to the motorway in the city of Essen. The construction works were often visited by high ranking politicians, among them Ludwig Erhard, Minister of Economic Affairs in the 1950s. When the tunnel in Essen was opened in 1970, Germany's President Gustav Heinemann (a former mayor of Essen) attended the festivities. The complex technical solutions needed to construct it across a metro line made the tunnel something special. It was celebrated as an act of liberation for Essen's inner city, which had almost succumbed to an increase in road traffic in the 1950s and

Happy

Politicians admire a model of the tunnel

Happy

Dancing girls during the opening ceremony of the tunnel

1960s. Huge crowds watched the spectacles that accompanied the opening of the tunnel. They listened to a miner's orchestra, admired the decorated floats and the group of dancing girls, costumed in fashionable glittering halter tops and metallic boots. After the show, the dancers were surrounded by young fans, eager for autographs. Yet only a few years later, the oil crisis of 1973 almost emptied the roads, with four Sunday bans on driving cars during that year. Town planners were subsequently forced to rethink their approach to traffic planning. The more critical public attitude that has grown up since then has had little effect on the influence wielded by the automobile lobby, but nonetheless it is very hard to imagine festivities like those in Essen being held for the opening of a road tunnel today.

Even at the height of motorway mania, it was not exactly usual for a group of artists to name itself after one, but in 1969, Helmut Bettenhausen, Bernd Damke, Günter Dohr, Rolf Glasmeier, Kuno Gonschior, Friedrich Gräsel, Ewerdt Hilgemann, Franz Rudolf Knubel, Ferdinand Spindel, Günter Tollmann and Thomas Grochowiak presented themselves in a gallery in Oberhausen as the 'Artists Group B1.' The name was chosen because all of them worked and lived near the motorway. They were convinced that the towns and cities connected by the B1 were going to claim a pivotal role in the development of contemporary art. Their intention was to stimulate a process of transformation of the urban environment by using production methods and source material indigenous to it. Their goal was 'optimal functionality, maximum aesthetics, and the greatest possible humanity.' In the catalogue they issued in 1969, they formulated a manifesto that focused on the relationship between the industrial environment and what they called 'rational object art.' Shortly after the exhibition in Oberhausen

Happy

they started to apply their concepts to real-life situations. In October 1969, the regional planning authorities initiated a spectacular event, a tour of the B1, to which artists, journalists, civil servants, civic dignitaries, traffic planners, architects and landscape architects were invited. The ideas of the participants – and even of the artists themselves – proved to be too diverse for a common position to be worked out. In the end, the group's optimistic attempts to spread their idea of aesthetics in the world of industry and commerce were abandoned. In the following years, some of the artists were at least asked to help decide the colour schemes of the baffle boards, but none of the larger projects of the B1 group were carried out. All that remained was an exhibition in the Folkwang museum in Essen in 1972 which presented some of the models and ideas of the 'B1 artists.'Only recently a group of composers, sound artists, musicians, poets and photographers tried another artistic approach to the phenomenon of the B1. Their performance was entitled 'Sound Spaces' and formed part of the programme at the national conference of Germany's Evangelical Church in 1991. A number of sound collages and lyrics were combined in a way reminiscent of chamber music and complemented by evocative photos of the cities along the B1, with the aim of making Dortmund, Bochum, Herne, Gelsenkirchen and Essen acoustically 'tangible.'

How do people live with the B1? In Essen, the B1 is cut into the ground so as to reduce the spread of noise, which is only partially effective. The houses next to the motorway are equipped with sound-insulating windows, but what good is that during the summer months, when you want to air the rooms? People have got used to the situation and though they are not always happy, only very few would like to leave. Living directly next to the street, many have seen how the B 1 has changed since the 1950s. Traffic has become heavier all the time; but behind the baffle boards one can find pockets of greenery, some used as playgrounds, others with benches where people can take a rest. The cars' occupants are not aware of this parallel world. If they are lucky, they have no time to wonder about the scenery, hidden or not, but can move on without being caught in traffic jams. In an area as densely populated as the Ruhr, the motorway exits come in quick succession, so that drivers need to concentrate if they are not to miss their turn-off. In Essen, the advantages and disadvantages of an urban motorway are especially clear. The exit to the 'centre' leads directly to the main railway station and also gives access to the Gruga Hall and Gruga Park. However convenient this may be, it means driving through a densely built-up area where the people are living practically on top of the street.

The Ruhr motorway has always been a barometer of the economy and the political state of affairs. Even though half of all its dwellings were destroyed in the Second World War and its industrial facilities seriously damaged, the region recovered economically to the extent that in the late 1940s and early 1950s it was nearly as important as it had been in the 1930s. A considerable part of the armaments industry had been concentrated in the Ruhr conurbation, which experienced a boom between 1936 and 1943. The Allies later dissolved the big industrial conglomerates, but they supported the industries crucial to Germany's reconstruction and their own aim of integrating it politically and economically with the countries of the western hemisphere. Germany's 'Economic Miracle' of the 1950s depended largely on the coal mines – and for many large and small companies proximity to the Ruhr was an important factor in deciding where to locate and invest in expansion. The region's infrastructure in turn was determined by these investments. Whereas streets leading from east to west lost their importance as a consequence of the Cold War, those running from north to south became vital. Centrally located in this network was the industrial area of North Rhine-Westphalia. This explains why the B1 became the vital artery for the reconstruction of West Germany. The Ruhr came to epitomise Germany's economic recovery and gave new life to the historical myth equating it with coal and steel. When the crises of the iron and steel producing industry started in the 1970s, politicians and planners were slow to react. It was only in the 1980s, as the situation deteriorated still further, that they began to rethink the destiny of the region, turning away from centralised state blueprints and stimulating regional initiatives.

What did this mean for the B1? The motorway no longer connected areas characterised by heavy industry, but rather nuclei of science. The Ruhr conurbation has one of the highest densities of schools and universities in Europe. In the immediate vicinity of the B1 there are six universities, seven technical colleges and the Folkwang College in Essen. All along the route of the B1, new research institutes are being set up, for instance in Dortmund, where the exit 'Dortmund University' also leads to its new technological centre. On the B1, the 'consumers' of knowledge, culture and products mingle with those on their way to and from work – often at service-oriented enterprises that also chose to be near the motorway. The Business Park Niederrhein, for instance, used by small and middle sized companies, occupies a vast area. Its integration in the landscape and its park-like entrance area not far from the motorway made it an immediate success with local people, who spend time in the park at weekends. Entertainment and consumer areas too are linked by the B1. They may be modest, like the mall near the Mülheim-Dümpten turn-off, or enormous and still expanding, like the Rhein-Ruhr Centre near the Mülheim-Heissen exit. The latter contains a chain department store, a Cinemaxx movie centre and a festival garden where people can take a leisurely stroll. Bochum-Ruhrlandstadion is the exit to take for the Ruhrlandhalle, the stadium and the latest addition: a musical theatre by the name of 'Starlighthalle.' People on their way to the cinema or the musical 'Starlight Express' take a seat on the terrace in front of the theatre, while traffic hurtles – or crawls – by on the nearby B1. An earlier development, the Ruhrpark shopping centre, to which a cinema and an 'Aquadrome' have recently been added, awaits those turning off at Bochum-Ruhrpark, while in Dortmund, one can find the Westfalenhalle, the Westfalen stadium and the Westfalen park directly next to the B1.

Not only for those living nearby is the B1 an important traffic artery. In 1997, Dietmar Petzina explored the possibilities of the old-new role of the B 1 in a catalogue entitled *Transit Brügge Novgorod. Eine Straße durch die europäische Geschichte.* Writing on the future of the Ruhr conurbation in view of the political and economic revolution that has taken place in Europe during the last decade, he stated: 'The old "Hellweg" is once again becoming part of an excel-

Happy

lent transit system between Eastern and Western Europe – the growing number of cars with licence plates from Warsaw and Szczecin is the sometimes noisy testimony of a new European normality'. Will the B1 remain as important as it always has been, or will its function change, echoing the recurring debate about a new high-speed railway system for the Ruhr region? Whatever may happen, it is likely that for those living alongside it, 'this terrible street' will always be 'their' B1.

Dancing girls during the opening ceremony of the tunnel

Happy

CONSU

IERISM

THE AMERICAN DREAM

What a wonderful, happy, optimistic scene: a stunning young woman, radiant with joy, a warm sunny beach, the ocean, the outlines of what looks like a holiday resort, and in the center a shining new car. A dream world for carefree people with lots of time for leisure, the Promised Land that fulfilled all the expectations raised in the Atlantic Charter, and more. The picture painted in this 1947 advertisement for a De Soto is a revealing one, showcasing a desirable lifestyle that, it was implied, was within everyone's reach. If anything personifies the 'American Century,' the wonderful world of advertising does, probably never more so than in the late 1940s and the 1950s, when the paradise-like visions shown on billboards and in magazines represented something of a social ideology.

Europe's fascination with America goes back a very long way. America is synonymous with freedom. In America, people are not tied to the dead remains of the past. 'There are no deeply rooted trunks of the feudal forest to be cleared away. There is no religious problem, nor one of ecclesiastical power or land ownership. There is no defense problem, nor the difficulties connected with political balance or political domination. There is no national problem and for a long time there wasn't even a social problem,' the famous Dutch historian Johan Huizinga wrote already in 1918. The unlimited possibilities the USA had to offer were well known in Europe, not least because America was the homeland of popular culture – a culture that could become popular only because it could be broadcasted and shown in movie theaters. In the 1920s and 1930s jazz triggered a dance craze all over Europe, and of all the movies shown in the Netherlands before the Second World War, no less than 85% were made in America.

America did not rely solely on its tremendous prestige and its fame as the land of unlimited possibilities to improve its reputation in Europe. After all, it faced the challenge of counteracting the formidable prestige of the Soviet Union, the superpower that had contributed as much as America had to defeating the Nazis. The Marshall Plan channeled millions of dollars into the reconstruction of Europe, luring many countries into allegiance with the superpower across the Atlantic. Complementing the Marshall Plan, a vast program of internationally circulating exhibitions was initiated. It was coordinated by the prestigious MOMA. The 'International Program' was openly anti-communist in character and intended to eliminate once and for all America's stigma as a country devoid of culture, since it was feared that the communists might exploit this biased view, which was so deeply rooted in Europe. 'American Design for Home and Decorative Use' and 'Built in USA: postwar architecture' toured Europe for two years, demonstrating the merits of the International Style. MoMA had been responsible for a similar program during the Second World War, and shows like 'Lessons of war-time housing' and 'Built in U.S.A.' provided many European magazines for years to come with examples of new building techniques and of suburban homes built in record time. The exhibitions stressed the most appealing qualities of American life: the endless opportunities open to everybody regardless of social position or class.

Undoubtedly the most famous of the exhibitions that the MoMA organized as part of this program was The Family of Man, a photography exhibition that between 1955 and 1962 attracted huge crowds in Germany, France, the Netherlands, Belgium, England, Italy, Yugoslavia, Austria, Denmark and Finland. The Family of Man celebrated mankind as being essentially the same all over the world, showing that people's natural propensities transcend geography, cultural identity and class distinction. And, at the same time, it promoted the United States as the country that was based on this notion of universal equality 'The first cry of a newborn baby in Chicago or Zamboango, in Amsterdam or Rangoon, has the same pitch and key, each saying, "I am! I have come through! I belong! I am a member of the Family." (…) Everywhere is love and love-making, weddings and babies from

Happy

generation to generation keep the Family of Man alive and continuing. Everywhere the sun, moon and stars, the climates and weathers, have meanings for people. Though meanings vary, we are alike in all countries and tribes in trying to read what sky, land and sea say to us. Alike and ever alike we are on all continents in the need of love, food, clothing, work, speech, worship, sleep, games, dancing, fun. From tropics to arctics humanity lives with these needs so alike, so inexorably alike.'

However benevolent America's new aura was, the most evocative aspect of the New World remained what it had always been: America was unique in offering all its citizens, regardless of their background (often poor immigrant families) material progress and the possibility of shaking off the stranglehold of the past. America was free of the social and religious prejudices that effectively blocked opportunities for progress in Europe. The ultimate sign of success was the ability to harvest the benefits of America's consumer society. Conspicuous consumption was a pillar of the new society, and American advertising campaigns inspired some of the most appealing icons of postwar European architecture and town planning.

If the icons collected in this book demonstrate anything, it is the overwhelming influence of the United States everywhere in Europe, on both sides of the Iron Curtain. Even the protest movements against everything associated with America – capitalism, the war in Vietnam – were modeled after American examples. Now, at the beginning of the new millennium, things seem to be changing. Has the American Dream outlived its promise? Have countries elsewhere learned how to emulate whatever it was that made American culture so successful? Has George W. Bush's allegedly totalitarian anti-terrorism alienated all his country's former allies? If so, this would mark the end of an era and one of the most fundamental cultural paradigm shifts in many decades. And it is not at all certain that Europe would be able to fill the lacunae all by itself. But maybe it doesn't have to.

Lijnbaan

Evelien van Es

The Lijnbaan is the counter-image of a history of suffering. A devastating air raid destroyed Rotterdam's inner city on May 14, 1940. Subsequent bombardments, the Holocaust, the scorched-earth tactics of the Nazi regime in the last years of the war, and a famine during the winter of 1945, made recovery hard to imagine. Not only did Rotterdam survive, however; it has become one of the emblematic cities of modern architecture and town planning, and the Lijnbaan is its most celebrated accomplishment. It anticipated the modern, carefree consumer society, even though in the decade following its inauguration on October 9, 1954, the masses of 'common people' could only dream about the promises of unlimited consumption. The Lijnbaan was a fragment of the future built in a city that was desperate to evoke the spirit of times to come. Its revolutionary concept combined a pedestrian shopping street and high-rise apartment buildings. The contrast between the black, two story, horizontal rows of shops and the bright, vertical towers with their green courts made the Lijnbaan an instant success. Lewis Mumford was enthusiastic. 'The effect of the Lijnbaan is warm, lively, almost gay: the daylight, the waving flags, the delicate acacia trees, the rectangular flower beds, the occasional benches, even a glass-enclosed café area plump in the middle of the mall – and, not least, the human figures, moving in and out between the shadows of the covered way and the open sunlight, in an area that is entirely their own. The unity and harmony of all this delight the eye, with just the right combination of the artful and the natural, the intimate detail and the clear over-all pattern.'

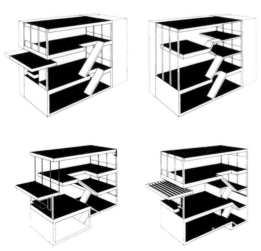

Section of the shops at the Lijnbaan

Happy

Right: In the late 1970s, the outward signs of the consumer society started to effect Budapest. Shopwindows became more elegant. More striking, however, was the widespread use of posters. The commercials of Fabulon cosmetics cheered up the city, they appeared everywhere, in railway stations, on the blind walls of tenement buildings. Shopping window on the Váci street, September 1982. Artist: Gábor Ruzsonyi. Poster: Fabulon – the guardian of your skin

Happy

Happy

BIOAKTÍV
ARCKRÉM
GYÁRTJA:
RICHTER GEDEON RT.

F. k.: Vörösházy Lajos

(Magyar Hirdető)

711544 Offset-nyomda — 4000 péd.

fabulon
A BŐRE ŐRE

Fabulon, the guardian of your skin

Happy

Fabulon cosmetics

fabulon

SZÉPSÉGÁPOLÓ SZEREK

Dresden, April 17, 2000.

Monday morning. Leaving the train I strolled across an empty space, empty because Lenin had already left it, having been given away to a collector who did not bill the city for the statue's transportation. The socialist style of hospitality had already departed, surrendering to Mövenpick and other such places.

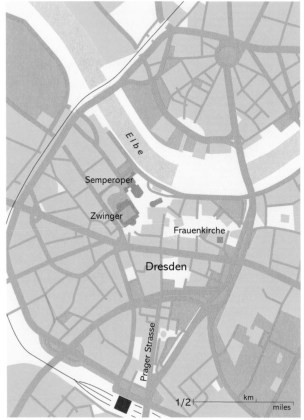

Elbe

Semperoper

Zwinger

Frauenkirche

Dresden

Prager Strasse

1/2 km miles

For visitors from the East, Pragerstrasse was once the gate to the promised land. Now the message carried by the large panorama presenting socialist society, which once was meant to greet visitors, was fading away, reduced to an absurd postcard. Yet, at the same time, it aroused nostalgia. When I met Kurt Sillack, the artist who created that panorama in 1968, I was taken back to that year, a year that shattered the foundations of West Germany. At that time, the East was still full of confidence; the 'socialist community' ('Sozialistische Menschengemeinschaft') was about to blossom, representing a precondition for unending happiness. Later that day, a young woman told me that I should not photograph her apartment from the road: two windows in the proud front of the Nationales Aufbauwerk of 1952. She considered the windows her property, the holes in the walls as marks of her private realm. Was I wrong to search for traces of happiness along the grand gesture of the Pragerstrasse? Was it not behind the curtain, the four walls encompassing the happiness of an intimate pursuit? **N.G.**

Happy

The Prager Straße in Dresden. Planned in 1963, built between 1965 and 1972

Niels Gutschow

'The socialist metropolis of Dresden is the hometown of happy people. It should also be the host town for happy visitors. Artful design should show that ours is a good city for loving people, since loving people need peace and a bright future to be happy.'

Motto of the 'General Plan for the architectural reconstruction of the city center of Dresden,' summer 1969

Dresden, for centuries the capital of Saxony in southeastern Germany, survived the war almost unscathed until a devastating air raid destroyed most of the old town in February 1945. This air raid soon proved to be one of the most controversial in more than four years of full-scale attacks on German cities by American an English bombers. Dresden was world famous, a veritable Florence on the Elbe, its famous Baroque Zwinger epitomizing its rich aristocratic culture. In 1945 it became part of the Soviet occupation zone, and in October 1949 it was integrated into the Russian-controlled, socialist German Democratic Republic. The remnants of the old Baroque architecture reminded the new political leadership of the 'parasitic' wealth of the historic ducal residence, and thus the socialist regime sought to demolish the remnants of that past, clearing the way for a new city that would reflect the values of a new society. This new beginning was celebrated at numerous party conferences. Successive phases, leading from a 'planned, systematic development on the basis of socialism' (1952) via the 'transitional phase' between socialism and communism (1963) towards the 'fully developed social system of socialism' (1967), were reflected in a series of specific town planning models, elements of which can still be recognized in the city as it appears today. In 1969, when the German Democratic Republic celebrated its twentieth anniversary, the direction of the road to happiness seemed clear and its final realization close at hand. In practice, however, the road was far from smooth and led through a sequence of very different town planning ideals.

Stalin's ideal: the beautiful compact city
The contrast between the Stalinist vision of the 'beautiful' compact city (1950-1953) and the ideal of the 'magnanimity of urban and physical planning' that was the professed practice after 1958 could hardly be more striking. The first phase is characterized by representative, closed spaces and axes that, in the typical socialist jargon, were labeled 'Magistrales'. In Dresden, this phase can be seen in the extension of the Altmarkt, which was dedicated to festivities and events for the general public. It was here that the newly formed community, showed the way forward. Parades on the first of May marked the road to a communist society with a continuously growing repertoire of slogans promising a happy life in the near future. Especially important in the reconstruction of the city was the plan for a high-rise apartment complex. A symbol of the power of the workers and farmers, it was meant to dominate the skyline, demonstrating that the people had, finally, become 'builders of the metropolis'. Even though it was relatively modest compared to the Marszalkowska in Warsaw, the socialist-realist stretch of the Prager Strasse is also intended to anticipate a glorious future. It was asserted that, as in the great cultures of the past, the people understood the 'language of architecture' and showed a true love for their city. Naturally, phrases like these suggested that in the years preceding the socialist experiment, people had become alienated and unhappy, having lost their relationship with the built environment. Trying to outdo the two grand boulevards in the neighboring states to the east, the Kreshtchatik in Kiev (1945-1952) and the Marszalkowska (1950-1952) in Warsaw, the urban spaces that were realized in Dresden before 1956 emulated 'national traditions.' If they referred to the real social situation in which they originated, they did so only in a very superficial way.

In 1955, Khrushtchev denounced Stalin's preference for wasteful exuberance, and in Dresden, as well as in most other cities in the socialist empire, this marked the end of the plans to beautify the city with 'Magistrales' lined with showy architecture. Financial problems and the Russian-inspired policy of strengthening the army led to a more economical approach, and during the subsequent phase of the 'Building of New City Centers' in the German Democratic Republic, everything was geared towards the development of the socialist version of the consumer society. The reconstruction of the Prager Strasse exemplifies this changing attitude. Before its destruction in 1945, the Prager Strasse already was the most prominent shopping street in eastern Germany; now it should mark the development of socialist society by the construction of new hotels and department stores. The street cut through the existing urban tissue in the center of Dresden and had become the principal artery between the railway station and the historic center with its castle, the Altmarkt (the old market square) and the Kreuzkirche. This has not changed since that time.

Happy

Perspective drawing from the design competition

Model, early version

Happy

Ulbrichts Vision: spaciousness At the end of the 1950s, the ideal of the compact city had been completely abandoned. It was succeeded by the vision of a 'magnificent', spacious architecture,' allegedly rooted in 'the spatial ideals and esthetic preferences of the people in a socialist society.' As president of the state council and general secretary of the Communist Party, Walter Ulbricht never ceased to comment about the road to socialism. Coining the phrase 'socialism will win' in 1958, Ulbricht declared that 'the transitional period from capitalism to socialism' had begun, and in 1962 he proclaimed that the aims of this intermediate phase had been achieved in the 'victory of the socialist production system.' All matters relating to power relationships 'had definitively and irrevocably been solved' by 'securing the state's borders' – the rhetorical slogan for the construction of the Berlin wall. Already at primary school, children were required to swear allegiance to the 'ten commandments of socialist morality' – these, too, pointed towards a future state of happiness that would dominate the reconstruction of the city.

The first plans for the Prager Strasse, which already by 1948 had been cleared of the rubble and debris of the air raid, demonstrate the architects' ambition to give the street a dominant position in the city's skyline. In these plans, which date from 1960, the street was meant to represent 'the strength and invincibility of socialism' and to become 'a valuable symbol for a new socialist culture.' A few years later, this role was no longer accorded to the street but transferred to a high-rise building connecting the street with the Altmarkt. Originally this tower was thought of as a 'House for Science and Technology,' but later it became a hotel. In 1962, on the eve of the seventeenth anniversary of the 'useless destruction of the city (the socialist establishment loved anniversaries since they offered a perfect setting for the proclamation of important decisions), a competition was organized for the reconstruction of the Prager Strasse. The street, now destined to symbolize the 'future victory of socialism', should characterize the urban space of the future and be 'magnificent' and 'spacious.' The moment when this happy stage would manifest itself, however, was continually postponed. Instead of completing the reconstruction in 1965, as promised in 1962, the date was now set at 1970. Although the first buildings and the fresco 'Dresden welcomes its guests' had been inaugurated by the time of the twentieth anniversary of the German Democratic Republic, it took five more years before the erection of a statue of Lenin marked the completion of the new city center. The festivities marked the twenty-fifth anniversary of the republic.

Unity and Spaciousness The designs that were expected to result from the competition in 1962 would, it was hoped, anticipate the 'ultimate state of socialist life.' Though not very outspoken, the members of the jury expected the designs to underline the 'unity of the Prager Strasse as a whole,' excluding ahead of time any proposals that stressed the individualistic character of the buildings. At the same time, they denounced the creation of closed street façades; and in doing so, essentially rejected all references to historic as well as Stalinist examples. The designs that were submitted, however, did not live up to their expectations – after all, society was still in the middle of the 'transitional stage.'

Happy

Parts of the original model

Happy

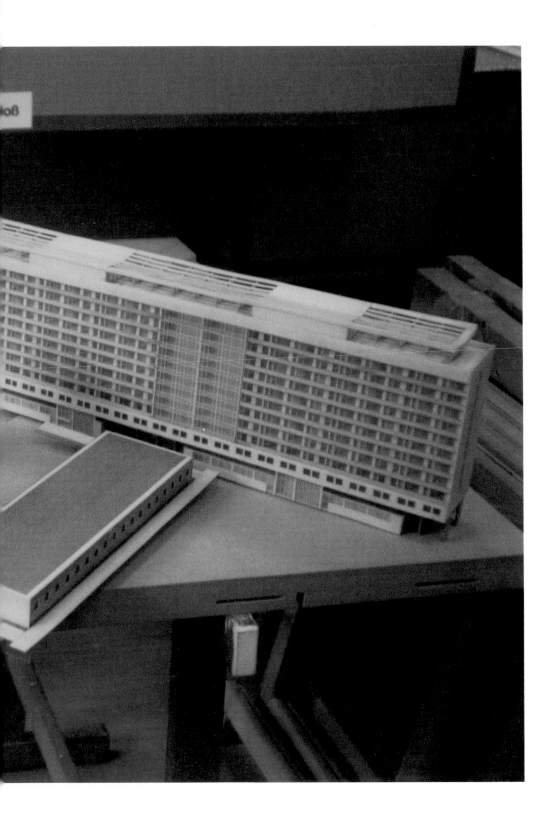

Happy

Until the autumn of 1963, the 'Komplexbrigade Prager Strasse' that was led by Hans Konrad, Kurt Röthig and Peter Sniegon – 'Komplex' refers here to new methods of design in a 'Kollektive', epitomized by the 'Brigade' – worked on a solution that was approved by the 'Politbüro' of the central committee of the Communist Party. Walter Ulbricht, however, could not resist the temptation to insist on a more open visual axis between the railway station and the House of Socialist Culture in the Altmarkt. He dismissed the sequence of urban spaces and opted for 'spaciousness' and 'unity', even though the distance involved made this hard to realize. Demands for 'more flatness' and 'uniform direction' dominated the discussion; and the plan, it was determined, should be directed at achieving 'unity of all the parts' and a 'harmonious fulfilling of all needs.' Already in 1958, one of the theorists of 'socialist architecture' had used these terms to describe what it should be like, equating 'unity' with symmetry and clarity.

'Festive spaces' for the 'friendship of all people'

Right from the beginning, it was decided that the design for the new Prager Strasse should underline Dresden's importance 'as a city of modern socialist industry, center of science and technology, and city of culture and socialist art.' Public spaces were to have more than merely representative functions: they should also be 'festive spaces and the framework for communal life, which in this center of tourism is characterized mainly by its international contacts.' In the 'general construction plan' that was presented on the occasion of the seventh Party conference, the Prager Strasse is described as a 'a road reflective of social experience' and a focus of the 'friendship of all people.' That is why, shortly after this conference, the painters Sillack and Lipowsky were commissioned to create a mural at the southern entrance of the street that was to express these intentions. Opposite the railway station, the socialist community welcomes visitors to the city. Between 1965 and 1969, numerous 'general plans' for the 'visual design' of the street were produced, all aimed at stimulating 'the development of a socialist state consciousness and love of the fatherland.' The large mural was expected to radiate 'optimism, joy of life and happiness as the immanent components of socialist realism'. All this should reflect a 'socialist, German national culture' and the 'realization of the challenge of the century: to establish the socialist culture of the German Democratic Republic.'

The Prager Strasse tells the story of the 'development and growth of the socialist community'

Architects and artists were called upon to contribute to the 'artful expression of the socialist view of humanity.' This ambitious goal, however, could only be realized 'by the conscious and creative use of the methods of socialist realism.' What was meant by this became clearer in May 1968, when the artists were asked to make a 'concrete contribution' to the twentieth anniversary of the Republic on the first of October, 1969. For this occasion, public buildings were to be designed in a 'vivid and beautiful' way. In the 'general plan' for the 'Komplex Prager Strasse', all objects were described in detail. 'Social partners' were assigned to all the artists, since it was believed that socialist art could flourish only when it developed in direct relationship with the population. For Sillack and Lipowski, this meant

Happy

that they had to communicate with the 'Town council for Trade and Services' and 'leading people from socialist trading companies.' Their design should 'welcome visitors to Dresden and explain the character and importance of the city.' In the little square in front of the mural, a sculpture ought to demonstrate how 'the socialist states represent peace in the world.' In the immediate vicinity, another sculpture expressed the theme of 'the socialist family,' which was supposed to induce the public 'to verify the socialist character of their own families.' The lay-out of the fountains in front of the railway station should radiate a 'cheerful, friendly and refreshing atmosphere,' and the water sculpture at the beginning of the Prager Strasse, was expected to express an 'optimistic tendency.' The mural on 'Meißener' ceramics on the outer

The Prager Straße in the 1960s

wall of the restaurant 'Bastei' was ready just in time for the anniversary. The government wanted this anniversary to be a 'people's festival,' radiating 'optimism and joy, a strong belief in the victory of socialism and the creative power of the citizens,' and testifying, as well, to both the 'development and growth of the socialist community' and the 'evolution of spiritual and cultural life.' And all this activity was necessary, as the general secretary of the Party never ceased to emphasize, because architecture should be directed at 'the formation of socialist educated, art loving and understanding people.'

Happy

On the road to the consumer society Hardly ever was the planning and realization of urban space accompanied by such an intense barrage of slogans about happiness. The spaciousness of the urban layout – which was marked by a 240 meter long, high-rise apartment building and three towers of eleven floors each – was promoted as a means of making people happy. The contrast between the almost monumental, horizontal apartment building and the towers expressed the 'unity' that, already in 1960, was proclaimed to be one of the characteristics of the plan. Between these two elements, numerous restaurants and shops were built. They demonstrate to what extent the 'Ministry of Commerce' directed the evolution of consumerism. In 1963, an economic reform forced the 'Kombinate' to adjust production to

The Prager Straße in the 1990s

the needs of the people and to allot at least two percent of their production capacity to consumer goods. This induced the shipbuilding 'Kombinat' in Rostock to start small work shops, where the only lawnmowers of the German Democratic Republic were produced. Most of these consumer goods were sold in the department stores on Alexanderplatz in Berlin, but part of the glow of the new consumer society reached the provincial capitals. In 1971, the 'Politbüro' proclaimed the 'unity of economy and social politics' as a new challenge. Erich Honecker, the new general secretary, opened up new vistas. Startled by the social unrest at the shipyards in Gdansk, in neighboring Poland, he had come to power believing that one

Happy

265

could never govern 'against the working population.' In the future, political acquiescence was required, and the best way to ensure peace and acquiescence was to provide the population with proper public housing and all the consumer goods they longed for. In the 1970s, the Prager Strasse flourished. The purchasing power of the citizens created a lively atmosphere. Where empty wasteland had dominated for more than twenty years, a veritable shopping paradise had developed. This is the impression the street gave the visitors of the 'world festival of youth' in 1973, whether they came from Kiev, Hanoi, Novgorod or Kaunas. The Prager Strasse was obviously the manifestation of a different world, one which echoed the consumer society in the West.

The 'socialist community' – the epitome of happiness
To better understand the nature of 'happiness' in socialism, a short analysis of the 'socialist community' may be useful, since the synthesis of town planning, architecture and the visual arts was supposed to reflect this community. When was this phrase coined, and to what utopia did it refer? After the sixth

Kurt Sillack, Rudolf Lipowski 'Dresden grüßt seine Gäste' (Dresden welcomes its guests), 1968. Sketches

Happy

party conference, more comfortable and more beautiful cities were called for in which 'new forms of a socialist society could unfold.' No longer would the impact of architecture be limited to individual buildings, groups of buildings or parts of a city. In the future, architecture would encompass the 'physical containers of life' at every scale, and gradually turn into 'a complex process of the creation of a socialist environment,' Bruno Flierl claimed. Man would 'visually embody and emotionally understand his social being and consciousness in architecture' party politics called for it. It was much easier to define the 'socialist community' in terms of where it ended – where people deviated from the official line, disturbing official visions of happiness. What made the socialist community 'happy' was the absence of ambivalence, and precisely this aspect connects the socialist community to its national-socialist predecessor, which also had made quite clear who belonged to it – and who did not. This explains why the future urban spaces of the socialist community would have to demonstrate 'unity.'

Sources

Quotes have been taken from the City Archive, *Akten des Oberbürgermeisters* 4.2.3. and *Stadtbauamt* 4.2.14

Johannes Bauch, 'Städtebauliche ensemble Prager Straße', in: *Deutsche Architektur*, volume 3, 138-159

Ruth Pape, Erika Neumann, *Bildenden Kunst und Architektur*, Berlin 1973, 100-126

'Grundsätze der Planung und Gestaltung der Städte der DDR in der Periode des umfassenden Aufbaus des Sozialismus', in: *Deutsche Architektur*, volume 1, 1965, 4-8

Bruno Flierl, Árchitektur im entwickelten gesellschaftlichen System des Sozialismus', in: *Deutsche Architektur*, volume 9, 1967, 390-391

Kurt W. Leucht, 'Zur Synthese von Architektur und bildender Kunst bei der Gestaltung des Stadtzentrums von Dresden', in: *Duetsche Architektur*, volume 3, 1969, 162-165

Georg Münter, 'Wettbewerb Prager Straße, in: *Deutsche Architektur*, volume 3, 1969, 133-156

Peter Sniegon, 'Die Planung des Gebietes Prager Straße in Dresden', in: *Deutsche Architektur*, volume 1, 1965, 9-14

Waltraud Volk, *Dresden*, Berlin 1984, 32-55

'Dresden grüßt seine Gäste' in the late 1990s

Happy

Utrecht, May 11, 2001.

Leaving the train at Utrecht Central Station, you enter a spacious hall. Here passengers can change trains, buy tickets at the vending machines, visit Hoog Catharijne, the huge inner city shopping mall, or they can go to the Jaarbeurs convention and exhibition center, but whatever it is they choose to do, it is bound to be some kind of temporary activity in a complex that is nothing but a transitional zone. You are not expected to spend too much time here, and when you're done you're supposed to leave. The only ones who are always there are the street artists, musicians and junkies who try to make a living out of this crowd of people-on-the-move. C.W.

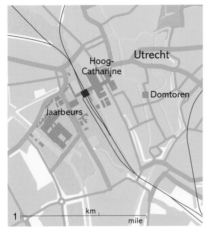

Hoog Catharijne: The Tomb of an Open Architecture

Aaron Betsky

The opening of Utrecht's Hoog Catharijne shopping mall and office complex in 1973 made me believe that a better world could be and was being built. Walking through the city of Utrecht from what was then the grungy canal zone and the confused marketplace into the skylit new entrance hall, where fountains played over marble steps and stores introduced the latest fashions to this provincial town, I rose up on the magic carpet of the escalators. From there I wandered past a square hovering over what had been the scary alleys leading up the main train station, past the fanciest restaurant in town, and onto a bridge. There you could watch cars zoom by on the sunken highway that had replaced the former canal ring while crowds waited in line at the new cinema behind you. Then I arrived, almost as if by a miracle, at the new hall of the train station, from where I could descend onto the platforms, which, though still old and worn, now served brightly colored yellow trains. Or I could pass over the largest transportation hub in the country into an even newer place where the tower of a Holiday Inn marked the presence of the ever-expanding convention center halls, and where it seemed that every week a new festival of gadgets filled the completely abstract hangars. Utrecht had joined the modern world, and it was a delight.

Hoog Catharijne was and still is the Netherlands' largest, most complete experiment in creating an integrated new world. It is not only its sheer size — with its millions of square feet of office space, its almost two hundred stores, and its immense train station — but the fact that all these elements constitute one more or less continuous whole that makes it such an astonishing complex. Utrecht produced the only real attempt to build the utopian dreams of an integrated replacement for the traditional city that was so much at the heart of the beliefs of architects and urban planners in the 1960s. That it is ultimately a failure says as much about those dreams as it does about the particular deficiencies of this building.

I grew up near Utrecht, and I had never liked the old town. Even Sybold van Ravensteyn's elegant train station seemed unpleasantly old to me. As a young boy, I had no sense of what had been lost with the construction of Hoog Catharijne, whether in terms of the varied patterns of streets and houses, or in terms of the sense of an intimate scale that still connected the city to its modest roots. I had no mental picture of what Hoog Catharijne could have been if the need to maximize profits, keep to building schedules, satisfy various political constituencies and, ironically, accommodate those protesting the new development, had not so severely impacted the complex's final form.

Nor could I anticipate how quickly Hoog Catharijne would become a glorified passageway from train station to inner city, a collection of low-class stores and a haven for the homeless and the drug addicts that were themselves the result of the change in the economic and social atmosphere from the optimism of the 1960s to the sometimes despairing and nihilistic atmosphere of the 1970s. The various attempts to clean the complex up, to open it up, and to improve its attractiveness to a varied clientele have had only a limited effect, though economically Hoog Catharijne continues to be quite successful.[1] Instead of a harbinger of a new world, it has become a standard-issue shopping mall and office complex in a provincial city, confirming both Utrecht's status and the problems that confront such commercial entities. The latest attempt to 'fix' Hoog Catharijne promises only to make it a better version of what are called mixed-use, transit-oriented urban redevelopment projects.[2]

The complex is the result of an ambitious urban renewal process that has its roots in a 1958 plan by the German traffic expert M.E. Feuchtinger for creating a more logical circulation pattern in the city.[3] This was followed by a plan by architect J.A. Kuiper that proposed a large-scale urban renewal scheme for the run-down city center,[4] which was meant to link the newly relocated exhibition and conference center (Jaarbeurs) via the central train station to the old downtown. Almost immediately, Empeo, a development firm that was part of the construction conglomerate Bredero, proposed a plan to realize this vision. The architects Spruit, Van der Grinten and Van Kasteel elaborated the plan in 1967 and realized its principal section in 1973. The design was partially based on trips to the United States, where they studied shopping centers by Victor Gruen and the integrated urban redevelopment project then nearing completion on the Green in New Haven, Connecticut, as well

1 It is difficult to judge exactly how successful, because the complex is currently under redevelopment, but according to the developer, Corio, its 30 million visitors make it the busiest (though not the largest) shopping center in the Netherlands. Cf. www.corio-eu.com. The lack of empty space in both the shopping center and the office buildings above is noted by the city government in its annual survey of real estate, *Vastgoedmonitor 2002/2003, www2.utrecht.nl.*

2 The current plan was chosen after a long political process, and is the so-called 'Scheme A,' which foresees both an expansion of Hoog Catharijne and the return of some of the original street patterns and canals under and around the complex. *Masterplan Hoog Catharijne*, Gemeente Utrecht, Projectorganisatie Stationsgebied, 2003.

3 M.E. Feuchtinger, *Verkeersonderzoek betreffende het toekomstig hoofdverkeerswegennetwerk*, Manuscript in the Library of the Technical University Delft, Delft 1958.

4 J.A. Kuiper, *Utrecht. Interim rapport van Ir. J.A. Kuiper*, Manuscript in Municipal Archives Utrecht, Utrecht 1960.

Happy

as to similar projects in Birmingham, England and Stockholm, Sweden. The plan for Utrecht itself was the most ambitious integrated urban renewal project in the Netherlands after the completion of the Lijnbaan, which replaced the bombed-out center of Rotterdam. It was also the last such large-scale scheme completed in the country.[5]

Hoog Catharijne is an amalgamation of different buildings, functions and styles. The train station, completed in 1978 to a design by K.F.G Spruit, individually, and expanded several times since then, is a reasonably successful example of the Dutch brand of structural expressionism.[6] Tall and broad, its main hall is an airy place in which the beams, columns and infill panels are clearly visible, and the articulation of these pieces at the ground level brings their scale down seamlessly to that of the human body. What is lacking, as in most examples of this style, is a middle ground in which some coherent expression is given to a collective, rather than an individual presence in a large space. This is what the axial hierarchies, ceremonial transitional spaces and other elements common to more traditional railroad stations did.[7] The experience of the main hall, moreover, did not extend down to the track level, which was left essentially unchanged, a windswept place where one is cramped and uncomfortable while waiting for the train.

A three-dimensional steel and glass grid acts as a transitional zone from the station to the shopping area of Hoog Catharijne proper. This area also acts as a food court for the shopping mall, and an access point to the buses. As it is a place for rapid movement and has no sense of its own identity, this area almost immediately became run-down and unpleasant in appearance. Moreover, because this area provides most visitors with their first impression of Hoog Catharijne, this situation presents a severe problem for any attempt to change the complex's image.

The shopping mall proper owes much of its design to American models, with respect to both the public spaces (by the firm of Wieger, Bruin, Vink & Van der Kuilen) and the shopping areas proper (by the French firm Thual). The slightly meandering pathways, the cut-offs on each corner, and the emphasis on slick and light materials to both reflect and not distract from the wares on display in the shop windows, are all elements in the recipe books of American shopping mall architect Victor Gruen and his followers.[8] Where Hoog Catharijne breaks with these rules, it falls apart. The main axis breaks apart into two parallel roads, which, although more common in European shopping malls and thought by some experts

5 For a very complete analysis of this process, see Eline Stomphort, Ewout Dorman, Thieu Caris, *Hoog Catharijne*, Groningen 1993. The only other attempt at an integrated development of this sort was the smaller New Babylon shopping center, which linked the Central Station of The Hague to the new national library. This area is now also under redevelopment.

6 Spruit designed one other train station, for Purmerend, in 1958. The firm itself did not survive the completion of Hoog Catharijne. See Bonas, *Archives of Dutch Architects*, Netherlands Architecture Institute, Rotterdam.

7 This is particularly ironic, given that the movement had at its core the architect van Eyck's interest in 'in-between' space that was supposed to provide social meeting places. Though this worked reasonably well in some of his earlier work and in several buildings by his follower Herman Hertzberger, the open structures that these architects designed were basically inimical to a sense of belonging. See W.J. van den Heuvel, *Structuralism in Dutch Architecture*, Rotterdam 1992.

Happy

8 Cf. M.J. Hardwick, *Mallmaker: Victor Gruen, Architect of the Shopping Mall*, Philadelphia 2003. For a further analysis on the functioning of stores and malls, see Paco Underhill, *Call of the Mall*, New York 2004.

to encourage shopping, in this case merely create confusion. Although the station is meant to act as an anchor for the complex, it cannot act as a counterweight to the close grouping of large department stores, including V&D, C&A and Peek & Cloppenburg, that clustered around the city side.

The shopping center is thus lopsided, with a transit space on one side and too many anchor stores on the other. Furthermore, too many cross-axes lead shoppers off to dead ends and cul-de-sacs. Though some of these routes connect to entrances and exits, they do not have their own anchors to draw visitors there (though some of this problem has been alleviated by the arrival of idiosyncratic tenants such as the supermarket Albert Heijn and the discount electronics giant Mediamart). One central section of the mall is one-sided, providing excellent views over the new highway, but without any strong elements that can either anchor this space or pull the visitor through it quickly. The central court provides too few eating and resting opportunities to entice the visitor to linger. The columns and circulation cores for the office and apartment blocks above intrude at strange points, creating many awkward (and dangerous) corners. Finally, the massive pedestrian flows lead to so much congestion that it is uncomfortable to shop at peak times, including both rush hour and Saturday afternoons.

The office and residential towers above the shopping mall, also designed by Spruit, Van der Grinten and Van Kasteel, are completely mundane in their appearance; they have few redeeming aesthetic features, and they offer no innovation in layout or special comforts. This defect would be of little significance if they offered something else, namely a clear identity, to the inhabitants or users. This could be achieved by clearly articulated imagery, but also by clearly defined entrance areas or common spaces. These, however, are entirely lacking. The office and apartment cluster could potentially use the roof for shared open space and facilities, but the latter do not exist. These towers could be anywhere, and the only thing that saves them from being an economic disaster is their central location.

The most tantalizing and troubling part of Hoog Catharijne is without a doubt the Vredenburg Music Center, completed in 1979. Designed by the only truly distinguished architect involved in the whole project, Herman Hertzberger, it is one of the most fully developed realizations of his ideas.[9] Here, too, structural expressionism provides aesthetic and organizational coherence to the spaces, but in this case the lack of a grand scale gives greater leeway to more varied social spaces. This is most true in the central hall, where the audience surrounds the orchestra and concertgoers can look at each other; and the transition to small balconies overlooking the public interior streets orchestrates the ritual of concert going with great style.

9 For the most recent and complete survey of Hertzberger's work, see his *Articulations*, Munich 2003.

The problem is that Vredenburg's achievements stop there. Here, as elsewhere, Hertzberger failed or refused to provide a facade, leaving the center to appear as a lump of grey concrete. The public streets do not so much intertwine with the Center, as they skirt its

Happy

edges, causing congestion rather than interaction. They also lead not to the center of the adjacent market square, but to its edges, divorcing them from the activity that takes place during market days. Although the manipulation of the individual building elements is often magical, creating intricate plays of light and vistas across spaces, these basic planning mistakes give the Center a sense of somehow not really being part of the life of Hoog Catharijne – a sense enhanced by its peripheral setting.

The edges of Hoog Catharijne, finally, are a combination of brutal impositions and less than elegant attempts to fit into the city fabric. The last part, Achter Clarenburg, was not finished until 1983 and, by then, the architect (F. Buitenrust Hettema) felt it necessary to clothe the buildings in abstracted versions of a generic historic architecture by using brick and gabled roofs. It is here that the various protest movements that started in the late 1960s managed to have their greatest impact on the design, creating a smaller scale and strange, irregular geometries.[10] Earlier sections present their bulky, cheaply constructed masses directly to the street, and the need to allow for service access, the lack of pedestrian entrances, and the inward focus of the whole complex make them all the more forbidding. The complex remains an alien presence in the city.

line Stomphort, Ewout Dorman,

u Caris, *Hoog Catharijne*, 47ff.

The problem of Hoog Catherijne is thus one of design, which is to say the specific ways in which the various parts and pieces respond to functional and contextual needs, establish a clear identity, and resolve the various demands on the building with an efficiently produced, but generously experienced construction. Here the complex fails in most places, except in the original design of the interior public spaces, such as the fountain court, the restaurant court and the main station hall.

Behind these specific failings, however, lies a larger problem that is also indicative of the transitional mode in which architecture and urbanism found itself during the time of the design and construction of Hoog Catherijne. The original vision for the complex came, as did most large-scale endeavors of this sort in Europe, from the government. Acting on the Feuchtinger plan and the analysis by the architect J.A. Kuiper of 1962, it wanted to create an idealized version of the city, not a collection of buildings. Employing a rational development entity, Empeo, providing subsidies and a tabula rasa bytearing down the existing neighborhood, and hiring a techno-cratic architecture firm, they asked for not just solutions to traffic and slum problems, but for an integrated vision of urbanity.[11]

11 Eline Stomphort, Ewout Dorman, Thieu Caris,

Hoog Catharijne, 39ff.

What emerged was a very large, but incomplete machine tending towards both integration and dissolution. In it, all of the aspects of the modern city were integrated, from infrastructure to movies to apartments. Its central feature was that it established a completely new reality, floating above and separated from the world around it. Ironically, its core was a passageway that led from one part of that old reality (the train tracks and the area of the Jaarbeurs or Convention Center) to the old downtown. This meant that, although it was a complete world in itself,

Happy

including shops, offices, apartments, services, theaters and restaurants, it had no core. Hoog Catharijne is an open grid hollowed out by circulation and only tenuously cohering as an object.

Accordingly, it highlights the focus on, and indeed obsession with circulation that characterized the thinking of late-modern architects and urban planners of the era. This tendency was present in the later years of CIAM, and can perhaps be related to the increasing rejection of the primacy of form in favor of planning and logistics that seemed to dominate both pre- and post-War concerns about construction.[12] Yet it did not receive a theoretical justification until the 1950s, and then in a somewhat unexpected form. With their publication of the Golden Lane Housing Project of 1952 and their emphasis on the 'street in the air', Allison and Peter Smithson proposed the space in between buildings as the positive result of the denial of form.[13] Buildings should be flexible, recessive, and adaptable, the Smithsons argued, and, as they said of the Sheffield University scheme of the following year, 'connection is the generator' of 'encompassing buildings' that would integrate but also subjugate functions to this great act of social cohesion.[14]

Ironically, this emphasis on pedestrian circulation within a protective and integrated environment was, of course, a theoretical version of the inward-turned shopping mall devised by Victor Gruen and later expanded into just such an 'encompassing building' by the likes of John Portman.[15] To Europeans, however, especially those who banded together with the Smithsons in the Team X movement, the encompassing, pedestrianized building would be a social condenser, not a place developed for exclusive occupation by a private developer.[16] In the Netherlands, the integrated development concept was championed by the most influential — and one of the most prolific — architects of postwar reconstruction, Joop Bakema. Believing it to be the task of the architect to design everything 'from the chair to the city', he proposed such megastructures as the Plan Pampus of 1964, in which a central traffic artery, through the system of streets branching off of it, supported an entire city.[17]

Whereas the Smithsons had argued for (and Gruen and his followers built) fortresses to shelter the street (the so-called New Brutalism), the Dutch took a different tack. Visionaries such as Constant Nieuwenhuis and John Habraken argued, instead, for a system of open skeletons, a completely flexible structural grid in which the street or circulation system would become the complete reality of a new, integrated urban

12 Cf. Eric Mumford, *The CIAM Discourse on Urbanism*, 1928-1960, Cambridge 2002; for pre-War emphasis on circulation, 59ff; for the post-War interest in large-scale traffic problems, 142ff.

13 Alison and Peter Smithson, 'Golden Lane,' in: Alison and Peter Smithson, *The Charged Void: Architecture* New York 2001, 86.

14 Ibid, 108.

15 For reviews of this development, see James Howard Kunstler, *The Rise of Nowhere: The Rise and Decline of America's Man-Made Landscape* New York 1994, and Margaret Crawford, 'The World in a Shopping Mall' in Michael Sorkin, ed., *Variations on a Theme Park: The New American City and the End of Public Space*, New York 1992, pp. 3-30.

16 Cf. Alison Smithson, *Team 10 Primer*, Cambridge 1974.

17 Hans Ibelings (ed.), *Van den Broek en Bakema 1948-1988 Architectuur en Stedenbouw: De functie van de vorm*, Rotterdam 2000.

reality. The building, both as static object and as functional container, would disappear in favor of the provision of services around an open space, presented in as neutral a manner as possible. For Constant, as he showed in his New Babylon project, this space would be a utopian place of complete freedom and joy. It is almost as if he were proposing an ideal version of Hoog Catharijne, at least in the interpretation of Mark Wigley: 'There are no volumes, only fields of countless shapes to be negotiated by roving inhabitants. The old ground-based cities with their static organization have been abandoned as an outmoded technology(...) it is the artificial landscape of the interior that dominations the attention, and changes like the weather. The suspended floors 'represent a sort of extension of the earth-surface, a new skin that covers the earth and multiplies its living space.'[18] For

Habraken, it would be a more sober 'carrier' that would allow an unending variety of 'infill.' For Aldo van Eyck and his followers, the structural grid would be democratic, given that it would allow a more humane society to encamp upon its clearly legible construction.[19]

18 Mark Wigley, Constant's New Babylon: *The Hyper-Architecture of Desire*, Rotterdam 1998, 13.

19 Cf. N. John Habraken, *Supports: An Alternative to Mass Housing*, transl. by B. Valkenburg, London 1972. It should be noted that Habraken developed his theories exclusively for housing, and never concerned himself explicitly with the design of shopping centers, office buildings or other large-scale urban structures.

During the 1960s, the grid and the endlessly flexible open space merged as an ideal in the work of another generation of architects heavily influenced by both the Smithsons and the Dutch thinkers. Unable to build as easily and at the same scale as their predecessors, but also more ambitious in their desire to introduce the latest technology into the field of architecture, they proposed 'plug-in cities' and world-encompassing grids. The dreams of Archigram,[20] Archizoom and

Superstudio, which appeared as published visions during the decade that Hoog Catharijne was being planned, developed and built, were the manifestations of the complete acceptance of the belief in an architecture of open circulation that subjugated any would-be definitive form to its corrosive activity, leaving only technological fragments adhering to an endless system.[21]

20 Peter Cook, Warren Chalk (eds.), *Archigram*, New York 1999; Peter Wang, William Menking, *Superstudio: Life Without Objects*, Zurich 2003.

21 In *Archigram 5*, 1964, Peter Cook proposed in his Editorial that 'This leads us to the proposition that the whole city might be contained in a single building. The concept of vehicular/pedestrian segregation is now an accepted part of planning theory. But once one accepts this and the idea of multi-level building, it is only logical to conceive of multi-level cities'. The most complete application of this 'plug-in' city concept was in the design for a shopping mall in Nottingham of the same year.

Such was the theoretical background within which Hoog Catharijne was produced. It is the largest, most complete and most revealing experiment ever undertaken in accordance with these notions. There was, of course, no explicit desire to create such an experiment. The architects and their collaborators positioned themselves pragmatically, and tried to find existing types on which to base their designs. Thus, the designers and developers toured shopping malls in the United States, as well as such European projects as the Norrhalm area in Stockholm.[22] Then, under the guidance of a hybrid aesthetic, these types were adapted to the local conditions of Utrecht. Where the buildings were at their most public, as in the train station, or were designed by stronger architects, the newly prominent structural expressionism was most evident. In the interiors, the bland and recessive surfaces of the ordinary shopping mall prevailed. The office towers presented a mixture of standard modern slabs and the more complex, hybrid shapes incorporating diagonals and polygons that were also evident in housing projects and in other office buildings in the Netherlands during this period. Finally, at the edges of Hoog Catharijne, where activist groups succeeded in reducing its contours and forcing it to integrate better with its surroundings, the nascent reassessment of vernacular forms and historical urban organization led to a breakdown of the monolithic forms.

22 Eline Stomphort, Ewout Dorman, Thieu Caris, *Hoog Catharijne*, 44.

Yet, pulling this all together was the need for movement through the complex, as well as the fact that it was actually a vast and, at least initially, delightful scaffolding. In this sense, Hoog Catharijne did resemble a new version of an urban structure. Without any proof of a causal relationship between it and the teaching and ideas of the visionaries of the time, one can point to the role of the government as producing, almost by default, the conditions by which Hoog Catharijne became an experiment in the making of integrated urban scaffolding around open space. The complex was the result not of one design, but rather of a variety of private initiatives that were coordinated by the government, which saw its task as threefold: allowing for and encouraging development by providing infrastructure and clearing away earlier construction; managing the development process by

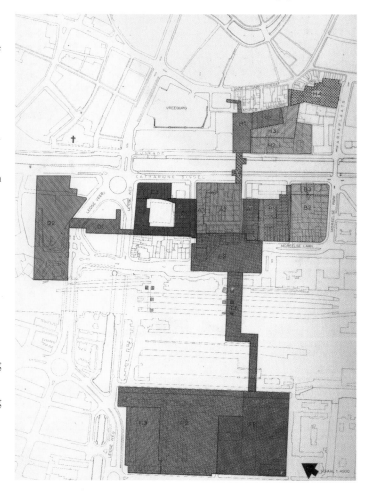

Happy

bringing together various parties and, at least initially, maintaining a strong voice through its guarantee and provision of loans; and, finally, defining the required circulation patterns, providing services for Hoog Catharijne, and, in general, acting as a manager of public space.

At first, the integrated urban scaffolding model worked well enough. Despite some disagreements between the various parties, and despite cost cutting by the developer, the result was at the time universally praised and immediately economically and functionally successful. Ironically, it might be said that the same problems that the traditional city must face in the modern era also arose at Hoog Catharijne as it matured. Circulation became congested at places where it had not been quite anticipated, while traffic bypassed less central areas, causing economic problems for the stores there. The public nature of the spaces meant that they were also available for those who either had no place else to go or who needed such environments to engage in illicit activities, ranging from pickpocketing to drug dealing. But the private nature of the space caused further problems, as the developers became loath to invest more money in upgrades or maintenance, tried to make more money by raising rents, and battled with those whom they did not see as appropriate inhabitants of their shining new city.

Yet, in the end, the dream fell apart into a collection of bad buildings, and the public space was not enough to hold the whole together. Hoog Catharijne did not have the ability of shopping malls or office parks to exclude 'undesirables' and perfect their interior environment as they learn from their clients or lessees. Nor could the city government act in a completely dirigiste manner, as it could and did in the center of the city, to provide a closely monitored, but open and flexible space. Finally, the open scaffold model, so favored by architects in the 1960s and now once again coming into vogue, proved to be a failure. The nature of investment is such that functions must be set; the rules of our civil society are that only certain kinds of activity can occur in certain kinds of spaces; and the nature of construction is that different uses mandate different forms. In the end, Hoog Catharijne was not an open web for pleasurable urban experiences, but a shopping mall, a train station, a theater and an office park, all combined by and hollowed out by a de facto pedestrian highway. The complex was killed, as it were, by the revenge of traditional types in architecture, which represent social and economic relations that turned out to be more rigid than either the architects or their clients had expected. In 1969, Giancarlo De Carlo, a friend and collaborator of Van Eyck and a charter member of Team X, still believed that 'This new conception cannot be formulated except by means of a more attentive exploration of those phenomena of creative participation which are dismissed as "disorder". It is in their intricate context, in fact, that we will find the matrix of an open and self-generating formal organization which rejects a private and exclusive way of using land, and, through this rejection, delineates a new way of using it on a pluralistic and inclusive basis.'[23] Yet the disorder was in the end only visual, as the planning processes demanded by investors and the government fixed relations and land uses. Here was the essential flaw of the dream of an open architecture: it was encased in a static building.

23 Quoted in Benedict Zucchi, *Giancarlo De Carlo*, Oxford 1992, 215.

If the station hall had been less abstract; if the planning of the shopping mall had been better; if more room had been made for commuter traffic flows; if the towers had been more elegantly integrated and had their own identity; and if Vredenburg had been given a more prominent place as a transition between city and enclosed complex, Hoog Catharijne might have been a success. None of the mistakes the architects and planners made were unavoidable. Yet they did not have models that would tell them what to do. All they could do was to use disparate types (shopping mall, train station, office park, cultural center) and glue them together, using a semi-utopian notion that the loose fit of these elements would create unexpected opportunities for urban life to develop. In a sense, they were right, but the kind of activity that emerged was not quite what they had in mind.

Now a major renovation process has started, and various developers are attempting to address these very issues. Ironically, this latest renovation comes at the same time as that of structures such as the Bullring, the spectacular shopping mall and inner-city highway intersection in Birmingham, England, and the New Haven downtown mixed use complex that had served as a model for Hoog Catharijne. What is of particular note is that in all three cases it is styling, produced by both the architecture and the interior design of the center, as well as the reintegration of the center into the historic fabric, that are meant to save the modernist machine from grinding to a complete halt. It is working in Birmingham, and it might work in Utrecht and New Haven. This means that all three centers are turning from machines to grind up the old civic structure in order to produce a new, free and better reality, into a highly functionally arranged producer of the image of that newness, one that will have to be adapted with every change in the fashion cycle.

Yet none of the plans addresses the basic problem that these uses may be incompatible in their current layout. There is no room for a central commuter zone, Vredenburg will remain shunted to the side, and the shopping mall is too spread out to be coherent. Ironically, the generation of architects who grew up in the Netherlands after Hoog Catharijne was opened has learned how to create what are now neutrally called mixed-use structures. Similarly, city governments have learned how to mandate integrated uses and provide adequate infrastructure. These efforts are shorn of their utopian, social engineering-based notions and are now pragmatic accommodations to market forces. They will not make us happy, but then again, neither did Hoog Catharijne. For that, we would need an altogether grander vision, whether by creating a truly integrated city machine producing happy spaces, as some companies are able to do in theme parks, or by tearing down behemoths such as Hoog Catharijne and letting the messy old city find its own way to happiness.

Happy

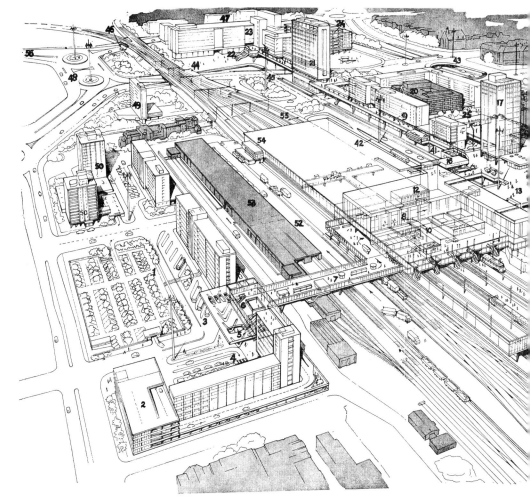

37 Verkeersplein over gedempte Catharijnesingel
38 Doorgaand verkeer
39 Aftakkingen voor plaatselijke bestemmingen
40 Streekbussen
41 Toegang parkeergarage onder winkelplein
42 Stadsbussen
43 Dubbele verkeersbrug over Catharijnesingel
44 Onderdoorgang Leidseweg-spoorbaan

45 Tunnel voor tweew
46 Nieuwe doorgang c
47 Nieuwe bebouwing
48 Dubbel verkeersple
49 Kantoorgebouw me
50 Woonflats met gara
51 Parkeerterrein N.S.
52 Goederenperron

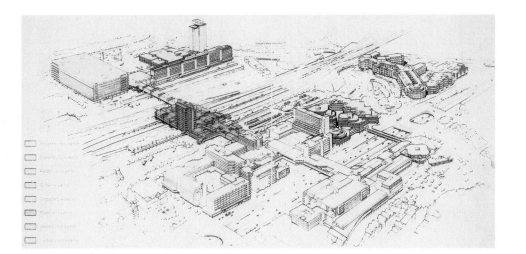

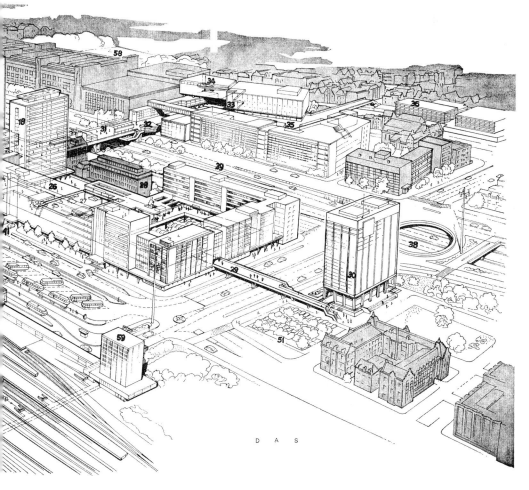

Moscow 2000, a Metropolis on the Verge of a New Era

Jörn Düwel

Moscow, which has over ten million inhabitants, is one of the largest cities in Europe and the capital of Europe's largest country. Even though its present size is quite impressive, plans were made to transform Moscow into an even bigger and more important metropolis. As the world capital of socialism, it was thought that the city should be improved and reconstructed, and thus become an almost tangible sign of a new, supposedly better world. Nothing less than the creation of a new kind of man was the ultimate goal and everything else was set aside to achieve this. For almost half a century after the victory over Germany, Moscow indeed succeeded assuming the role of a capital that exercised power far beyond the physical boundaries of the Soviet Union. It was the center of the socialist empire, and the fate of nations and people were decided there. Moscow was synonymous with Soviet politics and the consequences of the policies that were elaborated there were felt in all segments of life and in cities all over Europe: Kiev, Tiflis, Kaunas, Dresden, Budapest, etc.

Moscow served as an example in more than one respect. It showed the way in the areas of town planning and architecture and it was supposed to usher in a new socialist way of life. What was meant by all of this could change overnight, and did so several times. What remained, however, was Moscow's aspiration to lead the way. Whether certain interpretations of socialism were allowed or not was decided there, and only there. In 1991, however, the situation changed dramatically, when, after almost fifty years, Soviet power collapsed. The first signs of Moscow's waning power appeared in the periphery of the empire, in Poland, Hungary and the German Democratic Republic. After these countries had won their freedom, power definitively slipped out of the hands of the old elite in August 1991, when a revolt by a small group of socialist diehards proved futile. The once powerful union of many states disintegrated, and now the map shows a multitude of sovereign nation states that have taken its place.

Happy

Happy

Of course, with its hundreds of thousands of civil servants Moscow remained the political and administrative center of by far the largest of the new states, but the region under its control became much smaller. Even more momentous than the collapse of the Soviet empire was the introduction of new political and economic structures, which caused a social and cultural upheaval that can only be compared to the consequences of the October Revolution of 1917. It was a kind of Copernican Revolution. The socialist experiment that had lasted for seventy years suddenly came to an end, and new social structures had to be created. This had a profound impact on all sectors of society. The socialist way of life was gone, the habits and rituals that it had fostered lost their meaning, social experiences from the past had become controversial and the social values that people had shared for so long now appeared to be obsolete. Nobody had yet experienced what it would be like to live under these new circumstances, and only vague hopes and dreams provided some form of guidance in this totally new world.

Ten years have passed since that time, and Russian society has thoroughly changed. Moscow has become a completely different city, having survived very difficult years marked by soaring inflation and massive unemployment. For all but the happy few, this has had devastating effects on the personal lives of its inhabitants. Now, things are much improved. Optimism prevails, and people appear much happier than they used to. Moscow has become a thriving metropolis, bustling with life. Young people crowd the many downtown cafes and throng the rapidly expanding commercial zones. The entire city gives the impression of a huge construction site. In the center, it is mostly hotels, office buildings and shopping facilities that are being built, while in the outskirts apartment buildings predominate. Most striking, though, are the numerous churches, monasteries and memorial sites that have been (re-)built during the last couple of years. They are proof of the new moral concepts that have emerged; as always, architecture and town planning reshape the city, giving expression to its cultural make-up. A new social consensus seems to have crystallized, based on traditions that the socialist regime wanted to obliterate. The religious buildings and the numerous memorial sites are the physical expression of the quest for spiritual guidance and the desire to give meaning to life.

Is Moscow a 'normal' city? A European metropolis like London or Paris? It definitely is not. The city is likely to keep its particular character, which reveals itself only to the inquisitive mind. Travelers from Western Europe, who are used to the routine of cultural tourism, are probably appalled by its aggressiveness, its noise, its violence and its griminess. They will be taken aback by its social callousness and the bluntness of its social Darwinism. In all likelihood, they will visit only the usual sites, Basilius Cathedral, Red Square with the GUM department store, probably the Kremlin's treasures, and the famous museums. If their program is limited to these tourist attractions, they will see nothing of the new Moscow, which can be witnessed in various places, some of which did not even exist just a few years ago. Take Riding School Square, for instance, which many cultured visitors from the West will find distasteful since it is the scene of an all-pervasive, aggressive commercialism.

Undoubtedly, Moscow is also the capital of chaos, of anarchy and of the Russian mafia. In this respect, it confirms all the clichés, as is constantly underscored by the convoys racing

Happy

Happy

Happy

down the main boulevards with howling sirens and flashing blue lights, ignoring all the traffic laws. Anyone with money and influence can easily acquire this equipment, and now one car out of a hundred uses it. Regular traffic comes to a halt when a large limousine, usually with darkened windows comes racing by. The possibility of obtaining these special privileges mirrors the social make-up of Moscow, with its lack of shared values and relentless quest for wealth and high status.

Traffic is a continuous source of annoyance even without these special convoys. Most of the time, the main boulevards with their six, eight and sometimes even ten lanes are jammed – the products of socialist town planning, they are designed for large-scale political parades. Since there are hardly any traffic lights for pedestrians, attempting to cross them is an extremely dangerous undertaking. In Moscow, the motto 'a free way for free citizens' is taken quite literally, and cars are not likely to stop when somebody does try to reach the other side of the street. The only safe way to get there is through the underpasses. There are quite a lot of those, but usually they are far apart. In the worst case, the place one wants to visit is exactly across the street, and the nearest underpass a twenty minute walk away, making a long detour unavoidable. What makes things worse is the absence of many amenities that people from Western Europe are used to. The inquisitive visitor may deplore this, but it gives him an excellent opportunity to discover many new things. He will be impressed by the ubiquitous billboards in the city, the density of which is unparalleled in the West. Not only are they bigger, but the intervals between them are also much smaller. Above all, they are more aggressive. On some buildings, additional structures have been attached in order to provide space for even more billboards. Some of them are shaped like oversized beer bottles; others evoke speeding cars through the use of comet-like bands of light. In most pedestrian zones and especially near the subway entrances, sandwich men stroll along, handing out leaflets. What appears to make all this acceptable to the residents of Moscow is that under socialism advertising was virtually absent. Now, they are feverishly trying to catch up. Attempts to adopt Western attitudes are omnipresent, and often the new version completely outdoes the original.

The new function of the former Hotel Lux illustrates the new era in an almost tragicomic way. In the 1930s it was the home of the German section of the Komintern. Most of the leaders of the East German Communist party stayed there, and many experienced denunciation, anxiety, terror and fear for their lives. During the Stalinist purges their ranks of the German communists were thinned, too. These events entered collective memory and found their way into the biographical literature, but the Hotel Lux also has an official status in the history of socialism. Today, the disrespectful attitude towards history in a city that is so full of it is astonishing. In Western Europe it would have been unthinkable to convert this hotel in a luxury brothel. In present-day Russia, however, one is very selective in remembering history. With the notable exception of the war against Germany, the socialist phase appears to have been erased from Russia's collective memory. Even so, today's Moscow can be understood only when the years of socialist rule are taken into account. Only then can we begin to understand why the people of this great metropolis are so keen on reaping the fruits of the new, post-socialist era.

Happy

Usually various levels of planning interfere when larger urban spaces are being upgraded. The reconstruction of Riding School Square is illustrative of this. There used to be an urban wasteland where a multi-story, underground shopping mall has been built. As a result of the Stalinist reconstruction scheme of the 1930s, a complete neighborhood was demolished. The skyscrapers that were foreseen for that location never materialized, and the destruction of entire blocks resulted in a vast open space that served as an assembly area for parades in the nearby Red Square. After the collapse of the Soviet empire, silence fell over Riding School Square, which came to be used mainly for parking. In the mid-1990s the Square again witnessed demonstrations, but these were critical of the regime, not supportive of it. Yeltsin's government was not amused and looked for ways to stop them. At first a fence was erected to seal off the Square. Then the idea emerged to use the upcoming 850th anniversary of the city for its complete reconstruction. Within a few years a four story underground shopping mall was built on one of the most prominent places in the Russian capital, accommodating numerous small companies purveying mid-range and top-quality goods. The architecture emulates that of imperial, Tsarist Russia, and the materials and design are reminiscent of a glorious epoch. The entrance areas are designed on a grand scale, and the floors and the balustrades are clad in white marble. The mall, which has direct access to a subway station, is meant to radiate luxury and elegance. Large glass skylights illuminate even the lowest levels. During the summer of 2001 there were always people in the Mall, which is the first of its kind in Moscow. The times of widespread poverty, when security personnel in black battledress outnumbered the guests, seem to be gone. The ground level in particular of this shopping paradise is remarkably busy. What makes the Square permanently useless as a gathering place for demonstrations is the creation of the many cafes and restaurants that now attract crowds of visitors. They are a new phenomenon in Moscow, having made their appearance only after the collapse of socialism. On warm summer nights, all the tables are occupied until late, leaving many people to drink their beer standing by the balustrades, or lying in the grass of the nearby Alexander Garden.

Bridging the short distance from the mall to Alexander Garden is an artificial canal furnished with fountains. Here, too, white marble is used lavishly. The slightly meandering waterway is lined with sculptures. The bronze animals and fairytale creatures from Russian folk stories foster a relaxed atmosphere. Casualness and a complete absence of politics have thoroughly changed the character of central Moscow. Where vast empty spaces used to dominate, awaiting the official celebrations that alone could furnish them with some measure of life, a new feeling now prevails.

Rise and Fall of the Countercultural Commune

SUBURBIA AS A STRESS MACHINE AND THE REVOLT OF THE COUNTER CULTURE

If a pronounced emphasis on the collective is characteristic of the first generation of 'happy' icons, the second wave has many examples that sought to break away from all kinds of collective constraints. This latter ideal, however, was often seen as very provocative. Since both the icons representing the Welfare State and those typical of socialist societies claimed to be rational and democratic, as well as generally sound —and on top of that part of a strategy to defuse the social time bombs that were seen as the deeper cause of the war and the Holocaust — criticizing the society that was built on these ideological premises was tantamount to political and moral subversion. And yet, some of the most influential experts and opinion leaders openly attacked the planning practices of the political establishment, including Lewis Mumford, who was among its harshest adversaries.

In Mumford's eyes, the promises of modernism had been perverted and the modern welfare state had failed to liberate man, who had fallen victim to the machine. 'As a result we have only replaced the old slavery of production with the new servitudes and compulsions of consumption; and in comparison with the power and resources at our disposal, the net human gain has been dismally small. (…) Whether he wears a white collar or a blue collar, the typical American now serves as a baby-sitter to the machine, or is geared into a collective organization that is itself a more formidable and all-embracing machine – a machine that can be run effectively only by bureaucratic personalities, punched and coded to perform a limited set of operations'[1] The modern state, Mumford asserted, turned citizens into slaves, and since all societies based on slavery had perished, so, too, would the welfare state. It might well not take generations to arrive at this tragic stage, given that the atomic bomb could annihilate civilization in a split second. This tragic fate could be averted only if the machine that modern society had transformed itself into could be dismantled, if the cities could decentralize without the disastrous effects of suburban sprawl, and if they could overcome their dependency on the motor car.

As in America, where suburban life had long before become ubiquitous, the suburbs became a symbol for the lonely crowds of organization men who tried to conform to the lifestyles inherent in suburbia. Writing about the way the Dutch decorated the interiors of their new houses, A. Kleyn complained that they had no taste and, therefore, could only imitate the taste of their neighbors.[2] Whyte, too, saw suburbia as '…the best place to get a preview of the direction the Social Ethic is likely to take in the future. This is the new suburbia, the packaged villages that have become the dormitory of the new generation of organization men.'[3]

Being alone, man lived in a physical as well as in a social void. In the desert, there were no traces of human occupation. There, man was always the first man, 'le premier homme.'[4] But what was he in the modern city? There, too, he was doomed to be the first. Far from symbolizing the new community that was to be created out of the ruins, the new, open, sunny housing estates only underlined man's isolation. 'Les hommes d'Europe, abandonnés aux ombres, se sont détournés du point fixe et rayonnant. Ils oublient le présent pour l'avenir, la proie des êtres pour la fumée de la puissance, la misère des banlieues pour une cité radieuse, la justice quotidienne pour une vaine terre promise.'[5] Having been conceived according to the principles of the International Style, the modern city was seen as the mirror image of the society that had shaped it, which amounted to the allegation that it reflected the character of corporate life and of the vast government bureaucracies. Leftwing critics equated the city with the economic power structure inherent in its layout. Decoding these ingrained layers of meaning was one of the goals of a number of movements in art, including the 'Internationale Situationiste,' 'Fluxus' and the 'Internationale Lettriste.'[6]

If society becomes oppressive – at least in the eyes of it critics – and if it refuses to do something to rectify this situation, claiming that it is on the right track, what else can one do but try to escape it?

Happy

Rejection of society became the common denominator of many of the movements of the 1950s and 1960s. As with so many of the phenomena that are typical of the postwar period, these movements originated in the United States. Describing Dean, the main character of *On the Road*, the famous novel that is often seen as the bible of the Beat Generation, Jack Kerouac made clear what drove him, and what set him apart from the 'intellectuals': '…Dean's intelligence was every bit as formal and shining and complete, without the tedious intellectualness. And his "criminality" was not something that sulked and sneered; it was a wild yea-saying overburst of American joy; it was Western, the west wind, an ode from the Plains, something new, long prophesied, long a-coming (he only stole cars for joy rides). Besides, all my New York friends were in the negative, nightmare position of putting down society and giving their tired bookish or political or psychoanalytical reasons, but Dean just raced in society, eager for bread and love; he didn't care one way or the other, "so long's I can get that lil ole gal with that lil sumpin down there tween her legs, boy," and "so long's we can eat, son y'ear me?"'[7]

Rock and Roll soon replaced jazz as the binding force of the Teddy Boys in England, the 'Halbstarken' in Germany and the 'nozems' in Holland, and invariably it was seen as an insult to society. The caption beneath a photo published in a Dutch photography yearbook in 1959, is telling: 'They are looking for a reason to live, and that reason appears to be hard to find for those who were born during the last World War. The total negation of decency and reasonableness that is a consequence of war has affected their thinking. They believe only in the moment – in the racing moment of motorcycle and car, in the minute they share with somebody they will not love anymore tomorrow. In all of Europe the result is: young people who are bored and longing to prove their existence by showing off. In Stockholm, Copenhagen, Paris, Berlin, London, Moscow, and Amsterdam, what awaits them is the loneliness of the bed that they will have to flee the next day, [and] sometimes the rubber club.'[8] Everything that characterized European youth was Anglo-Saxon and American: the music, the language, the cars, the cigarettes, the clothes and, of course, the haircut. These things symbolized a protest movement that captured the better part of an entire generation within a decade, leveling social and political differences. In Germany, the beatniks were regarded as a dangerous species. They were studied in a deadly serious way, using the most modern means available: science and planning. What else could one do but try to create order through thorough scientific research? And some of these surveys were nothing if not thorough 'Rock and roll performances often put them in an ecstatic mood. Daring rock and roll scenes, whether on stage or on the movie screen, provoke tumultuous reactions. Some whistle with their fingers, others use whistles, claxons, horns, alarm clocks, bicycle bells and other instruments to make noise. Still others jump up from their seats, make wild movements with their arms high in the air, gesticulating ecstatically, while they undress and yell. They growl and whistle wildly. Favorite slogans are "Rock and Roll! Mambo-Rock-He, Mambo! Hau-ruck!" and "Pfui-Polizei!" Some dance in the streets as if they are drunk, surrounded by a rhythmically moving crowd. Finally, they group together, answering the order of the police to go away with loud yells and whistles; often, this results in riots, and thatt is precisely what they want.'[9]

Less panicky were the reactions in France. Obviously, the younger generation constituted a great force. 'Of the French population, eight million are between eighteen and thirty years of age today. None of them represents anything, or anyway, not much. A woman, a man, "this miracle without importance". Nothing. Yet, all of them combined, they can make or destroy the future, transform or disturb society. Without them, nothing will happen. Against them, nothing can be done. They represent our youth. Youth, you know? What is known as "our beautiful youth," when they let themselves be killed, and this "rotten youth" when they kill."'[10] Who were they? An opinion poll, the first of its kind in France, questioned them about their lifestyle. They turned out to be anti-political 90% blaming politics for everything that was wrong in society.

They didn't believe in anything. 'Distrustful of all ideologies, they vehemently expressed the desire not to be duped any longer, a desire that amounts to the search for a personal morality, a morality that is lacking and that they will have to build in solitude. How terribly alone they are, the boys and girls of the "nouvelle vague."[11] They were, in other words, as lonely as 'le premier homme,' part of but in no way integrated into the 'lonely crowd.' The only thing they were interested in was the pursuit of private happiness. 85% claimed to be happy. But precisely that made their lifestyle unacceptable. 'In a country with a Christian civilization, where happiness had a bad reputation for a long time – and still has – and where people are inclined to see happiness as something vulgar, like some kind of spiritual failure, the statistics don't lie.'[12] 20% named Jean-Paul Sartre as their favorite author, 9% favored Albert Camus, and Mauriac also scored 9%. Interestingly, 27% believed that France was on its way to socialism, and 25% hoped it was. So, there they were, the 'nouvelle vague' of the late 1950s. Were they dangerous to society? Maybe, but probably not. They might even be the generation that could rescue liberty and democracy, the interpreters of the poll concluded. 'Not only does this generation possess powerful means of information, but also a lucidity that is completely fresh and aimed at separating the truth from mere lies. If this lucidity kills their enthusiasm, too bad for their enthusiasm, because it was dependent on blindness anyway. They also have new means to better understand man and his motives, since Freud has "troubled the sleep of the world."'[13] What this generation had at its disposal that its predecessors lacked was, obviously, the rapidly unfolding potential of the electronic mass media.

Renewing itself continually, the younger generation's much feared negativism ran parallel to the harsh criticism of the artistic avant-garde. Beatniks and hippies borrowed many of its ideas and gradually a kind of revolutionary movement with leftwing, anarchist traits developed, uniting workers, students and their peers in an attempt either to revolutionize society, or, at the very least, to create countercultural niches in it. The philosophy of Herbert Marcuse and the Frankfurt School, turning the traditional Marxist hierarchy of economic structure and cultural superstructure upside-down and stressing the ontological essence of creativity and play, bridged the gap between the avant-garde's allegiance to the 'homo ludens' and the New Left's ideals of a society shaped by the imagination of ordinary people once they were freed from the entanglements of the modern establishment. The central theme revolved around people's individual creativity, a topic usually clothed in New Left jargon. In its vocabulary, the Second World War represented the nightmare vision of modern society. This denunciation of the establishment intensified with the emergence of a new conflict, one that modern Western society was increasingly engaged in, the Vietnam War. The first war ever to be televised, it set in motion a growing tide of criticism.

The counterculture manifested itself as a strictly bottom-up movement, the complete opposite of the top-down organization it so detested in modern society. Assuming that individuals and small groups could very well do without the collective arrangements of the Welfare State, if they made proper use of science and technology, the beatniks and the Teddy Boys, the Hippies, the adherents of Flower Power, the Punks and the protagonists of the New Age movement, as well as all their successors, created a fascinating series of total works of art, often combining environmental art and happenings, transforming life into an ongoing series of theatrical events that, in their view, were inspired by the natural qualities inherent in mankind, qualities that all too often were frustrated by the alienating effects of man's social and physical environment. In the 1960s, the counterculture showed itself to be no less collective a force than the establishment it wanted to transform, but starting in the mid-1970s the movement became less homogeneous. Music remained the binding force, and creativity and criticism always went together. The ultimate goal, evidently, was the Commune, and on the one occasion that something like a revolt actually occurred, namely, the

Happy

May 1968 uprising in Paris, references to the famous Paris Commune of 1871 were hard to miss. The rural communes – invariably founded by city dwellers – were of a different category, and often inspired by the natural philosophies of Thoreau 's *Walden* and the anarcho-socialist ideals of Bakunin and Kropotkin. Pop festivals often looked like temporary communes. Squatter settlements, which were always located in an urban setting and sometimes comprised entire districts, were organized as strictly regulated communes as well. And in all these cases, the commune took the form of a countercultural 'Gesamtkunstwerk'.

1 L. Mumford, 'California and the Human Horizon', in: *The Urban Prospect*, London 1968 (first published in 1956), 4, 9.

2 A. Kleyn, *De volkshuisvesting in Zweden*, 's-Gravenhage 1952, 119.

3 W.H. Whyte jr., *The Organization Man*, New York 1956, 10.

4 A. Camus, *Le Premier Homme*, Paris 1994.

5 Albert Camus, *L'homme révolté*, Paris 1951, 377.

6 C. Hollevoet, 'Wandering in the city. "Flânerie" to "Dérive" and after: the cognitive mapping of urban space', in: *The Power of the City/The City of Power*, New York 1992.

7 J. Kerouac, *On the Road*, Middlesex 1978, 13, 14. First published in 1957.

8 'Zij zoeken naar een reden om te leven, die moeilijk te vinden schijnt te zijn voor hen die tijdens de laatste Wereldoorlog zijn geboren. De absolute miskenning van fatsoen en rede, die oorlog teweegbrengt, heeft hun denken aangetast. Zij geloven alleen in het moment – in het race-moment van bromfiets en auto, en in de minuut van samenzijn met degene die zij morgen niet meer zullen liefhebben. Het resultaat is in heel Europa: jonge mensen die verveeld zijn en hun existentie willen bewijzen door op te vallen, vaak door straat-terreur. In Stockholm, Kopenhagen, Parijs, Berlijn, Moskou en Amsterdam, waar zij nozems heten, wacht hen meestal de eenzaamheid van het bed dat zij de volgende dag opnieuw moeten ontvluchten, soms de gummi-knuppel.' J. Blokker, G. Albrecht, 'Jeugd', in: *De wereld nu. Foto's en feiten '58-'59*, Amsterdam 1959, 118.

9 'Rock'n'Roll-Veranstaltungen, aber nicht nur diese, versetzen sie regelmäßig in Hochstimmung. "Gekonnte" Rock'n'Roll-Szenen auf Bühne und Leinwand lösen bei ihnen ein tumultuarisches Getöse aus. Einige pfeifen auf den Fingern, bedienen Trillerpfeifen, Autohupen, Almenhörner, Wecker, Fahrradklingeln und andere Lärminstrumente. Andere wieder springen von ihren Sitzen, gestikulieren mit erhobenen und ekstatisch zuckenden Armen, entledigen sich ihrer Oberkleidung und schreien wirr durcheinander. (...) Also pfeifen und grölen sie wild. Beliebt sind Sprechchöre von Rhythmen wie: "Rock and Roll! Mambo-Roch-He, Mambo! Hau-ruck!" und "Pfui-Polizei!" Wie trunken tanzen einige auf der Straße, von einer sich rhythmisch

Happy

egenden Menge umgeben. Schließlich rotten sie sich zusammen und beantworten

mungaufforderungen der Polizei mit lautem Johlen und Pfeifen, so daß es regelmäßig zu den erwünschten

einandersetzungen miet der Polizei kommt.' Günther Kaiser, *Randalierende Jugend. Eine soziologische und*

nologische Studie über die sogenannten 'Halbstarken', Heidelberg 1959, 25, 26.

Huit millions de Français ont aujourd'hui entre dix-huit et trente ans. Chacun d'eux ne représente

, ou pas grand-chose. Une femme, un homme, "ce miracle sans importance". Rien. Pourtant, ensemble,

ont construire ou détruire l'avenir (…), transformer ou perpétuer la société. Rien ne se fera sans eux,

ne se fera contre eux, parce qui, ensemble, ils composent la jeunesse. La jeunesse, vous savez? Celle

on nomme "notre belle jeunesse" lorsqu'elle se fait tuer, et "cette jeunesse pourie" lorsqu'elle tue.'

nçoise Giroud, *La Nouvelle Vague. Portraits de la Jeunesse*, Paris 1958, 9.

La méfiance à l'égard de toutes les idéologies (…), cette grande volonté si fortement exprimée de

plus être dupe aboutit à la recherche d'une morale personnelle qu'il leur faut, pour le moment, édifier

s la solitude. Solitaires, garçons et filles de la Nouvelle Vague le sont jusqu'à la moelle des os.'

nçoise Giroud, *La Nouvelle Vague. Portraits de la Jeunesse*, 11.

Dans un pays de civilisation chrétienne, où le bonheur a eu longtemps mauvaise réputation – il l'a

ore – et où l'on est encliné à le considérer comme une manifestation vulgaire, comme le signe d'une

e d'épaisseur d'âme, ces chiffres sont éloquents.' Françoise Giroud, *La Nouvelle Vague. Portraits de*

eunesse, 11.

Elle dispose non seulement de puissants moyens d'information mais d'une lucidité toute fraîche pour

êler le mensonge de la vérité. Si la lucidité stérilise l'enthousiasme, alors tant pis pour l'enthousiasme

n'était qu'aveuglement. Elle dispose aussi d'instruments neufs pour mieux connaître l'homme, ses

ivations, ses mécanismes depuis qui Freud est venu "troubler le sommeil du monde"'. Françoise

oud, *La Nouvelle Vague. Portraits de la Jeunesse*, 19.

Happy

The Free State of Orange

Koos Bosma

After its overwhelming success had forced the Provo movement to disband itself, Roel van Duyn, one of its spokesmen, founded the 'midget movement.' The midget, bent on improving the world and a prototype of a creature that brings happiness, became the symbol of a harmonious relation of man and nature. 'A new culture and a new type of man.— the culture midget, who would eliminate the tension between nature and the old culture.'[1] Small plots of land, roof gardens and ecologically viable agriculture would be the best alternative to the polluted cities and their over-abundance of cars. He combined the playful character of the Provo with the happiness of an ideal, anti-authoritarian state. The Russian geographer and famous anarchist Peter Kropotkin – hailed by Van Duyn as one of the prophets of the 'counterculture' – taught him that mutual assistance was one of the most important modes of behavior in the animal kingdom, and Van Duyn made it the cornerstone of his alternative society. The idea of a state within the state, anti-monarchal and more a parody of the state than a serious alternative, strongly appealed to him. In October 1969 his picture was taken in front of a Renault 4 with a roof garden on top. Inspired by the philosophy of the so-called 'midget movement', he stressed the need for a green, environmentally sound city.

The small but noisy group of Amsterdam Provos focused its program on the untapped potential of people's leisure time, on playful actions and provocative meetings, and on the emancipation of the enslaved consumer so that he might become a mature citizen.[2] In their propaganda and 'teach ins,' they expressed their critical views on

1 'Een nieuwe kultuur met een nieuwe mens: de kultuurkabouter, die de spanning tussen de natuur en de oude kultuur zal opheffen. Die de dieren verstaat en de mensen in liefde verenigt, die de eenheid tussen al wat leeft herstellen zal.' Roel van Duyn, *Schuldbekentenis van een ambassadeur. Nota's, beschouwingen en vragen van een ambassadeur van Oranjevrijstaat in de Amsterdamse gemeenteraad*, Amsterdam 1970, 24.

2 Virginie Mamadouh, *De stad in eigen hand. Provo's, kabouters en krakers als stedelijke sociale beweging*, Amsterdam 1992.

Happy

300

the most diverse topics, ranging from air pollution to the housing shortage, from the deterioration of the natural environment to the lack of green spaces, from traffic congestion and the devastating consequences of office building in the inner cities to the deterioration of the historic centers. Once the Provos were done provoking the authoritarian society, '…the midgets started the big job of realizing all their ideas, however clumsily, while showing great skill in sabotaging society wherever possible.[3] Three manifestos: *Amsterdam midget town* (1969), *Note on Sabotage* (1970), and *The proclamation of the Free State of Orange* (1970) expounded the ideology of the midget movement.

The Free State of Orange was the culmination of ten years in which Holland wanted to guide the entire world by proposing its own unique solutions to such controversial issues as drug use, euthanasia, the royal family, non-violence, sexual freedom, homosexuality, order and authority, civic disobedience, and cooperation between various religions, norms and values. Inspired by the growing tide of critical studies, foremost among them those of the famous 'Frankfurt School' with its curious mix of Marxist and Freudian theories, the intellectual elite questioned the very premises on which its own existence was founded. It started to attack the imperfect world with its social and political injustice, the excesses of the consumer society, the 'in-hospitality' of the metropolis, and the large-scale

3 Roel van Duyn, 'Voorwoord', in: Hans Verploeg (red.), *Peter Kropotkin Tekstboek*, Amsterdam 1972, 9-10.

modernization plans proposed to replace the historic centers. Alienation became the key word, i.e., the loss of personality brought about by capitalism. Herbert Marcuse, its most eloquent spokesman, invented famous phrases such as 'one dimensional man,' and 'repressive tolerance' (referring to society's capacity to appease those believed to be likely to criticize the establishment by presenting them either as a part of the prevailing culture, or merely a marginal variation of it).[4] To escape the

[H]erbert Marcuse, *One dimensional man. Studies in the ideology [of ad]vanced industrial society*, Londen 1964.

stranglehold of rationalism, Marcuse tried to define niches for people's subjective experiences (their authentic desire, according to the Freudian 'pleasure' principle), identifying the capacity to think in utopian terms as an instrument for criticizing existing society.

Happy

Alas, in the real world such a state could not survive, even though it had no less than 12 'people's departments,' a Soviet-style democracy and even its own national hymn. The Free State of Orange was simply not militant enough. 'It has nothing in common with the old socialism of the clenched fist, but rather represents the entwined fingers, the erect penis, the flying butterfly, the moving eye, the holy cat. It's anarchism.'[5] The squatters' movement and the leftwing student movements, refusing categorically to participate in the official procedures of parliamentary democracy, remained active much longer than the ambassador of the Free State of Orange, Roel van Duyn. Its most telling success was probably the celebration of the 25th anniversary of Liberation Day on May 5, 1970, which was proclaimed National Squatters Day, when many empty buildings were 'liberated.'

5 Roel van Duyn, *Schuldbekentenis van een ambassadeur. Nota's, beschouwingen en vragen van een ambassadeur van Oranjevrijstaat in de Amsterdamse gemeenteraad*, Amsterdam 1970, 26.

One of the lasting successes of the Provo and midget movements was the way they demystified order and authority. Civil disobedience and 'actions' outside the official framework of parliamentary democracy were no longer seen as subversive, but rather as 'the democratic right of the people who feel engaged in the restructuring of specific spaces.'[6] The 'sensorial deprivation' characteristic of the modern neighborhood should be countered by greenery, toys, home improvements, and, especially, more intense relations between the individual and the community. Apart from all that, the adolescent counterculture (long hair, deviant ways of dressing, leisure, music and drugs) was provided with all the cultural entertainment facilities it could wish for. In their squatted houses and 'sleep-ins,' they could experiment with happenings, pop music and drugs, a development which led Amsterdam become the Mecca of the alternative youth movement.

6 Virginie Mamadouh, *De stad in eigen hand. Provo's, kabouters en krakers als stedelijke sociale beweging*, 108.

Barcelona, June 5, 1999.

Every Saturday evening at about seven o'clock people put down their shopping bags and start to dance. Nowadays, the new square in front of the cathedral is where this happens; in earlier years this 'sardana' could be seen anywhere in Barcelona. A mixed audience of young and old is swirling around in circles

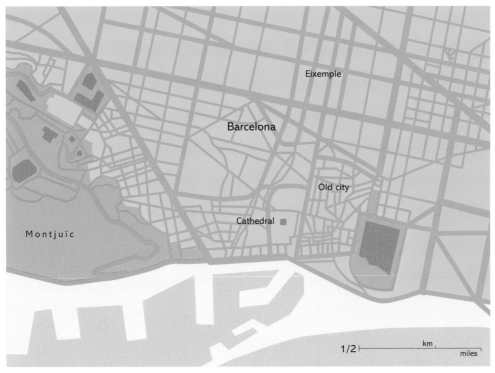

composed alternately of men and women. Some circles are large, others small; there are even some with only three people. The circle spins first to the right, then to the left, while the dancers hold each other's hands. Every now and then, they raise their hands. Of course, this dancing is not totally spontaneous: somebody always makes sure that there is a small orchestra of at least a few wind instruments and a bass. It's an example of the kind of folklore that is completely integrated into the normal, everyday life of the city, without museological mustiness, nationalist undertones, or the intention to please tourists. **R.B., H.H.**

Happy

Walden 7

an Architectural Dream

The Promise of Another Way of Life in Spain

Ronald Brouwer, Helma Hellinga

Distrust those who teach you lists of names formulae and facts and who keep on repeating the cultural models that represent the heritage you hate. Don't stop at learning things but think about them build situations and images that abolish the borders that appear to exist between reality and utopia

José Agustín Goyitsolo
Translation: Ronald Brouwer

This poem is written on a mosaic near the parking spaces of the condominium Walden 7 in Sant Just Desvern, a small city near Barcelona. It is typical of the atmosphere of the early 1970s, when Walden was built as a response to a mixture of old and new dreams about alternative ways of living. The name Walden refers to the famous novel of Henry David Thoreau, and the sequel to it, written almost a century later by B.F. Skinner (Walden 2). Combining the ideals of the two novels, along with those of 1968 and the movements that sprang up in Paris and

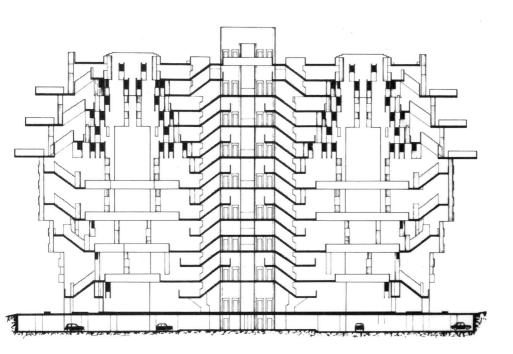

San Francisco, Walden 7 epitomizes the vision of the Catalan intellectuals and artists who opposed the Franco regime.

The initiators of Walden 7, members of Taller de Arquitectura, belonged to the Catalan leftwing movement, which was a very diffuse one. In 1969, when the idea for Walden 7 first evolved, the Taller comprised 40 people, most of them architects (among them Ricorado

Happy

Bofill and his sister Anna), but also the poet Goytisolo, the literary critic Salvador Clotas, and the economist Julio Romea. Anna Bofill, who guided the theoretical preferences of this multi-disciplinary group, had read Skinner and was fascinated by a slogan of his: '...imagine what it would mean to an architect to design an entire community as a whole!' According to her, the intention of Walden 7 was to create a closed community that was isolated from the repressive world outside it. Unlike ordinary housing estates, where families had to cope by themselves, Walden 7 was to be a community of individuals. The individual was expected spontaneously to establish multiple contacts with other inhabitants, encouraged by the community's supportive environment.

The ideas of the Taller could be realized because the Taller owned a piece of land and acted as its own client. On a whim, Ricardo Bofill had bought the old cement factory in San Just Desvern. The factory was demolished, with the exception of some architecturally interesting parts. It became the Taller's main office.

By offering a fundamentally different way of living, Walden 7 was likely to attract the same kind of intellectuals and artistically-minded people who made up the Taller in those days, and, not surprisingly, a number of them decided to move to Walden.

Translated into stone, the ideals of the Taller resembled a collage of the ideas that were current at the time: the 'City in Space', the vertical urban community or, in this case, the high-rise neighborhood. The concept of Walden foresaw constructing a number of linked modules. The basic module, which was 30 square meters, was seen as a 'pret à porter' (ready to wear) apartment for one individual. It contained all the basic amenities: a kitchen, a bathroom, cupboards

Happy

Happy

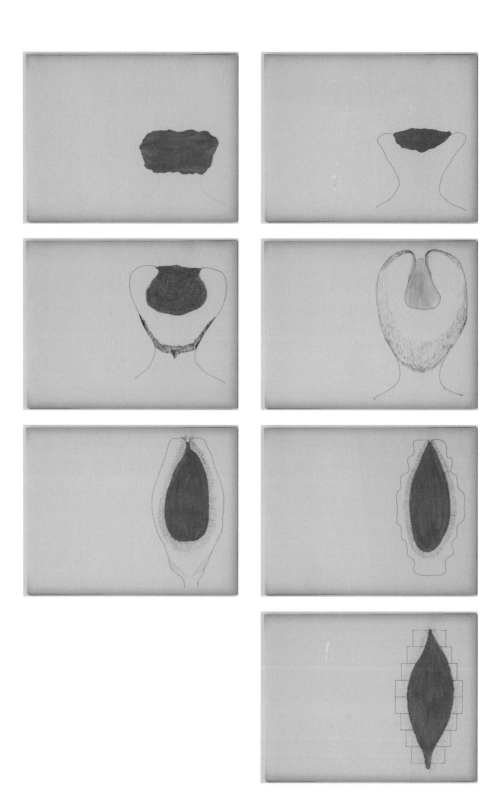

Happy

placed against the walls, a table, and mirrors the size of an entire wall. According to its designer, it provided everything the individual inhabitant needed. Joined together, the modules could house a group of people, each of whom had at least one of these basic modules at his or her disposal. Half-open walls separated the individual cells in their housing units. There were no doors and the cells shared the kitchen and the bathroom. Four of these units were designed, ranging from 60 to 120 square meters, either on one or on two floors.

Walden was surrounded by collective open spaces. A labyrinth of alleys, squares, patios and gardens created a pedestrian zone that spread out horizontally as well as vertically, providing pleasant rest areas and meeting places. A large hall on the ground floor offered extended opportunities for various activities, and the building contained numerous public amenities: a cafe, shops, a school, a library, and a roof garden with two swimming pools. From a distance, the huge, labyrinthine building of sixteen floors built around a common open space looks like an enormous rock with dark caves. The blue tiles of the outer walls, alternating with yellow and green accents, make this impression even more intense.

Financial difficulties forced the Taller to downsize the project from the originally planned four blocks to only one. Other problems soon followed. Faulty construction caused the walls to crack and the tiles fell down because the wrong type of glue had been used. Indeed, Walden became synonymous with falling tiles; they figured in cartoons and were running gags in a number of movies. The deterioration of the building had apparently been foreseen from the beginng; for there exists a drawing that shows Walden as a ruin. In the late 1980s, however, Walden was restored as a symbol of the ideals of the late 1960s.

Happy

Copenhagen, May 7, 2003.

'Wonderful, wonderful Copenhagen', these magic words resonate in one's mind when leaving the wonderful train station heading for the center of town, the Radhusplads near the Tivoli gardens. Capital city of one of Europe's smaller countries, Copenhagen is nevertheless something like a metropolis.

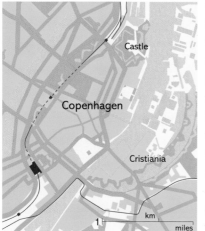

Its historical core has not been bulldozed away to make place for huge office blocks and multilane thoroughfares, the fate that struck neighboring Stockholm. Whereas in the 1950s and 1960s town planners and architects flocked to the Swedish capital to admire its transition into the main city of the world's most luxurious Welfare State, Copenhagen was often ignored by them, because it lacked the money to emulate these universal ideals – and that is probably what saved it. Even so, Copenhagen was the epitome of a liberal city for many years – until the good-natured but insensitive combination of political correctness and the vast bureaucracies of the Welfare State suddenly lost control. As in other Western-European countries, part of the population spoke out against the old, modernist establishment, fearing that it harmed rather than furthered their interests, believing that it had lost contact with the everyday situations they had to cope with. Sitting in a cafe, it is hard to guage the impact of this unexpected change. Not so far away from the center, however, the by now historical commune of Christiania may well be one of the victims of the new winds blowing through the streets of Copenhagen. **C.W.**

Happy

Poster, 1990

Happy

And page 313. Self-made homes, 1980s

Happy

The famous commune of Christiania started in 1972, when the first settlers
occupied a derelict parcel of land within the old fortifications of the city,
literally expropriating it from the Danish army, which owned it. Christiania
soon developed into a lively community of about 1,300 people, a true
paradise for dropouts. Many built their own homes, realizing their personal
dreams of happiness. Owning private property ran counter to the commune's
social ideals, and thus if people moved elsewhere, they simply left their
houses to their successors. Christiania's best known commodity is the bicycle
that is produced here. Since the middle of the 1990s, Christiania has
become a tourist attraction. Rumors are that it has outlived its promises and
lost part of its popular support, allowing the authorities to think seriously
about closing this one-time model of the revolutionary ideals of the 1960s.

Happy

Chairs designed by Anders Hansen

Poster, celebrating the 19th anniversary of Christiania, 1981

Happy

Cologne, March 18, 1998.

The best way to go to Cologne is by train. The railway station, a cathedral of steel and glass dedicated to the nineteenty-century notion of unprecedented progress, is built in the shadow of the famous Gothic cathedral that is Cologne's landmark. It, too, derives its present shape from a strong ambition to organize the world according to very specific schemas – everything should be as explicit an expression of the ideals of its origin as it possibly can be. So, a cathedral designed to have two towers should have two towers, and if only one of them was built, the omission of the other one should be corrected. Accordingly, the second tower was built, albeit centuries later than the first one. The cathedral became a building expressing time. Also expressing time is the rebuilt urban core of Cologne – a pure expression of the social and urban planning ideals of the 1950s. Possibly the most direct examples of environmental design expressing cultural ideals were realized by the countercultural opposition movements of the 1960s, 1970s and 1980s – but all of them have become history by now. All that remains of the Stollwerck commune, for instance, is a very low profile residential area – nothing the authorities will have to worry about. **C.W.**

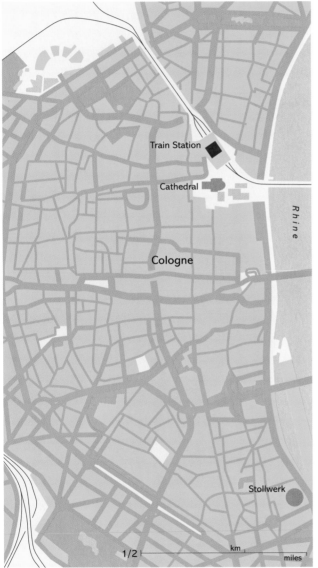

Train Station

Cathedral

Rhine

Cologne

Stollwerk

1/2   km   miles

Happy

STOLLWERCK

Stollwerck is the name of a chocolate factory in Cologne. This name became synonymous with the punk scene that found a home in the old factory in the 1980s, transforming it into a total work of art. Maybe Stollwerck represents the last phase of the counterculural commune, a far cry from the 'soft,' rural hippy experiments of the 1960s, a violent explosion of color in an atmosphere of urban debris, and a machine to promote a specific way of living and thinking, and, to quote the German author Bodo Morshäuser, 'thoughts that without such a space would not have been thought.'[1] As in the earlier alternative communities, however, music was still what it was all about. 'Have people ever before talked so much and so passionately about music? Music is playing everywhere, and afterwards people feel obliged to offer their views on it. When we're at home we hear music on the radio or from an LP, while we take a bath, are on the telephone, eat or put on make-up. We are particularly fond of music when we want to talk to each other. If we want to see each other, we get into the car and start out only after putting a tape in the cassette player.'[2] In the 1980s, the local government decided to tear the factory down, appeasing part of its habitues by building low-cost housing instead.

1 ...Für Gedanken, die ohne solchen Raum nie hervorträten'. Bodo Morshäuser, *Die Berliner Simulation*, Frankfurt am Main 1983, 30.

2 'Ist jemals so viel und dürftig von Musik gesprochen worden? Überall klingt sie auf, und kurz danach geben die Menschen ihre obligatorischen Geschmacksäußerungen über sie ab. Wir sind zu Hause und hören Musik aus dem Radio oder von der Platte, während wir baden, telephonieren, essen oder uns schminken. Besonders gern haben wir die Musik, wenn wir miteinander sprechen wollen. Um uns zu treffen, setzen wir uns in Autos, in denen wir erstmal eine Kassette einschieben.' Bodo Morshäuser, *Die Berliner Simulation*, 48.

THE BIRTHDAY PARTY

. . . die härteste Live-Band aus LONDON

einziges Konzert in NRW

Aus Köln

Jimmy, Jenny & Jonny

17.11. 20 Uhr

Halle im Stollwerck
Annostraße 24, Köln

Vorverk.: 7.– DM, Abendk.: 9.– DM

OUT OF NOWHERE: On a Friday night, the Birthday Party gave one of the year's truly brilliant performances.

Before a small and apathetic audience at the Ritz, Birthday Party (in a support slot to the Au Pairs) turned in a dangeorus, aggressive, literal, fierce show. When's the last time you found a rock band truly horrifying, both in intensity and power? Their 'music' is music as the raw animal, not just primitive but beastly, always brutal, always working, always sweating genuine tension and fear.

Happy

Happy

Happy

Thomas Wechs's Spiritual Town Planning

Herman van Bergeijk

Thomas Wechs, Don Bosco Church, Augsburg, 1960-1962

After the First World War an avalanche of books appeared dealing with town planning and its specific problems. They ranged from utopian propositions to thick manuals explaining technical problems and solutions. Remarkably, the Second World War did not produce a similar stream of books, although the destruction it caused was far worse. One of the reasons for this apparent lack of enthusiasm to write treatises and manifestos may have been – apart from the huge quantities of work awaiting architects and planners – the fading importance of handbooks. There was no need for them, nor was there a market for euphoric pamphlets. The prevailing mood was one of pessimism. Sigfried Giedion saw the loss of faith in progress as the main characteristic of the postwar period. The future was no longer people's primary concern. Solving acute problems was far more important for 'Germania anno Zero.' Nevertheless, some interesting plans were presented immediately after the war. One can think of Walter Schwagenscheidt's *Raumstadt* (largely conceived before the war) or Max Taut's optimistic book *Berlin im Aufbau*.

Only during the Fifties were more 'theoretical' proposals published and did town planning again become a hot issue in ideological debates.[1] The standard modern concepts, dear to the members of the C.I.A.M. congresses, were heavily criticized, and numerous alternatives were developed. In the international building exhibition 'Interbau Berlin 1957,' the city of tomorrow was again on the agenda. The concept of the 'Stadtlandschaft' as an alternative to the 'city of stone' was introduced, a clear illustration of the growing importance attached to the construction of free-standing elements in the landscape. The book *Die Stadt von Morgen*, compiled by Karl Otto, tried to give Germans some sense of the amount of work to be done by architects and planners in order to arrive at a city that would provide happiness to all. Children and elderly people would, thanks to new methods of production, find houses adapted to their needs. The book contained a number of essays, richly illustrated with scenes from contemporary life, along with realistic proposals for some general if not generic cities. It sought to show what the reorganized city of the future would be like and to promote the notion of 'the formative structure of a well-organized society.'[2]

A more schematic approach was taken, for instance, by Wilhelm Seidensticker in his book *Umbau der Städte*, dating from the same year. The author, who was not a well-known expert, took the contradictory reality of the city as the starting point of the evolution towards a more satisfactorily functioning metropolis. By reviewing recent history, Seidensticker identified the problems that exist between man and traffic. In order to do right to both, he pleaded for a restructuring of the city. The book, however, is rudimentary: it reduces analysis to traffic schemes and fails to propose any specific solution.

Criticism of functional planning's apparent inability to respect the ways people wanted to live was expressed by members of the 'New Brutalism' movement. Reyner Banham speaks of the 'moral crusade of Brutalism for a better habitat.'[3] He stresses the moral implications of

overview is presented by Gerd Albers in his *Entwicklung der Stadtplanung in Europa,* nschweig/Wiesbaden 1997.

om the 'Geleitwort,' in: Karl Otto (ed.), *Die Stadt von gen. Gegenwartsprobleme für alle,* Berlin 1959.

Happy

3 R. Banham, *Brutalism in der Architektur. Ethik oder Ästhetik?*, Stuttgart/Bern 1966, 133.

his proposals without ever specifying what kind of ethics are implied. The very term 'ethics' is in danger of being nothing but an empty shell, and it remains an open question why Banham introduced it. Nevertheless, it indicates a shift in approach. Life, art and architecture have to be less determined by idealism and should be considered as equal factors in the constitution of a 'new' environment. In his seminal book Banham discusses various churches but has difficulty in accepting a direct relation between Puritan esthetics and Puritan ethics. Therefore, he focuses on their architectural features. Banham's remarks are interesting because they illustrate the problems that arise when architecture and ethics work together and exert a decisive influence on how a building should be conceived.

In practice, the ideological foundation for solving urban problems relied more on sociological studies, however superficial, than on ethics. Many architects became amateur sociologists. In Germany, Hans Paul Bahrdt analyzed the different concepts that were introduced in this domain in the 1950s. Despite this flirtation with sociology, the gap between sociological studies and architectural and town planning solutions was never bridged. Architects distrusted the straightforward scientific manner of the sociologists' investigations, fearing that it would limit their creative possibilities. It is this distrustful attitude that Bahrdt criticizes in his book, which reads like a 'political brochure' and is in fact a plea for the use of sociological methods as a way to arrive at a more human city. In it he discusses the concepts of 'Verdichtung' and 'Auflockerung,' which had been in the center of architectural debate since the publication of J. Göderitz, R. Rainer, and H. Hoffmann's *Die gegliederte und aufgelockerte Stadt* in 1957.[4] Bahrdt tries to bring some clarity to the discussions that had been raging since the appearance of that work.

4 J. Göderitz, R. Rainer, H. Hoffmann, *Die gegliederte und aufgelockerte Stadt*, Tübingen 1957. The book dates back to 1945.

Much has been written about urban conditions in the 1950s and on the development of town planning. Yet some contributions have remained in the shadow. One of the most remarkable proposals is one that the Bavarian architect Thomas Wechs presented in a little book of scarcely more than fifty pages entitled *Ypsilon*. Although the book was sent to many friends and institutions, it did not receive much attention in the professional world, and no official town planner ever asked Wechs for further information. When it appeared, its publisher, a small local firm called 'die Brigg', observed in the accompanying prospectus that it was written in the belief that 'man [is] the mirror of things'; [he] is the beginning and the end. (...) The things around him may be hostile or friendly to him, they may change him or leave him indifferent, but they cannot harm his inner being.' The author states that his notes and observations date back to 1920 and that he had expressed some of the main ideas at conferences that he had attended in 1926 and 1929. During the Hitler regime and the war he had hardly any work, and thus he had sufficient time to rethink and systemize his thoughts.

Wechs (1893-1970) had been a complete outsider in the debate on the city. He had never actively participated in the struggle for modern architecture and town planning in

STADT YPSILON

Happy

Happy

Germany, although some of his pre-war architectural work had received local attention. The realm of Wechs's activity was limited to the area of Bavaria, and in particular, to the city of Augsburg and its environs. His housing complexes, Lessinghof and Schuberthof in Augsburg (1928-1930), were considered to be among the first examples of modern architecture in Bavaria. The facades of white stucco and the flat roofs, as well as the urban composition, make these works stand out in a city that is largely domi-nated by tradition. Nevertheless, as Norbert Lieb wrote: 'The synthetic form endows our open land-scape with an urban character.'[5] Soon after these two highlights his career came to an end. Considered to be a modern architect, Wechs was attacked by the Nazis and had to retreat into the realm of church architecture. Only there could he continue his career as an architect. In 1935 he had won a competition for a Stadthalle in Augsburg but Hitler had 'corrected' the design himself, and the project was never built.

5 'Die zusammengefaßte Gestaltung gibt einem offenen Gelände städtischen Charakter' Norbert Lieb, 'Thomas Wechs', in: *Zwiebelturm*, 1968, no. 4, 92.

Wechs cannot be regarded as a man with much town planning experience. In 1926 he had participated in a 'Denkschrift des Augsburger Verkehrsverein zur Stadtplanung,' which resulted in a new plan by Theodor Fischer for expanding the city. Wechs was a student of Fischer's in Munich and is certainly one of the few who closely followed him in making the transition from traditionalism to modernism. Fischer's interest in local conditions must have attracted Wechs, who thought of himself above all as a modern, middle-of-the-road regional architect. He kept a low profile and was in no way dogmatic. He preferred to follow his own path and his work was far from provincial. Wechs who wrote only a few articles, cannot be considered a prolific writer, and thus it is all the more surprising that he took the time to write *Ypsilon*. But, after his partial blacklisting ('Kaltstellung'), he had plenty of time for reflection, and he put it to good use.

Religious considerations were not at the core of Wechs's booklet. In contrast, for example, to Rudolf Schwarz, who shortly after the war had published his astonishing book *Von der Bebauung der Erde*, he does not mention God in it. Wechs certainly knew Schwarz's book. Schwarz, a Catholic, had made a name as a church architect and had also written a book on church architecture. His book on town planning is completely different from contemporary books on the subject. The relationship with and even dependence on the landscape is continually stressed. In his view, God shows himself through the landscape. It is one of the first ecological books; for here Schwarz makes preservation of the environment and the lessons that nature teaches us the central issues. One commentator has stated that 'The construction of the world is depicted in tones so evocative that studying this text should be made obligatory for geologists.'[6] The apocalyptic war experiences were also incorporated into this book. A reflection, in a way, on German nature, it is definitely not a book with a practical aim, and its discourse is characterized by abstraction.

6 'Der Bau der Welt wird – according to Wolfgang Pehnt – mit einer Evokationskraft geschildert, die den Text zum Pflichtstudium jedes Geologen machen sollte.' Wolfgang Pehnt/Hilde Strohl, *Rudolf Schwarz. Architekt einer anderen Moderne*, Ostfildern 1997, 113.

Happy

Only in the illustrations did Schwarz refer to some of his own town planning schemes. His message is perfectly clear: 'The city for the masses has lost its meaning and it would seem that

7 'Die Massenstadt verlor ihre Begründung und es scheint, als erfinde die Geschichte vierlei Vorwände, wenn sie eine Gestalt wieder einziehen will. Sie hatte sich selbst bis an die Grenze des Möglichen getrieben und dabei überwunden (...) Stadt und Land sind ins Fließen gekommen und aus ihrer trüben Vermischung setzt sich die Stadtlandschaft ab. Das überspannte Gebilde der Großstadt zerreißt.' Rudolf Schwarz, *Von der Bebauung der Erde*, Heidelberg 1949, 205.

history provides four reasons for this: the city for the masses has exceeded the scale at which it is still feasible. City and country have become fluid and their unclear mixture leaves its marks on the urban landscape. The metropolis has become an overstrained form that is breaking apart.'[7] The big city has no future and it is time to start thinking of how decentralization can save it. In another publication Schwarz stated that town planning was 'a play with utopias. We're only good at our work when we make prophesies and

8 'ein Spiel mit Utopien. Wir genügen unserm Beruf nur, wenn wir prophezieren und weissagen, das ist aber schwer. Es ist gar nichts Schlechtes dabei, wenn man einem Städtebauer sagt, er *handle nach Utopien*, sondern eher ein Lob'. Quoted in: *Die Städte himmeloffen. Reden und Reflexionen über den Wiederaufbau des Untergegangenen und die Wiederkehr des Neuen Bauens* 1948/49, Basel, Boston, Berlin 2003, 188.

predictions, however difficult that may be. It is in no way a negative thing to tell a town planner that he is dealing with utopias, but rather a word of praise.'[8] Ideal schemes give birth to new directions.

A contrary opinion about the big city was expressed by another architect who had an interest in town planning and was influential in Southern Germany.[9] His views were closer to those of Max Taut. We are referring to Adolf Abel, who before the war had been a professor of town planning at the

9 For biographical data see: *Süddeutsche Bautradition im 20. Jahrhundert*, München 1985, 149-180.

Munich Polytechnic. In 1950 Abel published his trilingual book called *Regeneration of towns*, the very title of which reflects his belief that the big city, far from being doomed, could still be revived. The book was dedicated to 'the art of living, to that sense of a possible harmony in the conditions of our life whose enjoyment goes beyond any purely rational order.' For Abel, Venice was the city that represented a useful prototype because there, as Le Corbusier had already observed, the different kinds of traffic flows were strictly separated, and Abel wanted to separate pedestrian and mechanized traffic.[10]

10 For an early discussion of his plans, see: Arnold Stöckli, *Die Stadt. Ihr Wesen und ihre Problematik*, Cologne 1954, 78-82.

Apart from a couple of concrete proposals, of which that for the inner city of Munich is the most interesting, Abel also presented an ideal plan. The drawings attempt to give an idea of how people would live in this town. One of them shows 'how the inhabitant of our new town will see things when he walks along one branch of the parkway towards the town center, which should again be dedicated to some monument, and not to some meaningless utilitarian building. It will give him the feeling that he is the master of his town, and not its slave.' In explaining the purpose of his project, he asserted that: 'Ideal schemes are like poetry, made from men's happiness, and to show them a certain direction, (...)'.[11]

11 Adolf Abel, *Regeneration der Städte*, Zürich 1950, 52.

Happy

In comparison with many of the books mentioned or with *Lebendiges Bauen* by the architect Wolf von Möllendorf (1953), Wechs's book has fewer scientific ambitions. Disguising his message as a tale, he introduces his unpretentious work with the observation that many exemplary plans have been made in the last years but that 'what I miss in most of them is the culmination of the town planning ideals of our times in religion and metaphysics. I consider them the key to the way out of the present helplessness and confusion.'[12] After these initial remarks the author presents an 'observation and assessment' in which he writes: 'Even if most people no longer live in dark rooms with no sun or fresh air, set in dull courtyards, still, in the long term, life behind expressionless facades or in overly-illuminated glass houses can hardly be enjoyable or attractive, despite the most comfortable furnishings and room arrangements.'[13] The air is polluted and traffic is responsible for many casualties. 'Today's motorized traffic is the blood altar of our materialistic-technological epoch. Every day, thousands of offerings are made, directly or indirectly.'[14] Cities have become cold places. 'The buildings that dominate our cities are no longer those representing spiritual or civic authority, but rather those of business and bureaucracy. They are competing in an attempt to dwarf each other and everything else.'[15] Wechs points to the responsibility of the town planner and states that 'the city should not be an elastic, doughy mass in which we suspect the existence of life only because we hear sounds and see movement. Rather, urban activity should emerge from the moral and spiritual life forces.'[16] After these poetically formulated sentences Wechs comes to his 'dream of Ypsilon' – the name of the city is itself a reaction to Babylon. This part of the book is written as a story. The narrative form takes up a long tradition which dates back to the Utopia of Thomas More. In the story, Paul lives in a terrible city and at night is tormented by nightmares. 'Revolving wheels, displays, clocks, manometers, wires tied up in knots, a mad mechanistic world dances before his eyes. Out of an electronic machine a robot emerges, and with its pincerlike hand reaches out for Paul's throat.'[17] In his dream Paul faints and wakes up in a different environment. He receives a letter from his brother Theodore who wants to visit him in

Was ich jedoch an diesen häufig vermisse, ist die Gipfeling städtebaulichen Denkens unserer Zeit in Religiösen und aphysischen, worin ich den letzten Ausweg aus der losigkeit und Verwirrung der Gegenwart erblicke.' Thomas hs, *Die Stadt Ypsilon*, Augsburg 1957, 6. A part of the book published in: *Das schöne Allgäu*, 1967, no. 1, 19-24.

Wenn auch die meisten Menschen nicht mehr in fast lichtlosen, nen- und luftarmen Räumen und an dumpfen Höfen wohnen, st das Leben hinter ausdruckslosen Fassaden oder in überbeteten Glashäusern, trotz der komfortabelsten Installationszellen die Dauer doch wenig beglückend und anziehend'.

Der motorisierte Verkehr von heute ist ein Blutaltar unserer erialistisch-technischen Zeitalters, auf dem täglich sende von Menschenopfern dem Moloch der Technik ct und indirect dargebracht werden.'

Die Dominanten unserer Städte bilden nicht mehr wie er die Gebäude der geistlichen und weltlichen Autorität; mehr ereifern sich Gebäude des Geschäftsbetriebes und Bürokratie, sich gegenseitig und alles zu übertrumpfen.'

die Stadt (...) keine elastische teigige Masse [darf] sein, in wir Leben vermuten, nur weil Bewegung und Lärm rgenommen wird. Vielmehr muß das, was sich bewegt, den irlichen, geistig-sittlichen und seelischen Kraftquellen des ens entspringen.'

Ypsilon, the city where he lives. After Theodore has arrived in Ypsilon by nuclear train, Paul walks him to his house, and on their way there he explains the city's layout. The visionary city is a metropolis consisting of around 500.000 inhabitants. A number of smaller towns, with between 10,000 and 20,000 inhabitants, make up this bigger city. Each smaller town has its own commercial areas, schools, churches, sport complexes, cultural and entertainment facilities, and each is governed by local authorities. For the most part the people live in setback, multi-story high-rise buildings. Each story has penthouse-like terraces. Smaller units and even farmhouses are also part of the smaller towns. Each person can arrange his apartment by re-arranging the inner walls. Ypsilon is governed by a city council that consists of representatives of the smaller towns. The city is conceived as a paradise for the pedestrian, who is not the flaneur of the metropolis but man in harmony with the natural setting of the 'Kleinstadt'. Motorized traffic is restricted to large roads that are divided into lanes for local and intercity traffic. Parking places and garages are constructed underground.

17 'Rasende Räder, Zählwerke, Uhren, Manometer, Tabellen, z Knäueln verwickelten Drähte, eine tolle mechanische Welt tan vor seinen Augen. Aus einer Elektronenmaschine trat ein Robo heraus und langte mit seiner Zangenhand nach Pauls Kehle.'

Although Wechs sent his booklet to many friends, magazines and institutions, the response was meager. As the architectural magazine *Der Architekt* noted, the book was conceived and written by a deeply religious spirit, who believes in order, and who is both realistic in seeing the facts and necessities of life and idealistic in striving for higher goals. 'One should read it, because compared to the huge quantity of town planning literature, its author leaves the beaten track and finds a way to go forward.'[18] Wechs starts his visionary tale with a critical attitude, but he does not present us with a doomsday scenario. On the contrary, by founding his beliefs on a religious, specifically Christian basis, he arrives at the image of a society based on happiness and on a certain set of morals. As Johannes B. Lotz wrote in a Heideggerian study of the city, 'in opposition to the chaos of today's city, Wechs 's vision proposes a new and true order, rooted in religious mystery'.[19] Ten years later, this was confirmed by Wechs when he wrote that the 'highest task of the town planner does not consist in giving life to a well functioning city organism, but in giving beauty to streets and spaces. It is here that the way of the technician diverges from the way of the artist. Here begins the realm of the mysterious.'[20]

18 'Man sollte es lesen, da in der Flut der Städtebauliteratur hier ein Verfasser weitab der ausgetretenen Wege auf einsam Pfad vorwärts wandert.' As [Alfred Simon], 'Stadt Ypsilon', in *der Architekt*, 1959, no. 12, 362.

19 Johannes B. Lotz, *Da religiöse Geheimnis der Stadt*, Münche 1958, 62.

20 Thomas Wechs, *Gedanken zum Städtebau*, Augsburg 1968.

The originality of Wechs's vision lies not in the description of the city in its different aspects nor in the way traffic is separated, but in the importance which it accords to the religious center, the church. The church, the center of the town, is 'completely space, formed by light.' It has to affirm the relation of man to God. In the only church Wechs actually built he tried to achieve this.

Happy

The Don Bosco church in Augsburg (1960-62) is one of the most beautiful examples in southern Germany. In the floor plan we can recognize an abstracted figure of man, but also the exterior has an appealing form, not necessarily connected solely to Christian religion.

In *Ypsilon* the order of the city is derived from the larger order of God. The ethical side of town planning is not neglected, but rather reinforced. Order does not produce happiness unless it is seen as referring to a higher, spiritual source. Town planning is not the means or the goal, but the result of respect for our natural resources, which are bestowed by God. Wechs's order is clear and so is his message. Yet the illustrations show us that Wechs did not have the traditional city in mind. Small houses and pitched roofs do not dominate his urban dreams. The book should not be read only as a novel but also as a realistic plan. Town planning has been raised from the level of knowledge to that of conscience, with material happiness being considered less important than spiritual happiness. His meticulous description contains incentives for rethinking the physical aspect of the modern city. One important point that is left untouched, however, is the question of land ownership. Unlike Bernoulli, who was also interested in the pedestrian city, Wechs does not advocate state ownership of the land.[21] In fact, private propriety is a characteristic of Ypsilon.

The last sentence in Wechs's visionary tale is derived from the poet Friedrich Hölderlin: 'Man is a god, when he dreams, a beggar, when he thinks.' And day-dreaming is, according to Freud, the motor of creative imagination. In this sense Wechs is a true poet.[22]

21 See: Hans Bernoulli, *Die Stadt und ihr Bodem*, Zürich 1946.

22 We are referring to the text: S. Freud, 'Der Dichter und das Phantasieren' [1907], in: S. Freud, *Studienausgabe*, Bd. X, Frankfurt a.M. 1969, 171-179.

Happy

Carimate, April 22, 2004.

Memories from a girlhood spent in Carimate in the late 1970s. 'We all had the same pieces of furniture. Every living room had its *Carimate* chair. Le Corbusier's *chaises longues* were everywhere. Many of our gardens were designed by the same Japanese architect. (...) Our dog, Lord Wilson Luca Maria I, an Afghan hound, always slept on the "Maralunga"' a couch by Vico Magistretti, awarded the 'Compasso d'Oro' prize in 1979. 'Every Saturday night, we held parties in one of our villas. The guest list was always the same. No outsider was accepted if he/she had not been presented by someone. Boys and girls from Cantù (the nearby city) always tried to sneak in, but we rejected them. There were big fights: I remember them throwing stones at us from behind a hedge. (...) Every year Count Radice Fossati organized foxhunting in his villa. (...) We did not mix with the people living in the old part of Carimate. We did not go to Carimate's public schools, but to private Catholic schools in Cantù. (...) We seldom went to the golf club. There were too many Milanese people. (...) Nobody really cared about the VIPs living there: Lothar Matthäus... Jürgen Klinsmann... It was not much fun, actually. We all watched that TV series, *The Prisoner*, with Patrick McGoohan, and felt it had a lot to do with Carimate.' A.C., F.d.P., P.S.

Carimate:
Happiness and Modern Design in Milan's Hinterland

Alessandra Coppa, Filippo de Pieri, Paolo Scrivano

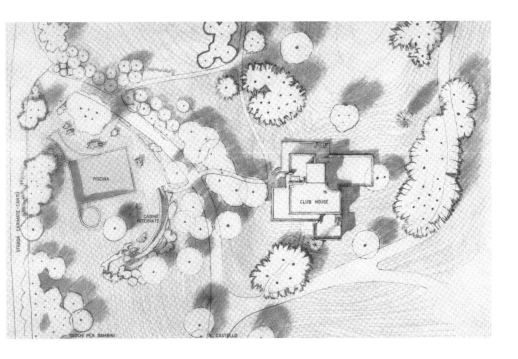

At first sight, Carimate is no different from many other upper-class residential suburbs built in Milan's hinterland in the period following World War Two. Situated some thirty kilometers north of the city, in the core of the Brianza, a region with a remarkable tradition in furniture production, this residential area was planned in the late 1950s, on an estate previously owned by an aristocratic family. The setting – the park of an existing castle – was green, almost pastoral. It was turned into a golf course, intertwined with large plots for single-family houses with gardens, soon to be occupied by members of the industrial elite of both Milan and the surrounding regionarea. Close to the Milano-Laghi highway (Italy's first high-speed road, built as early as 1924), the development was made possible by the growth of private automobile ownership in the region.

Happy

From the start of its construction, Carimate seemed to embody cultural values and lifestyles that were directly connected to the emergence of the Milanese area as one of the centers of Italy's economic boom. Located in the core of the Brianza, a region with a remarkable tradition in furniture production and one of the birthplaces of modern Italian design, Carimate was for a few years a place where architects and advocates of new trends found a favorable context for their work. There, the transformations brought about by the impact of a new visual culture and economic wellbeing on everyday life seemed more visible than elsewhere.

Golf courses had been built in Italy since the beginning of the century, but their appearance in the big urban areas, as in the case of Carimate, was a more recent phenomenon, signaling the game's growing role in the leisure habits of the urban upper classes. Several attempts to combine a golf club and a suburban residential development were made in the early 1950s. Carimate, an example of this trend, quickly stood out for its architectural quality. The building company behind the development was the Rome-based 'Società Generale Immobiliare' (SGI), an enterprise whose roots could be traced back to the years of Italy's political unification in the nineteenth century. In previous years, SGI had been responsible for the development of the Olgiata golf club and suburb, situated in the Roman countryside. The English golf course architect C.K. Cotton, who had designed the master plan for Olgiata, was hired as a consultant for the new project.

In Carimate, SGI's role was initially limited to the subdivision and resale of plots of land, with almost no responsibility for building design and construction. The golf clubhouse was an exception: the first building to be erected on the site, it was also one of the few to be directly commissioned by the Società. The center of life in the new community, it was meant to provide a visual background for its exclusive rituals. The architects chosen for its design were two young professionals emerging on the Milanese scene, Vico Magistretti and his associate Guido Veneziani. Their involvement signaled SGI's intention to give the development a strongly defined architectural character. Their building successfully translated the large scale of Carimate's garden utopia into a playful variation of modern architectural themes.

The building was widely published by the Italian architectural press: both *Domus* and *Casabella* presented it to their readers in 1961. In the latter, it appeared along with an article written by the review's editor, Ernesto Nathan Rogers; and the unsigned article that accompanied its publication in *Domus* was strongly supportive. Carimate was praised as an example of a modern residential development appropriately inserted in Italy's 'beautiful landscape' and 'entrusted from the very beginning to the best Italian architects.' Actually, it should be noted that the publisher of both *Domus* and *Casabella*, Gianni Mazzocchi, was a very early Carimate resident. The magazines were part of his small publishing empire, which included *Quattroruote*, a weekly magazine about cars that played an important cultural role in the mass diffusion of the automobile in Italy. In subsequent years, *Domus* continued to support Magistretti's architectural activity, as well as to publish houses built in Carimate.

The list of Carimate's early inhabitants included other interesting names: Cesare Cassina, for example, who was the owner of the furniture company of the same name, and one

Happy

Happy

of the businessmen behind the boom in Italian design of the mid-1950s. For his house in Carimate, Cassina had initially contacted Carlo Scarpa, who went on to submit a few projects. But it was Magistretti, the architect of the clubhouse, who was finally chosen for the work. The villa was built in the early 1960s, and, inevitably, it was published in *Domus* in 1966. In the meantime, Magistretti started designing furniture for the Cassina Company, thus giving birth to a long-lasting and successful partnership. Significantly, one of the first results of this collaboration was the mass production and distribution of the wooden chair that Magistretti had originally designed for Carimate's clubhouse. With its domestic, handcrafted feel, the 'Carimate' chair was a remarkable commercial success.

Other Carimate residents followed a similar path in their architectural choices, showing that for at least a few members of the diverse community that met in Magistretti's elegant golf club, 'taste' did matter at least as much as wealth. A modest tradition of architectural patronage soon became a recognizable feature of the development, with villa designs commissioned from such architects as Marco Albini, Luigi Caccia Dominioni, Jacopo Gardella, Afra and Tobia Scarpa, and Luigi Vietti. Not everyone shared this commitment, however, and the very success of the development soon paved the way for other, less exclusive types of architectural intervention. This was apparent in the way SGI changed its role in Carimate, with a gradual shift to building construction and the opening of a local architectural office that offered to potential customers semi-standardized projects in the areas opened up for new development.

Today, Carimate is lost in the ubiquitous urbanization of the Milanese region, and has absorbed part of its more common traits, including an inevitable penchant for building fences and gates. Over the years, however, it has kept its reputation as quite a special place, although admittedly for mixed reasons. The training ground of the Inter F.C. is not far away, and local residents have included several famous football players. Pop singers have also been seen on these grounds (and playgrounds) for some time, because part of the abandoned Carimate castle was used in the late 1970s and early 1980s as a recording studio, the so-called 'Stone Castle', where some classic albums of modern Italian pop music were recorded, most notably (for those who may be interested) Paolo Conte's *Un gelato al limon* and Fabrizio de Andrè's *Creuza de mä.*

The atmosphere is now different from the heroic times of the early 1960s, when the building of Carimate virtually epitomized the changes that simultaneously affected Milan and its hinterland, along with a significant part of Italy's architectural culture. These were: the growing scale of Milan's agglomeration; the development of new forms of conspicuous consumption and urban sociability; the alliance between the Milanese furniture industry and a small group of designers; and the commitment of both architects and their clients to promoting residential developments characterized by a recognizable 'modern' style. A reflection of these phenomena, Carimate, for a moment, witnessed the combined action of developers, architects, and an elite, who, in their quest of new cultural symbols, came close to shaping a new upper-class utopia for the years of Italy's economic boom. There the golf course still lies, its Stone Castle now eroded by the waves of suburbia.

Happy

Happy

The City as a Catalyst of Revolution

REVOLUTIONS

Revolutions always start in cities. The act of being involved in a revolution is usually an uplifting experience. It forges a close bond with one's fellow revolutionaries, and if the revolutionaries succeed in taking over the city, it is usually transformed into an urban commune (with the Paris commune of 1871 serving as the prototype). Often, the urban commune is a scale model of the new society – except, obviously, when the revolution fails. During the revolution, something mysterious shapes the masses, transforming them into a formidable force, with the city guiding its direction. In his monumental novel, *A Book of Memories*, Nádas describes this process during the – failed – Hungarian uprising of 1956: 'That is how it was at that hour, too, in the balmy evening air; we showed our combativeness only in that we were marching together, so many of us; of course our marching was directed against something or some people, but it wasn't yet clear what or who these were; everyone could still think what he wished, bring along his own private grudges, ask his own personal questions without having to come up with definitive answers, and if anyone did come up with one, he couldn't know how the others would respond, which is why he spoke in slogans, yelled, or remained silent. (…) After we managed to press through the human bottleneck on Marx Square and ran to catch up with the others, something in me changed irreversibly; I simply forgot that moments earlier I'd wanted to go home, and it was the city that made me forget it, turning stones into houses, houses into streets, and streets into well-defined new directions. (…) And from that point on things followed the course dictated by the law of nature: a spring wells up from the ground, branches into streams, flows into rivers rushing toward the sea; it was this poetic and this simple obeying the attraction of the larger mass; human bodies propelled themselves out of the noisy, gaily seething side streets towards the boulevard and pressed themselves into the larger crowd there; (…) people were rushing at us from behind, thrusting us forward, all of us sweeping along in the direction of Margit Bridge; yet even this

Happy

did not mean that these countless individual wills all at different temperatures, igniting one another with sheer friction but in the absence of real fuel causing only sparks that flared and quickly died – could heat up to a single common will; yet a change did occur, and everyone must have sensed it, because the shouting ceased; there was no more laughing, recitations, speeches, or flag waving, as if crowding into this one and only possible direction, everyone had retreated into the smallest common denominator of the moment: the sound of their own footsteps.'[1] The city and the revolution appear to be one and the same thing. Some revolutions are violent, others take the shape of a carefully staged urban spectacle – the way a revolution manifests itself does not seem to affect its outcome. In commemoration of the traumatic revolution of 1956, Imre Nagy, its leader, was reburied in June 1989. Apparently there was nothing revolutionary about the theatrical drama performed on one of Budapest's main squares, but the effect was more revolutionary than '1956': it marked the beginning of the end of the Soviet empire. Again, the city and the masses virtually merged, starting the process that ended with the fall of the Berlin Wall in November, only five months later.

éter Nádas, *A book of Memories*, London, New South Wales, Parktown, 1997, first published in Hungary 986, 504-506.

Lisbon, February 17, 2001.

A small café in a narrow alley in the Barrio Alto. I am sitting in a corner, drinking *vinho verde*. It is the beginning of the evening and there aren't many people around. Then they start coming, all at about the same time, as if they have a date with each other. There isn't much room. A group of young women settles down next to me, and some elderly people take a seat in front of me. They seem to be Portuguese. After a few minutes, two men appear, one with a *guitarra* in his hands. So that's what the people came for. Good to have my video camera with me. It had been on the table the whole time, but now the girl next to me whispers to put it away. They don't like it, she says. Well, I just leave it where it is, nobody can see me recording anyway. When one of the musicians sees the camera, he turns off the light and everybody is in the dark. Then the music starts. The singer sings his song full of *saudade* with a raw voice and sustained notes. It is beautiful. To my surprise my camera sees in the dark what I cannot see, so I keep it running. But then, just when I glance at the camera, the music stops and the singer comes up to me. 'The fado is for the Portuguese,' he says, and puts his hand in front of the lens. H.H.

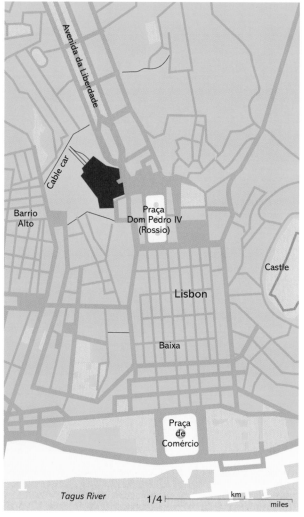

Happy

The Carnation Revolution

Helma Hellinga

April 25, 1974. Shortly after midnight, Rádio Renascença played the forbidden song: Grândola, Vila Morena:

> Grândola, little scorched city
> Origin of brotherhood
> Nowhere people are better organized
> Than in you, o city.

For a group of officers of the Movement of the Armed Forces, this was the sign to rebel against the old regime. The MFA (Movimento das Forças Armadas) thereby started what later became known as the carnation revolution. Early in the morning their tanks entered Lisbon, and in less than 24 hours a dictatorial regime that had wielded power for more than 48 years was overthrown. The legacy of António Salazar and his successor, Marcello Caetono, was destroyed. With little opposition, the revolutionaries took control of the radio and television stations, the airport, and the army headquarters.

As soon as the success of the revolution was announced, crowds flocked to the streets, celebrating the soldiers as heroes. Days of celebrations and festivities followed, as people everywhere discussed Portugal's new future. Political exiles returned, among them the Socialist leader Mário Soares and the Alvaro Cunhal of the Communist Party, political prisoners were set free, censorship was lifted and the freedom to hold political meetings was re-established. May 1 became an official national holiday. Soldiers and civilians alike wore carnations in the barrels of their guns, a symbol of renouncing violence, and of the revolution. The images of tanks riding the streets, full of happily gesticulating people, joyous crowds on the squares, and soldiers wearing red carnations, were televised all over the world. The revolution was to last for two years,

Happy

two years of euphoria but also of conflicting views and of political battles over Portugal's future.

The revolution led by the MFA inspired a massive people's movement. At all levels of society, people set themselves free and took control of their daily lives. During the honeymoon phase of the revolution, prostitutes freed themselves from their pimps, and one hundred slum dwellers occupied a new housing estate in the outskirts of the city. Creativity was unleashed, expressing itself, for example, in murals depicting scenes of militant activity. Streets were renamed, the most important bridge across the Tagus River, previously named for Salazar, now became known as the 'Bridge of April 25'. Before the revolution committees of workmen were not unknown, but during the revolution they spread everywhere, organizing strikes and seeking to overthrow the existing power structures. At the street level, neighborhood committees were formed. They wanted to improve healthcare and they organized self-help groups.

Having started in Lisbon, the movement soon spread across the entire country. It was particularly successful in Porto, Portugal second largest city, and in the rural south, where farmers and their employees began to oppose the landowners. A golf club in the south was opened for everybody except its own members. All told, two thousand new houses were occupied throughout the country. Everywhere people were engaged in political discussions. 'Viva o poder popular' (long live the power of the people) became a popular slogan and the motto for the new Portugal.

The Western world was caught by surprise. Portugal was known mainly as good place to go on a holiday. That it was a poor society of farmers suffering from a dictatorial regime was also a familiar fact. Thanks to the revolution, Portugal made the headlines. A revolution as momentous as this recalled the dreams of 'Paris 1968,' even though Paris was the capital city of a modern and industrialized nation scarcely comparable to the backward agricultural society of Portugal. The leftwing movement, already fragmented and lost in ideological controversies at the time of the events in Lisbon, gained new hope. Many people went there to experience the revolution first hand and to join one of the numerous revolutionary groups.

What came to the Western countries as a complete surprise had long been in the making, but the processes leading up to the revolution were overshadowed by other, more visible political events elsewhere. The roots of the revolution lay in Portugal's colonial wars in Africa. In the decades before 1974 Portugal had chosen to isolate itself from the rest of the world. For Salazar and for Caetano, who succeeded him in 1968, this was the only way to maintain the military dictatorship. Cooperation with other countries would inevitably have led to questions about Portugal's less than democratic governmental structure. Economically, isolation didn't hurt Portugal very much; for it had resisted the widespread movement of de-colonization and lived by exploiting its huge colonial empire in Africa: Angola, Mozambique, Guinea-Bissau, São Tomé e Príncipe, and the Cape Verde Islands. The unlimited resources offered by its colonial possessions enabled Portugal to keep its economy going, but this required it to maintain an autocratic way of managing the colonies. Severe repression was the only way to maintain the colonial empire, because Portugal became involved in a seemingly endless series of wars against a growing number of resistance movements. Conflicts grew steadily worse, starting in 1961.

Celebration on the Avenida Almirante Reis

Waging wars in the colonies led to increasing numbers of victims. Thousands of soldiers died, a growing portion of Portugal's national income had to be invested in the army and the war economy. Thousands of people who could have contributed to the economic development of the country were sent to Africa, while thousands of others fled the country to escape war and poverty, and thus all sectors of the economy suffered from a shortage of workmen. Caetano did nothing to change Portugal's colonial policies. He did, however, initiate some modest political reforms. Elections were allowed, though they were strictly controlled, the ban on labor unions was lifted, and student movements could be organized. Shocked by the results of these liberal policies, Caetano soon reversed them and returned to the strict rule of Salazar, but it proved impossible to contain the powers he had unleashed. The return to outright oppression and the persistence of the wars in Africa resulted in deteriorating labor conditions and growing dissent in all layers of society. Strikes became ubiquitous. These were the conditions that fostered the idea of a coup, a coup that would prove to be much more fundamental than a mere change of regime.

Happy

The years preceding the revolution saw growing discontent in the army. From top to bottom, the military was dissatisfied with the catastrophic wars in Africa. The hopelessness of the situation was diminishing the army's prestige, and the two most influential generals, António Spinola and Costa Gomes, both of them commanders of the army in Guinee-Bissau, openly criticized the official policies. In February 1974, Spinola published a book, *Portugal and the future*, the contents of which made it clear that Caetano could no longer count on the loyalty of the army. Both generals were fired, but that did not help much to contain the growing unrest in the armed forces. In the beginning of 1973, 136 army offices had met at a secret place in the countryside, and this 'special farmhouse barbecue' turned out to be the first meeting of the MFA. Six months later, the MFA had built up a network of about 300 officers and formulated the first draft of its program, entitled 'Democracy, Development and De-colonization.'

On May 15, 1974 the first 'provisional government of national unity' was formed. It was headed by General De Spinola, the most influential critic of the old regime. He was, however, not a member of the MFA. Apart from moderate forces in the army, he also included Socialists and Communists in his government. The MFA saw this curious combination of a military junta and leftwing political parties as the best means of finding a political solution for the colonial conflicts. One of the tasks of the coalition was to organize free elections. Already in September, however, the MFA sent De Spinola home. He was considered too conservative and expelled to Franco's Spain. Several provisional governments took over, in some of which the MFA as well as a few of the smaller leftwing groups participated.

On April 25, 1975, the first free elections were held for the Constituent Assembly. The results were surprising, since the big winner was the Socialist Party of Mário Soares, a party recently founded in exile, lacking political experience and with an electoral base that

The MFA as the promoter of cultural dynamism

Left: Poster commemorating April 25, 1974

Happy

345

was hard to define. The Socialists wanted to create a parliamentary democracy and voiced their ideals in terms so vague and ambivalent that their program appealed to almost everyone. The Communist Party, on the other hand, lost badly. Led by Cunhal, it had a long tradition of opposition to the dictatorship and strong backing from the labor unions, especially in the industrial areas near Lisbon, but it was precisely there that they lost heavily. A fierce political battle was fought between the Communist-oriented labor unions, which wanted to consolidate their position, and the non-aligned labor unions that were trying to provoke social upheaval and gain control of the factories.

The results of the election radicalized part of the MFA. A new movement, the New Left, developed and attacked the reformist wing for its willingness to help create a 'bourgeois' democracy of the Western European type. It concluded a pact with the committees that had developed in the popular movement in 'the street', the factories and the countryside. The open forum, where every new course of action was debated for days and nights on end, now became part of official politics. During the 'hot summer' of 1975, however, the radical movement headed for a dead end street. All over the country there had been confrontations with its political adversaries, culminating in the realistic threat of a rightwing coup and the return of dictatorship.

While revolutionary elan was ebbing away, the political center was gaining importance in the successive provisional governments. The Socialists and Social Democrats became the leading political forces in the elections of 1976. Soares was appointed prime minister, the first who did not originate in the military, although the president was still a general: Ramalho Eanes. The next milestone on the road to a Western democracy came in 1986, when Soares was elected president – the first civilian to hold that office in 60 years – and Portugal joined the European union. The carnation revolution set in motion the processes toward democratization, but the dreams of the popular movement that initiated the revolution went much farther than that. The Portuguese who engaged in the revolt will always remember these years as the happiest of their lives.

The emblem of the revolution, João Abel Manta

Happy

347

Madrid, August 15, 2001.

A hot summer's day, the feast of Assumption. Madrid celebrates the Virgin of the Dove. A party for ordinary folks in a village-like city. The neighborhood association organizes a karaoke party and a competition involving traditional dresses. The penetrating smell of barbeque fills the air, and small barrel organs are playing. It is Zarzuela – a typical, *the* typical Madrid variant of a light opera — in the open air, in the neigborhood of Lavapiés, in a traditional musical theatre in a rundown part of the city that is being hastily renovated by the municipality. Bohemians and squatters are leaving, and foreigners are taking their place. Bazaars full of kitsch stuff and drug dealing are everywhere. At night, bored young people and immigrants from all over the world take to the streets. The annual Zarzuela performances can be seen in the galleries of the old corralahouse. Far more interesting than the show for tourists is the real life on the balconies, the sight of people eating while gazing at the singers. Afterwards comes the ball.   R.B.

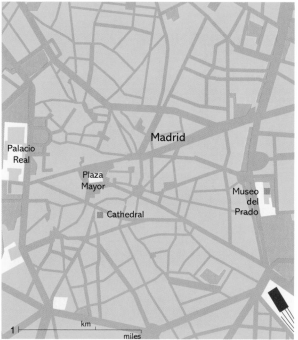

Madrid

Palacio Real

Plaza Mayor

Museo del Prado

Cathedral

Happy

MADRID VERSUS FRANCO

Ronald Brouwer

Fear and hope in Spain On November 20, 1975 General Franco died. Francisco Franco, dictator of Spain since the Civil War (1936-1939), had already made the arrangements for his succession: King Juan Carlos I was to become the new sovereign. Attempts to prolong Franco's life as long as possible had reached their limits, the Basque secession movement, the ETA, had succeeded in murdering Franco's right hand man, general Carrero Blanco, and the regime's hold had weakened in the years preceding Franco's passing away. Yet, all these signs of growing weakness cannot conceal the fact that outside forces were not the main reason why the regime collapsed. It came to an end because it committed suicide – to quote the historian García de Cortázar. In the first months after Franco's death, the consequences of the change of regime did not become manifest. The young king appointed people known for their loyalty to Franco, trying to make the transition to democracy as smooth as possible. Strikes, student revolts and a belated counter-revolutionary movement reminiscent of the 1960s could not be prevented, but looking back on what is known as the Transition, it is safe to say that it was relatively painless. In 1981 General Tejero tried a coup that, in the end, only strengthened the position of the king. One year later, the socialists won the elections. They stayed in power until well after 1992, the year of the Expo in Seville, the Olympic games in Barcelona, and Madrid's election as cultural capital of Europe. In 1993, the value of the peseta dropped. It signified the end of the linear, upward movement that had predominated since 1975. Money ran out, and the optimistic phase was over.

Happy

1975 'In the refrigerator, the champagne was waiting to be opened. On the streets nothing happened. Nobody did anything. Maybe because there was nothing one could do.' This is how Jorge Semprún remembers the day when Spain awaited the news of Franco's death. Paraphrasing a well known poem, he wrote: 'Madrid is a city of a million corpses, or, more correctly, a million people who keep their mouths shut.' Then, suddenly, in the middle of the night the long awaited word came. One hour before it was officially confirmed, a telex flew across the country: 'Franco is dead, Franco is dead, Franco is dead.' Spain heard the news. Tension did not subside. The bottle of champagne was opened but without a loud bang. No outbursts of happiness were heard, people's relief was still saturated with fear. The precautionary measures taken by the government proved superfluous. People waited passively, some communists and rebels went into hiding. The next couple of days, hundreds of thousands of Spaniards paid their last respect to the deceased head of state. Long lines took possession of the center of Madrid, leading to the palace where Franco was transported. Many lined the streets when Franco was brought to his grave: a basilica outside the city, hewn out of the

Happy

TIME

NOVEMBER 3, 1975

SPAIN AFTER FRANCO

Juan Carlos

rocks by political prisoners. Spain was deeply divided between the followers of Franco and his critics, but what united them all in these days was the fear of what might happen. The new king was not welcomed very warmly. People felt suspicious about the new head of state who had been appointed by Franco and who evidently did not want to make a decisive break with

Happy

351

the past. Amnesty for the political prisoners, for instance, was not granted until some time later. Franco's death did not trigger massive festivities; it only led to a lot of confusion, fear, and a feeling of disappointment. Gradually, hope won the day. People wished for political changes 'cambio' without remorse, 'libertad sin ira,' in the words of a popular song from these years. Even today, this song can still be heard, especially during demonstrations against the ETA – according to Semprún 'the last smoldering remains of Franquism' – and during the celebrations of the neo-fascists on November 20, the day Franco died. Franco's equestrian statue still stands in Madrid, and in many a Spanish city the street named after the generalisimo has not yet been renamed. Franco still isn't dead.

1981 The year is chosen more or less randomly. Let us, however, take the failed coup of Tejero as the starting point for the Movida Madrileña, the so-called Madrilean Movement that was typical of the growing hope for democratic reform and an atmosphere of increasing optimism. The movement represented an anti-political youth culture. Going out at night, pop music in the Spanish language, provocative behavior, and a kind of urban consciousness were its characteristics. The movement helped Madrid overcome its stigma as the hated capital of Franquism. La Luna de Madrid – the moon of Madrid – was the voice of this elusive movement. In it, the now famous film director Pedro Almodóvar wrote: 'Something is happening in

Madrid. Something dangerous: Madrid is starting to become self-conscious. Its inhabitants never had roots. People lived there, but might as well have lived somewhere else. Nobody cared about Madrid. And now people are talking about a Madrilean culture. You can be proud about the city where you live. That is not so good. In this way you don't feel yourself anymore, but become merely a part of the city.'

The Madrilean Movement was embodied by pop bands such as Kaka de Luxe, and the 'Muse' with colored hair, Alaska, singing songs entitled: 'Horror in the Supermarket,' or 'My friend is a Zombie.' Sex, drugs and Rock Ola

Happy

(the dancing where it happened). The television show 'The Golden Age' presented international-al pop stars and Movida heroes. This was the period of the first, still rather primitive movies by Almodóvar (*Pepi, Luci, Bom y otras chicas del montón,* and *Labertino de pasiones*), and of revived activity in the visual arts, fashion, etc. The movement attracted attention from abroad, and the popular mayor of Madrid, Tierno Galván, exploited its publicity value – either cunning-ly or because he believed in the movement. It is even whispered that the city council gave the movement its household name.

The Movida concluded the story that had begun with the Civil War, led to the dictatorship, and culminated in the Transition. The Transition was still far from complete and the Movida had an ambivalent ring. It was an optimistic movement characterized by a high degree of 'catch as catch can,' but it also was a punk movement voicing disappointment about the newly established democracy. Shortly after Tejero appeared in parliament shooting his gun, people imitated him during the carnival parades, wearing a moustache and the cap of the Guardia Civil. Fear quickly turned into satire. According to Almodóvar: 'The playful and independent character were essential. People did things just for fun. Frivolity almost became an ideology. The apolitical aspect of these years was a sound reaction to disastrous political activity that had led nowhere.'

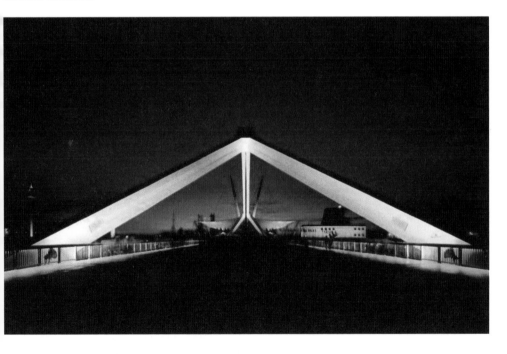

1992 After the period of fear and robust vitality, 1992 was a year of celebration. The Olympic Games were held in Barcelona, Seville hosted the World Expo, and Madrid became the European Cultural Capital. And the discovery of America, which had been the outcome of a Spanish initiative, was celebrated in a series of festivities.

Happy

The flawless Olympic Games in Barcelona suddenly gave Spain the same status as the other European nations. Catalonia was recognized as a region with its own language and culture, and Barcelona was able to greatly improve its infrastructure. Seville probably profited less by organizing the World Expo, even though the event did provide the occasion to build a super-fast train that covers the distance to Madrid in less than two and a half hours. These two top events overshadowed the festivities in celebration of the discovery of America and the exhibitions and events organized as part of Madrid's election as Cultural Capital of Europe. Even more important than the economic profits of this celebratory year were its social-psychological effects. The events increased Spain's self-respect. Spaniards were proud of what they had

achieved in a very short time. Some feared the hangover after the party, and their fears came true: the peseta had to be devaluated, unemployment soared, and corruption scandals were numerous. The dream was over. Spain went to bed rich and woke up poor, as one of the newspapers put it.

Even so, the World Expo attracted 42 million visitors, Spain gained 22 medals at the Olympic Games, thirteen of them gold, the country became a theme park, presenting its culture in a huge show, and the city was transformed into a stage with shining bridges and cosmopolitan boulevards, all according to the latest fashion: in 1992, Spain indulged itself in the grand party it forgot to celebrate in 1975.

Happy

The Reburial of Imre Nagy and the End of the Socialist Empire

Henriett Szabo

On June 16, 1989, a huge crowd gathered at the Hösök tér (Square of the Heroes) in the center of Budapest, in front of the Arts Hall, a turn-of-the-century museum for temporary exhibitions on contemporary art. The columns marking the building's main entrance had been draped in black, and so had the tympanum they carried, while the facade behind the columns was wrapped in white cloth. Although this was vaguely reminiscent of Christo's wrapped buildings, it was also quite clear that something else was going on here. The building was not what it was all about; it was just the backdrop for a dramatic event. Several coffins were placed on a scaffolding that was part of Lászlo Rájk's design for this event. They contained the remains of the leaders of the failed revolution of 1956, the most renowned being Imre Nagy. Earlier, these coffins had been dug up in Budapest's main cemetery, where they had rested for more than thirty years. The crowd stood silently, clearly moved by the ceremony that was taking place. When it was over, the coffins were carried to their final destination. They had been rescued from enforced oblivion and officially re-introduced into Hungary's history.

The second funeral of Imre Nagy and his comrades triggered a process that could not be stopped. On August 19, some two months later, the 'pan-European picnic' was organized at the border between Hungary and Austria. What was intended to be simply a symbolic gesture – the cutting of the iron curtain – proved to be the beginning of the exodus of many East Germans, who were on holiday at the time in Hungary. They stepped through the hole in the border and left the Soviet empire forever. In November, the Berlin wall came down, and the Soviet empire was no more. The second funeral ceremony marked the beginning of what

Happy

turned out to be the most dramatic event in the history of Europe since the beginning of the Cold War. The outcome of this carefully staged drama was even more drastic than the usual results of a civil war, and when the Committee of Historical Justice, founded by former political prisoners, and the leaders of the Communist Party were organizing this event, they knew very well that what they were contemplating was a revolutionary deed.

The reburial ceremony cured Hungary of a national trauma. The revolution of 1956 hardened the harsh political realities of the Cold War that had divided Europe since 1948. For more than thirty years, the iron curtain remained a barrier that was never seriously debated, as long as the two political powers that dominated either side of it managed to preserve peace in Europe. That was the political lesson of the 1956 rebellion in the streets of Budapest, which had been led by Imre Nagy, himself an ardent communist, but one very much opposed to the Soviet occupation. Several factors led up to the revolution, including the policy of forced socialization, the suppression of those who opposed the system, and the process of industrialization with its attendant low level of investment in housing and consumer goods, causing many hardships in a country that used to be quite wealthy. People felt embittered. Since the death of Stalin in 1953, opportunities to voice opposition had increased. With the departure of the Russian army from Austria in 1955, Hungary was no longer encircled by socialist countries and their military power; now it bordered on the American-dominated, Western bloc. On October 22, 1956, students of the Budapest Technical University issued their famous 16 point declaration, calling for, among other things, the withdrawal of Soviet troops from Hungary, freedom of the press, and free elections. This unleashed a spate of acts of resistance that lasted about two weeks. Hoping to counteract the rebellious sentiments, the Communist Party choose Imre Nagy as a member of the Central Board on October 24, and Nagy soon became the leader of the revolution. Adding to the confusion of these days was the uncertainty about which elements of the military and political system supported the rebellion, and which ones opposed it. At the time of Nagy's appointment, for instance, members of the state security forces were shooting at a demonstration, and the next day guns were fired at a crowd that had gathered to listen to a speech by Imre Nagy. As the rebellion gained momentum, Nagy called for a cease-fire and urged the Soviets to withdraw their troops from Budapest. By that time, the Hungarian army had joined the side of the uprising and most of the police and military institutions had stopped resisting it. Moscow refused to give in to Nagy's demands, and on October 28, Nagy decided to take Hungary out of the Warsaw Pact, the Soviet counterpart of NATO. In the beginning of November, the Russian troops started to crush the rebellion. The fight lasted for days, and the bullet holes that can still be seen today in some parts of the cities testify to its ferocity. NATO did not react. It allowed the Soviet troops to take control, and a new Communist Party, led by János Kádár, replaced its predecessor. Part of the city suffered severe damage, and more than 200,000 Hungarians left the country. On June 16, 1958, Imre Nagy and the other leaders of the revolution were shot. The political lesson of this turn of events was that the Iron Curtain could not be challenged. NATO was not going to start another European war, and neither were the Russians. Whenever rivalries between the two

Nagy Imre *art üzente...*

Union of Liberal Democrats. Artist: Ducki 89 Art

blocks caused military conflict, it was elsewhere – in the Middle East, in Vietnam, in Latin America. Paradoxically, the Kádár regime transformed Hungary into the 'most joyous barracks' of the Soviet empire. Clinging to the slogan that people who were not resisting the regime should be treated as supporters of it, political suppression was relatively mild. Economic policy was now geared to the needs of the people. Public housing, for instance, became a major concern, and starting in the second half of the 1960s, massive new housing estates, built with large concrete panels produced in 'housing factories', changed the image of many cities. The standard of living rose, Western tourism was promoted, and something like a socialist version of the Western welfare state came into being. In the 1980s, however, the Hungarian economy shared the fate of all the socialist economies. Stagnation became ubiquitous, but since it was not seen as prudent to lower the standard of living, the state had to borrow huge amounts of money. Facing similar problems in the Soviet Union, Mikhail Gorbachev decided on a fundamental political change, summarized in his policies of perestroika and glasnost. Since the empire could no longer be sustained using the old tactics, central control had to make way for different me chanisms. The people in the occupied countries had to find their own way to socialism, and Gorbachev suggested that he did not want to interfere in their home affairs the way his predecessors used to do. For the reformist politicians in the Hungarian party, this was the sign that change was again a real possibility – a situation reminiscent of the events leading up to the revolution of 1956. Kádár was relieved of his post in 1988. One of the first steps on the road to reform was the re-evaluation of the 1956 uprising. The final outcome of this process was the second funeral in June 1989, which eventually caused the entire Soviet empire to collapse.

Happy

June 16, 1989. The reburial of Imre Nagy and his associates.

Happy

Happy

vals

FESTIVALS

The city has always been a setting for popular festivals. They attract huge crowds who either participate in the show or line the streets watching what is going on. Festivals never continue for more than a couple of hours, a day at most. Sometimes they are organized on a regular basis, for example May Day parades, which tend to recur year after year. Since festivals always require a lot of organization, they never happen spontaneously. Those organized by the state are often testimony to a coercive regime, but even in this case people often find opportunities to enjoy themselves. Festivals are aimed either at society at large – the ones initiated by the state invariably are – or at specific lifestyle groups. Political parades are usually organized as a festival, and the idea of using the city as a catalyst for festivals probably originates in this type of event – political festivities have a tradition that reaches back to antiquity. What they have in common with contemporary dance festivals, gay parades and a growing number of urban sports events is their brief duration, skillful organization, and the often massive crowds they attract. Sometimes the streets and squares of the city are entirely redecorated to accommodate the festivities. Sometimes they are just left untouched, their architecture and urban design being thought sufficient to create the required atmosphere.

Happy

THE CITY AS A SPORTS ARENA: THE URBAN MARATHON

Koos Bosma

No city can afford to ignore the phenomenon of large-scale events like marathons. Better opportunities to promote a city are hard to imagine. Few sport events are better covered by the media. They attract massive crowds of spectators and offer a perfect opportunity to present the city to an international public.

In 1897, Boston organized the first urban marathon, and it immediately became a yearly event. It was only after the Second World War, however, that urban marathons became fashionable in Europe too, although only on a modest scale. It took the 'marathon boom' in the United States in the 1970s to make the urban marathon immensely popular in Europe as well. The prime example was, of course, the New York marathon, which leads its participants through all its five boroughs, uniting the entire community of the metropolis. Some European marathons also succeeded in becoming massive events attracting hundreds of thousands of people.

The marathons of London, Berlin and Rotterdam since 1981, became immensely popular in the following years. The London marathon starts in Greenwich and runs from there via Tower Bridge and the prestigious new projects on the north bank of the Thames to The Mall, the center of the British monarchy. In the 1980s, the motto of the Berlin marathon was 'run against the Wall'. Until the Wall came down, the route was limited to the western half of the city. The marathon of 1990 became legendary: only a couple of days before the official reunification of Germany, it crossed the former political border and covered all of Berlin. Deeply rooted emotions surfaced when the 25,000 participants reached the Brandenburg Gate. Rotterdam's

City marathon in Berlin, 2001

marathon is as famous as those of Boston and New York. Its winners include some of the most famous athletes, and its reputation as one of the fastest urban marathons is enhanced by no less than two world records, in 1984 and 1988. Each year, the organizing committee tries to find a route that is immune to the surprises of the Dutch climate. The most impressive moment is the crossing of Rotterdam's famous Erasmus Bridge.

However attractive the route may be, in the end all marathons are judged by their results. The winner probably couldn't care less whether he finishes at the Mall in London, the Kurfürstendamm in Berlin or the Coolsingel in Rotterdam. Even the municipalities of the organizing cities are more impressed by world records than by the sights of Canary Wharf, Potsdamer Platz or the Erasmus Bridge. The true beauty of the marathon lies in the distance of 42 kilometers and the exhausting battle each of the athletes has to wage. It always takes some time before the competition reaches a decisive phase. Things really become exciting in the last eight kilometers. Thousands of people encourage the athletes, cheering them on the street while the VIP's watch the race on a big video screen suspended above the tribune at the finish line. The first athletes arrive after about two hours, hoping for a new world record, or at least to break their own personal records. Then the winner breaks through the ribbon at the finish, followed by the runners-up and the average participants, those for whom running a marathon has become something of a routine, and finally the majority of athletes who only participate for fun. Those who do not arrive before the set time limits are not mentioned in the list of the final results. But even for them, running a marathon is a gratifying experience, as long as they succeed in reaching the finish line. When the marathon is over, the crowds

start to move, heading home. Dressed in plastic capes, the athletes try to find their way through the crowds, while some of them sit down on the floor, exhausted, helpless. For most of them the show is over, although the professionals are already thinking about the next marathon on the yearly calendar. Which one will it be? Rome? Vienna? Paris?

Happy

A PARADE OF SHEEP IN MADRID

Helma Hellinga

Once a year, the city of Madrid is taken over by the countryside. At the end of October, 2,400 sheep herded by four shepherds and eight dogs enter the Spanish capital, providing the occasion for a famous folk festival. Dance groups and musical bands in traditional costumes accompany the sheep on their way through the city, and traditionally decorated bulls make their appearance. For one day traffic comes to a standstill and the sheep take over.

What are all these sheep doing in the city? This is definitely not the usual kind of street party. The route of the herd through the city is part of a 700 kilometer itinerary that starts in the Picos de Europa, the mountain range in the north where the sheep spend the summer, to the Southwestern Extramadura where they stay during the winter. For centuries, sheep herds have moved from north to south each autumn, as the 'cañadas reales', the trails they left behind in the landscape, demonstrate. During the Franco regime, the tradition stopped because of heavy competition from industrial sheep breeding. In the early 1990s it resumed, but by then many of the old tracks had deteriorated. In areas near cities, they had been asphalted, houses had been built on them, and railway tracks and highways blocked them. The four routes that originally crossed the region of Madrid suffered most.

In 1993 the activist Suso Garzón started a movement dedicated to the reconstruction of the cañada trails. About 124,000 kilometers of them would have to be restored if the traditional ways of farming were to be successful. Headed by Garzón, the Proyecto 2001 made a precise inventory of all the obstacles. Contrary to what one might expect, the motives of the Proyecto are not inspired by romantic conservatism, but by a very modern notion of the equilibrium of ecosystems. It would also have been possible to maintain the traditional meadows in the north and south and transport the sheep by truck. However, since the old trails serve more purposes than just being traffic thoroughfares for sheep, it was decided to restore them. They

Happy

are corridors for wildlife and also were used as pedestrian roads between the villages. Apart from their practical use, they are testimony to a rich cultural heritage: the shepherds' cabins, springs, historical signs marking the trails, poems and songs all recall this old culture. Hikers and mountain bikers have discovered the 'caminos silenciosos', the silent ways, and travel agencies try to sell the 'cañadas' as a typically Spanish version of eco-tourism.

That makes the sheep parade, however festive it may be, above all a sign of protest against the decline of the trails, and a way of urging the municipality of Madrid to restore them. This also explains the ceremony that is part of the parade. Starting in the woods west of the city, the Casa de Campo, it leads to the Calle Mayor, where the alderman for environmental issues meets with the shepherds. Their leader hands him 100 *maravedíes*, which was the amount of money needed in 1418 for permission to cross the city. After a celebration with lots of songs, the parade continues its way via the Puerta del Sol — the geographical center of Spain and the main square for manifestations and demonstrations — the wide Calle de Alcalá, and the Plaza de Cibeles to the Puerta Alcalá, where an ancient pole made of stone marks this old trail. It is the only one left in the city. Since the goal is not really to reinstate this part of the trail, the parade turns around here and goes back to the Casa de Campo, where the yearly event culminates in the Shepherd's Festival (the Fiesta del Pastor), before continuing its way southwards.

Happy

Happy

Monu

nents

MONUMENTS AND THE CITY AS A MONUMENTAL STAGE

Monuments refer to memorable events, mostly heroic or tragic facts in a nation's history. Monuments come in all shapes and sizes, and usually the crowds pass them by without noticing them. Occasionally they are the centerpieces of meetings where the events they celebrate are commemorated. The crowds that gather around them are either representative of the entire nation, or only of specific groups. When they come together, the monument comes to life. For a short time, it makes its presence felt, expressing the virtues of the event it symbolizes, or merely the virtues of commemoration itself. Their varying popularity reflects the political and cultural evolution of society. Sometimes they are removed, and their role in the history of the city comes to an end. When hated regimes collapse, their monuments are often destroyed, but sometimes they are harbored in far-away parks where they enjoy the benefits of political asylum – though only if they pay for their maintenance by attracting enough paying visitors.

Lviv, June 10, 1999.

Arriving at the railway station in Lviv: the platform is full of people waiting for trains, for relatives; passengers are carrying big wicker baskets with fresh produce from their gardens to the market in Lviv. They spill down the stairs onto cobblestone streets, leaving behind the monumental iron construction from the days of the

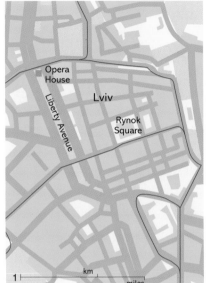

Habsburg era along with the smoky smell of coal-fired loco-motives. On the way to the center, it becomes clear that Lviv is a jewel created by centuries of Western civilization, just outside the new political border that separates the Ukraine from the European Union. The former Jesuit gardens, now Iwan-Franko Park, are full of people: male students from the nearby Iwan-Franko University drinking coke and flirting with well made-up girls in high heels dressed in the latest fashion, retired people playing chess and heatedly discussing the latest political events, and young mothers pushing strollers. Streets, cafés, and restaurants in the center are filled with people; cheap Ladas, taxis, and expensive makes of Western cars create a daily traffic jam. It was here in Lviv that in January 1990 Ukrainians took their fate in their hands, formed a human chain to Kiev, and started the process leading to Ukrainian independence and national development. It was here in Lviv that all those statues of Lenin were completely removed in 1990 and 1991, clearly signalling where its citizens belong. The square in front of the opera house has become the symbol of the city: the opera house functions as the beloved sign of its Western heritage, the empty pedestal where Lenin once stood, as a sign of the hated Soviet past, and the memorial to Shevtchenko as a shrine of Ukrainian identity, with fresh flowers placed there daily, betokening strong hopes and beliefs. **E.H.**

Happy

'Everybody wanted to see the symbol of the ideology disappear.' Construction and Demolition of Lenin's Statue in Lviv.

Bogdan Tscherkes

On July 27, 1944, Lviv was conquered by the Red Army. Until that day, Lviv had been a Western city – the capital of Galicia and Lodomeria until 1918, and a multinational city from time immemorial. On the eve of the Second World War, 345,000 people lived in Lviv.

Liberty Prospect in Lviv (Lenin Prospect in the Soviet era) derives its particular characteristics from the way it was reconstructed in the early twentieth century. The wish to extend the medieval city center and the desire to introduce a 'Ringstrasse', following the example of Vienna, were the guiding principles in creating this 700 meters-long boulevard. (The 'ring', however, was never completed.) As soon as the shops, restaurants, banks and museums settled there, the Poltava River was regulated, a pedestrian zone introduced, and the center moved from the 'Ringplatz' to the new street. This process culminated in the opening of a new opera house, designed by Zigmund Gorgolevskij.

Happy

Liberty Prospect in Lviv, 1910

Operahouse, 1912

The Soviet occupation forces soon designated the Prospect as 'remarkable', and henceforth this was the place where political parades were organized. Especially spectacular was the parade held on November 7, 1947, in commemoration of the Russian Revolution of 1917. The main facade of the opera house was 'embellished' by a larger than life-size portrait of Stalin. Portraits of Vjatscheslav Molotov, Minister of Foreign Affairs, and Kaganovitch, Secretary of the Ukrainian Communist Party, were overshadowed by the face of Stalin. The motto of the entire event was 'The sun of Stalin is rising above Lviv.' The second great leader, Vladimir Lenin, founder of the Communist Party and of the Soviet Union, was represented by a group of players from the local theater. They portrayed Lenin as he proclaimed the Revolution, surrounded by soldiers, working people and farmers. The actors were playing on a truck that drove along the Prospect, followed by a column of demonstrators. In this way the great leader showed himself, albeit only during the parade.

Around the same time, A.V. Nataltschenko and G.L. Schvezko-Vineztkij, both of them sent from the Soviet Union to Lvov, started working on the first reconstruction plan for the city. Focusing their attention on the city center, they proposed the creation of an 'urban compositional axis'. Lenin Prospect was to become its centerpiece, and therefore needed to be lengthened from 700 to 3,000 meters. The opera house remained in the center of the new

Parade of the soviet troops, November 7, 1947.

Happy

composition; in front of it, a statue of Lenin was to be erected, and behind it a 'central square'. The Soviet planners considered the lack of a sufficiently long 'Magistrale' and of a square where parades could be organized to be among Lviv's most important deficiencies in terms of planning. The new square, which was to be created by demolishing the remains of the Jewish ghetto, would be 250 x 160 meters, making it Lviv's biggest square. Not even the historic 'Ringplatz', measuring 142 x 129 meters, could compete with it.

The opera house was integrated into the facades of the new square, the climax of which was to be a new statue of Stalin, erected in front of the new Party headquarters. The statue and the building were situated on a platform above the square. A staircase of about 100 meters in width led to this ensemble; during parades it could be used as a tribune for Party functionaries, the military and high-ranking Soviet leaders.

ЕСКІЗ ЗАБУДОВИ ЦЕНТРАЛЬНОЇ ПЛОЩІ м. ЛЬВОВА

A.V. Nataltschenko, G.L. Schvezko-Vinezkij, general plan for the Lviv, central area, 1948

The statue of Lenin was to play a primary role in the reconstruction of Lviv. The first plans envisaged two statues of him. A birds-eye view by A. Nataltschenko and G. Schvezko-Vinezkij from 1948 shows the first Lenin monument in front of the opera house, in the axis of the

Lenin Prospect, and the second on a hill overlooking the city. It was proposed that a 1,200 meters-long 'Magistrale' be created leading from this second and most important statue of Lenin straight to Lenin Prospect. Standing on the hill, the main statue of Lenin would have towered 190 meters above the Prospect. With its pedestal, this monument would have been at least 50 meters high, and from its strategic position on a hill 138 meters high (furnished with yet another flight of stairs), it would have dominated the entire city. Obviously, this monumental trickery suggested that Lviv, historically oriented towards the West, was now integrated into the Soviet empire. Creating this 'Magistrale', pointed in the direction of Moscow, would have required the destruction of a large part of the historic city.

These megalomaniac projects were soon abandoned, although some elements were built. Sergei Merkurov, Stalin's favorite sculptor, was responsible for the first statue of Lenin, which

Liberty Prospect with newly erected Lenin statue, 1956 Right: S. Merkurov, sculptor, and S. Franzus, V. Sharapenko, architects, Lenin statue

was erected in 1952 in front of the opera house. Since the main monument was to be situated on the hill, the dimensions of Merkurov's work were relatively modest: a bust of about 1,60 meters on a pedestal of a little over 8 meters. Even so, standing in the axis of Lvov's liveliest street, it was a continuous reminder of the new political situation. In the Soviet era, all parades and demonstrations started here; Lenin seemed to be blessing all the people participating in them as they prepared themselves to promote the ideals of Marxism-Leninism. It is not difficult to understand the role of this statue in the lives of the inhabitants of Lviv, if one realizes that at least twice a year, on November 7 and on May 1, when these parades were held, the Party made sure that everybody who could possibly participate in them was actually there. For the leaders of the Party, the military, Soviet politicians, representatives of official institutions, their

Happy

friends and relatives, and all those who believed in the communist ideology, this statue was a symbol of justice, the rightness of their convictions and the eternal values of the Soviet Union. For them, it was more than a monument. It was a symbol of their life, and its meaning was quasi-religious. For the majority of Lviv's inhabitants, however, this monument was a symbol of the Soviet occupation, the massive deportation of the people of Galicia to the concentration camps of the Gulag Archipelago, the expropriation of their possessions, the demolition of religious and national monuments, and forced 'Russification.' After 1985, the reform policies initiated by Gorbachev resulted in a process of growing polarization between the two groups. Pro-communist immigrants wished to hold on to the Soviet Union, whereas local people wanted to do away with it. The Lenin statue became the epicenter of the ensuing clashes.

Then came the year 1990. Hardly anybody could imagine the Soviet Union had less than a year to survive. In July 1991, George Bush Sr. tried to convince the Ukrainian Parliament in Kiev that the wisest thing to do was to remain part of the Soviet Union. The Communist Party, the secret service (KGB) and most of the official institutions were still operating at full capacity, and most people could not imagine that statues of Lenin, the idol of communism, could ever be destroyed. That made the decision taken by the City Soviet of Lviv on September 14, 1990 all the more remarkable: it was decreed that the monument should be removed. That was the revolutionary outcome of one month of fierce debates and continuous demonstrations on Lenin Prospect. Local newspapers were full of articles by protagonists on both sides. The anti-Soviet group took possession of the boulevard, and on September 13 this culminated in massive riots. By that time, the statue had already been attacked and defaced by posters. The authorities had lost control, and on September 14 the crowds in the streets started to bring the statue down. The decision of the City Soviets only sanctioned what was already going on.

The entire episode is documented in a movie made by the Ukrainian Studios for Documentary Productions. A telling fact is that the people who made this film are unknown. Danger and fear still reigned supreme, and the authors did not want their names to appear in the credits at the end. The documentary shows the most important events. Tens of thousands of people gather on the Prospect, pushing each other, some full of expectation, some petrified; some are convinced that things will work out all right, while others are doubtful. Women in tears are waving the forbidden Ukrainian flag. Holding up the portrait of Lenin, students of the political and military academy display similarly intense zeal. Next to this portrait, somebody holds out a poster of a skull that is supposed to symbolize the victims of the Soviet regime. The statue itself is covered with the slogan: 'Lenin out of Lviv!' Posters claiming that 'In Lviv there are people who protect Lenin' are torn to pieces. Then a crane and a truck appear on the scene. Workmen come to the fore intent on bringing Lenin down. Today, they are the heroes who will remove the statue. All attention is focused on them, and it doesn't matter that the place where everything is happening is just a small scaffolding normally used by electricians for repairing electric cables. They act. They are giving a performance against the background of the opera house: they have become the actors. The masses of people are waiting excitedly.

Happy

В.І. ЛЕНІН
ЛЕНІНА
ЗІ ЛЬВОВА!
І ВСІХ
ЛЕНІНЦІВ З
УКРАЇНИ!
ЗА ВАНДАЛІЗМ НАД
СВЯТИНЯМИ,
ЗА СПРИЯННЯ ГОЛОДОМОРУ,
ЗА ЧЕРВОНИЙ ТЕРОР,
ГАНЬ-БА !!!
ИЛЬИЧ!
ВАКХАНАЛИИ
ОРГАНІЗАТОР
ЧЕРВОНОГО
ТЕРОРУ!

Previous page: The Lenin statue in September 1990. This page and page 382: Stills from a film documenting the removal of the statue

Happy

They want a victim. It doesn't matter that this victim is nothing more than a bronze bust. People have been told that this statue represents the leader, and they have feared this image for almost fifty years. Today they will bring him down. Finally, fear has left them. They wrap the statue in cloths and around his neck they attach a steel cable. Old communists start to cry; they bring flowers to their idol. With his removal, a whole era comes to an end. Nobody laughs. The statue starts to move from its pedestal. 100,000 wide-open eyes follow his every movement. An old lady spreads her arms, crying for joy. She has waited for this moment for ages, and now it has finally arrived. In Lviv, Lenin is pushed aside and hoisted up on to the truck. Moved, some people climb on the truck and start to kick at the bust. This night, Lviv will not sleep. Everybody awaits the dawn of the next day. Nothing happens. The statue lies in the storage room of the city's department of economic affairs. He is the leader no longer. Without the masses, the street and the square, he is just a piece of bronze. His empire is breathing its last breaths. He is paralyzed.

It didn't take long before the pedestal was removed as well. During Christmastime, a Christmas tree took its place. The next summer, somebody started a bicycle rental service for children at this spot. Today, photographers hang around, waiting for clients to have their picture taken in front of the opera house. The workmen who brought down the statue of Lenin have played their historic role, the most important of their lives. Traveling between Moscow, Warsaw, Berlin and Lisbon looking for jobs, they remember this eventful day. It does not often happen that happiness comes to the man in the street.

Happy

Gori, August 8, 2000.

An opinion poll conducted in the spring of 2000 left no room for doubt: the vast majority of the Georgian people still sees Stalin as one of their greatest countrymen and one of the leading politicians of the twentieth century. Taking this into account, the sight of Gori, Stalin's birthplace, is striking. Almost sixty years have

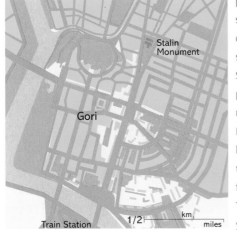

passed since Gori was transformed into a pilgrimage site. The town planning projects and the architectural decisions supporting it still dominate the urban landscape. They changed the city and made the house where Stalin was born the center of it. All axes and all visual perspectives lead to it. Even so, time has left its mark on most of the buildings, streets, boulevards and parks. It is not that they are neglected: everything is immaculately clean. But life has left the glorious 'Magistrale' that leads the visitors directly, and in a straight line, from the railway station to the holiest of all places. There is hardly any shop left that did not close its doors years ago. Urban life returned to the spots it evacuated sixty years ago. There, alongside centuries-old commercial routes, shops abound, makeshift stables occupy the streets, children play while cars and wooden carts try to make their way. Stalin? Sure, he was Gori's great son, everybody agrees. Nowadays, however, the people of Gori cannot make a living out of Stalin any more. The two cities unite: the glorious memorial site, and an ordinary town in the Caucasus.   J.D.

Happy

Gori: the Forgotten Mecca

Jörn Düwel

Obscurity had overtaken Gori long before the great reconstruction scheme that was supposed to transform the city into a communist Mecca had been completed. The ambitious project did not fail because of a lack of building materials, the usual reason for building projects to run into difficulties in the socialist plan economies, but because the political context had changed. Originally designed to make the city where Stalin was born a destination for socialist pilgrimages, the project became meaningless after the demise of the socialist regime. The new government stopped the project and Gori disappeared from public consciousness in most of the new republics that once formed the socialist empire. When the glorification of Stalin reached its climax, train loads of construction workers and delegations of various organizations from all over the Soviet Union visited this Georgian city to bow their heads in respect at the place where Stalin was born. In the 1950s, after Stalin's death. the political propaganda machinery ignored Gori, thus putting an end to the campaign to promote the formerly unknown and unimportant city at the foot of the Caucasus. This, however, could not prevent Gori's fame from lingering on. The city had acquired an aura that still attracted many admirers of Stalin. In the years between the start and the premature end of the project, Gori witnessed major changes. Even today the city is dominated by the impact of the project, and monuments to Stalin still decorate many of the city's squares. The movement that erased most of the socialist statues and memorial sites in the former Soviet Union did not reach Gori.

Most readers will wonder where to find the city of Gori. They probably have never even heard its name mentioned before. Is it really possible that now, at the beginning of the 21st century, there still is a city that is entirely dedicated to Stalin, who is generally considered to be one of the worst criminals in the history of mankind? Is there still a place where he is worshipped? In the beginning of 2001, the Georgian communists claimed that Stalin was 'one of the most able politicians of the twentieth century,' a statement that was followed by a plea for his rehabilitation. What made them pursue this course, they said, was President Putin's decision to restore the old Soviet hymn as the Russian national anthem. In Georgia, and particularly in

Happy

Gori, people are proud of the city's most important son. As in the old days, schools, companies, streets and squares bear his name, and the city's museum is dedicated exclusively to Stalin's good deeds.

In the same year in which Stalin and Hitler secretly made their diabolical treaty to divide up Eastern Europe, the leader of the Soviet empire also ordered his architect to reconstruct Gori. His intention was to transform his birthplace into a secular Bethlehem. In order to realize this ambition and transform the city into a socialist symbol not only for Georgia, but for the entire Soviet Union and even beyond, Stalin, inevitably, ordered its complete reconstruction. Under his direct leadership, the first plans were drawn up within a few months. Already in 1939 the plans began to be realized, but in 1941 war brought work to a halt. Immediately after the victory over Germany, work was begun again, still on the basis of the original plans from the 1930s. German prisoners of war were brought to Gori and forced to help rebuild the city. Just after the war, when the Soviet Union had beaten Germany in the Great Patriotic War, as it was called in Russia, Stalin's power was at its zenith, and the propaganda machinery painted a picture of the wise war lord and outstanding statesman who so well embodied communist ideals. Stalin now had the aura of a universal father, who, in a way, had already become immortal. That is why everything possible was done to transform Gori into an impressive pilgrimage site.

The reconstruction plan was centered on the small cabin where Stalin was born and lived with his parents and a shoemaker couple. Located in a poor neighborhood far from the historical quarters, it was not much more than a shed, and the houses surrounding it were of a similar kind: one story cottages consisting of a single room for living quarters and a separate storage room, with virtually no public space left open between the houses. This neglected neighborhood of the socially deprived now became the new center of the city. The area

Happy

around Stalin's house was cleared of all the adjacent buildings, and a temple was built over the original house, which now assumed the appearance of a precious shrine within a sanctuary.

Behind the temple, a museum was built to honor Stalin. Temple and museum together mark the end of a monumental axis that is designed as a 'Magistrale' and leads straight to the railway station, where trains full of visitors start their solemn walk to the shrine. In order to create this 60-meter-wide boulevard, a densely built up area had to be cleared. The small houses were replaced by multistory buildings with tenements, but also by restaurants and hotels designed to welcome the worshipping crowds. The Magistrale was planned as a pedestrian zone, and it is interspersed with a number of squares that form a rhythmic sequence of alternating urban spaces. Walking along the promenade, one experiences what appear to be differences in speed. Even though a considerable part of the project was realized before the middle of the 1950s, the dreamed of 'Gesamtkunstwerk' remained a torso. The most important elements were realized: the axis, the temple and the museum, as well as the buildings lining the Magistrale. The untouched parts of the old city were scheduled to undergo the same ambitious upgrading, but Stalin's star had faded before this could happen. In 1956, Krushtchev put an end to the personal cult of Stalin, but it proved impossible to remove Stalin's Krushtchev statues from Gori's townscape or to free the museum of his dominant presence.

Travelers who want to visit Gori have to take the train or rent a car and start from Tiflis, Georgia's capital. It takes about four hours to arrive at Stalin's birthplace. Whether one opts for the train or the car, one should be prepared for a tough journey; for there is no money to maintain or repair the deteriorated infrastructure. It had already been neglected during the last years of the Soviet empire, and the civil war that raged in parts of Georgia in the 1990s made things even worse. The relatively short distance takes, therefore, a disproportionately long time. Shortly after leaving Tiflis, one sees huge railway facilities. Where once freight trains arrived to bring their goods, there are now endless rows of abandoned cars and locomotives, that haven't moved for ages. The war in Abchasia takes its toll, paralyzing the economy and the transport system. The transit route that used to be very busy is now a dead end street. With great difficulty the train with its wooden seats enters the part of Gori's station that is used for regional travel. The great hall of the station was clearly built in the period of the reconstruction project. The first statue of Stalin that confronts the visitor is located underneath a canopy on the main facade of the waiting room with its decorative colonnade. Inevitably, this confrontation arouses feelings of alienation: the Georgian people apparently accept this scenery as something natural, something which is hard for foreigners to imagine. Half a century later, they are still living with these images, these representations of Stalin, whose name is present everywhere in Gori. This may explain why they are neither shocked nor afraid of his ubiquitous presence. For most people in Gori, Stalin has always been there. They have grown up with him, and he has become part of their everyday life.

Whereas in the cities of Western Europe statues are continuously vandalized, the people of Gori clearly respect the monuments to Stalin. Though the statue at the railway station shows signs of being several decades old, it is obviously taken care of. Those who are in the station waiting for their trains do not seem to notice the statue, and they are surprised if a tourist from abroad starts to take pictures of it.

Right behind the station, which is located in the outskirts of the city, the foothills of the Caucasus Mountains start to rise. On the opposite side, in the direction of the center, the view

appears to be blocked. It is easy to find one's way, however, since the obvious route to take climbs to a square near a bridge. This is the beginning of the Magistrale that leads to the temple and museum. On the other side of the bridge, a triangular square opens up and the character of the Magistrale as a 'via triumphalis' becomes clear. Even today the city's architecture and planning give a sophisticated and artful impression: the railway station is situated on the other side of a river, which has to be crossed before the Magistrale is reached. After climbing to the bridge, the visitor sees the goal of the visit straight ahead. If he looks backwards, he sees the mountains in the distance, a symbol of infinity. In a metaphorical way, this view signifies eternity. The route to the temple has been luxuriously designed. The facades along the Magistrale are richly decorated. The frivolity of the ornamentation, which was partly derived

Happy

from local traditions, reminds one of a spa town. Walking along the Magistrale, one also notes that it is only a fragment of what was originally planned; for there is nothing behind these blocks. Their isolation gives one the impression of coming upon a Potemkin-like decor. Looking down the alleys separating the blocks, one can see small houses that would appear more appropriate in a village.

Late in the morning on a summer's day, the heat causes the dusty street to be almost empty. Abandoned shops and closed windows lead to the inevitable conclusion that the situation will remain the same in the afternoon. Only Stalin Square is more lively. Here, a huge granite statue of Stalin stands in front of the town hall. It is always the same pose: upright, his right

leg and left arm slightly forwards, dressed in a smooth uniform with the jacket half open – the image of the unwavering war lord.

The statue's base can also be used as a tribune. Towering above everyone sitting there is Stalin, the personification of an idea transformed into material power. If the tribune is being used as a platform for demonstrations, Stalin is always present. Remarkably, the statue is framed with fir-trees even though in Georgia, they are not indigenous. The next stretch of the Magistrale is slightly wider and then culminates in the square that is the goal of the pilgrimage. Even when blinded by the strong summer sun, the outlines of the temple and the museum are easily recognizable. The Magistrale, long since transformed into a traffic thoroughfare with sidewalks, here becomes a public square containing a small park with the temple and museum on the far side. Here, too, fir-trees have been planted. In the center of the symmetrical square there is a pond with several small fountains. The greenery and the small, seemingly lost bridge over the pond – which appears to be in urgent need of repair – give an impression of unimpeded vitality. There is no sign of military rigidity, even though Stalin's celebrated birthplace is nearby. What a colorful scene it must have been when large crowds of visitors paraded the boulevard! While he was still alive, Stalin wanted to create a symbol of his benevolence and wisdom,

Happy

and therefore the layout is free of any suggestion of either aggression or fear.

The temple that was erected above the original cottage enhances this effect. Far from being an impressive, awe-inspiring copy of antiquity, it is designed as a sophisticated architectural treasure. Looking at the temple more closely, one cannot fail to see that its ornamentation is, once again, derived from local traditions. In fact, what one sees is not really a temple, and the columns are not real columns but rather support beams crowned with freely designed capitals. A remarkable detail is the large square skylight above the cottage. Its corners have been decorated with the same hammer and sickle that were also incorporated in the Soviet flag. Its center, however, has been designed in plain colored panels around a Soviet star, and when the sun shines through this glass an almost supernatural radiance fills the hall. Usually the cottage itself is closed, and then the only way to look inside is through the windows. What one sees is the way poor people furnish their homes – a handmade bed, two chairs, a table, a fireplace, and some relics of Stalin's parents.

Behind the temple, the Stalin museum arises, as does a wall that closes the Magistrale. The seemingly Moorish architecture of the two story building contrasts with the temple. The museum's entrance has been placed outside its central axis, beside the tower. The spatial layout is generous. Behind the luxurious foyer lies a wide double staircase, which obliges visitors to advance at a dignified rhythm. Even though there were no big crowds in the museum during my repeated visits in August 2000, there was a constant coming and going of visitors. Near the entrance they are welcomed by a guide who leads them through the entire museum.

The festivities for the centennial of Stalin's birth in 1979 were the occasion for the last changes in the museum's exhibition layout. Since then, everything has remained the same: the phases of Stalin's life are presented in chronological order, and one cannot fail to notice that not much material is shown relating to his youth and adolescence. Numerous objects underscore the poverty and deprivation of these years, however. By far the largest part of the exhibition is dedicated to Stalin's revolutionary activities and his subsequent development as an unwavering, steadfast communist. One is given the impression that the history of the Soviet Union coincides with Stalin's personal evolution. Documents that re-interpret this view in the light of post-socialist history are nowhere to be found. It is as if the exhibition is entirely based on the ideals of the Georgian communist party, which obviously thinks it owes its role model eternal respect.

The central hall is remarkable for its almost ghostlike atmosphere. The walls are black, and the room is only dimly lit. In the center stands a circle of marble columns, some of the them only knee high. The floor within this circle, which has a red covering, is slightly depressed, and there we find another marble column that carries a coffin with, on top of it, the bronze death mask of Stalin. The depressed floor and the ring of marble columns surrounding it prevent visitors for coming too close. The final expression on Stalin's face, therefore, remains unseen. Here, in this semi-religious space, the cult of Stalin, the sacredness that forms an aura around his name, reaches its zenith.

The temple and museum still attract people to Gori today, even though the demystification of Stalin that started very soon after his death prevented the city from becoming the radiant

Happy

symbol of soviet communism that he once dreamed of. And they keep coming – the people who see in Stalin an example to be followed. Even the ritual of newlyweds having their pictures taken in front of the temple still persists, in spite of how thoroughly the political and cultural context has changed.

Has Gori become the victim of the town planning ideal that endowed it with a Magistrale from railway station to the temple and museum? Life has left the Magistrale, and what remains is an empty void. Business activity has shifted back to its old location, in the busy, narrow King Street underneath the centuries-old castle on the hill, where the Georgian rulers once resided. Had Stalin been able to pursue his plans, this street, which has regained its former role as the main axis, would have been remodeled a long time ago. The ideal of a 'Gesamtkunstwerk' failed, because the rulers in Moscow were no longer interested in it. What remains are promises of happiness from a distant past, which have left their imprint on the city's architecture and planning.

Memorial
sites

Koos Bosma

In the urban happiness factory, desires manifest themselves suddenly and then disappear
again. There is a paradoxical ring to this longing of people for favorite places in the city, or
episodes from the past – as long as people feel it, they experience a sense of loss, but as soon
as a dreams comes true, desires evaporate.

In the vicinity of city X in the Ukraine, I witnessed how an entire historical era was
stored away in a secret religious depository, which preserves a collection of about 2,500
wooden and stone sculptures, icons dating back to the sixteenth century, along with about a
thousand paintings. A long time ago, when the socialists' anti-religious campaigns reached
their climax, this shadow collection was secretly assembled by a museum director. Risking his
life, he crossed the entire Ukraine in a freight truck, trying to rescue as many works of art as
he could. One might suppose that, given the religious renaissance of the last decade, someone
would have considered the possibility of returning these works to their original homes. But
the displaced items, mediators of religious feelings, cannot possibly be restored to the sites
where they were once contemplated, for they have acquired an artistic dimension that represents
a considerable monetary value on the Western European art markets. Bringing them back
home without adequate security measures in place would increase the risk of their being
stolen by the globalized mafia. Times may have changed – more than 5,000 new churches
have been built in the Ukraine since the collapse of socialism, most of them according to the
archaic typologies – but now, this collection must remain underground. Perhaps someday it
will be transferred to a museum, but these wonderful works of art will never go back to
where they belong.

In Lithuania I was initiated into the intricacies of cultural identities. This happened in
the town of Y, where I visited two colleagues. Years ago, they were part of a living chain of
people connecting the capital cities of the Baltic states, a ribbon of people meandering from
Vilnius via Riga to Tallinn. When Vilnius was liberated in a battle where people actually died,
they had occupied the front lines. Now they were honored by my visit to them – a sign of
respect for their work. These passionate and conscientious researchers took me with them to
their apartment in a neighborhood consisting of high-rise apartment buildings constructed
with large, industrially produced panels: a Spartan place on the ninth floor with only two
rooms, a kitchen and a bathroom. The sanitary equipment did not work, and the building

Happy

showed signs of leaks. After a heavy shower, not only was the wooden statue of Christ that was hanging on one of the walls crying; the walls themselves also appeared overwhelmed by emotion. This effect could only be studied on one wall, since all the others were buried behind research material; the room functioned as an archive, a library and a studio all in one. Hardly any place was left for eating, drinking and sleeping. The rest of the room was filled to the ceiling with piles of boxes and rolls of drawings, alternating with preserving jars and some inherited ceramic pots. A huge bookcase occupied half of the hallway, stuffed with books and files. The kitchen had been transformed into a working room, and only a tiny part of the kitchen sink could still be used for cooking and washing dishes. The second room was completely full as well. There were three chairs that could not be moved, a table buried under piles of papers, and a small table next to the couple's bed. The flood of research material was the result of more than fifteen years of work and constituted a treasury of documents concerning the disappearing rural culture of Smaller Lithuania, the region bordering on the Russian enclave of Kaliningrad. One box contains 60,000 note cards and almost as many photographs of historical objects: decorated wooden sheds, graveyards and funeral decoration. A collection of topographical maps shows how the successive Nazi and communist regimes rampaged through this region, bulldozering away an entire culture.

Wooden house, Smaller Lithuania, Memelland

Wooden house, Smaller Lithuania, Kaliningrad region

Happy

Do Memorial Sites Make People Happy?

Niels Gutschow

Good memories, bad memories Sometime during the summer of 2000, German scholars discovered that memorial sites recalling bad experiences had lost their public function, whereas those reminiscent of good experiences had become rare. This was thought to reflect the public attitude in a country feeling guilty for having started two world wars, a country that, as the German philosopher Karl Heinz Bohrer stated in June 2001, was robbed of its long-term memory and thrown into a peculiar state of amnesia. How different from the situation in Eastern Europe! There, both the distant past and the memory of recent years are present in people's consciousness. Bohrer suggests that this type of historical relationship, or historical construction, stimulates cultural coherence. Historical memory, he thinks, promotes a type of identity that emerges only within a specific cultural setting and that fosters feelings of self-assurance.

In the autumn of 2001 an avalanche of reports announced plans for memorial sites that were meant to commemorate recent experience and suffering. They refer to terrible events and were not meant to forge new identities; they are hardly likely to promote feelings of solidarity that could be experienced as being happy. Within a week after the terrorist attack on the World Trade Center, the official 'nomenklatura' court artist Surab Zereteli from Moscow presented President Bush and Mayor Giuliani with a plan for a monument that would symbolize victory over terrorists. Less than two weeks later, rescue workers removed a seven-story-high fragment of one of the towers from the rubble with the intention that it serve as the centerpiece of the future monument.

Kaunas After 1989, societies in Eastern Europe expressed a strong desire to rediscover cultural identities that had been lost during the Soviet era. Though the socialist system did acknowledge the existence of 'nationalities,' it ignored their precarious history and the often uneasy historical relationships between the nations in their empire. Since their liberation,

Happy

numerous monuments in both Poland and Lithuania recall events in recent and distant history, giving them a direct link to the present. The inauguration of new memorial sites and the demolition of monuments that were associated with socialist rule created an atmosphere of happiness – the dignity of the nation appeared to be restored.

Usually monuments require an urban setting. They occupy specific places, the symbolic context of which is often known only to insiders. Both Poland and Lithuania were independent states from 1918 until 1939. In the latter year German and Russian troops invaded and started a conscious policy of destroying places and monuments that promoted feelings of national pride. Building the new socialist state presupposed the construction of a communist identity. The struggle for a national civilization is best illustrated by the history of monuments in the

Statue of Freedom

Lithuanian city of Kaunas. Already in 1921, a statue commemorating the casualties in the war for independence was inaugurated in the garden of the museum that is dedicated to Vytautas the Great. The stones covering the small pyramid were collected on the battlefields of 1918. In 1928 a Freedom Statue was built. In 1949, the Soviet regime ordered the demolition of these monuments, and the destruction of all memorial sites in Kaunas. The inhabitants were very embittered when the memorial dedicated to the casualties of the war of independence was replaced by a statue for Feliks Dzierzynski, the Vilna-born, Polish president of the much feared Russian Tscheka, the Special Committee for the struggle against counter-revolutionary movements and sabotage. A more terrible reversal could hardly be imagined. Remarkably,

Happy

the original statue was kept intact and temporarily stored in a Russian Orthodox church that had miraculously survived the war and had been transformed into a museum.

In 1984 the Russians erected a monument at the entrance of the city, dedicated to the victims of fascism. This monument was part of a program that endowed many cities throughout the Soviet Union with similar monuments in memory of the Great National War (1941-1945). Creating sites that were meant to promote feelings of socialist solidarity, the superpower on the wane apparently tried once more to legitimate itself.

In the 1980s, signs of dissatisfaction and even of quiet resistance became increasingly manifest in the Baltic States, as well as in other parts of the Soviet empire. In 1988, the national architectural office in Kaunas started work on a design for the reconstruction of the monuments in front of the War Museum, where, as in many other cities, a statue of Lenin had been placed in 1972 to commemorate the 100th birthday of the founder of modern communism. Private funding provided the means to create a new Statue of Freedom, which was inaugurated on February 6, 1989, the anniversary of the declaration of independence in 1918.

Monument to Vitautas the Great

Six months later, tens of thousands of people from the Baltic States formed a living chain connecting Vilnius to Talinn, in a dramatic gesture against the heritage of the Molotov-Ribbentrop Treaty of 1939. On March 11, 1990, the Lithuanian parliament proclaimed independence.

In the years before 1991, not only were busts of eight national heroes resurrected and placed next to the Statue of Freedom; the restored group was also completed with references to forgotten heroes. Finally, the names of all those who in the era of tsarist occupation smuggled Lithuanian literature into the country are now chiseled in granite. The pyramid was reconstructed and again covered in original stones from the battlefields.

Another spectacular reconstruction took place in the heart of the old city, on the Boulevard of Freedom (Laisves aleja). In 1932 a statue had been erected for the legendary Vytautas the Great, who laid the foundation for the great Lithuanian empire that, in the fifteenth century, stretched from the Baltic to the Black Sea. It was inaugurated on the occasion of the 500th anniversary of the day he died, and is located in the outskirts of the city near the officers' barracks. Allegedly, Soviet tanks were obliged to make quite an effort to destroy it in 1951.

In created the conditions that allowed numerous private societies to organize a competition for its reconstruction, at a time when the Soviet army was still occupying the barracks. Many alternative locations were proposed and offered to public scrutiny before the decision was made to erect the new monument, designed by Jurgis Bucas, next to the Palace of the Communist Party on the Boulevard of Freedom. It was meant to 'remind people of the years of independence and the barbarian years immediately following it, when the national monuments were destroyed and the past of the nation deliberately violated' (Bucas, 2001).

A huge rock was collected in Tannenberg and served as the foundation stone for the memorial site, which was to be inaugurated on the 580th anniversary of the Battle of Tannenberg (1410), when Vytautas and his Polish-Lithuanian army proved victorious over the troops of the Order of the Teutonic Knights. The festivities were marked by a parade of the 'Vytautas Regiment,' which consisted of men who were born in 1930. An oratorio, composed in 1930 to honor Vytautas, formed the musical setting for the event.

In the following years, ever more memorial sites have been erected, and still more are being planned. We should mention the ones erected in honor of two more heroes of the nation, the pilots Darius and Gireno; these had been conceived already in 1939 but could only be realized in 1994. Striking, too, is the seemingly endless concrete slab in the park surrounding the Vytautas Statue. It is the monument for Romas Kalantas, who, in protest against the communist regime, set fire to himself in 1972. The flowers that are brought there every day make it clear just how much this event has become part of the collective memory of the Lithuanian people, and, therefore, part of their new identity.

Warsaw The first memorial site for the country's freedom fighters was erected in October 1945 in Praga, on the eastern bank of the Vistula River. It anticipated the creation of a socialist society. In the winter of 1944-1945, the Red Army had its camp here, postponing the liberation until the uprising in the city had been crushed by the Nazis. As in Berlin, Vienna, Auschwitz, Ulan Bator, and many other cities, the monument hailed the victorious troops as heroes.

The second monument was built in 1946 at the gates of the former ghetto. It was dedicated to the 'heroic struggle for the dignity and freedom of the Jewish people.' A little later, an inscription at the public square from which the Jews had been deported recalled the 'victims of the National Socialist genocide.' On April 19, 1948, a prominent memorial site was inaugurated in honor of the 'heroes of the ghetto.' Amidst the urban wasteland created by the German's systematic destruction of the entire ghetto, it stood out as a reminder of a dramatic tragedy. It was here that Willy Brandt went down on his knees in commemoration of the victims, confessing the guilt of the German nation. Many inhabitants of Warsaw believed that Brandt did this in the wrong place, since in Poland raison d'état still forbade acknowledgement of the uprising of 1944.

Happy

Monument to Darius and Gireno

Happy

Another monument from this period is the statue of Copernicus that was erected in 1948 in the heart of the city to honor of the man who was of paramount importance in shaping the Polish 'national civilization.' His importance was indisputable, and it is no coincidence that when Roman Polanski, the famous film director who had left Warsaw in 1962, made a cinematographic journey to the painful past of the city where he was born – his mother was murdered in Auschwitz – he had two squadrons of the Wehrmacht march in front of this statue. Nowhere else in the entire city could the history of Polish culture be experienced so intensely. Another indisputably famous national hero was King Sigismund III (1582-1632), King of Poland and, for a time, also of Sweden. In his honor, a column had been erected in 1644, designed by Constantino Tencalla. Destroyed by the Germans in January 1945, it was rebuilt in 1948 as part of the first reconstruction plans. As a symbol of national continuity, it had figured prominently on the posters that called on Poles to volunteer for the army and fight alongside the Russians to conquer Berlin: 'Warszawa Wolna. Na Berlin!'

Monument for the victims of Soviet aggression in 1939

Three years later, the creation of a statue of Dzierzynski heralded the rule of the Soviets, just as it had done in Kaunas. This monument, which presented him as a hero of the Polish labor movement, symbolized the power of the political police, who had succeeded in suppressing all opposition. The demolition of this monument during the first free elections, in September 1989, was seen as the final victory over a hated regime, and cheerfully celebrated as such.

Only in 1964 did it become possible to install a monument on the square in front of the restored opera house. In the figure of Nike, the powerful Warsaw Nike, it honored the 'heroes of the city.' Who these heroes were was a question that was deliberately left open. As far as the recent past was concerned, the answer depended on which side one was on: the London-based government in exile and the national army, or the communist committee that was created in Lublin in 1944 with the support of the Red Army. A few days after the first papal visit to Warsaw in 1979, a statue was inaugurated on which was inscribed, in large numbers, the year '1939,' in commemoration of the barricades that had been erected in September of that year to fend off the German attack. In a way, this was the least problematic common denominator of nation and city, since at that time the nation was not yet divided between two mutually exclusive political ideologies. Two years later a committee was formed to create a monument for the 'heroes of the Warsaw uprising.' Until then, a wall of silence had hidden this revolt, since to commemorate it would implicitly praise the 'wrong' heroes. In December 1981, however, a state of war was declared and it became impossible to continue the project. The political crisis returned the heroes of the revolt to their state of political adversaries of the system. It was not until August 1989 that the memorial could finally be inaugurated. But even afterwards the meaning of the uprising in the collective memory of the Polish people remained unclear, as was demonstrated by the vehement conflicts accompanying the 50th anniversary of the uprising in 1994. In the 63 days the uprising lasted, 180,000 inhabitants were killed and the Polish capital totally destroyed. After the war, this traumatic event had become one of the constituents of Polish national consciousness. The uprising is bound to stir up controversies even now, since the question whether it should be seen as 'necessary and unavoidable' or as the superfluous byproduct of amateur politics has still not been settled. Monuments, clearly, tend to avoid this type of controversy, emphasizing honor and 'honorable death.' As a result, they demonstrate the problematic aspects of Europe's commemoration cult.

Monument for the heroes of the Warsaw revolt

Happy

Since April 1988 a different type of monument recalls the genocide of the Polish Jews: a memorial route leads from the former ghetto to the square from which the Jews were transported to the concentration camps. Only after the collapse of the Soviet empire did it become possible to create monuments that called attention to hitherto suppressed memories of suffering. In April 1993 the entire 'nation', as the inscription reads, honored 'the casualties, those who were killed in the East, the victims of Soviet aggression in 1939,' with a new monument. For the first time, the aggressor in the East could be called by its name, and finally the victims of the Russian labor camps could be commemorated. And it is only a short while ago that the Polish officers who were killed by the Russians in Katyn finally received their monument. Another monument honors Stefan Starzysnki (1993), the city president who was murdered in 1943, and in 1995 the monument of Marshall Pilsudkis, who was seen as a freedom fighter after 1918, was restored to its old place in Victory Square.

There seems to be no end to the urge to furnish Warsaw with more monuments. When the national army and King Jan II Sobieski got their memorial sites in 1999, the Polish magazine *Architektura* felt the need to warn against an 'invasion of monuments.' Similar criticism is heard in Berlin, where some people fear that the city is threatened by 'a flood of monuments.' It led the journalist Wolf Jobst to speak of a 'presumptuousness of the penitents'.

The twentieth century seems to have outdone itself with regard to monuments. Nevertheless, occasions for the erection of memorial sites still abound. In 2001, the massacre in Jedwabne on July 10, 1944, for instance, was commemorated with rough granite blocks that mark the site of the barns where the Jews were burned by their own neighbors. President Kwasniewski apologized there in the name of the entire nation.

Ever more monuments In Germany, too, the creation of ever more monuments and memorial plaques has become almost a daily routine. A monument to Van der Lubbe, the Dutch communist who allegedly set fire to the Reichstag, however, was stolen by those who opposed it. At the airport in Frankfurt a plaque commemorating those who were expelled from the country was unveiled on May 26, 2000. It was removed the very same day, as had been agreed upon with the authorities beforehand. But the story continues. In May 2001 the German Social Democratic Party suggested that at the railway station in Frankfurt a monument be erected for the first generation of foreign workers, who began coming in the late 1950s, and who have been followed by others in ever increasing numbers since then.

Projects of a completely different nature abound as well. Consider for instance the 'Harburg Warning Sign against Fascism, War and Violence – for Peace and Human Rights,' conceived by Jochen Gerz and Esther Shalev-Gerz: a steel column over 12 meters high and clad in lead. It was intended to sink into the earth, carrying along with it the names etched in it. In the course of the deliberations on the new Holocaust memorial Berlin, the suggestion was made to treat the Brandenburg Gate as a sign of penitence; according to this view, it should be demolished and ground to dust.

Happy

No more monuments! On my journeys to Warsaw, Kaunas and Vilnius, my encounter with so many monuments was not completely a matter of my own free will. What I mean is that, in these cities, a gap appeared between me and my hosts as soon as we discussed monuments. My hosts were looking for historical continuities and points of reference. The re-creation of destroyed monuments was stimulated by reactions against the political circumstances that caused their removal in the first place. Now history has reversed course, appearing to proceed in tandem with the integration of these countries into a new, unified Europe. I was surprised by the sheer quantity of new monuments in Warsaw, but I was also deeply moved, because they were testimony to the need for a three-dimensional expression of historical memory and the wish to integrate them into specific places in the urban landscape. Of course, the new Holocaust monument in Berlin had been discussed for over a decade. I was so captivated by this project that I even submitted a plan myself: I wanted to fence off the entire terrain by a glass wall in which the names of the concentration camps would be engraved as the coordinates of a terrible past. The terrain itself I left as it was. In the future, I felt, someone in the next generation would be certain to find a convincing way to commemorate the perpetrators and victims.

I try to avoid monuments because I see them as signs of frozen emotion, thoughts that are not thought any more, fragile memories. Monuments dedicated to the Second World War, for example, which tell about heroism and honor — I consider them to be the secret glorification of violent conflicts. The creation and demolition of monuments demonstrate how short-lived are the ideas that pertain to specific political systems. I remain skeptical about national commemorations, whether decreed or spontaneous.

Paris, August 31, 1997.

The second night after the tragic accident of Lady Di and Dodi Al Fayed, I decide to take a look. At the crossing of Place de l'Alma, on top of the tunnel where it happened, thousands of people are hanging around, though it is already around midnight. Hardly any tears are shed. People are loitering. Nobody knows where

to look. Inaccessible to pedestrians, the tunnel underneath the square is filled with the noise of cars racing by, as if nothing had happened. Bending over the entrance, I count the thick concrete columns, trying to locate the exact spot of the crash. The newspapers mentioned that Lady Di's car ran into the thirteenth. On it, I see black stripes, but they are on the other columns as well. There are no skid marks. The grassy slopes that line the road towards the tunnel are buried under masses of flowers, bouquets, letters, photos, and messages. In a godforsaken corner of the square, above the tunnel, a kitschy statue representing a gilded flame has been erected, a recently made copy of the torch carried by the Statue of Liberty in New York. The flowers and messages surrounding it make it clear that the crowds gathered here have immediately adopted it as the memorial site for Lady Di. P.U.

LADY DI'S DEAD END TALE

Pieter Uyttenhove

Once there was an accident... (This sounds like the beginning of a fairy tale, but it is one without a happy ending. It's an urban fairy tale, moreover, and probably the most urban one anyone can imagine.) A young, unhappy woman dies in a car crash just when she is enjoying a new love affair. What a sad story. It would not have been half as sad had it not been for this new, amorous happiness that came to an end so sadly. There is no justification for it. A simple story, almost banal, as is so often the case in fairy tales. Only those banal stories, however, that are exemplary, become fairy tales. When she was still alive, the British princess Lady Diana Spencer, the young woman of our story, was already almost a goddess. If she wished to heighten the contrast with her grayish, dull prince, she could hardly have done better than to start a love affair with Dodi Al Fayed, an extremely rich Egyptian businessman.

The tragic accident that terminated Lady Di's life could only have happened in Paris. Paris is the second protagonist of this fairy tale. Paris is not only the place of the story, it is also an actor in the plot. Hidden behind the mask of the brilliant, illuminated stage setting for tourism, the true Paris is hard to grasp. It lies in the shadow of a glorious past, with one part of the city inspired by fiction, myth and legend, and the other by hard reality, complexity and uncertainty. Lady Di's fairy tale oscillates between fiction and reality. For this type of pendulum movement, Paris offers prefect scenes and scenarios.

The eighteenth century, the Age of Enlightenment, wanted to provide happiness. The city, it was hoped, would become an ideal, transparent place to live in. But one century later this dream was transformed into a spectacle of steam, electricity and technology. The enlightened city became a collage of wealth, boulevards, monuments, the great masses crowding the streets, and entertainment. This parallel city, which masks the smoke of factories, stations and the misery of the poor neighborhoods, produces pure fiction: a schizophrenic process that places members of the well-to-do middle class along with industrial tycoons, princes, kings and dandies in a dream world with artificial lighting, mirrors, and an abundance of luxury goods. Lady Di spent the last hours of her life at the Ritz, Paris' most luxurious hotel (and one owned by her lover's father). Located on the Place Vendôme, one of the most prestigious squares in the City of Light, it is home to the largest jewelers and banks. Her last ride, in a

Happy

Happy

405

black Mercedes, led through the most expensive parts of Paris: the Rue de Rivoli, the Tuileries, the Place de la Concorde, and the parks lining the Champs Élysées. Illuminated boats glide along on the nearby Seine under colorful bridges, close to floodlit monuments.

The other Paris is characterized by the social underclasses, poverty, neurotic behavior and phobias, all of them side effects of an industrial society. This inescapable reality needs to be kept from public view and is therefore almost completely suppressed: death, dropouts, unskilled workers, the transportation of all that is necessary to keep the city alive, in short, the technology and labor behind the fiction of Paris. At the beginning of the twentieth century, cadavers were piled on top of each other in quarries under the surface of the city, which became known as the 'catacombs.' Sewer systems, a vast infrastructure of pipes for water, electricity and the pneumatic post, subway tunnels and, later, tunnels for streets and highways, likewise disappear into the earth. Haussmann's 'urban block,' on the contrary, embodies the childlike happiness of enclosed spaces, the same theme that dominates some of Jules Verne's novels on space ships, submarines, mysterious islands and floating cities. Paris is a merger of all of this. It's a huge, maternal body that either incorporates, transforms or discards every-thing. The driver of the car at the time of the crash, who strikes one as a character from the world of Victor Hugo, is drunk. Place de l'Alma is a complicated intersection with five lanes, a veritable 'chaos mouvant' to quote Baudelaire's description of Paris's busy boulevards, and underneath it, in the stomach of the sweet and divine Alma Mater, there is a tunnel. There, in the darkness of the catacombs and the quarries, in the tunnel with its heavy traffic, in a slight curve to the right, the Mercedes hits the thirteenth concrete pillar, one in a long row that sep-arates this lane from the one leading in the opposite direction. This tunnel leading towards death is like the gate of the inferno where Dante, upon entering hell, read the words: 'Eternal love has also shaped me.' Closed to pedestrians – what would Paris be without the 'flaneurs?' – and open only to motor vehicle traffic, the tunnel is one of those unique creations that represent modernism.

The nineteenth century invented the duality of structure and skin, the anatomy of the skeleton and the organs, of grammar and meaning. The structure is transparent but subordinated to the skin. Unnoticed, iron construction and steel skeletons have shaped the metro tunnels, cupolas and glass facades of Haussmann's Paris. Where the structure is trans-parent, the skin is opaque and closed: it separates the inside from the outside and frames the boulevards with the monuments and symbols of the nation. The process of industrialization, Haussmannization, the Belle Époque – all of them always refer only to themselves. Paris is a closed city. It is also a city that dresses up, a clothed structure. After the World's Fair of 1889, voices could be heard arguing that the Eiffel tower was too light, rational and transparent and had to be clothed as well. In those years, France made a gift to America: the Statue of Liberty – 'la Liberté éclairant le monde' ('Liberty illuminating the world'). It is the work of the sculp-tor Bartholdi, but what keeps it upright is a steel construction made by Gustave Eiffel. It was inaugurated in the harbor of New York, a city built on an open grid that contrasts with the closed urban tissue of Paris. In New York, nature provides the vanishing point of all streets, as Sartre noticed long ago. Gilles Deleuze recognized the merits of escape: 'Escape does not mean that one does not act. On the contrary: nothing is more active than escaping. It is the opposite of imagination. It includes the act of making things escape. Not so much other people, but rather things. Making things flee and dissolve, as if drilling in an open pipeline.' Drilling in a pipeline... In a hectic attempt to escape, Lady Di is evading her persecutors. She is on the run, trying not to fall victim to the tabloid paparazzi. Is it possible to escape in a closed network? She is immersed in the city. The entrance of the lethal tunnel is next to the Place de la Reine Astrid, named for the Belgian queen who died in the deadly embrace of a car wreck before the war, just like Lady Di. The lawn near the entrance fills with thousands of her mourning fans.

On top of the tunnel, there is an incredibly kitschy monument: an enormous, gilded flame on a black marble pedestal. It is a copy of the torch held by the Statue of Liberty. For the hundreds of visitors who flock here looking for a symbol, it serves as a focus for their hard-hit feelings, and it has become a tourist attraction, the goal of a continuous pilgrimage. Clad in newspaper articles and attractive photos of Lady Di, it is buried under declarations of love, along with verbal abuse directed against the alleged perpetrators of Lady Di's death. The walls nearby now carry the sentimental 'displacement' of sorrow, like Jim Morrison's grave at Père Lachaise cemetery. 'To see the location of the accident, go to the other end of the tunnel,' a message in graffiti reads. What do we find there? Only another symbolic site. 'Go to Althorp (UK) Diana is there, not here!', another hastily written message states. The Parisian 'flame of freedom' has become a mystical place, where there is nothing to be seen: no drama, no sensational sight, no official sign, only memories and a kind of Hollywood-like, overly sentimental sculpture that concentrates Paris's fiction machinery in one striking gesture. Diana, in the meantime, has become the object of a veritable cult, a goddess, the 'queen of heaven.'

Beach

Cities

A CITY OF BODIES: BEACH CITIES

The spread of radio, television, telephone, the internet and e-mail have made urban culture dominant all over the world, even where there are no cities. In a way, urban culture has become independent of the physical structure of the city, even though electronic means of communication will never replace its physical qualities. Intermingling with one's fellow citizen and enjoying one's body (and possibly the body of others) are just two of the activities that can only be experienced by actually engaging in them. They are recreational activities and part of everyday life, and therefore part of the program every city offers. They are also a favorite pastime during holidays, and no place offers better opportunities to enjoy them than holiday beach resorts. Huge crowds populate them each year, some stay overnight, losing themselves in the discos and restaurants, others go home. Continuing a century-old tradition, those who can afford it buy small bungalows; in some coastal regions the sea is separated from the land by a fringe of bungalows, restaurants and camping sites. They are instant cities, some of them hundreds of kilometers long. In summer they are crowded, if the weather is hot, and the crowds are incredibly dense. In winter, some of these cites are completely abandoned. Beach cities celebrate freedom, and the escape from the moral strangleholds of everyday urban life. The spread of beach cities since the 1950s has been fueled by increasing numbers of people who can afford a holiday abroad, one of the blessings of the new society.

Benidorm, July 26, 2001.

No, I have never been in Benidorm. It's just that on this date I saw a film, *Barrio*, in which Benidorm appeared to be an unattainable goal for a lot of people in Spain, whereas we usually see it as an ordinary place where 'everybody' goes. In *Barrio* we see Benidorm only on a television set in an apartment in one of

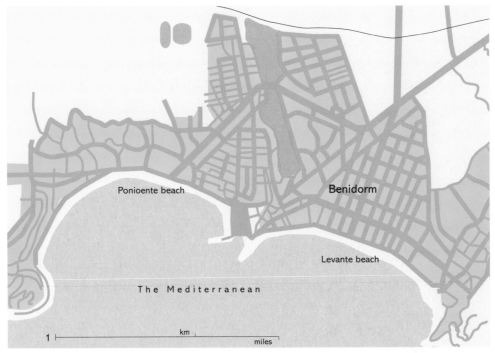

Ponioente beach

Benidorm

Levante beach

The Mediterranean

km
1 |—————————————————————————|
miles

Madrid's poorer neigborhoods. It makes you sweat, for you know it is August; it's terribly hot and the people in the story have no money to go to the coast. In an attempt to escape the neighborhood, a boy enters a competition, a kind of publicity stunt, and he wins ... a great big water scooter. But who will take him with his prize to the sea? The water scooter has to stay in Madrid, too, tied to a lamppost like a bike. H.H.

Happy

Benidorm, Europe's pleasure city in Viva España

Helma Hellinga

If there is one city that represents happiness as an ephemeral phenomenon for the masses, it is Benidorm. Vacation is celebrated there: the sun, the sea, the beach during daytime and, at night, the dancing, the booze, the romancing. These are the principal ingredients for going wild in an atmosphere eloquently expressed in several Dutch songs: 'Una Paloma Blanca,' 'Vino, Vino!' and 'Viva España!' Music with a familiar ring to it, two or three Spanish words incorporated into Europe's mass culture. As an Englishman (and the English are by far the largest group), a German or a Dutchman, you definitely find yourself in a foreign country, but so many things are so well known that there isn't anything strange or scary about it. You want sun, you need to party, but things shouldn't be too exotic. In Benidorm, you're a tourist among tourists. There are always your fellow countrymen around. With them you can laugh — they understand. You join them hunting for kicks in the bars and the discothèques. You're more daring here than you would be at home. Your daily troubles are far away and the group offers you safety. You can beat the whole world. Tiresome husbands get drunk and start to dance on the table, cheered on by the group. The most exotic thing that can happen to you here is to have a love affair with a Spanish guy or girl, provided he or she is in the mood for partying and not looking for a steady relationship. Very important, of course, is the menu in the restaurants: if you want, you can eat the same dishes you are used to at home. There are hundreds of simple fish and chip restaurants, and even the food in the Spanish restaurants has been adopted to suit the visitor's taste. And everything is cheap. Benidorm is, as you may have guessed, a holiday paradise for the masses, and not only for young people but for the elderly as well.

Benidorm has been Europe's largest tourist city for the last 25 years, if the number of visitors and overnight stays is taken as the main criterion. It is also the most popular destination for Spanish tourists, especially for people from Madrid. The city has grown spectacularly

Happy

Happy

since the rise of international mass tourism in the 1960s. More than 82,000 people live there permanently nowadays, as opposed to a mere 6,000 in 1960. Naturally, the number of tourists who stay in hotels and apartments is disproportionately large: about 325,000 each year, compared to a mere 9,000 in 1960. Seen from the sea, the city looks like a metropolis, such as Chicago or New York, mainly because skyscrapers dominate the skyline. Even so, it is smaller than it looks, the zone of high-rise buildings being relatively narrow and limited to the northern side of the city's older sections. The surrounding landscape can be seen from practically anywhere in the center. What makes Benidorm fundamentally different from every other major city is that it is completely focused on tourism. There are hardly any office buildings, industry is nowhere to be found, and the theaters and concert buildings that are so essential for a 'real' city are notoriously lacking. Benidorm's character is determined by its monoculture of bars, restaurants, and discos. The high-rise apartment buildings are almost exclusively occupied by hotels, most of which are empty during the winter season.

What are all these people looking for when they rent a small apartment with a tiny balcony in one of these hotels? The answer is simple: nothing at all. In Benidorm, tourists spend less time in their apartments than in any other Spanish holiday resort. The apartment is only a halfway between the beach and the city, between sun bathing during the daytime and enjoying themselves in the bars at night. A shower, a bed, a balcony for drinking a beer – that is all they need. Refreshed, they leave their tiny cubicles and go to the boulevard. That is where the evening starts, a perfect place to meet people, and if there is nobody to socialize with, there is always more than enough to see. Everybody is parading through the streets because everybody else does. Architecture and esthetics have no meaning here; the buildings lining the boulevard are successful because of their simplicity, which makes people feel at home. The same applies to the restaurants, bars and discos. Benidorm isn't really a city, but rather a conglomerate of facilities and public spaces that together create an atmosphere where people find what they are expecting: the perfect holiday feeling of ephemeral happiness.

La Grande Motte, August 21-22, 2001.

I've a lunch appointment at 12 o'clock with Jean Balladur, architect of the remarkable new holiday town of La Grande Motte. I arrived the previous day, rented a bike and explored the city. We meet at a restaurant in the marina. Mr. Balladur orders fish, a

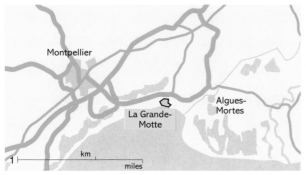

bottle of wine, desert, and coffee. After lunch we have a long conversation, walking along the beach, the lanes, the squares and parks. Every now and then we stop, allowing me to record fragments of our conversation on video. The interview lasts for three and half hours. He never stops smoking his pipe, and talks incessantly: his views as a young architect, his philosophical training, the incredibly fascinating challenge of designing this new town, the obstacles he met while working on it, the criticism it met, and the success of the project. This is 'his' town. He owns a condominium here, knows the dignitaries on the local board, and feels at home. Every corner, every building has its story. Here, architecture is adventure, message, a social project. I have the impression that all the vacationers are happy; there is a sense of freedom, a mixture of archaic habits and the discovery of new horizons. Behind me, I can hear tunes coming from the organ of an old merry-go-round.   P.U.

Happy

La Grande Motte, Venus's Hill

Pieter Uyttenhove

La Grande Motte is a holiday town that was created out of thin air. The decision to create it, the planning process and the actual construction were all part of a single, sweeping gesture. Nowadays, this would be highly exceptional, especially if it is the state that is sponsoring the project. In their longing for visionary, modern plans, French President, General De Gaulle, and his prime minister, Georges Pompidou, designated the coastal region of Languedoc-Roussillon as the place to accommodate the rising tide of mass tourism that crowned the booming economy of the 'Trente Glorieuses.' In those days, politics demanded the 'effect du prince,' a large degree of political sovereignty, a striking social gesture, and a good familiarity with the technocratic ways of planning and realizing this type of project. All these aspects came into play in the development plan for Languedoc-Roussillon.

Heroism   The first phase of this project for the physical reconstruction of the coast dates back to 1962. Between that year and 1964 the administration came up with the general outlines of the plan. Under the direct auspices of Pompidou, several ministries jointly issued the assignments for the construction of seaside resorts. The architect Georges Candilis was asked to expand Leucate Barcarès, and Raymond Gleize and Édouard Hartane received a similar commission for Guisman; Pierre Lafitte and Herni Castelle were made responsible for the estuary of the Aude, Jean Lecouteur for the spit of land called Cap-d'Agde, and Jean Baladur for La Grande Motte.

If there is one thing every architect dreams about, it is the construction of an entire city. Not merely daydreams that are destined to remain paper projects, for which he needs only the mental space of his own imagination, but a real city in a real situation. From Egyptian antiquity onwards, only a select group of especially blessed people were allowed to work on such unique projects: royal palaces, necropolises for deceased pharaohs, colonial cities, fortified towns, new towns … All these are highly exceptional projects for completely new settlements, each specific to a certain civilization, reflecting its particular culture, economy and political system. There is something heroic about such projects, something sublime. They represent something that exceeds everyday life, that appears to escape mortality.

For Jean Balladur, who was only 38 years old when he received this assignment, building La Grande Motte became his primary task in the following years. But where did he have to build his dream city? Could it be done on this narrow band of inhospitable dunes between the sea and the land? Where strong winds blew incessantly, carrying away the land in large clouds of sand and dust? His task was to transform this wasteland into a place where people could be happy. Is it possible to build a city on sand? Jean Balladur grasped the opportunity with both hands. He spent endless hours staring at the piece of land from the crest of the dunes that frame the beach, making sketches and trying to come to grips with this terrain, a task that was

Happy

to demand the utmost of his architectural skills. The beating of the sea, the howling of the wind, the unlimited expanse of the barren land – these were the things he had to cope with. But life isn't a rational thing, Albert Camus had taught him, and neither is the city.

There are moments in the life of an architect when he absorbs the site, reads the landscape, internalizes the atmosphere, does the 'work' he is destined to do and builds his dreams, projecting them onto the site, testing the results, modifying his vision. During these special moments, he prepares to become something of a god, the creator of earthly life and happiness. Maybe that is the real 'work' of an architect. Poised at the crossroads of a social and functional program, of the peculiarities of the site and the technical difficulties that are inherent in turning a project into reality, he distils his *oeuvre* out of this complex knot, and this oeuvre then justifies his own unique place in the universe.

Heroism becomes manifest in the actions of an obsessed man working to coordinate a giant's tasks, encompassing digging the harbor with giant draglines and building dikes and breakwaters with enormous rocks that were transported from the Cévennes and then dumped into the sea, as well as the distribution of endless miles of infrastructure: sewage systems, electricity cables, pipes for drinking water, and roads. All this was provided by the state, and the state also forested the area, got rid of the flies, and generally did whatever was necessary to make the region fit for its new role. The actual construction of the city started in 1966. In 1967, De Gaulle visited the site, crowded with construction workers from France, Portugal, and Algeria. The first high-rise apartment buildings in the eastern part of La Grande Motte were completed in 1968.

Ethics La Grande Motte is a typical product of its time. The emergence of the leisure society was foreseen in French scientific circles, which believed that it was based on a solid theoretical foundation. In their theoretical exercises, sociologists and economists like Joffre Dumazedier and Georges Friendman sketched the emergence of a welfare society characterized by ever more time for leisure, the increasing impact of automation in industry, in the public realm and in everyday life, and the growing importance of everything related to culture, religion, family life, and sports. It was believed that car, train and airplane traffic would increase exponentially. The future was painted in euphoric terms, populated with happy people who could boast of possessing all kinds of utilitarian, decorative and luxurious objects and material things. State policy was geared towards the realization of this image.

The modern welfare state called for new concepts of mass society, ones that would enable the planners to direct and mold it. Since the masses comprised everybody, they coincided with democracy itself. Most prominent in this view, however, were working men and the lower middle classes. In France, this led to a paradox. By stimulating the emergence of an American-inspired consumer society, the masses became a self-perpetuating phenomenon that had to be respected by the state's imperious politics. Conservative principles combined with a policy of state intervention. The 'Datar' (Direction pour l'aménagement du territoire et l'action régionale), for instance, itself a product of this particular context, developed into one of the

Happy

major agents of the government's initiatives on a national scale. La Grande Motte together with the accompanying reconstruction of the Languedoc-Roussillon region was one of the results.

The '3 x 8' principle, which was concocted by sociologists and economists, defined a 'time budget' that divided the day into three equal parts that coincided with three different ways of spending one's time: eight hours of work, eight hours of sleep, and eight hours of leisure time to spend with one's family, including rest, recreation, travel and culture. This division into three temporal segments did not presuppose that people divided their time into three monolithic blocks, but it did enable the planners to calculate the consumption of time on the basis of statistics, and to use these calculations as the framework to program time, the nature and number of amenities that should be provided, and the use of space.

The top-down character of the entire operation means that the construction of La Grande Motte should be seen in an economic context. The intention was to emulate the example of the Italian, Spanish and Greek coasts. Seen in a regional setting, this meant that the new beach resort was to be the heart of an 'unité touristique' along the new highway from Palavas-les-Flots to Grau-du-Roi and Port Camarque. Alternating the urbanized sections with the natural beauty of the untouched and inaccessible parts was one of the project's explicit aims. In a broader context, the goal was to stop the masses of tourists from hurrying to the Spanish coasts that were rapidly being developed at the time. Therefore, the French projects had to be endowed with all kinds of amenities and businesses, along with harbors where the rich could moor their yachts. Even more importantly, the area had to be cleared of flies!

This policy called for a carefully balanced relation between costs and quality. The new beach resort should not exceed one hundred beds per hectare, nor a maximum of six hundred vacationers per hectare of beach along a fifty-meter-wide strip. This meant that the total capacity was to be fixed at about 43,000 beds, even though the actual number of guests is much higher during the high season. There are four areas with specific categories of residences: high-rise apartment buildings, individual houses, hotels, and camping sites and holiday villages.

These four areas determine the ground plan of La Grande Motte, which itself makes explicit reference to nature and the organic. La Grande Motte du Couchant ('of the sunset') occupies the western part. Demarcated by Lake Ponant, La Grande Motte du Levant ('of the rising sun') is located in the east. Separating both areas is the harbor in the center. To the south lies the vast expanse of the Mediterranean, and the Étang de l'Or marks the northwestern border. The way automobile use is regulated suggests that the architect, even though he had to reach a compromise with this noisy and space consuming machine, succeeded in finding an acceptable modus vivendi that makes the car look almost natural. Integrated into a green band, a comfortable 'parkway' at about 600 meters from the beach acts as the backbone of the project. This road separates the areas with apartment buildings from the residential neighborhoods with individual houses and the camping sites. Alongside the road there are various parking lots with plentiful parking places allowing motorists to reach the beach on foot in less than ten minutes. The main boulevard is intersected with secondary roads leading directly to

Happy

the beach and to the residential areas. Access to these neighborhoods is facilitated by streets in the form of loops, the axes of which are continuously shifted to prevent speeding. They connect a series of small squares separating small groups of individual houses that appear to hide between the trees, as if they are floating in a sea of greenery.

Eroticism In these endless wet plains against the backdrop of hills and mountains, a city composed of buildings in the shape of pyramids and shells provided a striking silhouette, a dialogue of curves and straight lines: La Grande Motte presents an environment one literally feels with one's senses. This sensation can also be felt in the city, where it is stimulated by architecture. One of the secondary meanings of the French 'motte' (elevation) is mount of Venus. The naked, untouched virginity of the wide beach contrasts with the natural setting of the inhabited parts behind it with their pines bent by the winds. La Grande Motte is set in a location molded by the winds, and its contours extend and strengthen the lines of the rural horizon. Point Zéro, which was constructed in the eastern part, functions as a shelter on the beach, including, as it does, some cabins, a café, and shower. Symbolically, it marks a start, the origin of the entire operation, the nucleus of an atomic blast, a new beginning. The ground plan is in the shape of a fish.

For Jean Balladur, who before immersing himself in architecture was a student of Sartre, town planning is all about the human scale. Roads, greenery and buildings should have the right size relative to the human body, just like the rungs of a ladder, a chair or a table. This view implies the need to create a humanist dimension, but also a physical, sensual dimension. Manmade, humanist environments call for an architecture that establishes a harmonious relationship between the human community and the sea, the wind and the sun. Balladur's intention was to give people an opportunity to experience their dreams, their loves and hatreds, by confronting them with the beauty and serenity of the natural setting he created. For him a place is real only if it is like a personality, if it has its 'own name,' unlike other things which are identified only in general terms.

Working within the technocratic and commercial framework of the overall project, the architect managed to exploit the sensual qualities of the site to the full. No abstract urban concepts like soulless 'green belts', but rather inspired nature that plays with the prevailing winds in the Languedoc: the Tramontana from the northwest brings the sand that forms the dunes; the Marin or Grec, saturated with salt from the sea; and the Grégau – called the Mistral in the Provence – that cleans the skies with cold winds from the mountains. Balladur learned from a book written in 1770 by a land surveyor named Ginet that it is impossible to stop the wind, but that by 'combing' it one can reduce its speed and allow the whipped up dust to settle down in the lee. The architect uses the city itself for this purpose: to the east of the harbor, he built apartment buildings in the shape of pyramids. They comb the wind. The pyramids are set on a plinth two-stories high containing shops and cafés that open on to the streets. Nature shapes a world of colors and sensual experiences, and, in the end, the earthly paradise resembles not a palace but a garden. Pines, parasol trees, plane trees, herbs and

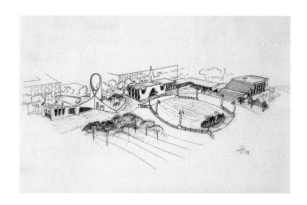

bushes of rosemary, tamarisk, laurel and lavender form a green texture with shady promenades, sitting areas, little squares and streets lined with shade trees where one can stroll in a leisurely fashion for hours surrounded by sweet perfumes and untouched by the wind. The garden precedes the city. Here Balladur was inspired *Les promenades de Paris*, a late nineteenth century masterpiece by Alphand, Haussmann's garden architect. At about the time Balladur built La Grande Motte, the first 'villes nouvelles' near Paris and the 'grands ensembles' in the urban outskirts made their appearance. The contrast between it and these horrible voids, where the human scale is lost and everything is deadly boring, could hardly be more striking.

The white pyramids contrast with the blue skies. Their playfully shaped facades include rounded parts that stick out like big noses – modeled, according to the architect, after De Gaulle's nose – or voluptuous breasts. The sharp angles of conformist international architecture are banished. Circles and parabolas, ellipses and diagonals dominate La Grande Motte. In the western part, the buildings are called 'conques the Vénus,' large shells that appear to have been stranded in the sand after delivering the most beautiful, Venus-like women from the sea. The waves of rising and falling buildings recall human bodies, lying prone in the sand. The shell buildings embrace exquisite courtyards and look out over the sea. In the part of La Grande Motte that was named for the setting sun – sometimes referred to as bishop's cap – the architecture evokes the female body, while the angular lines of the pyramids appear more masculine. Near the harbor is the Great Pyramid that symbiotically combines both shapes and is the city's landmark. The building's silhouette mirrors the Pic Saint-Loup that dominates the horizon in the far distance.

La Grande Motte is a clearly defined urban structure charged with organic, metaphorical, erotic and anthropomorphic references. Strolling along the pedestrian bridges, each shaped in its own evocative way, one encounters names like Lampodofores, Abysses, Monsters, and Snails. The columns in the conference center have human shapes, and the beach gallery in the western part appears to emulate anatomical structures. The Square of the First of October is dominated by a large fountain, the town hall, the church of Saint Augustine and the cultural center. The pavement is in the shape of a maze. The old church bell, which dates from 1603 and is a gift, bears the inscription 'My sound calls the people.' There is also a Pond of the Moon and a Wall of Meditation.

Although designed as a beach resort for mass tourism, La Grande Motte also invokes all kinds of intimacy in the endless gardens around the buildings, in the playgrounds and the parks, on the beach and on an old merry-go-round somewhere along the boulevard. Underneath the pines in the woods near the camping sites, groups of boys and girls enjoy their freedom. The masses of people in themselves also display a kind of erotic charm. In the busy shopping street of the Couchant, the half naked bodies of hundreds of vacationers swarm in a sensuous movement around the ice cream venders and the kiosks that sell meats and fruits, T-shirts, sun hats and beach balls. They crowd the café terraces with their colorful parasols. The well-known atmosphere of places crowded with tourists finds its proper setting in a civilized and open urban atmosphere.

Esoteric The chain of lagoons 180 kilometers long in which La Grande Motte is situated is very young. Its topography is less than one thousand years old. It has two nature preserves: the Petite Camargue in the east and the zone from Maguelone to Frontignan in the west. Its geography is relatively young and at the same time extremely old. The sea dominates everything, and here nature looks fragile and desolate. The architect's task was to enhance these qualities and give shape to the human imagination that is triggered by this strange topography. La Grande Motte has a certain esoteric dimension. Interfering in nature – if God alone has the power to decide over the essence of creation, man can at least change the way it looks – the architect allows mankind to regain the position it lost when it was expelled from Paradise. Balladur believes that the architect, working in the shadow of God, should arrive at a synthesis of everyone's aims and opinions. The architect knows things other people do not know and when this insight can be used to create unknown forms, the architecture is endowed with an extra dimension that only a few people understand. The pyramids of La Grande Motte, for instance, were not inspired by Henri Sauvage's terrace-shaped constructions, but by those of Teotihuacan in Mexico, which were built on a wet plain surrounded by dead volcanoes and protected by the sun god Quetzacoatl, the bloodthirsty plumed snake. Along the beaches and in the surroundings of the Great Pyramid are images of animals reminiscent of the figureheads of the Viking ships that once landed on these coasts. Altogether, this creates a world of gods, animals and mysterious creatures.

Balladur's philosophy leads back to the spirituality of the human instinct. Despite his great inventions, and his technology and machinery, which is becoming more powerful every day, man himself does not change. His steps are the same size they used to be, each day he fearfully awaits the mystery of the night, and he is still intoxicated by the perfumes of wild flowers. The solid matter of buildings and plants plays a similar role as the clothes of the invisible man in H.G. Wells's book: making the invisible manifest itself. Architecture is the clothing of an esoteric body. In La Grande Motte, the duality of male yin (upward movement) and female yang (lying down) becomes a physical reality. The evolution and destiny of material objects, the earth, the wind, the plants and living creatures in general, are positioned in a field of tension between good and evil, light and dark, mind and matter.

Happy

Artek, August 5, 2001.

For me, the name Artek, the summer camp Artek, built to provide recreation for 5,000 of the 'best' pioneers (adolescents aspiring to future leadership roles in the state or the Party), evokes images of the Crimea, the Black Sea, Bear Mountain, beaches, cypresses, sunshine and the Soviet Union. Artek was the symbol of

childhood in the USSR. Although I grew up in the USSR, my own childhood, however, had nothing to do with Artek, because I was not one of the 'best'. I saw Artek for the first time on a hot July evening in 1971, when I was 18 and working as part of a construction crew digging trenches for telephone lines in the hard Crimean rock. In the evening we were brought to the stadium in Artek, where a bonfire was burning – very typical of the Soviet times. My friends and I were to meet Leonid Brezhnev or somebody else from his politbureau, but we were late, and they were already playing the national anthem of the USSR. I stood still. Then somebody else moved on, and so did I, and for the first time in my life I understood that you do not have to stand still when the national anthem sounds, even if you are going to meet the Secretary General of the Central Committee of the Communist Party of the Soviet Union. After the collapse of the USSR I was often in Artek. I admired the architecture of young Poljanskii, which seemed to hover above the ground in the midst of cypresses. I even wrote about it, but I could feel decline everywhere. It is not only the architecture and infrastructure of Artek that needs repair. All that expensive Soviet educational and ideological machinery could not be adapted to the new post-communist life. The people who ran the Soviet Artek left or were dismissed, and the new people who came were already products of the new era.

When I was last in Artek, in the summer of 2004, I understood that it had ceased to exist as the fairy tale scene of a happy Soviet childhood. A total reconstruction had begun. The pioneer camps and their airy summer buildings are vanishing and a new complex of closed hotel buildings is being built, totally ignoring the architecture of Soviet Artek. What is left is the sea, Bear Mountain, the cypresses and some old camps which have not yet been torn down, and the memory that you do not have to stand still even if the national anthem is being played. B.T.

Happy

'ARTEK, ARTEK! - JOY OF MY HEART!'

Bogdan Tscherkes

'Artek' as concept Artek is the name of the city of childhood happiness on the shore of the Black Sea on the Crimean peninsula. Approximately 32,000 children, cared for by 2,000 adults, spend their holidays there every year, with up to 5,000 children staying there in summer, at the peak of the holiday season.[1] The city runs along the coastline for 7,5 km and spreads out over an area of 300 hectare.[2] It is without any doubt the world's largest scout camp (or 'pioneers' republic,' in Soviet terms). Until the decline of the Soviet Union in 1991 it was called 'The Lenin All-Union Pioneer Camp "Artek."'[3] Many things were named after Lenin in those days, but in this particular case 'the leader of the world's proletariat' actually did have some distant connection to the idea of creating this 'model children's spa', as Artek used to be called during Soviet times. In 1925 the revolutionary Zinovij Solov'jev, chairman of the Russian Red Cross and Lenin's friend, brought the first children from Moscow to Artek.[4] Solov'jev suffered from tuberculosis and

1 Vladimir Tshuklinov, 'In my poems and songs I live totally in "Artek"', in: *Artekovets*, 15 June 2001, no. 8-9, 6.
(Владимир Чуклинов, «Я весь в моих стихах и песнях об «Артеке», в: Артековец, 15 июня 2001, №8-9, с.6)

2 Olga Pochol'tshuk (ed.), 'Triple Jump into the third millennium. Result of the Century', in: *Artekovets*, 28 December 2000, no. 14, 2.
(Ольга Похольчук (Ред.), Тройной прыжок в третье тысячелетие.Итоги века, в: Артековец, 28 декабря 2000, №14, с.2)

3 Artek, in: A.M. Prochorov (main ed.), *Soviet Encyclopadic Dictionary*, Moscow 1985, 79.
(Артек, в: А.М.Прохоров(Главн.ред.), Советский Энциклопедический Словарь, Москва 1985, с.79)

4 German Tshernyj, Viktor Krjutshkov, Roman Ozerskij, Eduard Alesin, *Artek! Peace! Friendship. Photo album*, Moscow 1985, 4.
(Герман Черный, Виктор Крючков,Роман Озерский, Эдуард Алесин, Артек! Мир! Дружба! Фотоальбом, Москва 1985, с.4)

Happy

Anatoli Trofimovitsh Poljanskij, *Artek*, 1966.

seemed to have tried to cure himself and these children by making use of the therapeutic powers of the Black Sea and the Crimean climate. Legend tells us that the first camp flag was hoisted on June 15, 1925, and so this date is considered to be the founding date of Artek. These mythical first four tents on Bear Mountain are mentioned in almost all books written about Artek, and they can also be admired in a model shown in Artek's museum.

Until 1960 Artek's expansion followed the usual Communist pattern: 'Expropriation of the Expropriators,' i.e. compulsory nationalization of formerly privately owned land, spas and parks, buildings and houses were part of creating Artek. 'Only the best for our children!' – proclaimed a famous Soviet slogan; nobody burdened his conscience by thinking of the legal aspects involved in owning property that actually belonged to somebody else. Suuk-Su is one of the more famous spas that was nationalized for the sake of Artek. Built at the beginning of the 20th century by the millionaire V.I. Berezin on the land of Earl O.M. Solov'jev, it was a favorite summer vacation spot of the intelligentsia of Czarist times. In 1937 this spa was turned over to Artek and became Camp 'Lazurnij'.[5] Even the name 'Artek' had been used before. It was the name of a property that belonged to Princess Potemkin in the 19th century and that, shortly before the Russian revolution of 1917, was bought by the Moscow merchant Ivan Pervushin.[6]

The word 'Artek' itself means quail in the Tartar language, and it was the name of the small stream running there along the edge of the forest. Given the location of modern Artek, between the mountain streams Artek and Putanis, on the shore of an easily accesssible bay, surrounded by

5 Michael Sidorenko, Sergej Erochin, 'Happy Birthday, "Lazurnyj"'!, in: *Artekovets*, 14 March 1997, no. 6, 1. (Михаил Сидоренко, Сергей Ерохин, С Днем рождения, 'Лазурный'!, в: Артековец, 14 марта 1997, №6, с.1)

6 V.S. Sergeev, *The Silhouette of Yalta's Shoreline. Historical-architectural outline*, Kiev-Yalta 1998, 125-128. (В.С.Сергеев,Силуэты Ялтинского побережья. Архитектурно-исторические очерки, Киев-Ялта 1998, с.125-128)

Happy

beautiful subtropical vegetation, it seems strange that no city had developed there previously, all the more so as this location is similar to, if not better than the location of the historical cities Yalta and Gursuf, and Alushta and Partenit on the Crimean southern shore. It seems that this place had to wait for its own very specific city.

The project 'Great Artek' by Ivan Leonidov

The idea of founding a youth camp in Crimea for the purpose of curing children belonged to the revolutionary and physician Zinovji Solov'ev, but the concept of building a city of childhood happiness belongs to the brilliant Russian constructivist Ivan Leonidov, a genius and at the same time a tragic personality.[7]

7 A. P. Gozak, *Ivan Leonidov*, Moscow 2002.

(А.П.Гозак, Иван Леонидов, Москва 2002)

It is interesting that hardly anybody ever refers to Leonidov's concept for Artek. Even Anatolij Poljanskij, the architect who planned and realized the concept of New Artek between 1960-1973, and who is also the author of a very famous book entitled *Artek*, never mentions Leonidov's name.[8]

8 A.T. Poljanskij, *Artek*, Moscow 1966.

(А.Т.Полянский, Артек, Москва 1966)

It can be hardly overlooked, however, that Poljanskij made use of Leonidov's ideas as they are set forth in his projected plan for Artek dating from 1937.[9]

9 I. Leonidov, 'The Project "The Great Artekt"', in: *Architekture of the USSR*, Moscow 1938, no. 10, 61-63.

(И.Леонидов, Проект 'Большого Артека', в: Архитектура СССР, Москва 1938, №10, с.61-63)

When selecting and analyzing the site, Leonidov already predetermined the future structure of modern Artek: 'The territory stretches from the West to the East – from Gursuf to the mountain Aju-Dag (Bear Mountain) and is very diverse in its terrain. The low seashore with beautiful beaches and vegetation reaching down to the water abruptly changes in many places, giving way to steep, rocky precipices. Forbidding cliffs, ravines with mountain streams, three park-like mountain-massifs with subtropical vegetation, the ruins of a Genoese fortress, vineyards and tobacco fields – all this gives the site a special charm and picturesque quality (…) Six functional units should be distributed over the territory of "Great Artek", kept apart from one another.' And this is precisely the scheme that was later carried out in the planning and organizational structure of modern Artek.[10]

10 Ärne Winkelmann, 'Typologie der Ferienzeit. Das Pionierlager Artek auf der Krim', in: *Bauwelt*, 2000, no. 16, 12.

Leonidov took the location's topography as the basis for his zoning plan. There was a coastal belt broken up by ravines, guaranteeing each section the necessary isolation within rather clear natural boundaries. The area near the sea was to serve as a coastal park for the whole camp, with beaches, water sports facilities and a small harbor. Farther up towards the north and bordering the territory of the camp, a highway leads to the main route running from Sevastopol to Simferopol. North of it are located the central buildings for administration and housekeeping.[11] If we compare this layout for Artek, described by Leonidov in 1938, to Anatolij Poljanskij's general

11 I. Leonidov, 'The Project "The Great Artek"', 61.

(И.Леонидов, Проект 'Большого Артека', с.61)

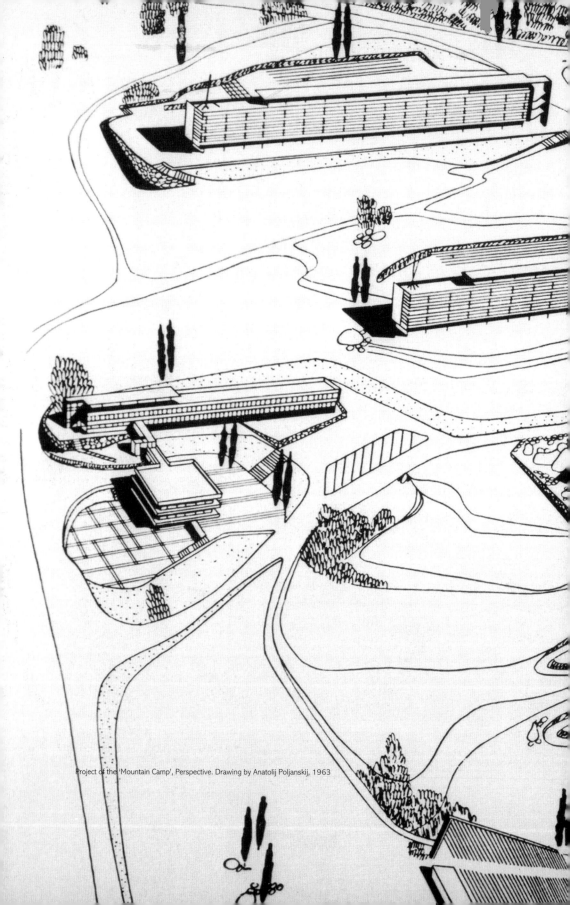

Project of the 'Mountain Camp', Perspective. Drawing by Anatolij Poljanskij, 1963

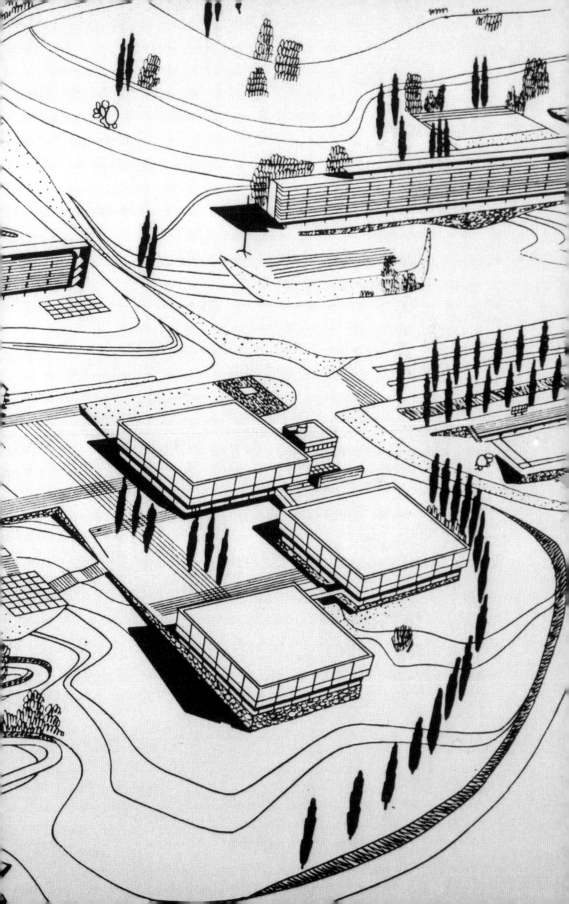

12 A. T. Poljanskij, *Artek*, 9. (А.Т.Полянский, Артек, с.9)

plan for the camp from the year 1961, it is not hard to see that the latter is practically a copy of Leonidov's ideas from 20 years earlier.[12]

Leonidov also determined Artek's organizational structure, including the number and nature of the buildings and the optimal number of children at Artek: 'Each section is planned for 450 children during the summer and 300 children during the winter and each has the same complex of buildings: 1. Sleeping quarters. Each building should house 60-90 children, 5-6 children in each room. 2. Dining hall and kitchen. 3. The House of Pioneers with a school. 4. Infirmary. 5. Beaches with medicinal pavilions. 6. Sports fields. 7. The Square for the Pioneers' roll call. 8. Park with flowerbeds. 9. Domestic area. 10. Administrative buildings and a hostel.'[13] Today, the number of children admitted to Artek is still

13 I. Leonidov, 'The Project "The Great Artek"', 62. (И.Леонидов, Проект 'Большого Артека', с.62)

very close to what Leonidov suggested, namely 500. This is the basis for dividing Artek into individual camps or – as they are also called – into children's towns. Only four of them operate all year round. The functional organization and layout of the buildings of the different sections is also inspired by Leonidov.

Leonidov's ideas that the camp's architecture should be subordinated to the camp's way of life and to the natural surroundings became very important for New Artek when Anatolij Poljanskij and his colleagues built it after 1960. 'The architectural solution has to be subordinate to life in the camp – to the routine of a day in the camp. Assembling for the roll call, raising the flag, eating and drinking, relaxing, swimming in the sea, sports, shows, going to school, working in technical stations, excursions – all this is part of the Artekians' day, developing in them a feeling of collective and individual responsibility and discipline as well as their organizational skills. This strict organization dictated a strict and compact architectural planning scheme for each section. The buildings in the camp are arranged symmetrically, in terraces, as dictated by the terrain. (…) The main facade of the buildings is directed towards the sea, the

Happy

very best solution under Crimean conditions: it is the best way to catch the breeze from the sea, it gives the best view of the sea (…) and makes orientation easy. The bright, light architectural structures surrounded by the beautiful Crimean flora, the small architectural forms – fountains, pavilions, booths, with their transparent lace-like delicacy – will blend harmoniously into the surrounding nature, rocks, blue sky and sea'.[14]

Another Artek dream that originated with Leonidov – who at the time of Artek's construction was a victim of Stalin's persecutions – was the ideal of a synthesis of the arts in the future city of childhood happiness: 'The architecture of sunny "Artek"

14 ibid, 62.

cannot be planned in isolation from the other arts. Within the beautiful Crimean nature it has to serve as a material world, embodying the very best that our happy socialist life can give the younger generation. We must ensure a genuine synthesis of the arts and have to invite the best painters, sculptors and illustrators for this purpose.'[15] It is clear that 'our happy socialist life' for Leonidov himself was anything but happy during the times of Stalin's repression. Leonidov actually never dropped the idea of a 'happy socialist life' to which he dedicated his famous constructivist projects of pre-repression times. Although he was

15 ibid, 63.

Children in the seashore camp 'Morskoj' (Sea-Camp), July 1962

page 434. Children at the beach in July 1984. page435. Pioneers in Artek in 1984

accused of 'Leonidovinism' and excluded from the architectural life of the Stalin era, he continued to develop his ideas in the years after the war by planning several versions of the utopian 'City of the Sun'. His project 'Great Artek' was Leonidov's very first 'City of the Sun'.

'New Artek'

Ivan Leonidov died in oblivion in 1959, a year before the planning and building of 'New Artek' started. Anatolij Trofimovitsh Poljanskij became its main architect and author of the concept of New Artek of the 1960s. This is the story that is told in the museum of Artek and propagated in all books that deal with Soviet architecture of that time. But there

is one more person besides Zinov'jev, Leonidov and Poljanskij without whom the idea of today's Artek could not have been realized. This person is the Soviet leader of that time – Nikita Khrushtchev. It was his idea to make Soviet society more human, to fight the tyranny of Stalinism, to improve life for the simple Soviet citizen and to start building houses in an industrialized way. In Stalin's Moscow 400,000 square meters of living space were built in 1949; by 1964, after ten years of Krushtchev's leadership, 3.8 million square meters of living space were being built in Moscow every year.[16] Krushtchev wrote: 'Because of an unbelievable housing shortage we were forced to take away all superfluous details when looking at the projects in order to satisfy the highest possible number of needy people. (...) People fight for the freedom to improve their lives and to satisfy their needs. They told the party leaders: 'Why do you tell us about a future happy life after death? Give us some earthly happiness today.' We had to hurry to satisfy the basic human needs.'[17]

16 Nikita Sergeevitsh Khrushtshev. *Memories. Selected Fragments.* Moscow 1997, 378, 395.
(Никита Сергеевич Хрущев. Воспоминания. Избранные фрагменты. Москва 1997, с.378,395)

17 ibid, 393-394.

When Krushtchev started actively to promote industrialized mass construction and the use of new technologies and materials in 1954, he did not get much support or understanding from the higher ranks of Soviet architects. They were still totally oriented towards the expensive, academic pomp of the architecture of the Stalin era. Krushtchev recalled: 'The architects were not happy with reinforced concrete. Each prefabricated part limits individualism. (...) At one time almost every house had its architect and something like a personality. The architect regarded a building as a monument of his time. I told them: "You can get houses quick and cheap only in a production line. We have to unify the production of details; this will allow us to produce them on a conveyor belt and manufacture them accurately; and qualified assemblers guarantee a flawless assemblage". An example is the production of cars and tractors. I did not want to have a conflict with the architects, whom I value and honor. We tried to find architectural forms that allow the houses to look differently so that the streets would not become boring. Resourceful architects could always do something'.[18] Anatolij Poljanskij, an ambitious and young architect from Donbass, the city where Krushtchev began his career, was one of these 'resourceful architects.'

18 ibid., 388-389.

Poljanskij could not only realize his creative personality in 'Artek'; he also won a place in the Russian architectural establishment, which was already difficult to join at that time. Indeed, he was very successful, becoming chairman of the Union of Architects of the USSR and winning the Lenin Prize; and until the end of his days he was respected by Party leaders. Poljanskij was indeed a talented and energetic architect, but the overall concept for 'Artek' was something he derived from Leonidov's writings. When working on the general plan of New Artek, planners studied in depth the natural qualities of this territory. The project 'New Artek' as a whole, as well as the plans for each of the six pioneer camps, avoids a dry geometric arrangement; instead, it is a lively composition embedded in the surrounding nature. The first camp, 'Morskoj' (Sea Camp), was opened in July 1961. It had seven dormitories and was

E. Tshepiga, 'The latest history. Year 2001. The Camp
orskoj" (Sea Camp)', in: *Artekovets*, 12 April 2001, no. 3-4, 9.

Чепига, Новейшая история. Год 2001. Лагерь 'Морской',
Артековец, 12 апреля 2001, №3-4, с.9)

designed to accomodate 500 people.[19] Unfortunately, Leonidov was completely forgotten. Not even Krushtchev remembered him. Times had changed. In 1966, when Poljanskij published his book on Artek, Brezhnev was in charge, and two years later Krushtchev became a *persona non grata* about whom it simply became dangerous to say anything good. Poljanskij understood the signs of the new times very well. Romantic dreams belonged to the past. Pragmatism was called for, and the hardliners within the communist leadership reigned supreme. Even so, Artek remained a symbol of Soviet idealists and reformers.

'Morskoj' was built on the same spot where Zinovij Solov'ev had set up the first tents of Artek in 1925, thus providing 'Sea Camp' with historical ties and a certain responsibility for ritual festivities. With its terraces, the camp is beautifully integrated into the uneven terrain. It is Artek's visiting card. The first five airy dormitory cubes of New Artek, made of glass and concrete, seem to float lightly above the beach and the blue sea against the background of the green bulk of the Bear Mountain. Even today, going there is still something that children all over the former Soviet Union dream about doing. Artek is a faraway city of happiness in the Crimea, on the shore of the Black Sea.

The two-story buildings along the sea measure only 10x15 meters, and they vary in height from 6 meters at the side of the magnolia alley to 10 meters at the beach. The buildings rise above the ground on white ferroconcrete support frames. Light constructions, recalling sails, rise up to three meters above the roof of each of the buildings, giving the whole composition the impression of ships sailing away. Each building has 4 sleeping rooms, two on each floor. On the first floor are the rooms for boys, and on the second floor, rooms for girls and the young Pioneer leaders. Each room houses 10-12 children, corresponding to the primary element of the social structure of Artek – the Pioneer brigade. Another element in Artek's social structure is the Pioneer group, which may consist of three to four Pioneer brigades. In other words, each of the 'Sea Camp' buildings are designed for one Pioneer group. The roof terraces of the buildings are connected by open stairwells to the ground level and to the galleries of the buildings. They are used for assemblies and exercises for everyone living there, in other words for one Pioneer group. Each of the buildings has been painted differently, and each of them has its own name: 'Emerald,' 'Red,' 'Blue,' 'Orange,' etc.

Besides the small two-story buildings that were placed rhythmically at the shore, two rather large three-story dormitories with a capacity for up to 150 children each were built in the heart of 'Sea Camp' at a distance of 40 meters from the sea and placed perpendicularly to it. In the center lie Friendship Square, which measures 27 x 27 meters, and the Lenin building, which during Soviet times was used for various exhibitions in his memory and for festive assemblies. From the side of the square, a mosaic can be seen on the Lenin building. The mosaic, created by the artists D.M. Merpert and Ja.N. Sripkov is dedicated to the friendship of the world's youth. It is said that it was exactly here on this square that Solov'jev put up the first tents and lit the first pioneer bonfire, and that is why the square and the mosaic continue

Happy

Pioneers in Artek in June 1954

Happy

to play a symbolic and ritual role in Artek's life right up until today. The mosaic shows the process of lighting the bonfire, an act that was meant to contribute to the happiness of different peoples and different races, who are symbolized here by the three main figures in the mosaic as they simultaneously turn to the sun. The rays of the sun illuminate the new buildings of Artek. The 400-meter-long 'Magnolia Avenue' is the main axis in the layout of 'Sea Camp'. All the dormitories, the dining hall, which is named 'Olive Grove', Friendship Square, and the Bonfire Place with its stands of seats overlook it. These seats also serve as a stadium and assembly place for 'Sea Camp' or, as it is called in Pioneer terminology, for the 'Sea Camp' brigade. 'Magnolia Avenue' starts from the dining hall, which is a special building because of the use of 15 construction elements in the form of mushrooms. Each consists of 4.45 meter-high ferroconcrete poles holding a hexagonal roof measuring 3.71 meters in diameter. Also noteworthy are the bright and dynamic mosaics on the glass barriers entitled 'Games of our planet's children'. They are the work of the artists T.V. Botsharova, I.M. Egorkina, O.S. Kuranskaja and Ju.I. Podogova. In the beginning, the dining hall was open to the air, and the mushroom-like constructions blended well into Artek's landscape. But with the years walls were built along its perimeter to protect the inside against wind and rain, and thus the dining hall lost its dynamic transparency. Besides the buildings already mentioned, 'Sea Camp' also has a reception building and an infirmary. The buildings of the camp lie in the midst of abundant subtropical vegetation consisting of cypresses, olive trees, and magnolias, as well as different flowers and bushes.

'Sea Camp' was New Artek's first camp. Its successful social, architectural, artistic and functional program influenced the development of all the other camps built at New Artek. In addition, it completely fulfilled Krushtchev's dream of using industrialized construction to achieve a new level of quality in architecture. Poljanskij wrote: 'Sea Camp' became the creative laboratory for the development of New Artek.' During its planning, several architectural and construction solutions were tested. Two important constructive elements were defined: one-story rectangular spaces, used for rooms of 40 m² with galleries and stairwells; and spaces determined by three poles with mushroom-like roofs. Each of these architectural-constructive elements consists of six ferroconcrete details: a ferroconcrete half-frame or a full frame of two identical half-frames; a ferroconcrete deck or tile floor; a ferroconcrete T-shaped console support for the flight of stairs; a ferroconcrete flight of stairs with half landings; ferroconcrete round poles with drains inside; and a ferroconcrete triangular element, reminiscent of a flower petal and formed after the assembly of the mushroom-like roofs. All of New Artek's 70 camp buildings consist of these elements.[20] Although all the buildings are constructed from the same components, they differ from each other in the number of floors, in length, in the way they are set into the landscape, in facilities for public services, in color, and in certain stylistic aspects.

A. T. Poljanskij, *Artek*, Moscow 1966, 86-88.

Т.Полянский, Артек, Москва 1966, с. 86-88)

After 'Sea Camp' Camp, 'Priberezhnij (Beach Camp) and Camp 'Gornij' (Mountain Camp) were built following similar principles. 'Beach Camp' occupies 30 hectares and was

21 V. Svistov, 'You are the youngest of all', in: *Artekovets*, 5 October 2001, no. 15, 3.

(В.Свистов, Из всех ты самый молодой, в:Артековец, 5 октября 2001, №15, с.3)

built in the former vineyards of the Stroganoff family.[21] The destroyed grape vines were replaced by approximately 35,000 saplings. 'Beach Camp,' which opened in 1962, is the biggest and the most complex camp of Artek, with a capacity of 2,000 children.

'Beach Camp' is four times bigger than 'Sea Camp' and consists, in fact, of four camps, also called 'Pioneer brigades': 'River,' 'Lake,' 'Field,' and 'Forest.' Each of these camps or 'brigades' has five identical two-story dormitories, 34 meters long and rising up boldly from the surrounding terrain. Each building can house up to 100 children, and each 'brigade' consists of 500 children. The fact hat there are no small, 50 meter buildings in the architectural composition of 'Beach Camp' makes this hyper-camp less rich aesthetically than 'Sea Camp'. The 'Mountain Camp' complex was built between 1966-1967 and is used all year round.[22] It consists of three buildings ('Amber,' 'Crystal,' 'Diamond'), each with a capacity of up to 420 children. In this case the principle is one camp

22 Vladimir Svistov, Olga Pochol'tshuk, 'All started 70 years ago...', in: *Artekovets*, 15 June 2001, no. 8-9, 2,4.

(Владимир Свистов,Ольга Похольчук, 'Все начиналось 70 лет назад...', в:Артековец, 15 июня 2001, №8-9, с. 2,4)

('brigade') – one building. 'Mountain Camp' has the largest and biggest dormitories of New Artek. All of them are four-story buildings, 100 meters long. In addition, 'Mountain Camp' boasts a reception building, an infirmary, a dining hall, a swimming pool, and a gym, as well as bonfire and sports fields.

Artek's gardens and parks, which occupy about 65% of its territory, con-

23 Vladimir Svistov, 'Know your camp. Our parks ar our wealth', in: *Artekovets*, 4 June 1992, no. 10, 4

(Владимир Свистов,Знай свой лагерь. Наши парки-богатство наше, в: Артековец, 4 июня 1992, №10, с.4)

stitute a world of their own.[23] Some of them, for example those in the 'Azur' and 'Cypress camps,' were laid out in the 19th century, while others were planned at various times in the 20th century. These parks can be classified as follows: historical parks, ritual parks, coastal parks, sport parks, botanical gardens, landscape parks, rock parks and natural parks.

Happy

Studying the parks seems to be a wonderful educational pastime in Artek.

Today, Artek comprises 36 dormitories, 8 dining halls, a school with 1,000 places, a health center, indoor sports facilities, a stadium with seats for 10,000 people, two pools with processed sea water, a yacht club, a harbor, a museum with an exhibition space, a building for watching television and films, a depot for 300 transport units, storehouses, studios, and domestic buildings.[24] Almost all of these buildings were constructed towards the end of the 1960s. Buildings which were added later, e.g. the gym complex which was finished in 1981 and the covered swimming pool of the huge 'Mountain Camp', display the totally different, pseudo-impressive architecture of the late Brezhnev era. They look light-years away from the first buildings of 'Sea Camp.'

Olga Pochol'tshuk (ed.), 'Triple Jump into the third Millennium. Result of the Century', in: *Artekovets*, 28 December 00, no. 14, 2.

льга Похольчук (Ред.), Тройной прыжок в третье сячелетие.Итоги века, в: Артековец, 28 декабря 2000, №14, c.2)

The last building constructed at New Artek is the Lenin monument, planned during the Brezhnev era and consecrated in 1985 by Gorbachev, who had just become Secretary General of the Party. Today this hyper-monumental, ossified Lenin, which has nothing in common with Artek's joyous architecture, towers 40 meters above all of Artek's buildings. It is interesting to note that Anatolij Poljanskij, the author of the original buildings, also designed this monument. At that time he was already spoiled by fame, and 30 years older. Perhaps the foundation was badly constructed, or perhaps nature does not like this Lenin, but today the monument is slipping slowly towards the sea, threatening to fall down on one of its last faithful admirers. Monuments and states have the propensity to decline. Only life continues. The same is true for Artek:

'When you stood before me for the first time
A crystal castle of unusual beauty
My heart and my soul suddenly knew
That crystal dreams here become true!
You are always full of warmth and tenderness
Of the crystal voices of "crystal" kids,
Of crystal songs, of crystal fairy-tales
Of crystal music from Artek's time'[25]

25 Vladimir Tshuklinov, 'The Crystal Castle', in: V.E. Tshuklinov, 'In my poems and songs I live totally in "Artek"', in: *Artekovets*, 15 June 2001, no. 8-9, 6.

(Владимир Чуклинов, Хрустальный замок, в:В.Е. Чуклинов, 'Я весь в моих стихах и песнях об'Артеке', Артековец, 15 июня 2001, №8-9, c.6)

Artek, propaganda and life beyond the propaganda

From the start, Artek was supposed to be not only a recreational camp for children but also an educational center for inculcating 'young Lenins' with the proper communist outlook — a 'school for the most active Pioneers, perfectly suited to be a training ground for communication and the friendship of peoples. Through excellent academic performance and exemplary social activity

Happy

26 Olga Pochol'tshuk (ed.), 'Triple Jump into the third millennium. Result of the Century', in: *Artekovets*, 28 December 2000, no. 14, 2.

(Ольга Похольчук (Ред.), Тройной прыжок в третье тысячелетие. Итоги века, с.2)

27 German Tshernyj, Viktor Krjutshkov, Roman Ozerskij, Eduard Alesin, *Artek! Peace! Friendship. Photo album*, 4.

(Герман Черный, Виктор Крючков, Роман Озерский, Эдуард Алесин, Артек! Мир! Дружба!, с.4)

a child could earn the right to be sent here.'[26] Soviet propaganda emphasized that 'Artek's fate is closely linked to the history of the All-Union Organization of Young Pioneers named after V.I. Lenin, founded and nurtured by the Communist Party and Lenin's Komsomol.'[27]

Propaganda often reflects reality. While staying at the camp, the children completed a program that for the most part did serve to prepare them for their future role as part of the socialist elite. The creation of monumental works of art in Artek served the same purpose. Even the daily rhythm in the camp followed ideological needs. There were many compulsory activities: obligatory parades of the Pioneers, assemblies, bonfires at night, and vows and oaths at all the possible ritual places near the memorial sites for those who had died in the battle for the victory of communism: 'Pupils of orphanages, activists of clubs for international friendship, junkers, standard-bearers and drummers, and participants in the sports competitions "The Starts of Hope," and young soldiers and young policemen regularly meet here.'[28] This quote from the year 1985 characterizes the group of children destined to go to Artek.

28 Ibid, 18.

In the Soviet era the Crimea was the favorite holiday resort not only for the Soviet leadership but also for leaders of the 'socialist brother countries', and Artek was visited by many famous communist leaders: Mao Tse Dung, Ho Chi Min, Erich Honecker, Janós Kadar, Todor Zhivkov, and of course the Soviet leaders Krushtchev, Kalinin, Brezhnev and Gorbachev. All of them became Honorary Pioneers of Artek. The camp became a model for the education of socialist youth, and of the Soviet organization of children's holidays. Artek always had an international character. Even today a huge globe occupies the place of honor in the hall of Suuk-Su Palace, where Artek's Museum is located, displaying the flags of the numerous countries of the world that have sent children to spend their holidays in Artek. On the seashore, close to 'Sea Camp,' a 'Monument to the Friendship of the World's Children' was built from stones brought by children from 83 different countries (the sculptor is Ernst Neizvestnyj; the architect Anatolij Poljanskij).[29]

29 V.S. Sergeev, *The Silhouette of Yalta's Shoreline. Historical-architectural outline*, Kiev-Yalta 1998, 130.

(В.С. Сергеев, Силуэты Ялтинского побережья, с.130)

It is obvious that this 'City of Childhood Happiness' was endowed with a generous budget. Artek was always under the direct control of the Soviet Party leadership, with the money coming directly from Moscow. That is why the end of the East Bloc in 1989 and the decline of the Soviet Union in 1991 had such an impact on the ideological and material principles on which Artek's prosperity was built. The Crimea became part of the Ukraine, and as an emerging new state, the Ukraine had other priorities at that time than supporting the international children's movement and the educational ideals of the disintegrating Soviet Empire. Russia also lost

Happy

interest in Artek, partly for ideological reasons, partly because it was now located on the territory of another state. Financial support dwindled and the 'Pioneer's Republic' had to finance itself by making money. Besides, after 30 years of intense use it was time to renovate Artek's buildings and infrastructure. People even considered the improbable idea of turning Artek into 'Artek Disneyland,' or of selling it and privatizing its individual buildings and camps.

We have to give credit to the management and employees of Artek, who at a time of social, economic and legal anarchy succeeded in preserving the main idea and goal of the 'Children's Republic'. In addition, they came up with many new initiatives and were able to turn the Soviet idea of an 'All-Union Camp for Pioneers,' which had exhausted its possibilities, into the new concept of an 'International Children's Centre "Artek."'[30]

Artek found its niche rather quickly in the new Ukraine as well as in all successor states of the former Soviet Union. Victims of all kinds of catastrophes are being cured there, coming, for example, from the area around Chernobyl in the Ukraine and from Jakutija in Russia when it was hit by severely flooding. Summer schools are organized; sport tournaments, competitions and festivals take place in Artek.[31] A University for Humanities was founded[32] and the 'International competition and seminar of school teachers' has been organized for the seventh year in a row.[33] Once more famous politicians are steady guests, among them Leonid Kutchma, Vladimir Putin, and Eduard Shevardnadze.[34] In fact, the camp attracts as many visitors today as it did during its heyday under socialism. Artek lives on.

30 Michail Siderenko, 'The main principles of the development of the International Children's Center "Artek"', in: *Artekovets*, 4 June 1992, no. 10, 2-3; Sergej Erochin, 'The Creation of a new model for "Artek"', in: *Artekovets*, 27 February 1992, no. 4, 1. (Михаил Сидоренко, Об основных направлениях развития Международного Детского Центра 'Артек', в: Артековец, 4 июня 1992, №10, с.2-3; Сергей Ерохин, Создать новую модель 'Артека', в: Артековец, 27 февраля 1992, №4, с.1)

31 E.L. Zolotych, 'For good times! Celebration!', in: *Artekovets*, 16 May 1997, 1; Natalja Ivanova, 'The new project "Artekt"' – "A Summer School"', in: *Artekovets*, 23 August 2001, 12-13; Olga Pochol'tshuk, 'Football in "Artek"', in: *Artekovets*, 20 September 2001, no. 14, 1. (Е.Л.Золотых, В добрый час, фестиваль!в: Артековец, 16 мая 1997, с.1; Наталья Иванова, Новый проект 'Артека'-'Летние школы', в: Артековец, 23 августа 2001,с.12-13; Ольга Похольчук, футбол в 'Артеке', в:Артековец, 20 сентября 2001, №14,с.1)

32 M. Sidorenko, 'Have a good life, dear graduates!', in: *Artekovets*, 27 March 2002, no. 5, 1. (М.Сидоренко,В добрый путь, дорогие выпускники!, в: Артековец, 27 марта 2002, №5, с.1)

33 'The Teacher – a name given by God', in: *Artekovets*, 18 May 2001, no. 7, 1-16. (Учитель-имя Божье, в: Артековец, 18 мая 2001, №7, с.1-16)

34 'Thank you, "Artek"', in: *Artekovets*, 23 August 2001, no. 12-13, 3. ('Артеку' – спасибо!, в: Артековец, 23 августа 2001, №12-13, с.3)

Happy

Re-inventing the European City?

RE-INVENTING THE EUROPEAN CITY?

Some time after 1945, in the late 1950s in some countries, maybe in the early 1970s in others, it finally happened: the great masses of people were rescued from poverty, backwardness and the need to spend most of their time struggling to stay alive. The great mission shared by politicians and economists in the wake of the war, whether their goal was the creation of the Welfare State or the fulfillment of the dreams inherent in socialism, had been accomplished. For the first time in history, the luxury of escaping from material concerns was extended to the entire population, marking the social success of the 'common man' and the laboring classes, who, in the socialist countries, were told that they were the new elite. One might expect that this historical achievement called for celebration. For a brief but telling moment, however, the authorities were not happy at all. They feared the loss of a powerful vehicle for motivating the masses. What better way to gain their support than by promising them a carefree future? Many of the icons collected in this book show how attractive these visions could be. Was there anything like them?

One of the most intriguing answers to this question came from A. Heckscher. In 1963, Heckscher, a member of John.F. Kennedy's brain trust, published *The Public Happiness*. In this book, he wanted to extend the scope of the Welfare State to include immaterial concerns, improving people's well-being while still maintaining that this would make society more secure. In other words: Heckscher wanted to promote public happiness – a phrase copied from the American Constitution. He called for a program that invited people to exploit their creative potentialities. In a way, everybody should become an artist. 'Here at least,' Heckscher argued, 'is a pursuit large enough, offering rewards sufficiently deferred and challenging, to make life again seem worthwhile.'[1]

Why had the introduction of such an ambitious scheme suddenly become so important? Heckscher's book contains some explanations, apologies almost. Times were changing, and for him the complete success of the Welfare State marked the end of the 'age of necessity.' People were no longer limited by the need to do whatever was necessary to stay alive. They had more and more time to spend on useless things – useless, that is, in terms of material survival. As their wealth increased and they had more time for leisure, the spectrum of choices offered to them expanded. That was a giant leap forward, but, Heckscher maintained, also a source of new dangers. If people are no longer limited by the need to secure the material basis of their livelihood and subsistence, they could easily be tempted to make the wrong choices. (Naturally, in the early 1960s the Second World War still stood out as the most terrible example of what this could lead to, a prospect made all the more dangerous by the threat of nuclear warfare.) What seemed to increase the danger that things might get out of control was the revolution in the electronic media. At about the same time Heckscher wrote his book, Marshall McLuhan coined the phrase 'The Medium is the Message', making the most of the electronic revolution epitomized by the spread of television, suggesting that reality was being replaced by artificial imagery. Freeing the media from the constraints of their contents, a whole new spectrum of possibilities seemed to present itself. Celebrated by some as a fundamental technological revolution with a positive impact on society, others feared that McLuhcan's discovery ushered in a world where the masses were bound to lose control of reality. That only seemed to prove Heckscher's point: as soon as the 'state of necessity' had been overcome, the masses were likely to lose all sense of direction.

Do the arguments supporting Heckscher's view contain the seeds of art as a social concern rather than art for art's sake? Do they mark the end of art as a window on reality? Is art something the state should subsidize not for cultural, but, ultimately, for political reasons? That is for historians and social scientists to decide. This much is sure: Heckscher's artistic program never materialized. Neither did the catastrophes he feared. So far, massive wealth has not culminated in massive revolution and the overthrow of political

Happy

power; neither the counterculture criticizing the bureaucratized Welfare State, nor the collapse of socialism in Eastern Europe can easily be attributed to it. If Heckscher's vision is destined to remain just a footnote in the post-war evolution of society, it is, nevertheless, hard to find better proof of the complete success of both the Welfare State and socialism – considered, that is to say, solely in terms of security and freedom of want. In the 1990s, the signs of a second social revolution began to appear in most Western-European countries, opening new vistas of a world not only rich, but extravagantly rich, where the 'new economy' appeared to have eliminated even the slightest risk of new economic crises. This is the backdrop of the fascinating and provocative picture painted by the French novelist Michel Houellebecq, a picture of a 'société érotique-publicitaire,' in which a generation that has become totally individualist and hedonist indulges itself in physical pleasure, because all other pursuits seem to have become trivial and unreal. In doing so, the protagonists of this lifestyle fully exploit the opportunities created by the Welfare State; though Houellebecq, of course, writes about France, he implies that this vision may eventually characterize all of Europe. (One of the recurring themes of our book is, obviously, the privatization of the collective, a tendency that manifests itself everywhere, even in today's post-socialist societies.) The combination of the successive revolutions in the electronic media and the end of the 'vie réelle,' to quote Houellebecq once more, again seemed to result in a world in which all 'real' messages have either lost their meaning or are no longer succeeding in reaching their audience.

At the beginning of the new millennium, these bright perspectives seem to have lost their basis in reality. All kinds of dangers seem, if anything, to have increased. The latest types of terrorism have freed the well-organized, very visible military-industrial complexes from the suspicion that hung about them in the 1950s and 1960s, i.e. that they increased the risk of suppression andannihilation. Big Brother, only a few decades ago synonymous with nightmarish views of totalitarian states, often modelled after the Third Reich, appears to have been accepted as a guarantee against vandalism and terrorism – there is hardly a shopping mall or a railway station where cameras do not keep a close eye on what is going on. The impressive social networks safeguarding the masses against poverty are in the process of being demolished, both in Western Europe and in the former socialist countries, exposing the 'common man' to threats that he believed had been eliminated, all the more so since the magic world of the new economy has collapsed. All this seems unreal, and the attack on the twin towers in New York on September 11, 2001 is the ultimate manifestation of this unreal reality – no wonder, then, that even the authorities looked to Hollywood for guidance in this apparently artificial world. In a way, the media finally did become the message, and what was feared until only a few decades ago now seems to be taken for granted. Rather than worrying about what may happen to everybody, people apparently prefer to focus on their individual well-being.

What does all this mean for the European city? Apparently, the fundamental characteristics of the public domain as a medium have been drowned in a *mer à boire* of messages radiated by an ever growing array of electronic media that, with the help of modern marketing techniques, are directed at specific lifestyle groups. Does the European city have to be re-invented because the public domain has become a medium without a message? Is that the ultimate outcome of Heckscher, McLuhan, Houellebecq, and 9/11? Has the concept of urban icons become meaningless? All the icons collected here relate individual happiness to people's social environment. They point out essential characteristics of human society as the result of deliberate, conscious choices and the resulting jockeying for power, in other words: as a historical setting for intrinsically historical phenomena. Has the public domain lost this meaning? Is that the necessary consequence of mankind's alleged emergence from the 'state of necessity,' where public happiness could still be presented as a prerequisite for private happiness?

Happy

Paradoxically, the public domain has become the only medium still addressing society at large. It never lost its particular character, and neither has the European city. There is no need to re-invent it; for it is continuously in the process of re-inventing itself and of coping with whatever challenges it has to face. Part of the process is the emergence of new icons that seem to have become more appealing. In the last article of this anthology, Charles Polónyi and Györgyi Konrád argue that cities are here to stay; that no matter how sophisticated the electronic media may become, they will never be able to substitute the unique character of the urban environment; that people will always flock to the cities because they both document and propel the evolution of society; and that, ultimately, there are no better places to witness and participate in this process – and what an exciting and sometimes dramatic process it is! The city will survive because it is a catalyst for mental and social processes that can only emerge there. No matter how sophisticated the electronic media may become, they will never replace the physical reality of the city.

1 A. Heckscher, *The Public Happiness*, London 1963, 10

Bologna, April 19, 2004.

'It's temporary!,' says Mario Cucinella. He clearly has a point. Yes, it is located in Piazza Maggiore, in the heart of Bologna, almost opposite the Cathedral. But it is temporary. We are talking with Cucinella about the 'eBo', the pavilion recently built by his firm MCA to host Bologna's municipal information center. The 'eBo'

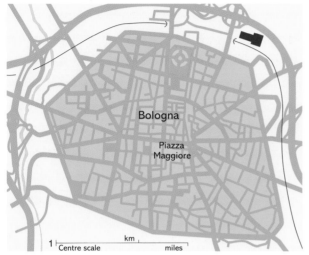

is small. Actually, it is nothing more than an entrance, since the exhibition is located underground, in a former pedestrian passageway. But the two 'bubbles,' built almost entirely of transparent plastic tubes which resemble giant bamboo stems, have provoked strong reactions. That the pavilion was built to promote the projects of the right-wing municipal government led by mayor Giorgio Guazzaloca, who held office from 1999 until 2004, certainly did not help to increase its popularity in Bologna's architectural culture. That it was built by a non-Bolognese architect (Cucinella is from Genoa, and his firm, now in Bologna, was based in Paris until 1999) probably did not help either. But the debate on the pavilion did not always follow these lines. Well known right-wing, non-Bolognese intellectuals violently criticized the 'eBo' after its opening in 2003, while a few left-wing, Bolognese architects and intellectuals came out in defense of it. The debate revealed how strong, widespread and deeply rooted is the idea that places like Piazza Maggiore should be left permanently untouched, not only by new buildings but also by any trace of modern architectural aesthetics. We have a friend in Bologna. He does not like to speak about the pavilion. If we force him to do so (friendship can be sadistic sometimes) he refers to its architect as 'Cucinotta'. The Italian actress. Does he mean that the pavilion's architecture is sexy? Probably not. **F.d.P., P.S.**

THE REVITALIZATION OF HISTORICAL BOLOGNA

Filippo de Pieri, Paolo Scrivano

'Dall'alto del colle si vede tutta la città. Nelle sue linee complesse e armoniose è scritta, attraverso i secoli, una regola civile che riconosce i bisogni della comunità e sa tradurre in spettacolo di pietra le più intime ragioni della vita quotidiana.' From the script of Renzo Renzi, Guida per camminare all'ombra

(written by Leone Pancaldi and Renzo Renzi, 1954)

The policies for the conservation of Bologna's city center carried out by the Communist-led local administration in the 1960s and 1970s are well known. In the late 1970s and early 1980s, especially, they enjoyed wide international attention, as possibly the best example of an ambitious program of socially responsible urban preservation, aimed at avoiding both physical destruction of the city's central areas and expulsion of the lower classes from them. In fact, Bologna's preservation policies changed over the years. They were embodied in a sequence of planning documents, two of which are of particular significance. The first was the plan for the conservation of the city center approved by the municipal council in 1969; the second was the affordable housing plan (Peep, 'Piano per l'edilizia economica e popolare') adopted in 1973. It was on the latter that Bologna's international reputation was largely

Happy

based: only after its approval, did the identification between social policy and preservation issues becaome a trademark of the Bologna experience. The previous plan, approved in 1969, has a more complex and less known history. Its roots lay both in Bologna's particular political situation in the 1960s and in a few basic elements specific to Italy's post-war urban and architectural culture.

Bologna was quite a remarkable place in the country's political landscape in the years following World War II. It was the only important municipality in Italy where the Communist Party (PCI) had governing responsibilities throughout the period. After the end of the 1950s, when the 'reformist' wing of the PCI gained power and influence in city politics, Bologna started adopting deficit spending policies and showing a strong interest in town planning issues. Starting in 1960, the planner Giuseppe Campos Venuti coordinated a sequence of projects that culminated in a new general plan for the city, which was adopted in 1970.

Most of these efforts (housing schemes, studies for a new business and trade fair center) dealt with the city's periphery. They were accompanied by reflections about the need to extend the scale of planning far beyond the municipal limits. They also involved a debate about centralization, in both political and planning terms. In 1962 the institution of the 'consigli di quartiere' ('neighborhood councils') marked the beginning of a process of political decentralization at the local level, pairing the physical re-design of the urban periphery with the creation of a new web of local powers aimed at enhancing citizen participation in the process of municipal decision-making. The attention devoted to problems concerning the conservation of the city center must be seen in this context.

The ambiguous notion of the 'centro storico' ('historic city center'), which lay at the core of the 1969 plan for Bologna, already had a long history at the time of the latter's approval. Italian architects and planners had been discussing it for at least a decade, attempting to figure out how 'modern' planning and economic development could be reconciled with the need for the preservation of Italy's many historic urban settings. The smaller cities of Central Italy embodied these problems in the most striking way, and it was actually in Gubbio, in 1960, that a group of planners, architects and preservationists approved the 'Gubbio Charter' for the extensive conservation of historic city centers, which may be thought of as a counterpoint to the 4th CIAM's 'Athens Charter.'

When, in 1962, the municipal administration of Bologna entrusted a research group, headed by Leonardo Benevolo at the University of Florence, with a study of the city center, these issues were still topical. The work of Benevolo's group, completed in 1965, explained why the visual and architectural character of the city center had to be protected in its entirety: the historical break produced by the 19th-century 'industrial revolution' had been so great that cities built in a previous period had become incompatible with most of aspects of modern life. In spite of their diversity, 'historic city centers' were unitary in their essence – the testimony of a bygone era and therefore a key element in the collective identity of modern urban societies. They could host only a few selected functions, and required the application of strong preservation policies.

Happy

Piazza Santo Stefano, 1969

Happy

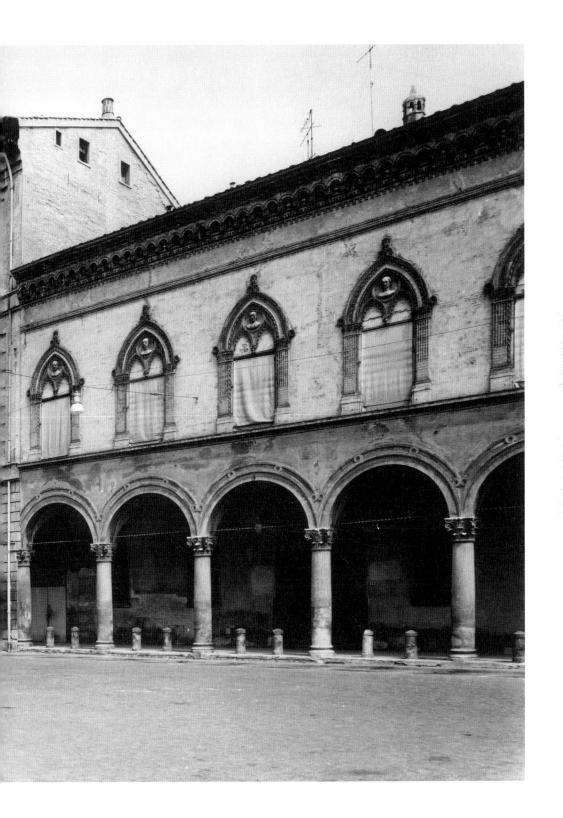

Happy

These arguments drew heavily on Italian modernist urban theories of the 1930s: previous decades (such as Gustavo Giovannoni's *Vecchie città ed edilizia nuova*, 1931). Having escaped radical change, the city center became part of a more comprehensive functional zoning that extended to the entire metropolitan region. The modernist orthodoxy was thus reconciled with the positions of radical preservationists like those gathered in the association 'Italia Nostra.' In planning terms, the analysis sketched by Benevolo's group (and which was incorporated in the 1969 plan, although Benevolo was not directly involved in it) was based upon a typological classification of the city's building fabric. The scheme, a simplified translation of Saverio Muratori and Aldo Rossi's typological research of the early 1960s, was supplemented by the identification of a limited number of possible interventions - from complete conservation to outright demolition.

Were these ideas about the need for preserving Bologna's 'historic' center supported by the city's inhabitants in the 1960s? It is difficult to say, but the public events organized by the municipality to promote the plan and win social consensus for the new conservation policies provide interesting material for a history of the pursuit of public happiness. The 'pedestrian-ization' of Piazza Maggiore and its environs began on September 18, 1968 and was promoted by the city as an initial occasion for re-appropriating the city's historic spaces. Two years later, in the summer 1970, the approval of the new plan provided the theme for an exhibition opened under the portico of Palazzo d'Accursio. The centerpiece of the show, suitably unsur-prisingly entitled Bologna Centro Storico, was a photographic campaign commissioned by the municipality from the Milanese photographer Paolo Monti. Presented as a 'photographic survey' of the historic city's architectural heritage, Monti's work, documented in thousands of pictures, provided a visual representation of the idea of a 'city center' that was not entirely consistent with the 1969 plan.

Monti was not new to the practice of making a photographic survey. In previous years, he had already been involved in surveys of the artistic and cultural heritage of the region, most notably in the Apennines. In the Bologna campaign, which was limited to a few selected parts of the city, he chose an approach that combined an insistence on recurrent elements of public space (the portico, the street), attention to architectural details (stucco figures, frescoes, paving, a poster, a crack in a wall), the visual conventions of architectural photography and, finally, an effort to reproduce the daily experience of the urban stroller (points of view were varied and kept at eye level, 'as occurs when one walks and stares'). Although a descriptive rendering was discernible in all the material, Monti's city was not devoid of utopian traits: it was an abstract setting where human presence was sporadic but perceptible, and the only documented activities were walking and talking. Car traffic was absent from many pictures, since most of the shots were taken in August 1969, when policemen blocked the streets during Monti's work. 'The Discovery of the Empty City' was the title chosen for a section of the the 1970 exhibition catalogue that presented the campaign; in a central part of the book, images of empty streets were published next to other images of the same places taken at rush hour and full of vehicles. The overall effect recalled N.A.W. Pugin's *Contrasts*, the 1840 book

Happy

The porticos of the Church of San Giacomo, 1969

Happy

Via Nosadella and Vicolo della Neve, 1969

Via Zamboni, 1969

Happy

that was familiar to many readers of Benevolo's works on the history of planning (*Le origini dell'urbanistica moderna*, 1963).

For all the interest and quality of Monti's images, he was actually building on a strong local tradition of photographic representation of the city. In the 1950s and 1960s, photographers like Enrico Pasquali and Walter Breveglieri had already engaged in interesting experiments in describing the city's architectural, spatial and social make-up. This tradition extended to cinema and literature, most notably including the work of the filmmaker Renzo Renzi, an important figure in the history of Bologna's postwar local culture. In a short movie of 1954, *Guida per camminare all'ombra*, entirely dedicated to Bologna's porticos, Renzi presented an idealized image of the city center: a 'homogeneous' setting where 'architecture has merged into town planning'; a place where 'women come back from shopping, artisans work in their shops, children play with the arches' cracked columns.' Renzi's subsequent book, *Bologna una città*, published in 1960, further elaborated these mythologies; the images which illustrated it, shot for the most part by Aldo Ferrari, provided one of the most direct precedents for Monti's work.

The impact of these representations and their contribution to the preservation policies of the late 1960s was immense. In spite of all the attempts to establish a 'technical' definition using such instruments as historical study, typological classification and zoning regulations, the notion of an 'historic city center' at the core of the Bologna plan also drew upon other, more commonplace notions of 'centrality,' inscribed either in the social discourse or in the visual conventions of urban description. Not all of these were 'modern' in their implications, nor were they always free of nostalgia for an idealized past. In the late 1960s, these policies helped to bring together different local cultures and to build political and social consensus around local preservation policies. Whether the contradictions inherent in the notion of 'city center' were also responsible for the subsequent failure poor results of the Bologna plans is for future historians to decide.

Tenerife, November 14, 2002.

Following the coastline, mass tourism occupies a densely populated, narrow band. Part of nature is crushed by the type of building that represents vacationing on the seaside: hotels and resorts. Even though the effects of mass tourism are felt all over the island, the band of recreational facilities is largely self-contained. Not even the few spectacular sites further inland are much visited, although well-paved roads funded by the European Union make them easily accessible. The coastline will always remain its eternal self.

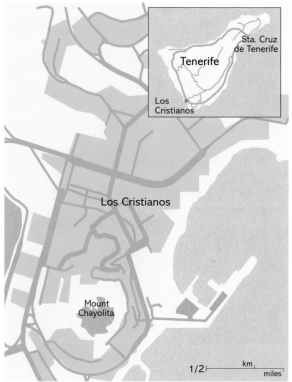

A bank of clouds hides the top of Tenerife's highest mountain. A cable lift on the south side exploits the mountain's recreational potential. Los Christianos is a transit station as well as a holiday resort. From the harbor, ferries head for the other Canary Islands. They carry people living on the islands who are trying to keep their small businesses going, but most of the passengers are crowds of noisy tourists, usually barely dressed and heavily packed. Los Christianos is also a city of dispersed tower blocks, manifesting the town planners agility in a kind of urban acupuncture. Alhough the outward appearance of these hotel towers shows slight variations, they all have a distinct feature in common: the vertical bands of balconies that mark the temporary character of the guests stay in a holiday resort. Contrasting with this verticality, the spaces that organize the vacationers social life spread out horizontally. All the facilities seem to cater for one of the many variations of walking: loitering in the hotel lobby, showing off on the beach, swimming in the pool, shopping in shopping centers and streets lined with booths, eating and drinking in the sidewalk cafés. Everything the holiday makers do is enveloped in a distinctly erotic atmosphere. K.B.

Happy

Atlantis

Koos Bosma

In the age of 'paper architecture,' that is, the years between 1975 and 1985, the Luxembourg-based architect Leon Krier became one of the protagonists of a nostalgic view of historic cities in their purest form. His design for the Arcadian settlement of Atlantis in Los Christianos on Tenerife in the Canary Islands was part of his quest for an alternative and, to some extent, socialist society. In the 1970s Krier had become an internationally famous social critic who hated modern architecture and refused to work for capitalist companies. Making paper architecture was a way to make a living that was compatible with his anti-capitalist beliefs. The architect, he held, should not collaborate with the enemy, but rather contribute to a better society by formulating theoretical concepts and designing alternative projects. Krier stuck to this attitude for a surprisingly long time. His alternative designs could only have been realized if an absolute monarch could be found who might be willing to support them – they had absolutely no roots in everyday reality.

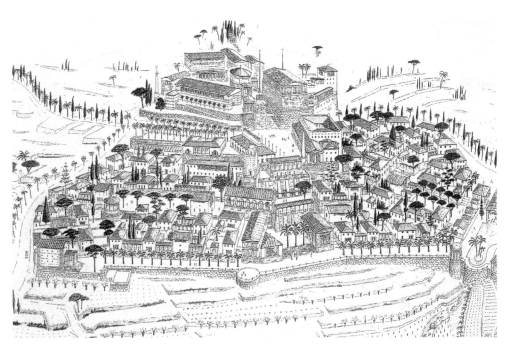

Happy

Gradually however, Krier's position started to change. The very same pre-industrial sentiments that characterize his critical work could be channeled into a form of 'revival architecture' that pleased the social elite. In the middle of the 1990s, Krier found a perfect patron in Charles, Prince of Wales. Charles was not exactly an absolute monarch, but he did have considerable influence and enough stamina to create the small city of Poundbury. Poundbury was built using techniques of the pre-industrial era, respecting the stylistic conventions of the past as well as the strictest ecological guidelines, although this does not mean that the most modern amenities are lacking. The houses are very comfortable and parking lots have not been omitted.

Atlantis, which ultimately was only partially realized in a completely different way, and, in the end, under capitalist conditions, looks less successful. Krier, in fact, refuses to have his name mentioned in connection with it. His intention was not a utopian dream, but rather a small-scale modification of a landscape not yet invaded by the masses of tourists who flock to the island all year long. A painting of Atlantis by Carol Laubin shows an idyllic landscape, the hills covered in shrubbery, some trees, scattered hammocks, and a spectacular view over the Atlantic Ocean. Crowning the spectacle is the small city of Atlantis on top of a hill. Another painting of Laubin depicts the center of Atlantis as an ancient agora clearly derived from the classical temple architecture of ancient Greece and Rome. The agora with the classical buildings of learning is the key to the design. Even the clothes worn by the figures populating this image are inspired by antiquity. The project in the harbor of Los Christianos differs from the painted project in two fundamental respects. First, even if it would have been built on top of a hill, it would have been dwarfed by the surrounding high-rise hotels. What all these hotels have in common is the endless repetition of endless rows of balconies, representing the ideals of the modern tourist industry. Second, the only part of the agora that can be found in Los Christianos houses the most capitalistic form of entertainment, the casino, even though it has been designed as a temple. The paintings and the present situation represent promises of happiness stemming from completely different epochs. Whereas the original project conveys the ideal of an authentic lifestyle, classical culture and low-budget tourism characterized by slightly drowsy people roaming the beaches, the townscape of Los Christianos radiates the atmosphere of hedonistic mass tourism, where contemporary urban phenomena such as discos, restaurants and casinos appear as the temples of modern entertainment while the original landscape and the remnants of Atlantis are crushed under their weight.

Bucharest, anytime.

It's all about the cars. Fancy cars, as nowhere else in the rich parts of the world, or just average cars. They are a parallel population, with exploding numbers in a shrinking city. Every day it takes longer to drive to one's destination and then to park. Every day brings confirmation that the world outside of the car, *your* car, is just hell. There are no more sidewalks for pedestrians: illegal parking has eaten them all up. There is no more air to inhale: the engines have burned it all up. And the logical limit of this spiral has been reached – there is no city any more: just a massive jam of powerful vans, four-wheel drive vehicles and limos, fully equipped with air conditioning and entertainment gadgets, enabling one to survive the standstill among the alien species crawling outside.

Two guys standing on the opposite sides of a boulevard filled with an endless stream of rushing cars. One shouts to the other: *How did you manage to cross there?* The other: *I didn't. I was born on this side.* **C.D.**

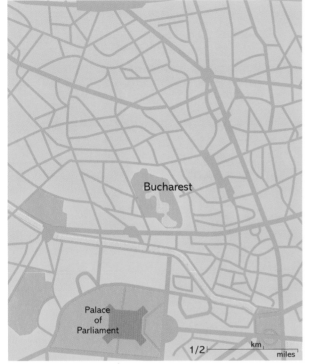

Bucharest

Palace of Parliament

1/2

Happy

Bucharest: Spritz, Concrete and Dusty Trees

Călin Dan

The city of Bucharest was established under the aegis of Vlad III Tzepes, better known as Count Dracula, through a document issued by his chancellery in 1459. This does not mean that Bucharest is a demonic place; it suggests simply that it was shaped through a complicated historical process into something more inspiring as a movie set than as a living environment. Probably that explains the perverse satisfaction people take from living in a city which gives its inhabitants a strange rush, as if they were involved in the making of a blockbuster film.

Situated at a meeting point of European identities, Bucharest initially developed not as a capital city but as a traffic hub for goods and people. Multicultural as far back in time as the oldest surviving records, the city was a gate between North and South, connecting, first, the Byzantine Empire with Scandinavia and Russia, and, later, the Ottoman Empire with its counterpart superpowers in the regional geopolitical game – the Austrians and the Russians. The convergence of economic and political interests made Bucharest the main city of the Romanian provinces, a process consolidated in the 16th century despite the disadvantages of its geography. In modern times, Bucharest was hit by two major waves of immigration. One internal – the Roma (gypsies) leaving the estates of Southern Romania, after being emancipated from serfdom

Happy

464

as late as 1848. And the other external – a flow of Galician Jews, seeking shelter in the aftermath of systematic pogroms in Russia in the same period. While trying to emulate the example of Paris as the supreme model in politics, economics, and life-style, Bucharest became a melting pot of Romanians, Greeks, Macedonians, Turks and Bulgarians, all of them strongly rooted in what could be called Balkan civilization, along with Germans and Hungarians originating in the neighboring provinces of Transylvania and Bukovina.

This course of events shaped Bucharest into a collage of decentralized sectors and stylistic mixes, both monumental and vernacular: Balkan architecture, fin-de-siècle eclecticism, art deco, early modernism. This cityscape changed dramatically in the postwar period, when the echoes of international functionalism were soured by the brutal import of Stalinist aesthetics. Later, the socialist regime became responsible for a little-known episode of ethnic cleansing that left entire historic neighborhoods subject to squatting by Roma: namely, the exodus of the Jewish community that was virtually sold to Israel for economic advantages. And, finally, the postmodern re-urbanization around the Ceauçescu Palace, which dramatically transformed the urban tissue, making the inner city a succession of unfinished ruins, empty areas reclaimed by vegetation (and used as dumps), and oppressive (sometimes absurd) construction fantasies. In 2004, the main construction initiatives are high-rise office buildings in the city center, and churches in the bedroom suburbs on the city's outskirts. As the principal urban features we can mention the fenced-off residential areas with prefab villas in the North and the plans for The Cathedral of the Nation, a mega-project meant to surpass even Ceauçescu's palace – including

And page 466-467. Călin Dan, Sample City, 2003, video, 11:45 min.

Happy

the destruction of an historic green area, one of the very few Bucharest still possesses.

There is no pursuit of collective happiness in the history of Bucharest. Even today, the city appears as a conglomerate of private solutions to general challenges, not to say crises. Since the eighteenth century, travelers and diplomats seem to agree – some in awe, some in admiration – that the dominant characteristic of the city stems from a strange blend of outrageous contrasts between the classes and an obsession with instant gratification through food, drink and sex. The high quantities (if not quality) of these three were seemingly guaranteed by the structure of both the land and its people, simultaneously capable of a generosity and of an unreliability so intense that they defy comprehension. The evolution of the city from a chaotic cluster of villages had to cope with what comes down to the sort of individualism that despises the collective needs (and values) of other individuals. For instance, the first strategic roads that make up the North/South axis follow a meandering route between lands and gardens once owned by the extravagantly rich, who refused to give up the immediate benefits of landownership for a conceptual phantasm – planning.

A medieval resistance to authority, and an authority ready to resort to medieval violence have been the twin forces primarily responsible for shaping Bucharest, from the initiatives of General Kisseleff (head of the Russian occupation in the Romanian provinces between 1829 - 1836), up through the novel kind of civil war waged by the late dictator Ceauçescu against his own people. The city dwellers cling to their fantasy about comfort, expressed mostly through horizontal structures filled with surrogates of individual freedom and of nature. The original

Happy

466

maze of courtyards, gardens and mud huts clustered around a manor were later fixed in a fractal pattern of streets boarded by vegetation. Those are the trenches against which the rulers built their own versions of fortresses: most recently snazzily designed office buildings and Disneyland-like fenced residential villages; and, previously, high-rise buildings, rectangular grids of connected villas, and squares for the gathering of disciplined crowds; or, quite simply, a castle for surveillance and defense, as the construction initiated by Ceauçescu so obviously appears to be.

The lower-class local residents are characterized mainly by immobility, almost never leaving their place (locus) of residence: self-sufficient enclaves where they hang out, sit in the shadow, consume, trade, and despise the city 'center' – usually perceived as being something bad and somewhere else. Pilgrimages are periodically organized to the source of the goods defining happiness – wine, meat, fish, fruit and fresh vegetables – brought from the small family farms situated in the villages surrounding Bucharest. The inner city is invaded by over-crowded busses and trams carrying people fulfilling the social routine of survival – the menial jobs, the hits, the stings. The fragmentary, bottom-up, semi-nomadic, and in some sense resentful perception these people have of their city is determined by an umbilical mentality, feeding from an ambiguous relationship with their peasant origin, where self-reliance and self-sustainability are the cornerstones of survival. A pervasive countryside is morphing into Bucharest, on both the physical and psychological levels, determining how the values of the citizenry are functioning in practice.

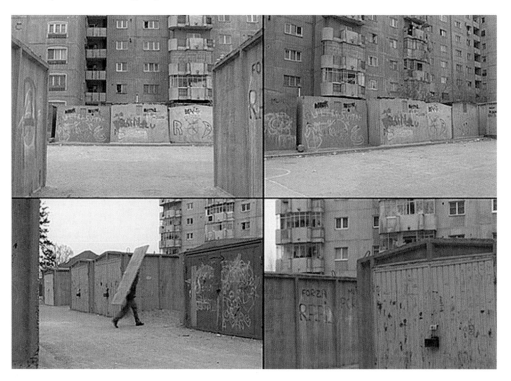

Happy

The upper classes are dynamic, always part of a larger scheme, counting their success by the number of days spent out of Bucharest and (preferably) out of the country, or at least by the number of kilometers separating their residence from their business operations. They see the city from without and from above, at the speed of the 4 x 4s nowadays, as in the recent past they saw it from motorcades flashing through boulevards emptied of any traffic and human presence except the shadowy silhouettes of the low-ranking secret service agents. For them Bucharest is a transit boulevard clogged by heavy traffic, a place for staging symbolic events meant to secure their grip on the city – a phenomenon with unsolvable malfunctions, a rebellious patchwork of failures impossible to contain, and yet the unavoidable place for the centralized exercise of power. Not too far from their own peasant origins, the rulers despise Bucharest both for what it is, and for what it could be, for its potential metropolitan value – alien to those who just want to accumulate goods from public resources and then consume them in the privacy of a golden exile, beyond legal complications.

The symmetric nomadism of the rich and of the poor, their reliance on the illusory consolation of 'nature' to compensate for the frustrating experience of urbanism, is introducing an interesting, twofold shrinking movement: both the neo-serfs and the neo-rulers are deserting the public space, becoming commuters between a private realm of happiness and a public no man's land where all the unpleasant facts of life are dumped amongst the garbage, car exhaust, stray dogs and beggars.

This sketchy picture lacks the refinement of detail which would allow a tiny middle class to insert its own standards of solid infrastructure, reliable services and democratic practice. But the notion of a middle class is just a cliché imposed by the propaganda intent upon integration into the Euro-Atlantic value system (if there still is one), with no roots in a reality that is based on the nostalgic pattern of the medieval republic, where competing local rulers held court and spread favors, mostly to undermine each other's interests, with little concern for the interests of their subjects. Imagology – this shadow discipline playing with the routines and commonplaces of cultural perception – might be the only instrument for dealing with overwhelmingly alien situations like the one Bucharest represents for the unprejudiced flâneur. Moreover, such a character is himself a paradox, since trying to acquire an innocent gaze is useless in an environment that swiftly punishes innocence. The only consistency recorded by the subjective perception in dystopian places is that of large-scale contrast and of appalling details, rewarding both our need for compassion and our need for comic relief.

There is a fluid pattern of recognition that familiarizes the flâneur with the alien city – chaotic grid, bad roads, decaying buildings, empty areas, confusion between periphery, office district and residential area, the dominance of the biological over the social, and of the nomadic over the sedentary. This induces an almost uplifting sense of déjà vu in the stressful act of experiencing a certain group of agglomerations – from South America to Africa to the Balkans to India. In all those places, our defensive memory projects over the complex reality a film of random violence, where the collision of interests between actors (the masters and the servants) cuts open the urban tissue into bleeding areas with decay as the only spectacular

Happy

continuity. Details don't matter any more, and this defensive way of looking induces a strange solidarity between the visitor and the locals, a mix of attraction and resentfulness along the lines of the complicity between the psychoanalyst and the patient, together with a spontaneous mutual manipulation, like the one that transpires between the anthropologists and their subjects.

Romania has produced its own series of (self) critical writings about the city, displaying both an enduring fascination with the subject and an identity crisis so deeply imbedded in the local culture that no therapeutic solutions can be expected in the foreseeable future. My text belongs to that brand of love/hate outburst, concocted mainly by the self-exiled who couldn't stand the perpetual state of conflict that defines this spastic city. My Bucharest is a mix of unresolved memories, the reality imposed by Ceauçescu's regime (subway, postmodern boulevards, modernist slums, ruins, no man's land) and the new developments unfolding in the lives of a generation that grew up in that fracture zone between freedom and oppression, for which the city is mainly a playing field for the exercise of global trends.

This generational change deserves particular atten-tion, because it has the potential to induce a paradigm shift in the self-perception of the city, and eventually to bring some peace to it. But then again, there have been moments of elation in the past as well, when the young and talented middle classes were building a better Bucharest. It is always a matter of more generous politics and bigger policies to sustain such a delicate process, and that is never certain – not in this place.

Until such dilemmas are resolved, or displaced by new ones, all the competing Bucharests will continue to coexist in a bacchanalian consensus. The city dwellers, old and young, rich and poor, feel and are at their best while drinking spritz and chatting around a coal-fired grill filled with various meats, on restaurant terraces or – even better – in their own domain, be it a (usually modest) courtyard or even a balcony, or, if possible, the lawn of a villa. This is the quintessential image of the Bucharestian – simplified perhaps, but highly suggestive – a gargantuan consumer and talker, enjoying a break between two intervals of Brownian spending.

Happy

FROM GOVERNMENT DISTRICT TO A PARADISE FOR TOURISTS: THE RECONSTRUCTION OF THE CASTLE DISTRICT IN BUDAPEST

Henriett Szabo

In the center of Budapest, hovering above the Danube, the castle district stands out as an island in the vast urban sea of this big metropolis. It is one of the oldest parts of the city, and is itself made up of two distinct parts: the castle and the small, walled city. Already in the Middle Ages, the Hungarian government established its seat in this area, which is located on a hilltop that commands a wide view over Pest; furthermore, it was surrounded by open fields, making it easy to defend. The castle district survived the vicissitudes of history almost unscathed – not even the Turkish occupation in the sixteenth and seventeenth centuries caused much harm. Budapest developed into the fastest growing city of the Austro-Hungarian Empire, experiencing an economic boom lasting from the last quarter of the nineteenth century until the outbreak of the First World War in 1914, and during this period the castle district became the seat of Ministries and their ever-expanding bureaucracies.

Happy

This is what the castle district looked like in 1944. Then things changed dramatically. As Russian troops advanced, the German occupation forces hid in the wine cellars of the old houses in the city of Buda, and only the use of small bombs could drive them out. Only one house remained completely undamaged; all the rest lay in ruins. To the surprise even of historians, the partial destruction of the houses unveiled the medieval origin of most of them. There were gothic hip-niches with stone lace in the doorways, original arches, and traces of old windows. Nobody had suspected the existence of this medieval treasury that, for centuries, had been hidden behind baroque and rococo facades. It gave Lajos Meczner, the chief architect of the reconstruction campaign, a unique opportunity to restore Buda to its former grandeur, without, however, erasing the most valuable contributions of the eighteenth century. Meczner did decide, however, to remove most of the extra floors added in the late nineteenth and early twentieth centuries to accommodate the growing number of civil servants working for the Ministries. It was decided to move the governmental departments to the opposite bank of the Danube, where they found space in the area near the Parliament buildings. Meczner also removed most of the historically uninteresting annexes that filled up a number of the courtyards. The urban density decreased, and the area became more airy. Working together with László Gerö, Meczner designed a detailed organization plan, containing precise instructions for each individual house. By 1951, the work was finished. The severe economic situation and the very severe housing shortage made it impossible, however, to modernize the apartments, and behind the beautifully restored facades modern amenities were usually lacking.

The question of how to fill in the empty plots between the restored houses provoked vehement professional disputes. Some architects tried to emulate the style of the neighboring houses, while others wanted to make reference to the modernist architecture of the 1950s and 1960s. Especially controversial was the implantation of the Hilton Hotel in the 1970s. The property of one of the first international hotel chains to come to Budapest, the Hilton was intended to boost tourism by targeting the upscale market of Western vacationers. Part of the plan for this large hotel was the integration of the Saint Nicholas tower and the ruins of the Dominican monastery, two buildings that had not yet been reconstructed. Béla Pintér

Happy

The weekend: leisure for a day - fresh power for a week! Travel week by week to a different countryside Information and ticket booking at the offices of the Ibusz Travel Agency1951. Artist: Tibor Toncz

Happy

Color schemes for the Buda castle district, A. Nemcsics

Happy

designed the new hotel within the framework of the medieval cloister; the wings of the new building, clad in prefabricated concrete panels, appear to embrace the plait styled facade of the Jesuit collegium.

One of the most fascinating aspects of the Buda castle district is its daring color scheme. Few people would suspect that most of the colors are completely new. Hardly any building has been painted according to historical models. Antal Nemcsics, creator of the 'coloroide', a color theory that attempts to integrate various approaches to the problem of coloring the human environment, was responsible for the color schemes of the entire city of Buda. The coloroide theory combines a specific, three-dimensional way to represent colors, a numeric system designating colors, and, most importantly, a vast database containing people's color preferences and color associations. If, in previous epochs, people colored their houses according to their taste, why should they stop doing so in the late twentieth century? The color schemes for Buda are believed to reflect the tastes of modern man in this particular era, and this is what sets them apart from the pastel colors of the baroque period, and the bright colors of the Middle Ages.

If one of the motives for this color scheme has been to please the inhabitants and visitors of Buda, it has been an overwhelming success. Since the late 1970s, tourists have been crowding the streets of Buda. Restaurants and boutiques are everywhere, minibuses and the luxurious limousines of international tourist operators ensure that the stream of visitors never stops. People adore Buda, not knowing that what they see derives its character entirely from reconstruction work in the 1940s and a color scheme made in the late 1970s, nor that the tourist industry superimposed on this pleasant urban scene every possible amenity it could think of. Buda proves how effective (semi-) historical imagery can be in fostering happy sentiments in an re-invented historical setting.

Happy

Tiflis, August 10, 2000.

The marriage cathedral rises impressively above the town of Tiflis, a landmark visible from afar. The closer one approaches it, however, the shabbier the once beautiful palace looks. Its facade is damaged, and parts of the mighty flight of stairs have broken off. Old female guards sit down near the entrance. Their task is

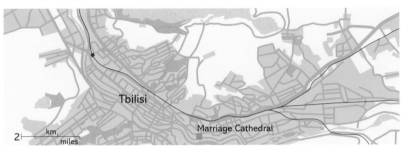

not to guard the palace; they really have nothing to do. They talk about the old days, less than twenty years ago, when the palace was built to rob the churches of their last function: marrying people in front of the altar. When socialism collapsed, the marriage palace became obsolete overnight. People have returned to the church to get married, as they have done for centuries. Slowly, the marriage palace is turning into a ruin.   J.D.

Happy

A Secular Marriage Palace

Jörn Düwel

In the middle of the 1980s, the architects of the Soviet Union faced a completely new type of assignment. They were asked to design imposing buildings for multiple weddings, temples of a pronounced secular character and, as such, without precedent. In the minds of the socialist leadership, these secular churches would destroy one of the last strongholds of the church, since marriage ceremonies would be taken away from the churches and performed in buildings designed especially for festive occasions. The authorities were convinced that this campaign could be successful only if these buildings were as opulent and rich as the churches, and they ordered the architects to rival the traditional church buildings, outdoing them, if possible. The campaign started in the country's regional capitals, that is, in the capital cities of the various Soviet Republics, and the resulting designs were meant to serve as examples for lesser cities to follow. Consequently, everywhere in the enormous empire church-like buildings appeared in the course of the 1980s. They were only used for weddings, and, apparently, they were very much in demand. The politicians encouraged the use of these secular churches, and since they also offered facilities for big parties – providing a rare opportunity in countries that continuously suffered from the lack of even the most basic goods – people quickly turned to these places to get married.

In Tiflis (or Tblisi), the Georgian capital, two renowned local architects designed an almost fairytale-like Marriage Cathedral. Slightly outside the city center, but easy to reach by foot, the palace is situated on a picturesque hill above the Kura River, which flows through the city. It occupies a prominent place between the historical center and the new living quarters surrounding it, and with its striking features it functions like a symbol when seen from afar.

Happy

Tiflis is situated at the border of Europe and Asia, and influences from East and West flow together in this Caucasian city. The resulting continuous tension between various tendencies that sometimes merge and sometimes keep their distance has often been described as an inspiring stimulus for pluralism. For centuries, this delicate balance has characterized Tiflis, and the pious religiosity of its inhabitants remained intact right up through the first decades of the twentieth century. Only when it was forcibly integrated into the Soviet empire did the city and its urban landscape change. In spite of all the attempts to abolish religion, however, the inhabitants of Tiflis have resisted these Moscow-directed campaigns, clinging to deeply rooted Caucasian myths. This residue of resistance was the source of an astonishing renaissance of Georgian national culture after the fall of the Soviet empire.

No restraints were imposed on the architects when they started work on the Marriage Cathedral. Whereas public housing fell to a deplorable level, they could do as they pleased, order the best materials, and design the building on a very large scale. The spatial program is sumptuous. When seen from a distance, the church-like structure evokes curiosity, bringing to mind a modern church, an association one is quick to discard when one remembers that no churches were built in the Soviet Union. What gives the building the appearance of a church, however, is above all the bell tower. Even today, people from Tiflis are convinced that in the design of the Marriage Cathedral, the architects deliberately referred to the sensual curves of human bodies in the act of making love. This reference is not only enhanced by the phallic form of the tower, but even more by the organic voluptuousness of the other parts, which

Happy

seem to celebrate fertility. This interpretation may not be so odd; after all, we are dealing with a cathedral for vital young people wanting to get married.

The building welcomes its guests with a festive gesture. Having climbed the winding road to the top of the hill by car, one enters the building through a flight of stairs that seems to defy the laws of gravity. Here, a much repeated motif returns that also characterizes the building's plan: the curves of life lead to the final destination, climbing the stairs one is on one's way to salvation. This anthropological explanation suggests itself because, time and again, the architects create secularized applications from traditional religious motifs.

The actual entrance to the Cathedral is located near the tower. The shape of the tower seems to be playing on references to church architecture, and this appears to be the case for the building as a whole. It seems to be a collage of several motifs, with snake-like forms dominating. Stretching their necks, they seem to create the shaft of the tower and so to symbolize the symbiosis of the two sexes. Radiating lightness and frivolity, the building lacks all seriousness and heaviness. It refers to youthful happiness, fulfilling itself in marriage.

Even though the tower is the central part of the building, symmetry has been carefully avoided. What lends the Cathedral an air of excitement is not the play of volumes, but rather the way the walls have been pierced by a multitude of different openings. The windows, which are mostly circular, have been inserted at irregular intervals and contrast with the arcade-like incisions. Nevertheless, both the ground plan and the elevation suggest a straight route that symbolizes the unequivocal meaning of matrimony. Obviously, it stands for order. This aspect is inherent in the circulation pattern through the building as well as in the rising sequence of its interior spaces, and it seems to stress the quality of marriage as a completely earthly form of happiness.

The Marriage Cathedral was not only a place to get married; it also provided the setting for the subsequent wedding party. On various levels, the building contains numerous spaces of varying capacity, all including more or less abundant catering services. This allows it to offer facilities for celebrating several marriages at the same time. This ability to provide for everything was one of the principal features of the Cathedral and was intended to make it a more attractive place to get married than a traditional church.

The joyous, carefree play of sensual forms continues inside the Cathedral. Spaces without right angles are kept open and seem to penetrate each other. The main feature of the interior is a kind of processional route for the wedding couple. It leads from the undulating flight of stairs outside to a lavishly decorated, awe-inspiring foyer and from there to a church-like apse, where the actual wedding ceremonies took place. This truly opulent hall is dominated by a large mural, which was painted by Surab Nischaradse. Born in 1928 in Tiflis, Nischaradse was something like a state artist, and in the 1960s he represented Georgia in the Soviet Union. In 1984, when he obtained the assignment for this mural, his fame was at its peak. The recipient of numerous official prizes, including the highly prestigious Lenin Order, he excelled in paintings that celebrated the workers of Georgia. Surprisingly, the mural in the Marriage Cathedral breaks with the official stereotypes of socialist realism. Instead, Nischaradse

Happy

painted an equally frivolous scene, which, at first glance, has little in common with the usual imagery of the Soviet Union, and which is hardly possible to interpret in terms of the well known historical and iconographic categories. One can only understand the painting in relation to the Cathedral's function. Any attempt to create overbearing propagandistic imagery was out of the question here. What was required was a visual language capable of captivating and

Happy

481

Happy

Happy

seducing the young couples, who were meant to perceive this building as the home of joy and untramelled happiness. Only an evocative visual language could achieve this goal.

The main action is painted horizontally over a band of windows. A group of people is depicted seemingly floating in front of an Arcadian landscape. In the center, a young nude couple, clearly happy, can be seen in an almost shy pose. Like Adam and Eve, bride and bridegroom personify innocence. In contrast to Christian iconography, this couple appears to be free from the curse of hereditary sin, and the two youngsters seem to embrace the earthly happiness awaiting them, having successfully loosened all religious ties. Leaving Christianity behind them, they announce the dawn of a new era, where people define their own lives. In a way, the painting can be interpreted as a vision of a new age of enlightenment. The couple is completely free and may choose its own way, liberated from old traditions.

The rest of the mural is built around this central couple. Behind them, towering high above everything, Nischaradse painted a mother with welcoming arms, embodying fertility. To the right of the bride three young ladies come foreward carrying presents. Apparently, they want to accompany the newlywed forever. This type of arrangement, in which traditional elements are used while acquiring a slightly different new meaning, is typical of the mural. Nischaradse played with conventional elements and rituals, without, however, identifying himself with them. Returning to universal values, he gave visitors the opportunity – in more ways than one– to recognize themselves in the scenery on the wall.

Remarkable, too, is a seated dwarf. Representing an allegory of a Caucasian lion, it is composed of a young man's body crowned with a lion's head. In his hands he carries a model in which one can recognize references to the Marriage Cathedral that is the home of this scene. Thus, this figure represents the homeland, Georgia, as the patron of this important building. To the left of the wedding couple, a deer dressed in the local costume is playing an instrument that looks like a bagpipe.

This surreal scene with its fairytale atmosphere also incorporates bright stars shining in the blue skies above the hills. The central parts are brightly painted, but the light fades as the outer scenes are reached, creating a nocturnal atmosphere. Though the entire painting radiates a vision of Arcadia, it is not hard to recognize Tiflis in it. The bridge that Nischaradse painted looks very much like the real bridge that can be seen from the Marriage Cathedral, and the sports stadium he includes is a reference to another big building project underway in Tiflis in the 1980s.

The horizontal sequence of the main scene is complemented by a vertical scene that is dominated by a big plant that seems to surge right out of the central part of the painting. It towers above the mother figure and rises from behind the wedding couple, at the same time forming a cross. One again, the visitor is confronted with a well-known motive from Christian iconography. One is surprised how easily the socialist state incorporated religious symbols in its programmatic building projects.

Equally surprising is the complete lack of references to the usual socialist imagery. Educative and propagandistic elements are found neither in the iconographic program nor in

Happy

the interior organization. The obligatory heroism of having started a new historical epoch is totally lacking. The iconography that had developed in the preceding decades to depict the historical evolution of socialism was deliberately discarded. What remained, however, was the ideal of creating a new society. The only thing that really changed, therefore, was the visual language. The basic values that pervaded society were not questioned, but even so, it is tempting to see this imagery as a precursor of the approaching fall of the Soviet regime. A comparison of this mural with a painting from 1970 may illustrate this point. In the latter we see a group of people celebrating a socialist wedding, and neither the shining red banners of the working-classes nor the usual imagery in praise of labor itself have been left out of the depiction. Fifteen years later, this victorious rhetoric is absent from the mural in the Marriage Cathedral. Giving up the usual rhetoric seems a sign of resignation, since all that we see now is the wedding couple, and the mother figure that dominates the entire scene. The socialist ideology seems to near its end, having returned to universal values that were seen as incompatible with it only a couple of years before. Then, the bridegroom would at least have been a muscular working man, a proud activist or even a cosmonaut, and the bride upgraded to an engineer, chemist or teacher – anything that allegedly surpassed her original role as a woman. There would have been many attributes that are now lacking: signs of social progress, the leading role of the party, the blessings of education and industry, labor and scientific research. The shift to a more contemplative attitude, to the origins of human happiness, however, could only be completed when socialist rule had come to an end.

The Marriage Cathedral was used for five years. Then silence fell on the fairytale building with its large mural. Since the collapse of socialism, no marriages have taken place in it. The restaurants have closed their doors, and all the furnishings have disappeared. In this once joyful building, traces of neglect are visible everywhere. The wall decoration has come down, the flight of stairs has lost some of its steps, and part of the electrical equipment has been stolen. Still, each day a number of employees arrive at the Cathedral, even though they have nothing to do there. They come because they used to do so in the old days and because they have no idea what else to do. They are civil servants paid by the state, however poorly and irregularly. By keeping the Cathedral open, they at least prevent it from being plundered. Perhaps, one day, the building will find a new function, but that would require a new sense of appreciation of the Palace, and we found no traces of this so far. Rather, the Georgian people feel an intense animosity against the recent past, especially against the cultural imperialism that emanated from Moscow.

It is very unlikely that the Palace will ever be used again as a setting for marriages – this function was too closely linked to the socialist regime that built it. The demise of socialism paved the way for a resurgence of traditional values, and this led to a strong revival of the church. Matrimony has returned to the churches, leaving the Palace an empty relic of a vanished time.

Happy

Almere, June 4, 2003.

Already in Amsterdam Central Station loudspeakers announce that those who want to participate in the activities of the *Libelle* Summer Week can take the train to Almere. An extra stop has been scheduled near Muider Beach. As soon as the train stops, crowds composed mainly of women get out on the improvised, wooden platform. In a long row they set out for the beach, where party tents have been set up for educational and recreational purposes. The latest novelties for the kitchen, for personal care and in home furnishings are on display. In the morning, the visitors are invited to create a new atmosphere for their homes, or visit fashion advisers who tell them how to improve their outfits. In the afternoon, there are bingo games and sushi workshops. For those who think all this is too much, a bar has been installed, and if people need to relax they don't need to worry, for a massage parlor has been provided. If all one's nails have been polished, the day is complete. Satisfied, the women return to the provisional railway station, carrying bags full of products guaranteed to stimulate afterglow. Determined to come back next year, they head for home, still enjoying what for most of them was their first visit to Almere. M.v.R.

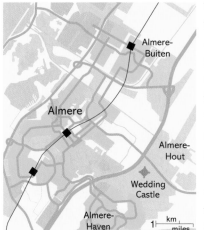

A Marriage Castle in the New Town of Almere

Marieke van Rooy

Only cities where people can get married, children are born, the dying are mourned, and where their memories are carried on to the next generation can be seen as complete urban communities. Cities that evolved slowly in the course of many centuries usually have places – the market square, the town hall or the cathedral – where the collective memory of the city can be celebrated and the feeling of belonging becomes one of the pillars of the urban com-

Happy

munity. In contemporary society the emphasis has shifted to the individual. Opportunities to feel part of the community have become rare, and hardly ever is a building erected that provides the proper setting for that type of sentiment. Probably the shopping mall is the only contemporary environment still fostering human contact, however superficially. And of course the Mosque, dozens of which are being built in all the major cities of Europe – but the Mosque does not address the community at large, only a select group of believers. In old cities, historic public buildings – i.e. buildings that serve a public function – may lose their original meaning, but they still remain important landmarks. Aldo Rossi wrote about this phenomenon in his *L'Architettura della città*: 'In all European cities large buildings or ensembles of buildings can be found that make up a considerable part of the city and only rarely are they used for the purpose for which they were once erected. The Palazzo della Ragione in Padua, for instance. When we visit a monument like that, we're struck by the quantity of functions that apparently are not determined by the building's form. Even so, the form is what we remember, because it is what we experience.' Such buildings are not likely to be found in New Towns. Neither does the city's overall layout encourage people to identify with their urban community. Everything communal seems to be missing in today's new towns.

Almere, a Dutch New Town only twenty-five years old, has determined that the lack of opportunities to forge a collective memory is a serious omission. Special, high quality architecture was always the intention when building Almere, and since the primary goal of this New Town was to alleviate housing conditions in the nearby cities of Amsterdam and Utrecht,

Happy

488

the focus was on accommodating as many people as possible. Although the housing program envisaged mainly the standard type of low-rise housing estates, experiments were made with giving some neighborhoods their own, specific identity. These experimental projects were named after the themes that guided their design: movies, color, music, islands. Interesting though these experiments have undoubtedly been, they failed as a means of endowing Almere as a whole with the clear identity the city apparently longed for. Therefore, the municipal authorities decided to embark upon a mission one is likely to associate with Rossi: the attempt to attract special buildings like a World Trade Center, a theater and a center for pop music. They were designed by renowned architects and have culminated in a reconstruction plan for the central areas of Almere. The plan, which was created by Rem Koolhaas, is dominated by office buildings, shops, parking garages and luxury apartments.

The already impressive list of interesting new buildings will shortly be joined by a 'marriage castle.' Almere's town hall does not fit the requirements of those couples looking for a romantic setting for their marriage, and many of them now look for more suitable locations in historic cities. The municipality was far from pleased with this development, and that led it to look for alternative solutions. It opted for a replica of an existing castle in Belgium, the 'Maison Forte Antoine.' The original castle is dominated by its donjon, a square tower used to defend the building against intruders that was built in the twelfth century. The addition of several wings in the seventeenth century completed the castle and gave it its present rectangular shape. In the course of the centuries, more wings were added, but in the end the castle suffered from

Happy

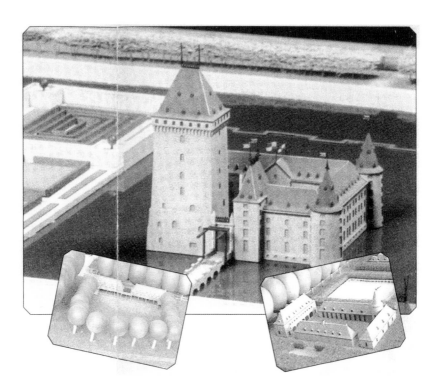

lack of maintenance. In 1997 it was bought by a realtor who soon came up with the idea of making a replica of it for Almere. The original plan was altered to fit its new destination: the main building was enlarged, some wings and a monumental garden were added. The new castle is built in concrete and clad with historic bricks from Hungary. Apart from the marriage hall, the castle comprises a conference room, a restaurant and a hotel. Even though the most modern techniques were used to erect the new castle, its outward appearance is that of an authentic, historic monument. Whereas the original building is situated in an unspoiled, natural setting, the replica is built alongside a highway. Not only does the highway guarantee easy access, it also ensures maximum visibility, which is vital if the castle is to become Almere's principal landmark.

When Almere was initially developed, the architects were still trying to reinterpret historical typologies. The center of Almere Haven, for instance, looks like a twentieth century version of an old coastal city. Twenty years later it is clear that this approach has failed, and therefore an existing model was literally copied. The new castle will find its way into the photo books of the couples who get married there, and their memories will become part of Almere's collective identity. Soon it will be forgotten that the castle is not real. People live to become part of a story, and it doesn't matter if these stories are full of artificial constructions – if people believe in them, the mission has been accomplished.

Happy

Praying in a Cathedral is Very Different than Praying in Front of the Television. New Estates Versus the Historical City

An interview with György Konrád and C.K. Polónyi

Cor Wagenaar

'The glory of Budapest is in part the opposite of a city that looses its character, a mixture of the gigantesque and the city's flamboyant expansion that coincides with the hybrid affiliation of the capital of Hungary with the Habsburg eagle and that is also reflected in the historical eclecticism of its architecture, for instance in the old Buildings of Parliament, or the Opera, that were built by Miklós Ybl in the style of the renaissance, or Imre Steindl's late baroque new Buildings of Parliament. The new entrepreneurial bourgeoisie wanted to create its own heroic past; it was the driving force that urged the city's feverish metamorphosis and its turbulent industrial development, that caused the seventh district to be labeled 'Chicago' and that was hidden behind the veil of sparkling lightness and that, the farther capitalist expansion let it away from its tradition, was the more urgently presented as essentially Hungarian. (…) This 'scale model of America' that Budapest actually was between 1867 and 1914 is saturated with lust for life and a careless tempestuousness. (…) Surely, Budapest can give one the impression of Europe after the show, but unlike Vienna it is not just a stage for memories of the glories of the past, but still also a robust, sanguine city that demonstrated what power Europe could and should have, if only it succeeded in evaluating its scattered energy and join forces instead of wasting them in an

1 *Claudio Magris, Donau. Een ontdekkingsreis door de beschaving van Midden-Europa en de crisis van onze tijd,* Amsterdam 1991, 262, 263, 265. Translated by the editor.

Happy

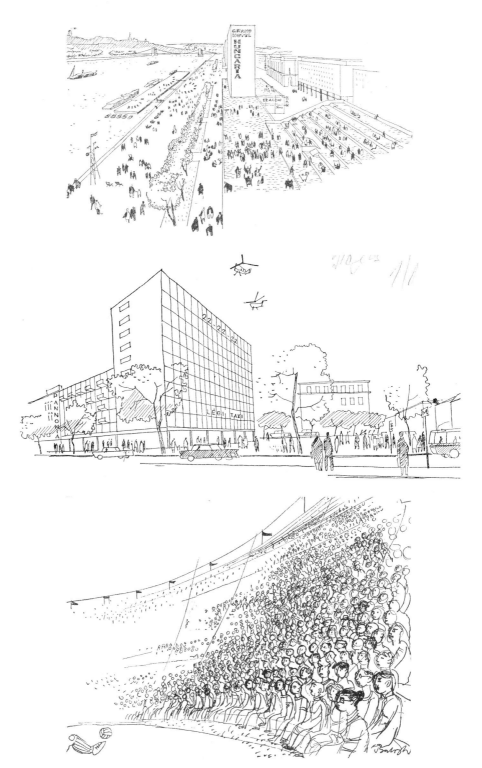

Drawings from Pál Granasztói, Károly Polónyi, Budapest Holnap, Budapest 1959

Happy

eternal process of opposite tendencies that neutralize each other in a permanent deadlock.'[1] Claudio Magris's lively picture of Budapest depicts this busy metropolis as one of the pillars of European civilization. Every revolution that occurred in Europe in the course of the twentieth century left its imprint on Budapest. As in so many cities, the Second World War resulted in large-scale destruction, which was repaired with remarkable energy. Then an even more fundamental drama evolved. A wave of modernization flooded Europe in the wake of the war, and in Hungary this took the shape of a battle for socialism. It was only after the failed uprising of 1956 that Hungarian society experienced its big leap forward. Simultaneously with the suppression of the rebellion, the Russians made Europe's division a permanent one: the iron curtain was there to stay for decades. In these years, reformist regimes alternated with hardline socialist governments.

For Károly Polónyi and György Konrád these events proved to be decisive. Between 1969 and 1975 Polónyi was in charge of the city's Department of Architecture and Town

Happy

Planning. During these years the modernization of Budapest was at its apogee. A ring of new housing estates, made up of prefabricated high-rise apartments, forever changed the city's periphery. New infrastructure was introduced to accommodate the ever-growing number of automobiles. At the time, Polónyi was convinced that these changes were necessary for the city to survive, and today he remains faithful to the views he held then. Living in the city is something special for him, something extremely valuable. The city is the 'market of ideas', and the 'cradle of civilization'. Even more importantly, in the city people first learned to respect each other's ideas. That makes the city the place where people can feel free.

In his many novels, Konrád conveys the same views. 'The big city is the most beautiful creation of human society. No work of art can equal the community of the metropolis. It is a phenomenon that constitutes itself, it is concentration and enlightenment, it represents the battle against the slow pace of objects and people, it is human concentration and the joining together of people as an act of creation.'[2] While studying the social changes that modernization triggered, comparing, for example, the new housing estates with traditional social patterns, Konrád became an expert on Budapest. In his work, the city lies at the core of a specific urban philosophy. According to Konrád, the city makes it hard to stay at home. In the city, there are so many things to attract attention, activities to participate in, gatherings, exhibitions and, above all, street life. The essence of the city is its public space, and Konrád relates its importance to the number of people that can be found in the streets and squares. He sees Budapest as a Geschichtenkalvakade, a collage of numerous stories, and as a catalyst of knowledge. 'I believe that people who live in cities know lots of things that one can only know in a city.'[3] Like Polónyi, Konrád sees the city as a place that generates freedom.

2 'Die Großstadt is die prachtvollste Schöpfung der menschlichen Gesellschaft. Es gibt kein Kunstwerk, das es mit der Lebensgemeinschaft der Großstadt aufnehmen könnte. Sie is ein sich selbst aufbauendes Subjekt, sie ist Konzentration und Illumination, sie ist Kampf gegen die Trägheit des Material und des Menschen, sie ist der menschlichen Zusammenschluß und die Vereiniging des Menschen als Schöpfung.' György Konrád, 'Von Schelmen, Harlekinen und Hochstapler. Budapester Marginalien', in: *Die Melancholie der Wiedergeburt*, Frankfurt am Main 1992, 24.

3 'Ich glaube, daß der Mensch in der Großstadt vieles weiß, was er nur dort wissen kann', György Konrád, 'Von Schelmen, Harlekinen und Hochstaplern,', Budapester Marginalien', in: *Die Melancholie der Wiedergeburt*, 50.

Konrád appears to continue the tradition of Baudelaire when he defines the city as the realm of the flaneur; for him, loitering on the streets is an act of self-affirmation. Only exhibitionists are really free; cities where people stay at home demonstrate a lack of freedom. The secrets of the city are most easily disclosed to the pedestrian strollers. Konrád sees Budapest as an essentially European city, the product of a culture that is obsessed with the passing of time. Precisely that makes the European city very different from its American counterpart, which is obsessed with space.

From this common vantage point, however, the views of Konrád and Polónyi tend to diverge. Whereas Polónyi is convinced that the city will always need planning and professional guidance, Konrád overtly questions the merits of planning. His urbanism is coincidental, analogous to the complex interaction of people on a busy street. In his book *On the Peripheries,* his 'retrospective diary,' Polónyi explains his personal motto: 'Remain loyal and preserve your rights'; in this motto, loyalty stands for fidelity to one's profession.[4] In his view, the work of the architect-city planner has two sides: on the one hand, it is a pragmatic discipline aimed at solving practical problems, but, on the other hand, it fosters idealistic visions of the city and its people. 'Planning is an opportunistic activity. Either you do what you have to do, and do it at the right moment, or you don't do it at all.' This attitude he summarized in his favorite metaphor: 'The planner is like a sailor. A sailor should not try to change the winds, instead, he has to make the most of them, whatever the circumstances may be.' However, Polónyi complemented this pragmatic approach with optimistic visions of a modernized world with better living conditions for everyone. He dreamed of creating new patterns of living that would accelerate the transition to modern lifestyles without disturbing the universal characteristics of traditional ways of living.

4 C.K. Polónyi, *On the Peripheries*, Budapest 1992.

Did this qualify Polónyi – in the eyes of Konrád – as the typical representative of the 'planner-God?' As the almighty bureaucrat who had struck a deal with the authorities? Did he belong to the caste of technocrats who, as Konrád and his colleague Iván Szelényi had written in *Die Intelligenz auf dem Weg zur Klassenmacht* ('The Intellectuals and the Path to Class Dominance') adapted themselves quite easily to the 'dictatorial administration,' even when they questioned its political motives?[5] Konrád much prefers places that are left untouched by the planners. In his famous *The City Builder* he glorifies the unplanned city: 'Let's face it: we like this city; it resembled us, and the colored drawings of children on the gray asphalt. We began to look into the labyrinthine streets and saw witty and mostly unorthodox solutions to tricky tasks, to which patient time had given its stamp of approval. We saw limber channels of motion amid stiff blocks... We even accepted the scattered bones in excavation ditches, accepted this complicated piece of work that has accommodated so much havoc, so much change, and that has come to resemble only itself.'[6] Konrád deplores the high-rise housing estates. For him, they represent the ultimate gesture of the planners. 'It shocked me to see colleagues of mine, nice, well educated people who meant well, gazed at the models of the new housing estates, and how they talked about fifty thousand people in this neighborhood, subway lines going in this or that direction. They behaved as if they were Gods. I experienced this display of superiority as an affront.'

5 György Konrád, Iván Szelényi, *Die Intelligenz auf dem Weg zur Klassenmacht*, Frankfurt am Main 1978, 324.

6 György Konrád, *The City Builder*, New York 1977, 27-29.

Here were two completely different men, working in approximately the same period, trying to improve the same city. One might expect that their different opinions would dominate our interview. Even though both Polónyi and Konrád completely agreed on the importance and the historical continuity of the city, their opposing views on the role of planning and the fundamental aspects of urban life were guaranteed to fuel a fierce argument. Unexpectedly, things took another turn.

Happy

Happy

Happy

497

Reformism and the narrow margins of politics The uprising of 1956, which acted as a watershed in the history of Hungary, marked the lives of both Polónyi and Konrád. Polónyi was born in a small town in eastern Hungary. After surrendering his initial ambition of becoming a journalist, he decided to study architecture at the Technical University of Budapest. Like Konrád, he was extremely critical of the regime, but the reformist period that permeated political life after the revolt prompted him to stay in Hungary. Instead of leaving the country, he wrote a book with his colleague Pál Granasztói, *Budapest Holnap* ('Budapest Tomorrow').[7]

7 Pál Granasztói, C.K. Polónyi, *Budapest Holnap.*

In the same years, Konrád watched the development of socialism with growing concern, and his skepticism started to affect his sociological studies.

Budapest Holnap eloquently illustrates the narrow limits placed on criticism of the regime. The manuscript of the book was completed in 1957, but it proved to be very difficult to get it published. 'We called upon a friend of ours who was a publisher. He read the manuscript and was willing to take the risk, but only if we could arrange some kind of official support. So we turned to a high-ranking employee at the Ministry of Planning, whom we knew to be rather liberal, for help. We succeeded in convincing him, and the book could finally be published in 1959. It caused a scandal at the Ministry. The hardliners brutally attacked us and wrote a review that was meant to appear in one of the weekly newspapers. The editor of this weekly was a friend of ours and was willing to hold the review back for one week. That gave us time to write a very positive review and get it sanctioned by yet another high-ranking official. This review appeared in the party newspaper, shortly before the weekly with the debunking review came out! Nevertheless, when they read our book people wondered why we didn't end up in jail. The book appeared to celebrate the past and criticize everything brought about by socialism.'

Budapest Holnap is a remarkable book indeed. Its aim was to restore the city to its former glory by making changes in it in accordance with the principles of modern town planning. The authors envisaged the old historical core — which was to be safeguarded against the all too brutal waves of modernization — surrounded by a wide ring that was to become the stage for more radical interventions. What made the inner city exceptionally valuable was its historical character. 'Each square meter there is invested with history, with life and all kinds of events, and carries more seeds of the future than any other place. The core has many faces. It is the political and commercial center, it houses the major universities, and it is the place where tourists flock together.[8] Polónyi and Granasztói stressed that cities are made by people, not by planning. 'The expansion and improvement of cities do not depend on projects and regulations, but above all on the strength and the will of the inhabitants.'[9] Even though they stubbornly maintained that they did not try to produce some kind of counter-proposal to official planning, the book nevertheless clearly manifests a way of thinking that is completely at odds with the mentality responsible for the rigid proposals emanating from the official planning offices.

8 Pál Granasztói, C.K. Polónyi, *Budapest Holnap.*

9 Pál Granasztói, C.K. Polónyi, *Budapest Holnap.*

Happy

The ideas promoted in *Budapest Holnap* reflect the spirit of Team X, the 'new' avant-garde that had evolved within CIAM. This movement also criticized the rigid dogmas and the explicitly technocratic approach to modernism that had originated in the United States and spread all over Europe. At the time of its publication *Budapest Holnap* did indeed represent an act of defiance against official planning. Polónyi, however, did not get a chance to realize his ideas. In 1960, he left Hungary to partake in the development of modern planning in Africa, at this time a continent effervescent with optimism as the process of decolonization created undreamed of new opportunities. His stay in Africa was to have a decisive impact on his further career.

A few years later, in 1965, Konrád embarked on his career as an urban sociologist. 'Together with Szelényi I wrote one of the first sociological treatises on the modern city. Around that time, sociology began to regain its position as a respected profession. This tendency even extended to architecture and town planning, which now recognized the need for at least some sort of sociological survey. Architects wanted to know what kind of apartments they should build. The future inhabitants of their housing estates couldn't tell them, since they had hardly any contacts with the architects. Public housing was initiated by the municipal authorities and the task of defining what a house should be like was now assigned to the sociologists. What captivated me was the way the changes proposed by the planners affected the structure of the entire city, and how this revolutionized the social stratification of the urban community. How certain strata moved from one zone to another, and how the social make-up of various neighborhoods changed completely because of the proposals of architects and town planners.'

Polónyi knew the work of Konrád and his colleagues, but decided not to join them. 'I knew Szelényi. In those days, Szelényi and I taught at Cornell University and Szelényi invited me to join him in developing and expanding the scope of social criticism. At the time, I was working on other problems: we faced the task of building an unprecedented number of houses in the next five years, because back then there was yet another social problem: each apartment housed three or four families, and often lacked a proper sewage system and fresh water. What interested me much more was how to use the limited means at our disposal as efficiently as possible. I didn't agree with Szelényi. For me, their efforts represented some kind of intellectual exercise based more on foreign literature than on the real problems in Budapest.' From that time on, Polónyi and Konrád went their own ways.

Large-scale urban expansion: modernization or oppression?

Having been called back to Budapest in 1969, Polónyi was appointed chief architect and town planner of the capital. His main task in the years that followed was the realization of large-scale urban expansion plans, specifically, the housing estates that were to be criticized so vehemently by Konrád. Polónyi believed that there was no alternative. 'In the 1960s, the housing shortage became acute. It wasn't caused by the growth of the population but by a strong increase in the number of families. The average number of people living in one apartment went down from 4.5 to 2.5 and, as a consequence, the number of houses had to double. For that there was only one solution: the large-scale construction of high-rise apartment buildings of the type already

Happy

499

Happy

in use in Scandinavia and France. We simply lacked sufficient construction workers to do it any other way. Of course, we could have transferred a part of the labor force from industry to the building trades, but state policy didn't allow us to.' The situation of the new estates was carefully studied. 'When Budapest was first built, those who could not afford to live in the city itself moved away, creating a ring just beyond the municipal border of Pest. After the communist takeover, this ring was annexed to the city. The communists hoped, thereby, to increase their share of the votes, since the periphery was predominantly leftwing. Between this semi-circular band and the inner city, there was an empty ring with gardens. By locating the new housing estates there, both the inner city and the periphery could profit from the new infrastructure. The introduction of new infrastructure was part of the building program. Even today I don't think it was such a bad idea to plan the new estates in this way, no matter how strongly we were attacked by the press – and not, by the way, by the inhabitants of the new apartments. What stimulated the critical attitude of the press was the fact that we were very late in adopting this kind of strategy. When we finally got a chance to build these estates, they had already become the object of severe criticism in France. We knew the literature and tried to learn from the mistakes made abroad. In many ways, our housing estates are much better, but in some ways they are worse, because we lacked sufficient funding.'

This pragmatic attitude coincided with an optimistic view of the modern city. In the early 1970s, Polónyi recalls in his retrospective diary, the city radiated optimism. 'Even though the laws and regulations from the 1950s were

Happy

501

Óbuda Housing Estate, 1972

still on the books, the climate had changed completely. The civil servants dressed elegantly, everybody wore a tie and most had a university degree. Everyone seemed to agree that the tedious official procedures, which still had to be respected, should be complemented by honest, amicable relationships. And we were enthusiastic about our task: to catch up with the rest of Europe.'[10] In only a couple of years, Polónyi succeeded in realizing many of the dreams he had published in *Budapest Holnap*: the historical city was spared, and modernization efforts were focused on the periphery. A temporary 'showroom,' where the latest plans could be studied, demonstrated Polóny's belief in the necessity of involving the citizens in the transformation of their city. The row of new hotels along the Danube, already presented in *Budapest Holnap*, and the idea of adding a public terrace to the new Hilton hotel located on the Buda side of the river also originated in this book.

10 C.K. Polónyi, *On the Peripheries.*

Konrád was far from enthusiastic. He saw the new housing estates as tools of a state-promoted anti-urban policy. 'Life had already tested this kind of functional town planning, and rejected it. The grands ensembles developed by the socialists are very unpopular —probably because they destroy the essence of the city. The city produced two fundamental things: the street and the square. The continuous street disappeared, and discontinuity was now the watchword. Visual stimuli are lacking. There is nothing to see. People want to gaze at shop windows, go to bars, visit restaurants, meet their fellow citizens on the street. In a society where the political police regarded a meeting of three or four intellectuals in a bar as highly

Happy

Textile Painting Company. Young workers watch their flats under construction, September 1973

suspicious (what could they be discussing?), we tried to increase the opportunities for people to meet. A bit of fun, entertainment, relaxation. What people try to avoid more than anything is being bored. The entire epoch of socialist town planning, of prefab housing and the rational distribution of services, infrastructure, heating, traffic roads and the calculated minimum amount of sunshine and greenery between the flats, was anything but a success story.'

For Konrád, the new estates constituted a threat to urbanity. He saw them as an instrument of oppression. 'We considered the new estates a perfect means of making the people apathetic, of transforming them into some sort of machines. And the way the new apartments were assigned, as a kind of premium for political correctness, a present, was also wrong. It reduced adults to children. It demonstrated the self-esteem and self-confidence of a fundamentally industrial mentality born of the scientific and technological revolution and the futuristic rhetoric that went with it, combined with socialism in Eastern Europe and capitalism in the West. We wanted to prevent the destruction of urban living. We wanted to demonstrate what people really wanted. Our message was: please, don't go too far. Less state, more society. Less rigid rationalism, more communication. Sensual communication. People should have a wide range of opportunities to come together.'

Polónyi was well aware of this criticism. 'But I should stress that this negative attitude wasn't half as severe as the criticism directed against the town planners who, over a century ago, tore down those beautiful, two story baroque houses in Pest and replaced them by the five story apartment buildings everybody loves so much today.' For him, the new housing

Happy

503

estates do not represent the town planners' readiness to surrender to whatever happens to be fashionable, and even less do they stand for authoritarian state planning. He is convinced that they represent universal values that are deeply rooted in the discipline of town panning. This type of modernization was indeed characteristic of the ideas of Team X. 'The views of Team X were always very important. I think that they will prove to be much more valuable than all kinds of fashionable novelties. I wouldn't say that these ideas make their comeback every now and then. They are always there. Again and again we rediscover them. It is fascinating to see that everything we stood for was already there at the turn of the century. At the conference that was held in London in 1910 all the themes that were important to us were already analyzed, including social criticism. Geddes was very important at this conference. All his books were republished in 1954, a memorial year for Geddes. And these books had a great influence on Team X. But even before, in 1951, there was a group that stated that our cities had become boring and ghastly, because we no longer followed historical examples. This criticism was inspired by Sitte. The history of the city was the theme of CIAM VIII, which dealt specifically with the core of the city. The Roman Forum, Piazza San Marco, the Capitol, the Champs Elysées, Rockefeller Center. Ortega y Gasset was often quoted: "the city is like a gun, the hole is the most important, the empty spaces where people meet. These should not be created by bureaucracy, but by art."'

Here, the interview reached a crucial point. Evidently, Polónyi and Konrád fought a common enemy: the bureaucracies that despised individual personality and were afraid of the social community expressing itself in the public realm. Both men believed in the unique value of urban lifestyles. Even their positive ideals, the public space crowded with people who celebrate their freedom, are very similar. At what point do they disagree? Clearly, Polónyi's views on society and on the conditions that should be met in order to create a socially supportive environment differ from the concern for the specific history of a given city that inspired Konrád. His plea for the automobile as a means of transportation that stimulates individual freedom, and his belief in the possibility of organizing a city by using a simple architectural structure or a repetitive urban pattern, are hardly compatible with the historical city and its subtle interplay of parcels and building lines, on the one hand, and architectural representation on the other. Even more importantly, the position of both men within the planning machinery and their views on professional responsibility were totally different. Polónyi claims that the possibilities of renewing Budapest's urban tissue have been used to the full. Given the prevailing political winds, no sailor could have done better. 'Our aim was to make use of the possibilities that presented themselves. Had we not done so, a quarter of the population would have lived in slums by now. Had we not created the second subway line and improved the city's infrastructure, our transport system would by now resemble that of Cairo, Teheran or Lagos.' At a more fundamental level, however, the two men fully agreed. Both believe in urbanity and in the city's capacity to survive whatever crisis may occur.

City in crisis: urban reality and its virtual enemies
Once again the city appears to be in crisis. Some philosophers predict the end of the city as a social model and

the emergence of new patterns of living. The media are thought to play a dominant role here. Is this fear justified? Polónyi and Konrád think not. According to Polónyi: 'There have always been people who disliked the city. Cities are the cradle of the urban masses, of the worst that mankind is capable of. Already during industrialization this became apparent. Rapidly deteriorating demographic tendencies always manifested themselves first in the cities. All major revolutions, whether leftwing or rightwing, always start there. That is why people from Jefferson to Mumford were always afraid of the city. In Hungary, we always have had two literatures: an urban and a rural one. For the populists, cities are bad and sinful. And now, at a time when national economies make way for international globalization and cities no longer can manage to pay for their own infrastructure, the city appears once again to be in crisis. They have lost their economic viability. The industrial phase is over. Industry isn't an urban phenomenon any more. The computer makes the industrial labor forces superfluous.' But does all this imply the end of the city? Both Polónyi and Konrád are convinced that the city will survive the latest crisis just as it did the many preceding ones. Polónyi observes that: 'Throughout history, cities have been successful in adapting themselves to changing circumstances. Budapest was the beautiful capital of the Roman province of Pannonia. In the Middle Ages it was the seat of the Hungarian monarchy. During the Turkish occupation, it became the capital of the region. When the Turks left it developed into a small city populated mainly by German immigrants. After the Compromise of 1867 it became the capital of the Hungarian part of the Austro-Hungarian Dual Monarchy. In 1918 it suddenly found itself the capital of a small central European country that had to accelerate industrial development in order to survive. This kind of story can be told of all important cities. If they have been capable of adapting themselves in the past, I'm convinced that they will be able to do so now.'

In Polónyi's views, the same reasoning applies to the new housing estates. 'One shouldn't think that they will always remain what they are now. They will surely be expanded and transformed. Florence and Bologna started as tiny cities that were founded by army officers who designed simple baracks, and from that time on they have continued to change. The apartment buildings in the inner city also change continuously, but the only way to expand them is to fill in their courtyards. To every second window of the apartments in the periphery, we could attach a hanging garden. And that will surely happen. Elsewhere, these buildings will be torn down because they have become slums. But cities always change, and it would be arrogant to believe that, just because we are the ones who built them, they have ceased to do so.' In Polónyi's views, nothing beats the reality of city life. 'What is there to show on television once there are no cities any more? After all, praying in a cathedral is not quite the same experience as praying in front of a television set.'

Konrád agrees. He doesn't see the modern media as a serious threat to urban life. 'For the far future, that might be an interesting thought, but for now, it isn't. People still flock to the cities, if they can afford it. The square meter price in Budapest is higher than in any other place in Hungary and in some parts has reached the same level as in Western Europe. The market doesn't show that people have started to leave the cities. I'm not so sure that, in general,

Happy

people can live just as well in the countryside, working on their computer without physical contact with other people. Life doesn't offer grounds for thinking that people can live like that. They like to come together, to go to a restaurant, loiter in the city and indulge in urban rituals at night. These longings are basic and cannot be changed by electronic revolutions in the media. I don't believe in the possibility that people's need to meet each other will disappear. And that implies that the city will never lose its function. If it has always been like that, why would it change now?

Happy

The contributors

Lucka Azman

Born in Ljubljana, Slovenia in 1961. Graduated from the Faculty of Architecture in 1986, gaining a MSc in 1993 and PhD In 2004. Granted by Norwegian and Finnish government and twice by European Community in years 1988 – 1998. Assistant professor at the Faculty of Architecture, University of Ljubljana. Published numerous articles in Slovenia and abroad, editor of several publications, organiser of numerous international symposiums and workshops, author of many exhibitions. Dealing mainly with themes such as architectural theory, architecture and archaeology, urban design and planning, contemporary architectural education.

Herman van Bergeijk

Architectural historian, works at the Institute of History of Art, Architecture and Urbanism (IHAAU) of Delft University of Techonology. One of his recent publications is *De Steen van Berlage* (2003). He will soon publish a study of the work of Jan Wils and a book about the Märzgefallenendenkmal in Weimar (in association with K.J. Winkler).

Aaron Betsky

Architect, architecture historian and critic and director of the Netherlands Architecture Institute (NAi) in Rotterdam. From 1995 to 2001 he was curator of architecture, design and digital projects at the San Francisco Museum of Modern Art (SF-MOMA). His publications include such titles as *Architecture Must Burn* (2000), *Landscrapers* (2002), *Three California Houses: The Homes of Max Palevsky* (2003) and *False Flat* (2004).

Koos Bosma

Architectural historian and professor at the Vrije Universiteit in Amsterdam. His publications are about infrastructure, housing and urban planning, e.g. the recent co-edited volume *Mastering the City: North European City Planning 1900-2000.*

Ronald Brouwer

Lives in Madrid since 1992 where he works as dramatist and translator of stage plays (works by Judith Herzberg, Gerardjan Rijnders, Karst Woudstra, and also Bredero and Hugo Claus; he also translates poetry of Hugo Claus). In 2001 and 2003, he was assistant director of the theatre festival 'Clásicos en Alcalá'. At present, he is writing a book on the history of the Teatro de La Abadía.

Lucy Bullivant

Architectural critic, author and exhibition and conference curator. She was the guest editor of *AD's Home Front: New Developments in Housing* issue. She contributes articles and reviews to *The Financial Times, Tate magazine, Archis, Domus, Icon, Building Design, a-matter, Metropolis* and *Indesign.* Exhibitions she has curated include Space Invaders: Emerging UK Architecture (British Council, 2001), The Near and the Far, Fixed and In Flux(XIX Milan Triennale, 1996), and Kid Size: the Material World of Childhood (Vitra Design Museum, 1997).

Alessandra Coppa

Teaches Architectural History at the Politecnico di Milano. She is a member of the editorial staff of the Italian magazine *Area* and writes as an art and architectural critic for several Italian newspapers. Her publications include *Francesco Paciotto architetto militare* (Milan 2002).

Cǎlin Dan

Based in Amsterdam / Bucharest. MA in Art History & Theory. Initial career as art journalist, free lance curator and cultural manager (with the Soros Foundation, Romania). From 1990 involved in various visual projects, independently and within the art duo subREAL. Developer of multi-media events in Romania and in the Netherlands (mainly with V2 Lab for the Unstable Media, Rotterdam, and as creative for rich media platforms - Lost Boys Interactive, Amsterdam). Contributions to mainstream and alternative publications on internet related topics. Various teaching positions (notably the Art University Bucharest and the Hogeschool voor de Kunsten, Utrecht). Presently developing a cross-platform research on the Emotional Architecture of medium-to-large scale metropolises.

Jörn Düwel
Professor of architectural history and theory at the University of Applied Sciences Hamburg. With Werner Durth and Niels Gutschow he co-authored *Architektur und Städtebau der DDR* (Frankfurt 1998) and *Baukunst voran* (Berlin 1995) and with Niels Gutshow, *Städtebau in Deutschland im 20. Jahrhundert* (Stuttgart 2001).

Evelien van Es
Studied at the Hogeschool voor de Kunsten in Utrecht and architecture history at the Vrije Universiteit in Amsterdam. Presently she works as a free lance architectural historian, writing articles on a wide range of topics in the field of architecture and town planning.

Niels Gutschow
Studied architecture in Darmstadt and wrote his PhD thesis on Japanese towns. From 1978 to 1980 he was City Director of Building Conservation in Münster. He is the author of numerous publications on the history of town planning, including *Documentation of the Rebuilding of the City of Münster*, with Regine Stiemer, and *Annihilation and Utopia. Town Planning in Warsaw 1939-1945*, with Barbara Klain, both in 1982, and the two volume work *the Fate of German Architecture in the War*, with Hartwig Beseler, in 1988. Recently, he published W. Durth, J. Düwel, & N. Gutschow, *Architektur und Städtebau der DDR*, 2 vols. Frankfurt a.M., New York 1999. Since the 1970s he dedicates part of his time to Asian architecture, spending several months in Nepal each year.

Helma Hellinga
Works as free lance urban sociologist. She was the curator of exhibitions for the Amsterdam Stedelijk Museum and the Amsterdam Historical Museum and published about public housing and urban planning. She was co-editor of *Mastering the City. 100 years of urban planning in Europe* (1998) and co-author of *Ernest Groosman 1917-1999* (2001) and specializes in public housing after Worldwar II. She is now working on a study of the urban renewal in the Western Garden Cities of Amsterdam.

Elisabeth Hofer
Researcher (education and training in higher institutions of learning in Russia and the Ukraine), trainer (personnel development in companies in Russia; personal skills development for junior diplomats and postgraduate university students worldwide), organizer (conferences, workshops, exchange programmes for students and professors). Since 1997 Director of Studies, Diplomatic Academy of Vienna, Vienna, Austria; 1994-1996 Head of Liaison Office Lviv of the Austrian Institute for East and Southeastern Euroepan Studies, Lviv, Ukraine; 1991-1993 Director of 'Team Training Russia', Moscow, Russia; 1988-1991 Director of Training Department, Wang Inc., Vienna, Austria and Boston, U.S.A.

György Konrád
Novelist, essayist and sociologist. His best known works are *The City Builder* (Budapest 1973; New York 1977), *A Feast in the Garden* (Budapest 1985; New York 1992), *Melinda en Dragomán* (Budapest 1991) and *The Invisible Voice* (Budapest 2000; New York 2000). His most recent novel appeared last year: *The Eclipse* (Budapest 2003).

Doris Müller-Toovey
Studied art history, history and theatre sciences at the Free University in Berlin and has worked over eight years for the German History Museum in Berlin. She has also worked on several exhibitions as a freelancer, for example 'Happiness City Space' at the Academy of Arts in Berlin in 2002. In 2003, she finished her PhD and in May 2004 she set up her own office, offering exhibition services, together with a former colleague in Berlin.

Filippo de Pieri
Holds a research appointment and teaches Planning History at the Politecnico di Torino. He is the editor of the planning section of the Italian monthly *Il Giornale dell'Architettura*. His publications include *Il controllo improbabile. Progetti urbani, burocrazie, decisioni in una città capitale dell'Ottocento* (Milan 2005, forthcoming).

Karoly Polónyi
Architect and urbanist. Assistant lecturer at the Technical University of Budapest (1950-1954), Chief engineer working on regional planning of Lake Balaton (1957-1960), Consulting architect of the Ghana Construction Corporation (1963-1969, Associate director, director in charge of the Department of Architecture and Town Planning of the

Happy

Municipal Council of Budapest (1969-1974), bilateral aid expert for the Ministry of Housing and Urban Development, Ethiopia (1977-1980), Research Professor at the Technical University of Budapest, 1080-1998. Held teaching post as visiting scholar at the Architectural Association School of Architecture, London and Nottingham, Cornell University, Ithaca (as a member of the TEAM 10 chain teaching), Middle East Technical University, Ankara.

Michelle Provoost

Architectural historian and co-founded the Rotterdam-based office of Crimson in 1994. She wrote articles for national and international magazines and was author and/or editor of *Asfalt* and the Crimson-books *Re-Arch, Re-Urb, Mart Stam's Trousers* and *Too Blessed to be Depressed*. Recently she became a Ph.D. with a publication on Hugh Maaskant and Dutch modernist architecture from the fifties and sixties. Since 2001 she has been one of the directors of WiMBY!, a social and fysical development project in a sixties New Town near Rotterdam.

Marieke van Rooy

Studied Art History at the University of Amsterdam. Works as free-lance publicist and curator. For the NAi she contributed to exhibitions on J.J.P. Oud, Stadiums, The architecture of mass recreation, Reality Machines, Start; in 2002 she was the curator of Moving Landscapes, art an architecture in the Netherlands, in Sala 1 in Rome. She contributed to many magazines and books.

Paolo Scrivano

Assistant Professor of Architectural History at the University of Toronto. His recent publications include *Storia di un'idea di architettura moderna. Henry-Russell Hitchcock e l'International Style* (Milan 2001) and *Olivetti Builds. Modern Architecture in Ivrea* (Milan 2001, with Patrizia Bonifazio).

Henriett Szabo

Architect, obtained a university degree in the Budapest University of Technology and Economics (BUTE), in 2001. Obtained a postgraduate degree in barrier-free design in 2003 in BUTE. Previously took part in the design process of the reconstruction of the Museum of Fine Arts, Urania Cinema and Páva Street Synagogue in the Mányi Architectural Studio (István Mányi), office building with Buda Architectural Workshop (János Kóris) and the National Theatre of Székesfehérvár with Artonic Design (Géza Szőkedencsi). Recently she is a postgraduate student in the BUTE and teaches in the Department of Industrial and Agricultural Buildings. Besides that, she works on projects of barrier-free design.

Ed Taverne

Architectural historian, emeritus professor of architecture and urban design history at the University of Groningen. His most important publications are: *Stedebouw. De geschiedenis van de stad in de Nederlanden van 1500 tot heden* (Nijmegen 1993), *Carel Weeber, architect* (Rotterdam 1989) and with Kees Schuyt *1950: Prosperity and Welfare* (Assen 2004).

Bogdan Tscherkes

Professor and director of the architecture faculty of the National University of Lvov. Member of the Ukranian academy of architecture and corresponding member of the Saksische Kunstacademie in Dresden. Professor at the Institute of Urbanism Design and Planning of the Vienna University of Technology. Writes regularly about Ukranian and Soviet architecture in Eastern Europe.

Pieter Uyttenhove

Associate professor in theory and history of urban planning at the Department of Architecture and Urban Planning of Ghent University, Belgium. His research and publications focus on 19th and 20th century city and landscape design, and planning theory. His PhD on Marcel Lods, at the EHESS in Paris, is under press. Was curator of the drawing collection of the Académie d'Architecture in Paris and coordinator of the architectural program of Antwerp European cultural capital in 1993. He currently also teaches in the New York Paris Program at Columbia University (Paris). Published numerous articles in international reviews and was author/editor of several books.

Cor Wagenaar

Architectural historian; works at the Institute of History of Art, Architecture and Urbanism (IHAAU) of Delft University of Technology. Publications include *Welvaartsstad in wording. De wederopbouw van Rotterdam* (Rotterdam 1993), and together with Ed Taverne and Martien de Vletter, *J.J.P. Oud. Poetic Functionalist 1890-1963* (Rotterdam 2001). Also carries out research into health care architecture for the University Hospital Groningen.

Happy

Illustrations

13 Photo's M. Borggreve, 28 Photo Károly Escher, Budapest, National Museum, Collection of Historical Photographs, 30 Photo David Seymour, 32 Photo's Noor Mens, 44 Photo Cas Oorthuys, 45 Budapest, National Széchenyi Library, Collection of Small Prints, 46 Photo Dan Weiner, 47 bottom: Photo V. Taresevich, 52-53, 54 top: Kiev, National Film-, Photo and Phono archives of the Ukraine, 54 bottom, 55 top (2): Kiev, Archive of the Institute of History and Theory of Architecture, 55 bottom (2): Kiev, National Film-, Photo and Phono archives of the Ukraine, 56 Kiev, Archive of the Institute of History and Theory of Architecture, 57 Kiev, National Museum of the Ukraine, 58 top and middle: Kiev, National Film-, Photo and Phono archives of the Ukraine, bottom: Photo K. Shamshin, 59 top and middle: Kiev, National Film-, Photo and Phono archives of the Ukraine, 60 Photo Anatolij Kudrytzkij, 61 Photo A.B. Poddubnyj, 62 top: Photo Bogdan Tscherkes, bottom: photo Ukrinform, 64-73 Stanislaw Jankowski, *MDM Marszalkowska 1730-1954*, Warsaw 1955, 83-89 Budapest, National Széchenyi Library, Collection of Small Prints, 105-107 Johanna Kint, *Expo 58 als belichaming van het humanistisch modernisme*, Rotterdam 2001, 110-111 Photos Daniela Walter, 114-115 Photo's J.A. Vrijhof / Nederlands fotomuseum, 124-126 Turin, Fiat Archives, 155 Photo Marieke van Rooy, 171, 174-175 Gross Max 178-181 Photos Marieke van Rooy, 220-222 Turin, Fiat Archives, 237-243 Rurhlandmuseum Essen, 250 Rotterdam, Gemeentearchief, 251 Hungarian News Agency, 252-254 Budapest, National Széchenyi Library, Collection of Small Prints, 277 *Hoog Catharijne. Een rekonstrukieplan* [s.l, s.a.], 283-287 Photo's Daniela Walter, 301 E. de Jong, M. Dominicus-Van Soest, *Aardse Paradijzen. De tuin in de Nederlandse kunst, 1770 tot 2000*, Haarlem, Enschede 1999, 304-308 Barcelona, Taller de Arquitectura Archive, 312-314 Photos Niels Gutschow, 316-319 Photos C.V. Dahmen, 331-335 Private Archive of Vico Magistretti, 343-347 Joaquim Viera, *Portugal Século XX. Crónica em Imagens 1970-1980*, Lisbon 2000, 358-359 Photo László Balogh P., Hungarian News Agency, 366-367 `B.V. Algemeen Nederlands Persbureau ANP, 375 bottom: Kiev, National Film-, Photo and Phono archives of the Ukraine, 377 Photos M. Koslovskij, 379 Photo P. Beresin, 385-388 Photos Jörn Düwel, 399-400 Photos Niels Gutschow, 405 Photos Pieter Uyttenhove, 417-424 Paris, Centre Pompidou-MNAM-CCI, 432 O. Volobuyev, *Greater Yalta*, Moscow 1979, 433 Kiev, National Film-, Photo and Phono archives of the Ukraine, 434-435 Photo: Roman Ozerskij and Eduard Alesin 454-458 Photos Paolo Monti, 1969. Bologna, Cineteca di Bologna, Archivio Fotografico, Fondo Paolo Monti, 471 Ed Taverne, Cor Wagenaar (ed.) *The Colour of the City*, Laren 1992, 472 National Széchenyi Library, Collection of Small Prints, 473 Ed Taverne, Cor Wagenaar (ed.) T*he Colour of the City*, Laren 1992, 477 Photo Jörn Düwel, 482 Photo Jörn Düwel, 492-493 Granasztói Pál, Polónyi Károly, Budapest Holnap, Budapest 1959, 496-500 Photos Cor Wagenaar, 502 Photo Rudolf Járai, Hungarian News Agency, 503 Photo Endre Friedmann, Hungarian News Agency

Happy

Acknowledgments

The publication *Happy. Cities and Public Happiness in Post-War Europe* is an initiative of Stichting Architecturalia. Architecturalia is a foundation that promotes publications in the field of architecture, landscape architecture and town planning. This book contains the findings of a project that was supported by the Netherlands Architectural Institute in Rotterdam and the Akademie der Künste in Berlin with the intention of organizing an exhibition on this theme. In October 2002, this resulted in an exhibition in the Akademie der Künste in Berlin, entitled Glück – Stadt – Raum. Abridged versions of Lucy Bullivant, 'Cumbernauld, Tomorrow's Town Today', Filippo de Pieri and Paolo Scrivano, 'The Italian Autogrill', Jörn Düwel, 'Gori, the Forgotten Mekka', Bogdan Tscherkes, '"Artek, Artek! – Joy of my Heart!"', and Pieter Uyttenhove, 'La Grande Motte' have previously been published in Romana Schneider, Rudolf Stegers (ed.), *Glück Stadt Raum in Europa 1945 bis 2000*, Berlin 2002, the catalogue of the above mentioned exhibition. An earlier version of the interview with Karoly Polónyi and György Konrád, 'Praying in a Cathedral is Very Different from Praying in Front of the Television. New Housing Estates Versus the Historical City' has been published in *Archipolis. Over de grenzen van de architectuur*, Delft 1994.

Architecturalia wishes to thank the Akademie der Künste and the Netherlands Architectural Institute for their support. This publication has been financed by the Netherlands Architecture Fund, Belvedere, the Van Eesteren-Fluck & Van Lohuizen Foundation. Jan Hoogstad kindly gave permission to use photo's of the Doelen in Rotterdam.

Edited by: Cor Wagenaar
Copy editing: Harvey Mendelsohn
Proof reading: Els Brinkman
Cartography: Frank van Workum, Willum Morsch
Translation from Russian and Ukrainian: Elisabeth Hofer
Project management: Véronique Patteeuw, NAi Publishers
Publisher: Simon Franke, NAi Publishers
Graphic Design: Rick Vermeulen, Natascha Frensch / Via Vermeulen
Printing: Drukkerij Die Keure, Bruges
Paper: Eurobulk, 135 grs.

Available in North, South and Central America through D.A.P./Distributed Art Publishers Inc, 155 Sixth Avenue 2nd Floor, New York, NY 10013-1507, tel +1 212 627 1999, fax +1 212 627 9484, dap@dapinc.com Available in the United Kingdom and Ireland through Art Data, 12 Bell Industrial Estate, 50 Cunnington Street, London W4 5HB, tel +44 208747 1061, fax +44 208 742 2319, orders@artdata.co.uk NAi Publishers is an internationally orientated publisher specialized in developing, producing and distributing books on architecture, visual arts and related disciplines.

www.naipublishers.nl
info@naipublishers.nl

Printed and bound in Belgium
ISBN 90-5662-408-3

Happy